Investment: a professional approach

Investment:
a professional approach

B Julian Beecham B Comm, MA, MEd, PhD
Director of Banking Studies, South Glamorgan
Institute of Higher Education, Cardiff

Pitman

PITMAN PUBLISHING
128 Long Acre, London WC2E 9AN

© B J Beecham 1988

First published in Great Britain 1988

British Library Cataloguing in Publication Data
Beecham, B. Julian, 1927–
    Investment: a professional approach
    1. Great Britain. Investment by financial
    institutions
    I. Title
    332.6'7154'0941

ISBN 0 273 02894 4

Printed and bound in Great Britain

Contents

Introduction

This book has been written to meet the requirements of the 1988 Chartered Institute of Bankers (CIB) Investment syllabus. The sequence of Chapters follows the layout of the syllabus contents. Chapter 1 gives advice on how best to utilise your study time and how best to deal with the question paper during the examination. Adherence to this advice will go a long way in helping you pass the examination you take.

Chapters 2 to 10 cover the 1988 syllabus adequately. Each chapter begins with the syllabus requirements for the topic covered in that chapter, followed by a brief introduction as an overview of the syllabus coverage. Then follows two sections dealing with the theoretical and practical aspects of the syllabus coverage, followed by a few carefully selected questions from the past CIB Investment examination papers, together with brief answers, and a model answer to a specially selected question: this should help you to gauge how to answer the question, the whole question and nothing but the question. Finally, each chapter ends with advice on how to update your knowledge of the topic covered in the chapters.

Starting with the May 1988 examination, the Investment question paper consists of three sections: Section A is compulsory with up to 20 short answer or multiple choice questions (20 marks). Section B is a compulsory choice of two essay-type questions out of four (40 marks). Section C, gives a choice of two out of four practical questions (40 marks). Since the separate section of the paper for candidates for the Trustee Diploma has been removed, one of the questions in Section C covers the practical aspects of investment by trusts and charities. Although the candidates now have to answer five instead of four questions as previously, there is now greater choice in Section B: 'two out four' compared with 'one out of two', as previously. There is now no need to memorize the tax and allowance rates: these are stated on the front of the question paper. The range of questions has widened over the past few years, reflecting the major changes occuring in the investment field. However, the overall standard required to pass the Investment examination remains the same as it has been since 1979, when the subject was introduced.

The text in each chapter is divided into clearly demarcated sections and sub-sections, giving you the opportunity to think upon and digest what you have been reading before proceeding further.

Finally, my *sincere* thanks to The Chartered Institute of Bankers for their kind permission for allowing me to use their Question Papers and Reports of Examiners and to John Petty, ACIB former CIB Investment Chief Examiner, for his invaluable expert advice and constructive comments in the writing of this book.

B. Julian Beecham
April 1988.

1 Study guide and examination technique

Prepare ye well, and thou shalt succeed

The two most important ingredients for achieving success in the examinations are: preparation and revision.

Preparation: private study

1   You should have in your possession (a) the *latest* CIB syllabus for Investment, and (b) the latest edition of a 'recommended' textbook. The textbook you choose should be the one which you can follow and with which you feel most comfortable.

2   Whether you are attending classes in Investment at a college, taking a correspondence course or studying the subject on your own, it is essential that you set aside a specific study-time for Investment, at least once a week of, say, two to three hours, and stick to it without fail.

3   Begin each study period by revising what you have learnt about the previous subject-topic. Do not proceed to the next topic until you are certain that you have fully comprehended the work done earlier. You can do this by answering questions from this textbook and comparing your answers with the answers provided or with the information given in the text on that topic. Remember: remedial work is as important, if not more so, than progressive work. Make sure that the foundations of your comprehension are firm and without loopholes.

4   In addition to studying the textbook you have chosen, read as much as you can of the financial pages of at least one leading newspaper, preferably *The Financial Times*, and especially the two-page FT Share Information Service normally printed at the back of the paper. Also look for relevant articles in the *Investors Chronicle*, a weekly magazine, *The Economist, What Investment* (published monthly), listen to 'the BBC's weekly radio programmes 'Money Box', and 'Money Matters' and watch the 'Money Programme' on BBC 2 and 'Business Programme' on Channel 4. These activities will not only update your knowledge over a long-term period, but will also make you feel at home with the technical terms. You will then begin to appreciate the context in which investment activity takes place. It will also assist you to do the homework set by your tutors satisfactorily.

5 You should do some written work on a regular basis and get it appraised by your tutors or friends who have passed the CIB Investment examination.

6 In addition to buying the textbook on Investment, buy the CIOB Reports of the Examiners for at least four previous examinations. Study these thoroughly to assess your understanding of the subject, and to see which topics cause most problems to candidates, and why.

7 You must read any 'Signpost' article on Investment in *Banking World*. These articles signal changes in the direction and emphasis of questions that will be asked in future examinations.

8 After completing each Chapter, *revise* the Chapter again to detect any area(s) in which your understanding is shallow. Do *not* proceed to the next Chapter/Lesson until you have mastered the one you have been studying.

9 Prepare brief notes of the salient points in each chapter on a regular basis. This will help you to understand the whole syllabus in depth, but *your* notes will also be an excellent aide for revision before the examination.

Examination technique

1. When you are given the question paper in the examination centre, do not be in too much of a hurry to start writing. Concentrate for a few minutes on reading the *whole* question paper, and in assessing what *each* question requires you to do.

2 Decide which questions you are best able to answer and start with one of these: this will give you confidence to tackle the remaining questions.

3 In answering each question, make a brief answer plan, identifying the main points you intend to cover. Arrange the points in each answer plan in a logical sequence. Write one paragraph, including calculations, on each point. Use headings, sub-headings and *tabulate* the points in your answer. This mode of answering Investment question papers is quite acceptable to the CIB examiners. Your full answer should be well-structured. Avoid emotive language and eschew political statements.

4 Allocate the time allowed appropriately, so that you are able to answer the required number of questions. Be brief and relevant; you will achieve no marks for irrelevant material, no matter how well it is expressed. If a question has more than one part, be sure that you answer all parts: answer the question, the whole question and nothing but the question.

5 You will be required to answer five questions, the examiner will mark the first five answers you have written and will ignore everything else. There will be one compulsory multiple-choice and short-answer question covering the entire syllabus. You must of course answer the compulsory question *plus* any four other questions (two each from Sections B and C).

6 Make sure that you have a few minutes left over after answering the required number of questions, use this time to read what you have written, correct as necessary, delete anything that does not make sense or is irrelevant to the scope of the question.

A final word

Remember: there is no substitute for **confidence**, in tackling examinations, and confidence arises from a thorough preparation, attention to detail and regular revision which assists recall.

2 Public company securities

Introduction

Greater need for capital brought into existence Partnership from Sole Trader. Similarly, Joint Stock Company developed out of Partnership for precisely the same reason. A public limited joint stock company raises its *initial* capital by the issue of its shares to the public. In order to attract all types of investor – cautious or enterprising, large and small, shares are issued with varying degrees of risk and right, and at popular nominal prices, usually between 5p and £1 per share. The share capital of a company may be broadly divided into two classes of shares: ordinary and preference shares. Investors in ordinary shares provide the *equity* of the company; they are the chief risk-bearers of the enterprise because they have a *residual* position both in the distribution of divisible profits and in the sale proceeds of the assets of the company if it is wound up. In return, the ordinary shareholders have the special rights to elect the board of directors of the company and through them to control the policy of the company (see Chapter 10).

Preference shares confer a preferential claim to dividends on their holders over ordinary shareholders, at a pre-determined fixed percentage, and sometimes priority of repayment of capital in the event of a winding up, but they have hardly any rights in running the company.

A company may acquire *additional* capital for expansion either by issuing the unissued capital (if any) or by issuing new shares (after its maximum registered capital has been fully paid up). However, if the directors thought that it would be more beneficial to raise the additional capital in the shape of loans, they would issue various types of loan stock, with varying degrees of risk and rate of return in order to attract all types of investor. Whereas the share holders of a company are its owners, the loan stockholders are its creditors, and as such their claims for interest payments and capital repayments come before any other class of shareholder.

As a business starts and expands, it is important to the continuing success of the enterprise that the directors are able to identify both the type of capital and the amount of finance the company needs. Investors to a company's initial and/or additional capital need to be aware of the inherent soundness of the company and its business activities and of the risks and rights attached to the company securities they intend to buy.

Theoretical aspects

The diagram below shows the capital of a fictional company.

Capital of XYZ PLC: £1 000 000.
Share capital: £700 000 in £1 shares

Cumulative Preference shares (10%)	75 000
Participating Preference shares (10%)	50 000
Convertible Preference shares (10%)	40 000
Redeemable Preference shares (10%)	35 000
'A' Ordinary shares	75 000
'B' Ordinary shares	75 000
Ordinary shares	300 000
Deferred Dividend shares	50 000

Loan capital: £300 000

8% Mortgage Debentures (fixed asets)	£100 000
9% Debentures (floating charge)	£80 000
10% Loan stock (unsecured)	£80 000
10% Convertible Loan Stock (unsecured)	£40 000
Issued and subscribed in full	£300 000

Issued capital	*Unissued capital*
£700 000	Nil
Paid up capital	*Calls in arrear*
£700 000	Nil

Equities

The term 'equity' implies the net assets of a company and is often used to denote its ordinary shares. A 'share' is a part of the ownership of a company, and ordinary shareholders, as owners of the company, are entitled to its equity, i.e. the residue of its assets after all debts have been paid. In return, the ordinary shareholders provide the 'risk capital' of the company, i.e. if the company does well they receive good dividends and if it does badly they may get no dividends at all, because after the claims of loan stockholders and preference shareholders have been met there may be no profits left to distribute to ordinary shareholders: they do not share profits but are entitled to the residual profits.

Ordinary shareholders benefit in geared companies, i.e. in which loan capital and preference shares finance expansion, because fixed interest commitments become a progressively smaller and smaller burden on increasing profits. However, gearing can also be dangerous to the ordinary shareholders if the company profits are fluctuating or falling, because the fixed interest commitment has to be met even if there are no profits, and not so beneficial when profits are not rising fast enough. Shares can be issued partly paid (e.g. 5% in the £1), the balance can be called by the directors at any time or at a specified time in the future when the company wants additional capital. But shares can remain partly paid only for a limited period.

Types of equity

In order to attract investors with different investment objectives, the capital structure of a company may have more than one class of equity. The difference between various classes of equity relates to voting and dividend rights, and this difference is reflected in the marked price of separate classes of equity. The various classes into which ordinary shares of a company may be divided are as follows:

1 Ordinary

Holders of the straight ordinary shares (which are described above) are entitled to have a proportionate say in company affairs; a proportionate share in its divisible profits if it prospers, in the form of dividends – usually twice a year, net of basic rate of tax, limited liability if it fails; and a proportionate return of capital from its equity if it winds up.

2 'A' Ordinary

These are non-voting ordinary shares, therefore not attractive to an offeror in a takeover bid (see Chapter 10), but rank equally with straight ordinary shares in dividend distribution. Their market price is normally lower than vote-carrying ordinary shares.

The issue of these shares has now practically ceased owing to the strong opposition to them by the Stock Exchange and others on the grounds that all shareholders who bear the same risk should have an equal say in the running of the company.

3 'B' Ordinary

They rank in all respects with ordinary shares except that instead of a cash dividend, their holders receive a free issue of share to the equivalent value. These shares are also sometimes called Accumulating Ordinary Shares. They were once very attractive to high rate taxpayers but since the Finance Act 1975, the value of such scrip issues is treated as investment income and not capital gain.

4 Deferred dividend

These shares have full voting rights and rank with straight ordinary shares in liquidation, but the payment of dividend on them is deferred until a specified date, and this point is reflected in the lower price as compared to straight ordinary share price, hence a greater capital appreciation which is attractive to high rate taxpayers. They have varying rights; in some cases the equity of the company may not be in ordinary shareholders' hands but rest with deferred dividend shareholders. In such a case ordinary shares will be similar to preference shares. The presence of deferred dividend shares must be disclosed in the company's prospectus.

Capitalisation issue

The residual profits of a company belong to its equity holders. However, the directors, with the approval of equity holders, retain a portion of such profits in the company as reserves to be ploughed back for future expansion.

Nevertheless, the reserves belong to ordinary shareholders; they are in effect postponed dividends.

In addition to the reserves of retained profits, a company may also have reserves of 'share premium'. A company usually issues its shares at a premium, i.e. at a price above their nominal value to take account of the excess value of its assets over the nominal value of its shares. When shares are issued at a premium the premium must be paid into a share premium reserve.

Furthermore, a company may have some other residue which is not available for distribution as dividends. A company may use funds from its above three reserves to issue fully or partly paid new shares to it's shareholders in proportion to their existing holdings, e.g. one new share for every five already held, i.e. a 'one-for-five' capitalisation issue. Although under a capitalisation issue new shares are issued to existing shareholders, no additional capital is raised. Capitalisation issue is a book-keeping device for converting reserves into share capital, it does not change the balance sheet equation of the company, nor is the value of shareholders' total holdings increased (see Practical aspects below). It is rather misleading to describe a capitalisation issue as a bonus or scrip (free) issue, since as residual reserves belong to ordinary shareholders they are getting back what is already theirs.

The reason for making a capitalisation issue is to bring the company's issued capital more into line with the scale of its activities. To enable the directors to make a capitalisation issue, an ordinary resolution (see Chapter 10) must be passed by the ordinary shareholders. The new shares will be sent to the ordinary shareholders, usually in the form of renounceable certificates. When a shareholder receives this certificate he may do one of two things: (i) sign the transfer form on the reverse of the certificate and sell it through a stockbroker or bank, or (ii) retain his share of the capital issue simply by holding on to the certificate in a safe place.

Rights issue

A nominal method for an existing company to raise additional capital for, say, expansion or to repay borrowings, is by inviting its existing ordinary shareholders to subscribe in full, or in instalments, to their allocation of a rights issue of ordinary shares, made strictly in proportion to their holdings. As per the requirements of the Stock Exchange and the stipulations of the 1985 Companies Act, the existing shareholders have the legal *right* of the first refusal to the rights issue allocation. If this were not so it would amount to outsiders buying the company's shares at below the market price – the new shares are issued at a discount to their current market price, otherwise no one would buy them – and reducing the claims of existing shareholders. The new shares have exactly the same rights as the old ordinary shares.

Rights issue is a relatively inexpensive method of raising additional capital; for example, the company does not have to issue a full prospectus, and the 'give away' element with discounted price is kept, as it were, in the 'family'.

The broad outlines of the *procedure* involved in making a rights issue are as follows. The announcement of a rights issue by a company quite frequently coincides with the release of the company's trading results. The company sends to each existing shareholder a Provisional Allotment Letter (PAL), informing him/her the terms and conditions of his/her allocation, rate of dividend after the rights issue, instructions etc. PAL, is, in effect, a kind of abridged prospectus.

The shareholders who receive the PAL have three options:

1   They may take up the allotment in full, and thereby maintain their proportionate ownership of the company. To do this the shareholders send the payment as required (free of government stamp duty and broker's dealing costs) along with their PAL to the company bankers. Soon afterwards they will receive the receipted PAL and, in due course, a proper share certificate.

2   The allottee may decide to buy some and sell the rest of the allotment of new shares. In that case he/she will sign the Renunciation Letter, which is on the reverse of PAL, and pass it on with the appropriate payment to a stockbroker or bank. The stockbroker will obtain from the company split allotment letters in the required denominations; one for the original allotee for his/her purchase and the other for the new buyer.

3   If the shareholders decide to renounce the allotment altogether (e.g. not enough cash available) and to sell it in full (e.g. the sale proceeds of nil paid shares could be more beneficially invested elsewhere), they will sign the Renunciation Letter and pass it on to a stockbroker or bank with instructions to sell it. Usually it should not take the stockbroker or bank long to sell the allotment of the discounted priced new shares, which can be purchased for a limited period free of stamp duty, and for the provisional allottee to receive the sales proceeds which, in theory, should be equal to the fall in the value of his/her investment in existing shares. Subject to fluctuating market conditions the shareholder should be neither better off nor worse off by taking up or renouncing the allotment (see below).

The Stock Exchange requires that the allotments of those provisional allottees (the existing shareholders) who neither sell nor subscribe for their rights, should be aggregated and sold on the Stock Exchange in nil paid form, and any excess receipt over the subscription price, less expenses, should be distributed pro rata among the shareholders to whom such shares were provisionally allotted.

After the expiry of the acceptance and payment date the new rights issue shares are dealt in, in fully paid form, up to the date of renunciation.

The buyers of renounced allotments can either sell them, without difficulty because PAL is a bearer document, or they may retain them by completing the Registration Application Form (on the reverse of PAL) and sending it to the company or its registrar with any payments due. The company will send them their share certificate in due course.

Unlike a capitalisation issue, a rights issue actually increases the assets of the company, and is therefore more significant. Like a capitalisation issue, a rights issue depresses the market price of the share concerned, but for different reasons (see Practical aspects below).

New issues

The Stock Exchange is basically a secondary market where all the securities of listed companies are traded. But these securities must have originated from new issues of one type or another. Companies already quoted on the Stock Exchange can issue *additional* stocks and shares to existing shareholders via rights issues, or as bidding companies in exchange for shares in the target company, or in exchange for shares in other companies in mergers and amalgamations. However, the technical phrase 'new issues' does not strictly apply to these additional issues of stocks and shares. It is when companies, seeking Stock Exchange quotation as 'listed' or 'unlisted' companies (see Chapter 6), in order to 'go public', float new shares, that *new issues* come on the market, and attract much attention in the media and from prospective investors and speculation. New issues tend to rise in price immediately after issue.

Generally speaking, partnerships and private limited companies 'go public' in order to obtain more funds and to enjoy the prestigious status of a quoted company, which enables them easy access of yet more funds from the money and capital markets. However, 'going public' and becoming a 'quoted' company is rather costly (see Chapter 6). The public exposure, and some loss of control of the existing owner, makes any public company a possible target for a takeover bid (see Chapter 10).

The *techniques* and terminology associated with 'going public', and the consequent 'new issues', are as follows.

There are *five* techniques of going public and creating new issues of shares: offer by prospectus; offer for sale; offer for sale by tender; an introduction; a placing.

Note: Irrespective of which technique is used, at least 25% of the new shares is made available to the stock market, for a market in these shares to be made.

1 *Offer by prospectus* A prospectus is in effect an invitation to the general public to purchase at a stated price the shares or loan stock of the issuing body. It accompanies a new issue and contains full and detailed (but not misleading) information on the issue and the issuer, as required by the Companies Act 1948, and by regulations superimposed by the Stock Exchange on the 1948 Act's requirements. In order to avoid the issue

becoming a flop, companies enlist the services of an issuing house. Issuing houses, normally merchant banks, live by their reputation and will not undertake to organise an issue which is remotely uneconomic or fraudulent. If an issuing house does lend its sponsorship to an issue, it is more likely to be fully subscribed; if it is not, then the issuing house, for a fee, underwrites the issue; so that the company will be certain to have its issue fully subscribed, one way or another. The company and its advisors aim to strike a balance between obtaining the best price and pitching the terms on a sufficiently attractive basis to ensure the success of the issue. The prospectus and the accompanying application form are published in at least two national dailies, and copies are made available to the public through the brokers and bankers of the issue. Offer by prospectus, or a direct offer, as it is sometimes called, is a rarely used method, although government stocks are issued to the public directly by a prospectus.

2 *Offer for sale* This method is favoured by the Stock Exchange Council. Under it a sponsor organisation, like a merchant bank or a firm of stockbrokers, buys the issue from the issuer, and then reoffers them to the public, again at a stated price. The issue is widely advertised in the newspapers, together with the prospectus and a cut-out coupon for applicants to complete and send in to the company's bankers by a specified closing date and time. The shares are then allotted to the applicants according to the state of demand. Photocopies of the application forms and multiple applications are rejected. If multiple applications are forbidden then applicants making them may be prosecuted.

If the issue is oversubscribed, because it was very popular or priced too low, allotments may have to be scaled down or sometimes even put into a ballot. Conversely, if the issue is not fully subscribed, because it was priced too high or for some other reason, the unsubscribed portion of the issue is taken up by underwriters with whom prior arrangements have been made. The procedure described above is very similar to offer by prospectus.

In the case of under-priced and/or highly popular issues, 'stagging' profits are made, i.e. quick capital gains by selling the share allotted at a higher price than the issue price. Advance stagging, merely on the expectation of receiving the allocation of the number of shares applied for, can backfire and cause losses to stags if their applications are not, or are not fully, accepted.

3 *Offer for sale by tender* This is a variation of offer for sale. Under this method only a minimum purchase price is fixed by the vendors. It is then up to the investors to decide whether they should tender a higher price. They should subscribe according to their judgement. After the last date for the receipts of application, applications are counted, working down from the highest price until the entire issue is absorbed, *but* every accepted applicant pays the *lowest*, or the striking, price. If the issue is undersubscribed then the minimum tender price will be the striking price. In practice, to ensure a wide enough spread of holdings, there is often some scaling down of the

accepted applications, and sometimes there may even be ballotting, in which case the striking price will be reduced.

The main advantage of this method, which has become popular since 1979, is that it prevents stagging, and if there is any stagging then the stagging profits go to the company. The main disadvantage is that it is rather complex and the ordinary investor has difficulty in deciding the price at which to apply. Financial reports or advisers should be consulted by the less informed investors.

4 *An introduction* When the capital of an unquoted British company is already 'widely held' its shares are traded on the Over-the-Counter market, (a market for shares not quoted on the Stock Exchange – see Ch. 6) and all it seeks is introduction to the Stock Exchange so that its shares may be quoted there, then, according to the Companies Act, it is not necessary for it to have a published prospectus. Nevertheless the Stock Exchange insists that a similar document be prepared for circulation.

The Council of Stock Exchange refuses to say in advance as to what spread it would deem to be 'widely held' for an introduction. It may well be that before an introduction is approved the number of shareholders may have to be enlarged, and the existing shareholders may have to make some of their shares available to the market.

In the case of the securities of overseas companies which are already quoted on their national stock exchanges, introduction is a natural method for these securities to be quoted on the Stock Exchange.

Note that although no new issues have been made, yet the share of *new* companies have come on the market for the first time.

5 *A placing* This comparatively less expensive method of making a new issue is suitable when the issue is small or unlikely to arouse much public interest. A sponsor organisation – an issuing house or a stockbroker – places the issue privately with the institutional investors or with its own clients. This method avoids the expense of issuing a full prospectus. Even so the Stock Exchange insists on newspaper advertisements carrying full details about the company.

Allotment of shares

The directors of the company cannot allot shares to prospective investors unless:

(a) they have been authorised to do so by the company in a general meeting or in the articles of the company;

(b) the amount of the minimum capital (as stated in the prospectus) has been subscribed for and the subscribed amount has actually been received by the company; and

(c) the maximum amount of capital offered for subscription has been fully subscribed or if not, then there is an express provision in the offer allowing allotment to be made even though the full amount has not been subscribed.

After the above provisos have been met, the directors issue *letters of allotments* to applicants. A letter of allotment is a temporary deed of title to shares (or stocks) given to the person named thereon. Allotment letters issued by the UK companies are almost always negotiable documents and being unregistered are renouncable, in whole or in part, without transfer forms. While allotment letters are used to notify successful applicants in prospectus offers and rights issues, in an offer for sale *letters of acceptance* are used for the same purpose. There is no practical difference between the two documents. Both contain: the name of the company, the allotee's name and the details of the issue, calculation of allotment based upon either the amount applied for or an existing holding, a timetable stating the date and time by which payments (if any) must be made, and the place where they must be made, the last dates for splitting, renunciation and registration, the date when the share certificates will be issued, and the renunciation and registration forms.

The company must deliver a *share certificate* to members within two months of allotment or the date when a transfer was lodged for registration. The certificate states: the names of the company and shareholder, the number and type of share held and the amount paid-up on them. Unlike an allotment letter, a share certificate is not a negotiable document, because it has been registered and entered in the company's Register of Members. It is a *prima facie* evidence of title, and should be kept in a safe place. Should the investor, however, lose it, or it is destroyed by some accident, the company may issue a duplicate on receipt of an indemnity signed by the holder and guaranteed by a bank, insurance company or a stockbroker.

Dividend payments

Unlike fixed-interest securities (see below), ordinary shares do not pay a fixed rate of interest. Instead they pay shareholders a share in the amount of net profits (i.e. after corporation tax) of the company. The dividend amounts will therefore vary with the prosperity of the company and its dividend policy. However, no dividend can be paid if it would render the company unable to pay its debts as they fall due. Thus the right of shareholders to receive dividends is not automatic, even if the company makes a profit.

The normal practice in the UK is for an interim dividend to be declared by the directors (profits permitting) between the Annual General Meetings, leaving the final dividend to be passed by the shareholders. Shareholders can approve or reduce, but cannot increase, the amount of the final dividend recommended by the directors. Dividends are paid, in cash or kind, proportionate to the amounts paid-up on shares. Cash payments may be made by cheques sent by post to the registered addresses of the shareholders.

Dividends may be paid by distribution of specific assets or paid up shares or debentures of any other company. It is becoming more and more common for companies to offer their shareholders the option to take additional shares in lieu of a cash dividend. Shareholders ought to consider the following points before accepting the option.

1   There is no income tax advantage in accepting the offer – only the *net* dividend is applied and higher rate tax, if applicable, is still payable as though the cash dividend has been taken.
2   The additional shares give book-keeping problems and Capital Gains Tax (CGT) complications. The small amounts are easily overlooked in making a sale, leading to further difficulties.

Dividends unclaimed after 12 years, may be forfeited and cease to be owed by the company.

Near to the date when dividends become due, shares are sold *ex-dividend* and marked 'xd' in the listed prices, which means that the seller of the shares, not the buyer, will get the forthcoming dividend. Hence the xd share market price is lower than the 'cum div' price, in which the buyer gets the dividend. UK companies generally declare and pay dividends as net pence per share, i.e. after basic rate of income tax. More important to serious investors than dividend per share is the dividend yield (see below).

Risks and rights of investors in equity

The *risks* that the equity holders accept arise from their 'residual' status in the company's assets and earnings. If the company fails they lose most or all of their capital invested in the company. If the trend of the company's earnings is downward, they will be last in the 'pecking order' in sharing the earnings; and since they have no automatic right to dividends, therefore the value of their investment will fall. Falling share prices could make the company a target for a takeover bid, leading to uncertainty of the shareholders' stake in the company.

The *rights* of equityholders are discussed in detail in Chapter 10, therefore only a brief outline is given here. Equityholders have the legal right to: appoint or remove directors; have a say in the company affairs and to interfere in the day-to-day running of the company; receive annual reports and accounts of the company; to attend, vote (in person or by proxy) and speak on any matter on the agenda of general meetings; share in the distributed profits of the company; to have the first refusal in the new issues of share and loan stock of the company; and to sell their shareholdings whenever and to whoever they please.

Fixed interest securities

Investors may wish to keep a proportion of their wealth in fixed interest investments to provide a regular income. A fixed interest investment may be defined as a guarantee by the issuing authority to pay a pre-determined rate of interest for specific periods and usually to repay capital at par or at a pre-determined price on a specific date or within a stated period, and to give the investor creditor status (except with preference shares, see below).

There are several fixed interest investments that may be considered by the investors. For example, term deposits with the building societies, banks and other authorised deposit-takers, National Savings Certificates and other Department of National Savings fixed interest products, local authority securities (see Chapter 3), gilt-edged stocks (see Chapter 4) and the industrial corporate fixed interest securities – and we are concerned with these here.

There are *five* main types of industrial fixed interest securities, viz., preference shares, debentures, unsecured loan stock, convertible loan stock and warrants.

1 Preference shares

Although preference shares are almost always grouped with the fixed interest securities, they, in fact, constitute a part of the company's share capital, and along with ordinary shareholders, preference shareholders are members of the company. As members they have no charge or debt against the company.

There are however important differences between the risks and rights of preference and ordinary shareholders.

Rights of preference shareholders

(a) They have preference over other classes of shareholder in respect of either dividend payments or repayment of capital or both. They have a fixed rate of dividend, expressed as a percentage of the nominal value of their shares, e.g. $7\frac{1}{2}\%$, which must be paid before ordinary shareholders receive anything.

In most cases the articles of the association of the company give them priority of return of capital, together with arrears of dividend. Dividends once declared must be paid out of taxed (franked) rather than pre-tax profits. They get the same rate of dividend year after year unless in any year the profits of the company are insufficient to pay preference dividend which, of course, takes priority over payment of dividends on ordinary shares.

(b) If the preference shares they hold are of the *cumulative* type, the company must pay the fixed rate dividend which it was unable to pay in a year when profits were insufficient in the subsequent years when its profitability improves: dividend arrears are carried forward to future years and paid as soon as possible, before the ordinary shareholders receive anything.

(c) If the shares held are *redeemable preference* or *cumulative redeemable preference shares*, the company, in addition to paying the dividend year in and year out, should redeem them at their nominal or face value at some stated date in the future.

(d) The holders of *participating preference shares* are entitled to a limited share in the profits of the company, in addition to the fixed annual dividends.

(e) The *convertible preference shareholders* have the right to convert to ordinary shares on specific future dates and prices, and until conversion continue to receive fixed annual dividend.

(f) Unless the articles provide otherwise, they carry the same voting rights as other voting shareholders.

Risks and drawbacks faced by the preference shareholders

(a) As income from preference shares is already taxed income, sound and easily saleable preference shares yield no more, sometimes less, than the more secure loan stock.

(b) The holders of irredeemable preference shares, like the equity-holders, have no capital protection and carry much the same risks but, unlike equityholders, they do not enjoy the potential rewards in the company when its profitability is on the upswing.

(c) Redeemable preference shareholders face two risks:
 (i) These shares will be redeemed at their face value, even though their market value might be higher than their face value.
 (ii) If on the redemption date the company is unable to redeem them, they cannot, unlike the redeemable loan stockholders, take legal action against the company, and must look for satisfaction in the clauses of the articles of the company.

(d) On liquidation of the company, they do not have an automatic right to prior return of capital. If the articles are *silent* on this point, they rank equally with ordinary shareholders (although in most cases the articles do give them the priority of return of capital).

(e) Their right to vote is usually restricted to issues which directly affect them, e.g. if their rights are being varied.

Advantage of preference shares to the issuing company

Fixed dividends can only be paid if the directors so recommend. If there are insufficient profits or the company is experiencing financial problems, dividends may not be declared.

Disadvantage of preference shares to the issuing company

They can be more expensive because preference dividend is paid out of the post-tax profit. Therefore the company may prefer to raise loan capital, especially if the corporation tax rate is high, because interest on loan capital is paid out of the pre-tax profit, i.e. interest on loan capital is a deductible item of expenditure in connection with the company's corporation tax liability (see Practical application below).

As investments, preference shares are attractive to institutional investors (such as investment trusts, insurance companies) because preference share dividends are 'franked' income for corporation tax purposes, i.e. dividend incomes in the hands of institutional investors are exempt from corporation tax since they have already been charged the advance corporation tax at a rate equal to the basic rate of tax, as shown in the tax credits which accompany dividend payments. They yield less than both the secured and unsecured loan stock, and are less secure than either of the loan stocks, therefore have little attraction for the private investor.

2   Debentures

The term 'debenture' has two meanings: a *document* by which the issuing company acknowledges its loan indebtedness to the debentureholder, and the *loan* itself. 'Debenture stock' is a loan secured on the assets of the issuing company, carrying a fixed rate of interest and normally a guarantee of repayment by a specified date. If the issuing company is being wound up, debenture stockholders rank before preferential creditors (e.g. unpaid wages, taxes etc.) for repayment from the sale proceeds of its assets. Payment of fixed interest on debentures ranks ahead of preference dividends and ordinary dividends, and ahead of preference and ordinary shares in repayment of capital on liquidation.

A debenture may be an individual debenture evidencing a large sum lent by one person to the issuing company, or the issuing company may create a debenture stock which is subscribed to by many persons, each subscriber receiving a debenture stock certificate evidencing the proportion of the debenture stock held by each subscriber. Not all indebtedness of a company can be described as a debenture; the loan must have some permanence to be classed as a debenture.

The *secured* debenture stockholders may have a *fixed* charge over a fixed asset (e.g. land, building, machinery) of the company. The company must keep the mortgaged asset intact, i.e. it should not be sold, exchanged or another charge created against it. The secured charge may be a *floating* charge, i.e. applying to all assets, not already mortgaged, which normally can be traded.

The debenture deed often appoints a trustee (usually a bank or insurance company) to look after the interests of stockholders. Amongst the debentures, there may be 'first' or 'second' or even third 'debentures' over the same assets. Debenture stock is *free* of government stamp duty.

Risks of investing in debenture stock

(a) With a fixed charge, although the stockholders know in advance exactly which asset of the company forms their security, the market value of the specified asset can fluctuate to the stockholders disadvantage at liquidation.

(b) With a floating charge, the company may dispose of the assets in order to ward off a disaster before the stockholders or their trustees realise it.

(c) Although the 'first' debentureholders are entitled to full satisfaction before 'second' debentureholders, there may not be sufficient assets, after the trade creditors have been paid off, to satisfy any class of debentureholder.

(d) An upward trend, in general interest rates *after* the debenture stock has been subscribed may cause both income and capital loss to stockholders.

(e) There is no hedge against inflationary loss.

Rights of debenture stockholders

(a) The basic rights of all debentureholders against the company are contractual.

(b) Unsatisfied stockholders may appoint a receiver to sell charged assets.

(c) They can sue as creditors for arrears of interest.

(d) Petition the courts to wind up the company if it is unable to pay its debts.

Prospective investors in debenture stock should be aware of the following points: (For details, see Chapter 7)

(a) The issuing company's 'interest cover', i.e. the extent by which its gross profits exceed its interest obligations.

(b) Its liquidity, i.e. the extent by which it cash inflows exceed its cash outflows.

(c) Its provisions, if any, for redemption of debenture stock, i.e., a sinking fund, into which a set percentage of annual profits are credited.

(d) If the issuing company is not a 'blue ship', there is greater risk, and therefore probably restricted marketability; the company will offer a larger yield on its debentures than offered by comparatively safe and marketable gilt stock.

3 Unsecured loan stock

The unsecured loan stock issue does not offer any asset of the issuing company as security against the loan. To compensate for the higher risk the unsecured loan stock bears a higher rate of interest and gives a greater yield than a secured debenture stock. The Stock Exchange does not allow an issue of unsecured loan stock, or 'naked debentures' as it is sometimes called, to be listed as debenture. Its listing must indicate that it is an 'unsecured loan stock'. Investors should be wary if an unsecured loan stock offers an above the average yield because it could imply the stock is a second-line stock, small in amount and narrow in marketability. Like the debenture stock, the unsecured loan stock is free of government stamp duty. In the event of the issuing company being wound up, stockholders are one place below the preferential creditors (e.g. rates, corporation tax, VAT, PAYE liabilities, wages etc.) and one place ahead of preference shareholders for repayment of capital.

Apart from the fact that the loan is unsecured, the risks and rights of stockholders are very similar to those of the debenture holders.

If the stock is listed, a summary of the conditions may be printed on the reverse of the loan certificate. The trust deed constituting unsecured loan stock will cover the following main matters: terms of the issue; restrictions on issuing further loan stock and further borrowing; restrictions on disposal of business and so on. The stockholder is entitled to be supplied with a copy of the trust deed on payment of a fee not exceeding 20p.

4 Convertible Loan Stock (or Convertibles)

The debenture and unsecured loan stocks are sometimes called the 'straight' or 'normal' loans, as distinct from the convertible loan stock which, in addition to giving holders a fixed interest return regularly and redemption (repayment of capital) usually at par at maturity, entitles them to convert their stock into the issuing company's ordinary shares at a pre-determined ratio and price. This gives the convertibles added spice as an investment.

Convertible issues are first made to the company's ordinary shareholders on a rights basis, who have the option to take up the offer or to refuse it. They may be able sell the offer in the market. However, if the convertibles were available to all comers at issue or if the existing equityholders do not take up the offer, then outsiders who buy and convert them into ordinary shares, would dilute the stake of the existing equityholders in the company.

Normally the conversion right exists for a number of years, and the company must give holders the notice of their right to convert in every year in which the right exists. After the expiry of the last conversion right, the unconverted convertible loan stock becomes a straight loan stock.

The additional right, i.e. additional to a fixed interest rate of return enjoyed by the convertibles is reflected in the yield on convertibles which, in the earlier years of the conversion right period, will normally be above that offered by the issuing company's ordinary shares. Therefore, investors interested in high, relatively safe income and with the added attraction of some capital growth potential, affording some protection against inflation, provided by the underlying equity link, would find the convertible issues of special interest.

However, before they decide to exercise their rights to convert, they should consider the following matters.

(a) The length of the conversion period remaining and the number of times that conversion can take place.

(b) The merits/demerits of holding ordinary shares in the prevailing market conditions.

(c) The higher yield on convertibles.

(d) The relative market values of the convertibles and the equity of the company.

(e) The future prospects of the company's profitability.

(f) The fact that the gains from the sale of convertibles, unlike gains from the sale of straight loan stock (and gilts), attract CGT.

For a practical example of conversion and allied matters see Practical application, below.

Rights of convertible loan stock holders

(a) They enjoy identical rights to straight loan stockholders in respect of fixed interest payments, redemption and higher pecking order in the earnings and assets of the company than preference and ordinary shareholders.

(b) The right to convert into ordinary shares at a fixed price if the company does well, otherwise right to redemption at par.

(c) The right to participate in the growth of the company by conversion into high priced shares at low pre-determined price.

(d) The right to receive fixed regular income and the opportunity to participate in the growth of the company which provides some hedge against inflation.

Risks of convertible loan stockholders

(a) Being unsecured loan stockholders they do not enjoy the same degree of safety of capital as debenture stockholders.

(b) The trend of interest rates may rise subsequently, and the company may perform badly during the conversion period.

(c) The inflation rate may rise rapidly.

The reasons for making a convertible loan stock issue

(a) A rights issue may not be successful because the market price of the company's ordinary share is not attractive above their nominal value.

(b) Shareholders may, at certain times, be more willing to subscribe to a convertible stock because of the spice of potential equity interest link.

(c) The issue of debenture stock may not be feasible because the company has at that time no large unmortgaged assets.

(d) Interest payments to all types of loan stockholders – and not just convertible stockholders – are deductible *before* corporation tax calculations. This tax benefit is not available if the company raised the required funds by the issue of preference shares; preference dividend payments are not deductible for corporation tax purposes (see below).

5 Warrants

A warrant is an investment offered by the company which, for a relatively small payment, entitles the warrant holder to subscribe for the equity capital in the company at some fixed future date or dates at a price fixed at the time of the issue of the warrants. Warrants are issued by companies, sometimes on a rights basis, to the existing shareholders to raise additional capital. In this form, warrants are an alternative and less expensive method of acquiring (like call options, see Chapter 6) a large potential equity interest in the company. Warrants may be listed on the Stock Exchange and the issuing company may normally have a register of warrant holders, but warrants do *not* form the company's share capital. On the Stock Exchange warrants are dealt in as ordinary shares, and treated similarly for CGT purposes.

Warrants are also issued by companies as an alternative to convertible loan stock to raise additional loan capital. They are also linked to the issue of a loan stock as a sweetener to make the subscription of the stock more attractive, by entitling the subscribers to the loan stock to purchase company's shares at a fixed price at a future date. Soon after issue, the loan stock and the attached warrants are dealt in on the Stock Exchange as separate entities. Warrants do *not* form a part of the company's loan stock.

Attraction of warrants to issuing companies

(a) They are a cheaper method of obtaining finance because on a loan stock with attached warrant rights, less interest is paid.

(b) No interest or dividend is paid to warrant holders.

(c) Since warrants are not a part of the company's capital warrant holders have no rights to attend and vote at ordinary meetings of the company.

(d) In a takeover bid, the bidding company may issue warrants in payments to shareholders of the target company.

Attraction of warrants to investors

(a) Warrants normally stand at a premium, i.e. the fixed price is less than the market price of the shares.

(b) Since the warrant price is related to the ordinary share price, therefore it can be expected to move more or less in line with the share price. This means that a similar price rise in both prices, in money terms, will represent a greater percentage gain on the lower warrant price than on the higher ordinary share price. Warrants can therefore provide the opportunity for long term equity 'gearing' to an investment (see below).

(c) If the company does badly and its equity share price falls below the warrant fixed price, the warrant holders do not have to exercise their right to buy the shares, thereby avoiding a much larger loss which an outright purchase of equity shares would have caused them.

(d) Warrants attract those investors who believe that the price of the underlying shares will rise during the subscription period, thus providing a substantial opportunity for capital gains.

Drawbacks of warrants for investors

(a) They receive no dividend or interest, whereas shareholders and loan stock holders receive dividends (hopefully) and interest payments respectively.

(b) Capital gain, the main objective of buying warrants, may not materialise if the underlying shares do not rise in price.

(c) Warrants confer no rights to attend company meetings and to vote.

(d) If the price of underlying shares falls and continues to remain below the fixed price, the warrants are rendered valueless and investors suffer capital loss.

(e) If the warrant rights are exercised and they are converted into ordinary shares of the company, the stake in the company and the amount of dividends of the existing shareholders will be diluted.

Practical application

Capitalisation issue

Balance Sheet of X PLC (before capitalisation issue).

	£
Issued and Paid up Ordinary Share Capital of £1 each share	500 000
Reserves	700 000
	1 200 000
Current assets	550 000
Fixed assets	650 000
	1 200 000

The company decides to capitalise £500 000 of its reserves on a '1 for 1' basis. After the capitalisation issue, the balance sheet of the company will look like this:

Balance Sheet of X PLC (after capitalisation issue)

	£
Issued and Paid up Ordinary share capital of £1 each share	1 000 000
Reserves	200 000
	1 200 000
Current assets	550 000
Fixed assets	650 000
	1 200 000

This example shows that while the number of shares has increased from 500 000 to 1 000 000, the reserves have decreased by £500 000 and the assets of the company have remained unchanged. Thus capitalisation is a book-keeping adjustment because it neither changes the balance sheet of the company, nor the *value* of the shareholders' total holdings: if the market price of XPLC share on the Stock Exchange before capitalisation was £1, after the '1 for 1' capitalisation issue, the market price will fall to around 50p (unless the share is very popular). Similarly if the shareholders were receiving a 20% dividend before capitalisation, they would receive a dividend of around 10% after capitalisation issue doubles this shareholding.

Note that the reduction in the *rate* of dividend does not reduce the dividend receipts of shareholders. Thus by bringing down an outrageously high dividend rate to a more reasonable rate, capitalisation issue avoids public gaze and therefore unjustified criticism. Furthermore a share price of 50p may be more acceptable to the general public than the same share priced at £1.

It is quite possible that after capitalisation the share price may in fact rise due to the fact that the new shares are obtained without any dealing costs, and, if renounced, are traded on a cash basis, and are therefore free from stamp duty, and at a lower price are more marketable and more attractive to the investor.

Rights issue

Dealings normally begin in new shares on the day after the PALs are posted by the company to its shareholders. The price of 'ex-rights' shares, i.e. after the rights issue is over, immediately falls to the average price of the old and new shares, because not all of the provisional allottees may wish to, or can afford to, take up the rights, or they may doubt the company's ability to achieve a satisfactory return on new capital and therefore may not want to take up the offer. This will increase the supply of and decrease the demand for the new shares on the stock market causing their price to fall, at least temporarily. This may be an appropriate time to buy or to increase a stake in the company.

Suppose a company needs additional funds to finance a project. The directors find other sources of raising capital (e.g. sale of assets, floating off a subsidiary, issuing new shares, borrowing from banks or in the eurobond markets) as unsatisfactory. They decide to make a rights issue to their shareholders of '1 or 4' rights shares at 250p. The current price of the shares is 300p per share. All those provisional allottees who take up the offer will own five shares for every four shares they previously held. The weighted average price of each share will fall, as shown below:

4 old shares at 300p	1200p
1 new shares at 250p	250p
	1450p
Weighted average price	$\dfrac{1450p}{5}$ = 290p

Note: the weighted average price is called the *theoretical ex rights price*. In the above example:

(a) *Theoretical ex rights price* is the price *after* the rights have been issued, i.e 290p. A *cum-rights price* is the price per share *before* the rights are issued, when the option to take up or sell the rights is still available, i.e. 300p. The *value of a nil paid share* is the excess of the theoretical exercise price over the discounted offer price, i.e. 40p (290p − 250p)

(b) The provisional allottees who take up their rights neither gain nor lose in money terms, because the total gain is neutralised by total loss. An allottee holding 4000 shares, takes up 1000 ('1 for 4') new shares:

Total gain = 1000 × 40p (290p − 250p) = £400
Total loss = 4000 × 10p (300p − 290p) = £400

(c) Similarly the shareholders who sell their rights neither gain nor lose in money terms. An allottee holding 1000 shares sells 250 ('1 in 4') new shares:

Total loss on existing shares 1000 × (300p − 290p) = £100
Sale proceeds of new shares 250 × 40 (290 − 250) = £100

However, by selling the rights the allottee will have a smaller stake in the company's increased capital.

(d) Whether the provisional allottees take up their rights in full or in part or sell them, or neither renounce them nor sell them, the company will, other things being equal, get the additional capital from those who take up the offer, i.e. from those who buy the partially or fully renounced allotments.

Note: The above calculations are theoretical to explain the concepts involved; they may not always work out in practice due to other market forces.

After PALs are issued to allottees and rights start trading, there is a period of about three weeks before the allottees have to take up the rights and send the required money or renounce the offer. If the price of underlying shares rises during that period, the price of the rights will rise proportionately more because rights are offered at a discounted price.

Suppose the current price of the old share is	100p
Rights are issued at	75p
nil paid premium on rights	25p

Suppose during the three weeks or so the price of the old share rises by 25p, the percentage rise in price is equal to 25 ($\frac{125 - 100}{100} \times 100$), but the percentage rise in price of nil paid rights, which will also rise by 25p, is 100% (from 25p to 50p). This proportionately higher capital gain attracts stags to speculate on rights.

If a large majority of allottees renounce their rights, this will leave the door open for a potential bidder to build up, without too much attention, a strategic voting share stake in the company.

A rights issue can be made to reduce unhealthy gearing in a company.

Suppose the share capital of a company is	£1 000 000
and the borrowings are	£1 300 000
Gearing ratio	130%

However a successful rights issue which raises the share capital by say £500 000 to reduce borrowing, will mean

Share capital	£1 500 000
Borrowings	800 000
Gearing	53%, which is much more satisfactory.

Dividend and dividend yield per share

Of greater significance to investors than dividend per share, is the yield per share, because yield is the return they get on the price they have to pay for the share. Dividend yield of a share is calculated on the current market price of the share, and not on its nominal value.

It expresses the gross dividend per share as a percentage of the current price of the share and therefore shows the amount of income a investor will receive per £100 invested in buying that share at the current market price.

For example, Company X PLC, whose 25p share currently costs 350p to buy, declare a rut dividend of 7.3p per share. This will give the shareholders a dividend yield of:

$$\frac{\text{Gross dividend 10p (net dividend + basic rate tax)}}{350\text{p}} \times 100 = 2.86\%$$

Suppose the market price of the share is 150p, all other things remaining unchanged, the shareholders will receive a dividend yield of:

$$\frac{(10\text{p} \times 100)}{150\text{p}} = 6.7\%.$$

Hence the lower the market price of the share the greater the income for every £100 invested by the investor.
(For the valuation of ordinary shares, see Chapter 7).

Convertible Loan Stock (CLS)

Example: On 1 January, 1978, Y PLC issued a 9% CLS 1995–1998 at par. The CLS holders are entitled to convert £100 of the stock into 40 Y PLC ordinary shares, on any 1 December from 1978 to 1995 after which the CLS will become a 'straight' and will be redeemed at par in the year 1998. On 1 December, 1978, Y PLC ordinary share was worth 150p. If the CLS holders wished to exercise their conversion rights they would have paid a *conversion price* of

$$\frac{\text{prevailing market price of CLS}}{\text{number of shares received per £100 stock converted}} = \frac{£100}{40} = 250\text{p}$$

i.e. a *conversion premium* over the market price of the share of

$$\frac{\text{conversion price} - \text{share price at issue}}{\text{share price at issue}} \times 100$$

$$= \frac{250\text{p} - 150\text{p}}{150\text{p}} \times 100 = 66.6\%.$$

Suppose on 1 December, 1987, the CLS and ordinary shares were worth £110 and 267p respectively, investors wishing to buy Y PLC ordinary shares via its CLS, would pay a conversion price $= \dfrac{£110}{40} = 275\text{p}$; i.e. a conversion premium of $\dfrac{275\text{p} - 267\text{p}}{267\text{p}} \times 100 = 2.99\%$ over the current share price.

The rise in the worth of £100 CLS to £110, other things being equal, was caused by a rise in the price of ordinary shares, hence the conversion premiums fell.

Note: The CLS *until* conversion or *after* becoming 'straight' till maturity, continues to provide a good, fixed and steady income to the holders.

CLS in relation to straight loan stock

(a) A rise or fall in the market price of the linked share will lead to, other things being equal, a rise and fall in the worth of a CLS, respectively, but the straight which has no linkage with the ordinary share will remain unaffected.

(b) Consequent upon a significant fall in the price of the linked share, the CLS holders will not be worse off than a parallel straight holder on account of the identical fixed interest return; CLS holders are not obliged to convert.

(c) Since the market value of fixed interest securities is *inversely* related to the movements in the general level of interest rates, both the CLS and straight will rise and fall in value when the general interest rate falls and rises respectively.

(d) A significant fall in the market price of linked shares causes a *conversion discount* on the conversion price, i.e. its market price falls below the conversion price. At this point it might be beneficial for investors to switch from ordinary shareholdings to CLS holding.

CLS in relation to ordinary shares

(a) In the event of a crash in share prices on the stock market, share prices can go into a free fall, but the value of CLS cannot go into a free fall on account of its fixed interest return net. Therefore the loss to shareholders can be extensive whereas the loss to CLS holders will be limited.

(b) When there is a boom in share prices, the holders of those shares whose prices have risen will enjoy a potential capital gain. However, if such shares are linked to a CLS, then CLS holders will also enjoy, indirectly, a rise in the value of their holdings.

(c) Usually the value of a CLS falls upon its becoming a straight, i.e. when the last conversion date passes. At this point it would be beneficial to sell it and invest the proceeds in some other investment giving a suitable yield.

Valuation of warrants

Warrant holders receive no interest or dividend, but hope to make capital gains during the subscription period. Therefore in valuing warrants several factors need to be considered, viz. the price of ordinary shares for which warrants may be exchanged, the fixed subscription price and subscription period, profitability trends of the company, the price of warrants, the dealing costs in acquiring the warrants and any income tax and CGT obligations.

If the share price falls and becomes equal to the subscription price, there is no capital gain, only expenses to be borne. Once the share price falls below subscription price, the investors will be making avoidable loss (capital loss + dealing costs) in exchanging warrants for shares. In such circumstances the length of the subscription period becomes significant: the longer the subscription period the better the chances of the share price rising above the subscription price, especially if the trend of the share price is upwards, and therefore the higher the value of warrants.

Warrants normally stand at a premium, i.e. the subscription price is less than the share market price. Therefore warrants have intrinsic worth. Suppose: the subscription price is 100p, share market price is 130p and the warrant purchase price (ignoring dealing costs) is 40p, then the conversion premium is 7.7%:

Warrant market price = 40p

Warrant conversion price $= \dfrac{100p}{140p}$

less market value of $= \dfrac{130p}{10p}$

Conversion premium $= \dfrac{10p}{130p} \times 100 = 7.7\%$

The conversion premium is the theoretical extra price which the investors pay for buying a warrant – assuming they hold it to maturity and exercise their conversion right.

Instead of locking up a sizeable amount of money in a block of a particular company's shares, the investor can buy warrants at a fraction of the cost which gives them the right to buy the same number of shares at a known subscription price sometime in the future. This releases the bulk of their capital to take up other investment opportunities.

Suppose a share has a market price of £1. A holding of 5000 of such a share would cost the investors £5000 (ignoring dealing costs). However, investors have an alternative of buying warrants over the same number of shares at, say, 33p a piece. The warrants give the investors the right to convert until year 1995 on the basis of one warrant per share at the price of 51p. The warrants cost only £1530 (= £0.51 × 3000), as against £5000 to buy 5000 shares outright. Investors can invest the balance (£5000 − 1530) £3470 in safe fixed interest securities. This difference in earning compounded over the life of the warrant is a significant factor in assessing its value.

In the above example, for the sake of ease, it is assumed that the holding of one warrant gives the right to subscribe to one share. If the conversion rate is, say, one warrant for three shares than the warrant price per share would be $\dfrac{33}{3}$ = 11p.

The warrant holders are not locked into their warrant investment until 1995. There is an active market in which warrants can be traded before their exercise date. The point to bear in mind about warrants is that the price at which a warrant is bought and sold on the stock market is entirely separate from the fixed subscription price at which the warrants can be converted into a company's ordinary shares, at a fixed date in the futute.

Gearing opportunities with warrants

Warrants offer major gearing advantages to investors seeking capital gain. Warrants do not pay any income but offer only capital gain (or loss) opportunities, i.e. price movements, up or down, are magnified in the corresponding movements in the warrants. Suppose the share price in the above example rose from £1 to £1.40 the 40p rise in the share price quite possibly pushes up the warrant price from 33p to 73p. However, whereas the percentage rise in share price is only 40, the percentage rise in the warrant price is 121. Therefore the gearing ratios in first and second prices are $\dfrac{100}{33}$ = 3 and $\dfrac{140}{73}$ = 1.9, i.e., the gearing ratio is reduced at the higher prices by 1.1. Similarly, a small fall in the share price will tend to produce a magnified fall in the value of the warrant.

Investment trust (IT) companies (see Chapter 5) are prolific issuers of warrants; currently there are some 30 issues which are actively dealt in. IT companies issue warrants for two reasons:

(a) Existing ITs issue them to raise additional capital cheaply. Investors buy them in the hope that if the issuing IT does well in the future its shares will rise in price, enabling investors to make capital gains on conversion.

(b) Managers of a new IT at its launch offer warrant attachments to shares in the hope that when the shares fall to discount to net asset value the warrants, which can be sold separately to shares, will attract the investors to subscribe to the shares of the new IT.

Advantages to the company of loan capital over preference shares

1   Corporation tax is charged on profits *after* interest on loan stock, but *before* dividend on preference shares:

	£
(a) Profits before interest	1 000 000
less interest on loan stock (assumed)	100 000
	900 000
less corporation tax at say, 35%	315 000

Profits available per shareholder	585 000
(b) Profits before interest	1 000 000
less corporation tax at say, 35%	350 000
	650 000
less preference share dividend (assumed)	100 000
Profits available for shareholders	550 000

Thus under (a) there is a tax saving for the company of £35 000 (£585 000–£550 000), and the true cost of the interest to the company is £65 000 (£100 000 − £35 000). A 10% loan stock would cost the company, £6.5%.

Formula:

$$\text{Nominal rate } \% \times \frac{100 - \text{corporation tax rate}}{100} = 10 \times \frac{100 - 35}{100}$$

$$= 6.5\%$$

2   A company can raise loan stock in the market when it is short of funds, and it can buy its own stock when it has surplus funds. This provides the company with flexible means to adjust its liquidity.

Selected questions

The following questions have been selected from the previous CIB Investment examination question papers because of their relevance to the contents of this chapter. After you have read and understood the topic of Public Company Securities try to answer briefly these questions before looking at the outline answers given below.

Q1   Describe the following methods of bringing previously unquoted shares to the stockmarket:
  (a) offer for sale;
  (b) offer for sale by tender;
  (c) placing;
  (d) introduction

Q2   Describe in detail how you would assess the investment merits of an unsecured loan stock issued by a quoted public company.

Q3   A UK registered quoted company is proposing to make a rights issue of ordinary shares to raise enough money to enable it to discharge its bank loans.

  (a) What factors are likely to have persuaded the directors to take this course, rather than to have issued an unsecured loan stock?
  (b) The rights issue is on the basis of 1 for 10 at 155p. If the ordinary

shares of the company are quoted at 210p on the day before the allotment letters are posted:

   (i) What is the value of the rights to existing shareholders?

   (ii) What is the likely premium?

   (iii) What is likely to be the quotation of the ordinary shares after the allotment letters are issued?

   (c) What other methods of raising cash might the directors of the company have considered?

A1 (a) In an offer for sale:

- A merchant bank buys a block of shares from the company or existing shareholders and invites the public to buy them at a fixed price.
- The offer is advertised in the press with a prospectus and an application form.
- If the offer is undersubscribed the surplus is taken up by the underwriters.
- If it is oversubscribed applications are scaled down or alloted by a ballot.

   (b) In an offer for sale by tender:

- A merchant bank buys a block of shares, offers them to the public *but* the price is not fixed in advance.
- Applicants are invited to name the price, usually subject to a minimum figure.
- Everyone pays the lowest price at which the issue is fully taken up, i.e. the striking price. (Exceptions to this practice are possible.)
- Applicants bidding below the striking price have their cheques returned.
- Sometimes the allocation is scaled down or ballotted to ensure a wider spread of holdings and an orderly market.

   (c) In a placing:

- Small issues, or issues unlikely to arouse public interest, are brought to the stockmarket.
- A sponsor (a merchant bank or a broker) buys the whole issue after charging a commission, places them with clients of his/her own choosing.
- Under Stock Exchange regulations 25% of the issue must be offered to the general public to ensure an orderly market, via market makers.
- For a fixed interest stock issue, the proportion is 10% plus 10% in reserve.

   (d) In an introduction:

- Shares already widely held are brought to the market, suitable for foreign companies, already quoted overseas seeking quotation in London.
- No published prospectus is required, but details are circulated.
- The Stock Exchange may ask existing shareholders to make available some shares to the market.

A2 *Four* main areas should be considered:

   (a) *Terms of issue*: These are incorporated in a trust deed; examine them to see:

- Where the stock stands in order of priority with other loans;
- Whether further stocks may be issued ranking in all respects with it;
- What restrictions are there on further borrowing;
- Repayment terms: has the company an option to repay before the final date? Is there a sinking fund and how is it operated?

  (b) *Status of the issuing company:* consider its:
- Size; financial strength; profit record; future prospects – by examining its published accounts and reports;
- The ideal issuing company will have a stable record and not be in a cyclical industry;
- If the stock has conversion rights, it must be assessed *both* as an equity and a loan stock – for a loan stockholder, security, as opposed to an ordinary shareholder, will be more important than earnings growth.

  (c) *Accounting ratios:* examine the balance sheet in detail to find out:
- Capital and income priority percentages. (see Chapter 7, for details);
- Calculation of capital and interest covers. (see Chapter 7, for details);
- Nature and value of assets;
- Extent of gearing; highly geared companies should be avoided.

  (d) *Market performance:* examine quality financial press and reports to:
- Compare its price with alternative fixed interest stocks;
- Calculate flat and redemption yields, for comparison (see Chapter 4, for details);
- A high yield might indicate above average risk;
- Ascertain the size of the issue and its marketability.

(e) *Investor's tax position and objectives:* these should be brought into the picture of their investment portfolios to establish the suitability of the loan stock for their investment requirements.

A3 (a)
- interest on loan stock, unlike ordinary dividends, is a charge for corporation tax.
- the yield on the equity must be fairly low and interest rates relatively high.
- its existing gearing ratio rules out a new loan stock issue.

  (b) (i) *value to shareholders* = 210p−205p = 5p: this in theory they would lose if rights are allowed to lapse.

  (ii) *premium:* = 205p − 155p = 50p: this the buyer would have to pay, over and above the subscription price; it is not the same thing as the so-called 'value of the rights' per share.

  (iii) *Ex-rights price* = $\dfrac{(210p \times 10) + 155p}{(10 + 1)}$ = 205p

(c) sale of assets; floating a subsidiary; raising cash in other markets, such as the sterling commercial paper Eurobond.

Specially selected question

A customer has received notification of impending conversion dates in respect of two convertible loan stocks:

1 ABC plc 12% Convertible Unsecured Loan Stock, 1995 is convertible into 25p ordinary shares on 25 October each year from 1983 to 1993 inclusive at the rate of 30 shares for every £100 stock. The market price of the ordinary shares is 280p. The market price of the convertible stock is £105. Net dividends per ordinary share in respect of the year ended 31 March 1988 totalled 9.8p.

2 XYZ plc 5% Convertible Unsecured Loan Stock, 1990 is convertible into 25p ordinary shares on 28 October each year from 1974 to 1988 inclusive at the rate of 38 shares for every £100 stock. The market price of the ordinary share is 370p. The market price of the convertible stock is £142. Net dividends per ordinary share in respect of the year ended 31 March 1988 totalled 7.77p (updated).

(a) Calculate the conversion premium (or discount) in each case.

(b) What action would you advise your customer to take? Give reasons for your advice and show any relevant calculations.

(c) What are the advantages of convertible unsecured loan stocks from the point of view of the issuing company?

Model answer

(a) Conversion price $= \dfrac{\text{convertible loan stock market price}}{\text{no. of shares per £100 of nominal stock converted}}$

(i) For *ABCplc*, the conversion price $= £105 \div 30 = 350p$

For *XYZplc*, the conversion price $= £142 \div 38 = 373.7p$

Conversion premium/discount = Conversion price − Market price of stock

(ii) for *ABCplc*, conversion prem/dis $= 350p - 280p$

$$= 70p \text{ or } 25\% \ (\dfrac{70p}{280p} \times 100)$$

For *XYZplc*, conversion prem/dis $= 370p - 373.7p$

$$= 3.7p \text{ or } 1\% \ (\dfrac{3.7p}{379p} \times 100)$$

(b) Effect of conversion in money terms:

(i) *For ABC plc*   *Capital value*   *Gross income*

£100 stock @ £105 $= £105.00$ £12.00 (interest rate on stock)

30 shares @ 280p $= \underline{£\ 84.00}$ $£\ 3.62 \ \left(\dfrac{30 \times 9.8}{73} = \text{gross dividend}\right)$

capital/gross income loss on conversion $= £21.00(20\%) = £8.38$ (69.8%).

Advice: Since the customer has until 1993 to convert he/she should defer a decision until a later date. Meanwhile he/she is getting a good return on investment with some prospect of capital growth.

(ii) *For XYZ plc* *Capital value* *Gross income*
  £100 stock @ £142 £142.00 £5.00 (interest rate on stock)

  38 shares @ 370p £140.60 $£4.04 \left(\dfrac{27 \times 7.77}{73} = \text{gross dividend} \right)$

Capital/gross income
loss on conversion = £1.40(1%) £0.96 (19.2%)

Advice: The last conversion date is 28 October 1988. Failure to convert will mean a huge loss on capital since the stock will then become a straight loan stock. He/she should either sell the stock in the market or convert. The decision will depend on his/her assessment of the company's prospects.

 (c) (i) As compared to issuing straight loan stock:
    • Cheaper than straight (i.e. lower yield basis) because of conversion prospects
    • company may not have security for a mortgage debenture issue
  (ii) As compared to share issue:
    • interest allowable for tax.

Updating

The ideal sources for updating your knowledge of the public company securities are the quality financial press announcements of and comments on such securities, *The Financial Times*, 'London Share Service', leading companies' (your own bank's) annual reports and accounts, the CIB *Examiner's reports, Updating Notes, Sign post* articles (in *Banking World*) and the financial statements in the annual budgets. Sometimes the Bank of England *Quarterly Bulletins* include useful articles in this connection.

3 'Cash' and direct interest-bearing investments

Syllabus Coverage

Investment products of:
  Commercial banks
  Building societies
  National Savings Bank
  National Savings
  Local Authorities
  Finance Houses
  Others
Advantages and disadvantages of investing in each product

Introduction

It is important for you to learn to distinguish between the concept of investment on the one hand and the concept of saving, hoarding, speculation and gambling on the other, so that you are able to answer your customers' investment queries correctly.

Generally speaking, *savings* are the surplus of income over essential expenditure. Savings are, in effect, postponed spending: the saver is providing for some known item of future expenditure (e.g. house repairs, replacement of the old car) or some unknown future contingency (e.g. redundancy).

Hoarding takes place when money is physically accumulated, say, under the mattress, from where it could be lost by fire or theft. Although hoarded sums are instantly available for spending, they earn no interest and provide no hedge against inflation loss in the purchasing power of the saved up sums: it costs money to hoard money.

Surplus money may be used for *speculation*. Speculation is based upon anticipated changes in the prices of financial and other assets and in interest rates, enabling the speculator to make quick gains. The speculator is not interested in the long-term ultimate worth of the financial venture, but by taking a calculated risk based on careful examination of available facts, accepts a high risk of loss in return for a quick capital gain.

Surplus money may be used for *gambling*. Although some of the considerations which apply to speculation also apply to gambling – for instance, the acceptance of a high risk/reward ratio, the characteristic which distinguishes gambling from speculation is the element of pure chance, as opposed to the calculated risk, for a quick gain.

Alternatively, surplus money may of course be *invested*. Financial investment differs from speculation in intent and degree: it implies a sophisticated and more considered process of seeking a steady and increasing income and *real* (adjusted for the rate of inflation) growth of capital invested.

In this chapter we shall be studying the advantages and disadvantages of investing in the investment products of the banks, building societies, finance houses, local authorities and National Savings.

There are four main categories of savers in the UK: private individuals, commercial companies, local authorities and public corporations. Of these four categories, the personal sector (savings of households and individuals) and the company sector (retained profits and depreciation provisions) are the largest contributors to the UK savings market: their respective savings contributions, in 1985, were £24 billion and £40 billion.

Traditionally, UK personal sector savers save with the building societies, banks and National Savings. However, unit trusts (particularly those with life assurance links), pension funds and investment trusts, are increasingly challenging the dominance of the 'big three'. At the end of 1986, the relative shares in the personal sector's liquid investments of the 'big three' were: building societies: 53.1%, commercial banks: 31.9% and National Savings: 15%.

Theoretical aspects

There are five main points which need careful consideration when choosing between several investment products of various deposit-taking institutions.

1 Liquidity

Liquidity investments are cash investments, i.e. they can be cashed quickly and without any risk of financial loss. Liquid investments have some in-built advantages: instant spending power to take up bargains in goods and financial assets, to meet sudden, unforseen expenses and no loss of capital through bad debts. With liquid investments, investors are in control of their own spending ability. On the other hand, liquid investments are unlikely to carry high rates of interest because if the deposit-taker lends short and borrows short the opportunity for profitable use of deposit is restricted.

2 Safety

Safety of investment relates to the creditworthiness and financial soundness of the deposit-taking institution: the more financially secure the institution the greater the safety of capital (savings) invested with it. Naturally investors expect a higher rate of return as compensation for investing with comparatively less secure deposit-takers. The element of safety in investment is of extreme importance, especially if the investors are old age pensioners investing their life savings – there is no second chance for rebuilding life savings once they have been lost in a risky investment.

The value of invested capital can be rapidly eroded in times of high inflation. During such periods, the safety of capital may be achieved by investing in index-linked investments. With index-linked investments the capital value of the investment increases in line with the inflation rate, as measured by the Retail Price Index, so that when investors get their money back, it is still worth the same in real terms as when it was invested. When the inflation rate falls and there is no reason to expect that it will rise again, index-linked investments become less popular than those offering a reasonable rate of return from interest or dividend payments.

3 Rate of return

This basically means the rate of interest (or dividend) paid by various institutions on their investment products. Generally speaking, the larger the amount invested, the longer the loss of liquidity and comparatively less secure the deposit-taking institution, the higher the rate of return offered. Another consideration with regard to making fair comparisons between the various rates of return on offer is the timing of interest payments. If different institutions pay interest at different intervals, it is then essential to apply a common standard for a fair comparison between the various rates of return. The method generally used to achieve a common standard is the Compounded Annualised Rate (CAR) of interest. For example, if institution X pays a 10% rate of interest annually, institution Y pays a 10% rate of interest half-yearly, institution Z pays a 10% rate of interest quarterly, then £100 deposited with each of the three institutions will produce the following CARs:

institution X: 10%
institution Y: 10.25% (5% + 5.25%)
institution Z: 10.38% (2.5% + 2.56% + 2.63% + 2.69%)

This means that £100 deposit with the three institutions will, at the end of the year, be worth: £110 (institution X), £110.25 (institution Y), £110.38 (institution Z). It is clear therefore, that although the nominal interest rates on deposits in the three institutions are identical, the highest CAR is earned on deposits with institution Z. Thus the more frequent the interest payments the greater the excess of CAR over the given nominal rate.

4 Tax considerations

If interest is paid gross (without deductions of income tax) the investment will be particularly attractive to a non-taxpayer who will not have the bother of reclaiming tax, whilst the taxpayer will have the use of the extra money until such time as the tax liability is paid. If interest is paid net the non-taxpayer may be unable to reclaim the tax deducted. Other things being equal, high rate taxpayers prefer investments which produce capital growth rather than high income because capital gains within the annual exemption are tax free.

The investment income is treated in four *different* ways by the tax authorities. These differences are important because they influence the choice of investment products by investors.

(a) *Investment income is free of tax* No tax is payable on income from certain investments, e.g. National Savings Certificates. Such investments are very beneficial to taxpayers, in partricular the higher-rate taxpayers.

(b) *Investment income is paid untaxed* Investors receive income from some investments, such as the interest payment by the National Savings Bank. The investors must declare such incomes and pay tax according to their tax positions. Such investments are excellent value to the non-taxpaying investors: for them the 'gross' income received is the 'net' income.

(c) *Investment income taxed at basic rate* Income from certain investments, such as dividends from stocks and shares, is paid after deduction of the basic rate of tax along with a tax deduction certificate (tax credit). The non-taxpayer can normally claim a refund of the tax deduction by sending the tax credit to the Inland Revenue. The basic-rate taxpayers have no further tax liability. For the higher-rate taxpayers, the income is 'grossed up', i.e. how much income they would have received if an amount equivalent to base rate of tax (25%) had been paid to them along with the dividend or interest; they then have to pay the additional tax due on that total.

(d) *Investment income taxed at composite rate (CRT)* Building societies, banks, local authorities, finance houses and life insurance linked investments that pay regular income are required by law to pay interest net of CRT to investors. The rate is determined each year by the Treasury (24.75% for 1987–88 and 23.25% for 1988–89) and is below the basic tax rate, because some investors are non-taxpayers. Non-taxpayers cannot claim the tax paid, basic-rate taxpayers have no further tax to pay and higher-rate taxpayers are liable for extra tax. The following receive interest gross of CRT: non-resident investors; National Savings Bank depositors; depositors of over £50 000; pension funds; friendly societies; registered charities; limited companies; and clubs and societies.

5   The comparative cost and ease of making and withdrawing investments

Naturally people will prefer those investments which involve no buying or selling costs, are easily bought and which involve no financial penalties, provided of course that other investment considerations – liquidity, safety, rate of return, tax considerations – remain the same.

The deposit-taking institutions discussed in this chapter are close competitors for the savings of the public. Therefore any increase in the rate of return offered, or the introduction of a more attractive product by any of these institutions, is bound to produce similar changes in the rates of returns and products of the other institutions.

Practical application

The demarcation lines that clearly separated joint stock banks, Trustee Savings banks, the National Giro bank, finance houses and building societies up to the mid 1970s, have become progressively blurred, certainly so far as the saver and investor are concerned. Depositors now have to look more closely at all the products offered by the above-mentioned institutions if they are to obtain the best return on their savings.

Commercial banks

This category of deposit-taking institution includes authorised, commercially oriented joint stock banks: The Bank of Scotland, Barclays, Lloyds, Midland, National Westminster, The Royal Bank of Scotland, the TSB Group and a few others. Of course, UK savers can also invest in the products of fringe banks, foreign banks and offshore banks.

The investment products of commercial banks, in terms of safety, are a close second to UK government stocks and national savings investments. In any case, should an authorised bank get into financial difficulties, the Deposit Protection Board guarantees that investors (up to £20 000) will get 75% of their money back.

Faced with keen competition on deposit-taking, commercial banks have had to produce attractive investment schemes for all groups of savers. The following are the main products which all major commercial banks with minor differences offer to UK savers:

1   Ordinary deposit accounts

This account is designed to make saving simple, safe and convenient.

Anyone, including children under 16, can open a deposit account with as little as £1. Money can be paid into the account at any branch of the bank.

Interest is calculated daily and credited to the account half-yearly, quarterly or monthly. Strictly speaking, withdrawals from the account require seven day's notice, but in practice banks allow withdrawals on demand subject to a seven-day interest deduction in lieu of notice.

Advantages

It is a very simple, convenient and flexible way of saving, with in-built liquidity and a competitive rate of return. If the investor has a current account as well, it is easy to transfer money between the two accounts, to avoid overdraft charges on the current account and to transfer surplus amounts from the current to the deposit account. Overseas depositors receive interest payments gross.

Disadvantages

The interest rate is comparatively modest, possibly four or five points below base rate and usually between one and a half and two points below the building society Ordinary Share rate (see below). If money is required quickly, then seven-day interest loss has to be borne. Interest is paid net of composite rate tax (CRT) which means that the basic rate taxpayer is not liable for further basic rate income tax; but this is a loss to the non-taxpaying depositor who cannot reclaim the tax.

2   Higher rate deposit accounts

Premium rates of interest are paid provided the balance remains above a specified level, say, £1000. In addition there is instant access to funds. Usually an 'interest ladder' is applied; the larger the credit balance in the account, the higher the rate of interest paid. Interest is calculated on a daily basis and credited half-yearly, quarterly or monthly.

Advantages

A high rate of return is earned. Instant withdrawals without financial penalties are possible. Transfers between a current account and this account are allowed, which assists adjustment of balances between the account according to the depositors' needs. Payments into the account can be made at any branch of the bank. Overseas investors receive interest payments without CRT deductions.

Disadvantages

Much larger amounts must be committed to the account to enjoy premium interest rates and instant withdrawals or transfers. Interest payments are net of CRT, hence are less profitable to non-taxpayers.

3 Regular savings accounts

Banks offer a slightly higher rate of interest on this account than they do on the ordinary deposit account. A regular amount, which can be as low as £10, is deposited in the account each month, usually from the current account (if the depositor has a current account) through a standing order. Interest is calculated on a daily basis and credited to the account half-yearly.

Advantages

There are various types of savings accounts, each with its own facilities. Regular savings are encouraged to produce large sums in due course. A higher rate of interest is earned. The depositor is usually allowed to miss one month's payment and make one withdrawal within specified intervals, usually six months, without losing the extra interest. This gives the depositor a measure of flexibility and liquidity.

Disadvantages

The extra interest advantage is lost if the committed amount is reduced. Non-taxpaying depositors (except overseas depositors) suffer because interest payments are net of CRT.

4 Investment accounts

Interest rates paid by the deposit-takers are sensitive to market conditions and can change significantly within a short space of time. If the investor takes the view that interest rates may fall and that their money will not be required during a specific period, then they may invest for fixed terms; a fixed rate of interest is guaranteed. There are three main variations of investment, or money market, accounts:

(a) Fixed term, fixed interest account. A fixed rate of interest (between 2.25% and 2.50 % below base rate) is paid if the depositor locks in their capital (usually a minimum of £5000 and a maximum of up to £30 000) for a fixed term of one, two or three months.

(b) Fixed notice, varied term account. The depositor selects a fixed notice period and deposits a large sum (a minimum of around £2000 and a maximum of between £20 000 and £30 000) in this account. In return they receive a rate of interest which may be 0.75% above the ordinary deposit rate and about 2% under the base rate. The bank is also bound by the fixed notice period: it will give the same notice period to the depositor of its intention to change the interest rate.

(c) Fixed term, varied interest account. If money is left in this account for a fixed term of one or more years, banks offer a high interest rate, often 2% above the ordinary deposit rate, depending upon the length of the fixed term for which the money is locked in. The rate of interest varies according to the movements in the money market rate.

Advantages

With fixed interest accounts depositors encounter the possibility of loss if interest rates fall during the fixed term. Even with varied rates, the returns are competitive since they are linked to the money market rates. At the end of the term the depositors may withdraw their money and re-invest it in the same type of account or in more appropriate accounts in keeping with their needs.

Disadvantages

Rather large surplus sums are needed to benefit from the high rates of return of these accounts; such sums are generally beyond the means of small investors. Apart from the fixed interest account, the rates are linked to money market rates, so they may go up or down during the fixed term period.

5   Monthly income accounts

Depositors with £2000 or more can open this type of account and enjoy the benefit of a high rate of return, paid into their current account every month on a day nominated by the depositor.

Advantages

High rate of interest is converted into a regular monthly payment to supplement and budget personal income and expenditure. Suitable for people receiving redundancy payments on losing their jobs.

Disadvantages

A lump sum of £2000 or more is needed to open this account. Interest payments are net of CRT which are unsuitable for people who are, or have become, non-taxpayers.

6 Higher interest cheque accounts

Usually not less than £200 is needed to open this account. Deposits of £10 000 or more earn high interest rates, paid quarterly. Usually cheques of not less than £200 may be drawn on this account.

Advantages

The account combines to a degree the convenience of a current account with the earning capacity of a high interest deposit account. Suitable for the personal and company sector investors, who can use the account as repository of their transaction and investment balances. Interest is paid quarterly which means that the CAR is higher than the nominal rate. Standing orders and direct debits can be operated through this account.

Disadvantages

It is not suitable for small amount depositors. The minimum amount restriction on cheques makes the account slightly inconvenient for quick payments of smaller amounts.

7 Treasurers (a large sum) deposit accounts

The amounts deposited tend to be between £10 000 and £50 000, depending on the period of notice the depositor wants to give for withdrawal: for seven days' notice the amount will have to be around £50 000, for longer periods of notice the minimum deposit may be smaller. The interest rate paid on the account fluctuates daily in line with the London Interbank Offered Rate (LIBOR), but is usually above the ordinary deposit rate. If the deposit is for a fixed term of up to one year, interest is usually paid on withdrawal. For longer term deposits interest is credited half-yearly to the depositor's current account.

Advantages

Suitable for the investment balances of businesses, firms, institutions and wealthy individuals. High interest rate, often 0.75% below the base rate, is earned by the investors.

Disadvantage

Large sums are locked in for fixed terms.

National Savings Bank (NSB)

There are two types of account offered by the NSB and operated through the Post Office:

1 Ordinary account

Anyone over the age of seven can open this account at any post office transacting National Savings business with as little as £1 and there is normally a maximum limit of £10 000. Accounts may also be opened in the names of children under age seven, but withdrawals are not normally allowed until the child is aged seven. Up to £100 can be withdrawn on demand at a post office. Larger amounts can be obtained within a few days by applying to the National Savings Bank in Glasgow. If a depositor has used an ordinary account at a chosen post office for at least six months, the account can be designated as a Regular Customer account, and up to £250 in cash can be withdrawn at the chosen post office.

Two interest rates are paid on ordinary accounts which for 1987 were 3% and 6% (5% and 2½% from July 1988). To get the higher rate, the depositor must keep the account open for the whole of the calendar year, then for each complete calendar month, during the year that £500 or more is kept in the account, the depositors will receive 6% p.a. For other months the interest rate will be 3% p.a. Interest is earned on the sums deposited from the first day of the month following deposit and ceases to accrue on the first day of the month in which withdrawals are made. For example, a deposit made on 15 July 1988 and withdrawn on 15 October 1988 would earn interest for two complete months of August and September 1988.

Advantages

The first £70 of interest in any one year is free of all UK income tax and capital gains tax and married men and women are each entitled to £70 tax-free interest a year. Interest is automatically credited to the account on 31 December of each year. There is simplicity in opening and operating this account which offers liquidity and a reasonable rate of interest. There is convenience too: there are 22 000 post offices offering longer opening hours than the banks. There are free standing orders for regular payments. The £70 tax-free interest income is advantageous to all taxpayers, especially to higher rate taxpayers. The two interest rates once announced – around November of each year – are guaranteed for the whole of the following year.

Disadvantages

No interest is paid on any amount not deposited for a full calendar month.

The facilities offered to an ordinary account holder are limited compared with a current account holder with a commercial bank.

2 Investment account

A much higher rate of interest is paid on this account, 8.5% p.a. from July 1988 and the minimum and maximum amounts of deposit are £5 and £100 000 respectively. The latest interest rate can be ascertained from most post offices. The interest is calculated on a daily basis and earned on each whole pound for each day it is held on deposit, and is automatically credited to the account on 31 December of each year.

Advantages

It offers a higher rate of interest than a deposit account at a commercial bank. It is particularly attractive to non-taxpaying individuals, charities and other organisations entitled to exemption from tax, since interest is paid without deductions of income tax, whilst taxpayers do not have to pay the tax until it is due.

Disadvantages

Unlike the ordinary account, there are no tax concessions. Withdrawals are subject to one month's notice which is longer than the period of notice required with a deposit account with a commercial bank. This makes balances with the NSB investment account less liquid than balances in the deposit accounts of commercial banks.

Finance houses

The 1987 Banking Act has 'authorised' the major finance houses for deposit-taking business. Consequently their activities are monitored by the Bank of England, and they participate in the Deposit Protection Scheme under the 1987 Act. Certain other finance houses are wholly or partly owned by the big banks. There are also many smaller independent houses.

Generally speaking, the creditworthiness of finance houses is considered below that of banks and building societies, therefore the interest rates quoted by them are above the banks' deposit rates and the ordinary share rates of building societies. They take deposits, normally above £500, for fixed periods of one, three and six months. Longer fixed term deposits with fixed interest rates can be negotiated with the houses.

When lending to a finance house, investors should check the nature of its major activities and ensure that they are not accepting an above-average risk. If a house is offering lenders above-average rates, then it suggests that lenders are wary of its creditworthiness and will lend only at above-average rates, and that the house itself is lending at above-average rates to borrowers who are considered too risky by more cautious and responsible lenders.

Advantages

Finance houses which are authorised under the 1987 Act and those which are wholly owned by the big banks can legitimately be considered as safe as banks. If interest rates are expected to fall then fixed interest-lending for longer term to the houses would be profitable.

Disadvantages

Withdrawals are not allowed, except on draft, during the fixed-term period. They pay interest net of CRT which is not very profitable to individuals or organisations not liable to tax.

National Savings

The Department of National Savings (DNS) and the Post Office are two different organisations. The DNS pays the Post Office a large sum annually to carry out DNS business through the innumerable post offices in the UK. Keen competition for savings has changed DNS a great deal; from the old patriotic voluntary savings body to a highly sophisticated and competitive investment institution. DNS products offer substantial investment advantages not only to the small saver but also to more sophisticated individuals, as well as (in certain cases) to trust, charities, voluntary bodies, registered companies and other corporate bodies. Investments in the DNS products, including the deposits in the National Savings Bank accounts, are in effect loans to the UK Central Government and therefore can be regarded as absolutely safe in monetary terms.

The terms of DNS products change considerably but the general characteristics of each remains relatively constant. In July 1987 the following products were on offer.

1 Fixed interest National Savings Certificate (NSCs)

There are two kinds of National Savings Certificate; fixed-interest and index-linked. NSCs offer a fixed guaranteed return, provided the investor holds them for a fixed term. They can be purchased free of cost at post offices and banks.

The 33rd Issue of fixed-interest NSCs was introduced on 1 May 1987. Certificates of this Issue are purchased in units of £25 with a maximum holding of 40 units (cost £1000), which is in addition to any holdings of units of previous issues. Each unit offers a guaranteed rate of 7% p.a. compound, if it is kept for the full five-year term. For example, four units of the 33rd Issue (cost £100) will, after five years, have a value of £140.25. The table below shows what rate an investor will get if certificates are encashed on or before their fifth anniversary:

Date of repayment	Compound interest earned from the date of purchase
Before 1st anniversary	0%
On or after 2nd anniversary of purchase but before 2nd	5.50% p.a.
On or after 3rd anniversary of purchase but before 3rd	5.75% p.a.
On or after 4th anniversary of purchase but before 4th	6.00% p.a.
At 5th anniversary of purchase date	7.00% p.a.

If a 33rd Issue Certificate is cashed before the end of the first year no interest is paid – only the purchase price is repaid. After the first year interest is earned for each complete three months and compounded annually on the anniversary of purchase.

Therefore, NSCs should not be bought as a short- term investment but with the intention of holding them for the full five years in order to obtain the full benefit from them.

Special facilities are offered for those people who are cashing in their holdings of earlier Issues held for at least five years and reinvesting the proceeds in 33rd Issue Certificates: such investors can hold up to £5000 of 'Reinvestment Certificates' of the 33rd Issue, in addition to any purchases made within the general £1000 limit. Holders of Reinvestment Certificates are entitled to interest at 5.5% p.a. for each complete three months if they encash them within one year of purchase. To obtain the Reinvestment Certificates, they should fill in a Repayment/Reinvestment form, available from most post offices and banks, and send the completed form along with their eligible NSCs, including Index-linked Issues (see below) and any inherited Certificates, to the Savings Certificate Office in Durham.

The 34th issue, introduced on 22nd July 1988, guarantees a tax-free return of 7.5% p.a. compound over five years. Investment is limited to £1000 per person, plus an extra £5000 for those reinvesting money from past NSCs that have matured.

Advantages

Fixed interest NSCs offer a return which is free of income and capital gains tax. The return is guaranteed for a five year period. They are particularly attractive to higher-rate taxpayers and to small savers requiring a safe investment. They can be bought free of cost at irregular intervals. At the end of the fixed term, tax-free interest continues to accrue at an attractive rate (see below).

Disadvantages

No interest is paid before the end of the first year, except for Reinvestment Certificates. The terms offered on each new issue depends upon prevailing interest rates and how keen the government is to borrow, e.g. the 32nd Issue offered an interest rate of 8.75% over five years. Any issue can be withdrawn from sale without notice. Interest accrued cannot be withdrawn without cashing in the Certificates, which will take eight working days.

General Extension Rate (GER)

This is a variable rate of interest for matured certificates of the 7th and subsequent issues when they have completed their fixed terms. GER is changed periodically in order to keep it competitive. The repayment value of a certificate is increased for each complete three month period held beyond the end of the fixed term. Interest is calculated separately for each completed month at the rate on offer at the beginning of the month. The interest for each month is one twelfth of the annual rate. At each anniversary of purchase, the return is 'capitalised'. This means that the interest for the previous year is added to the capital sum and rounded to the nearest penny. The whole amount then continues to earn interest, which is of course tax-free. The GER from October 1987 was 6.51% p.a. The GER, from 22nd July 1988, is 5.01% p.a. There is almost a 2.5% incentive to switch into the 34th issue.

Earlier issue

Investors may retain earlier issues of fixed interest NSC, after the end of the guaranteed period. As they continue to earn interest at the GER they are particularly attractive to higher-rate taxpayers, bearing in mind the maximum holding limits placed on new issues. The 33rd Issue introduced a new method of calculating the value of NSCs based on specified rates of interest. Earlier issues grew in value by the addition of specified increments, usually every three or four months from the first anniversary, moving on to the GER at the end of a specified period. The first six issues, which were sold up to 1939, may be held indefinitely, but the return is now very low (less than 2% p.a.) making them relatively unattractive.

2 Index-linked National Savings Certificates

These certificates can now be bought by any person above the age of seven from most post offices and banks. Certificates may also be bought in the name of a child under seven years of age but may not normally be encashed until the child attains the age of seven. The 4th Issue of Index-linked NSCs became available in August 1986. An investor may hold from £25 to £5000 in these certificates and they can be bought in multiples of £25. The £5000 maximum is in addition to holdings of all other NSCs. These certificates are held for a full year from the date of purchase. If cashed before the first anniversary then only the purchase price will be repaid. To get the maximum benefit the certificates should be held for a full five year term, as can be seen from the following table.

Purchase Anniversary Value		Index-linking for year		3% of purchase price		1st anniversary Value
Purchase Anniversary Value	+	Index-linking for year	+	3% of purchase price	=	1st anniversary Value
1st Anniversary Value	+	Index-linking for year	+	3.25% of 1st Anniversary Value	=	2nd Anniversary Value
2nd Anniversary Value	+	Index-linking for year	+	3.5% of 2nd Anniversary Value	=	3rd Anniversary Value
3rd Anniversary Value	+	Index-linking for year	+	4.5% of 3rd Anniversary price	=	4th Anniversary Value
4th Anniversary Value	+	Index-linking for year	+	6% of 4th Anniversary Value	=	*5th Anniversary Value*

This adds up to an overall return of 4.04% p.a., on top of inflation proofing, if the certificates are held for the full five years.

The index-linked value, according to the Retail Prices Index, will be calculated as $V \times \dfrac{B}{A}$, where 'V' equals the value of the certificate at the beginning of the index-linked period (ie, the purchase price or the value at anniversary). 'A' equals the index figure applicable to the calendar month in which the first day of the index-linked period falls (i.e. the purchase date or an anniversary of it).

'B' equals the index figure applicable to the calendar month in which the final day of the index-linked period falls (i.e. an anniversary date or, where repayment is being made between anniversary date, the most recent date which is one or more complete months after two previous anniversary dates. For example, for a certificate purchased on 18th July the final day of the index-linked period will fall on the 18th of August).

If the certificates are held beyond the 5th anniversary date, they will continue to earn interest and index-linking on such extension terms as may be announced by the Treasury.

Advantages

A tax-free rate of return which matches the rate of inflation plus a tax-free rate of interest are guaranteed. If the Retail Price Index falls, the value of a certificate at an anniversary date will never be less than an amount equal to (a) its purchase price or its value at the immediately proceeding anniversary date plus (b) interest at the rate for the relevant year as shown in the above table.

Disadvantages

Repayment is at purchase price only if the certificate has to be cashed before the first anniversary of its purchase date. In times of low inflation the return on index-linked certificates may not prove attractive when compared with some other types of investment.

Earlier index-linked issues

Investors may retain earlier issues of index-linked NSCs which continue to earn an attractive inflation-proofed tax-free return. Of the three earlier issues the 3rd Issue is similar to the 4th Issue, but with a slightly lower overall rate of interest for the first years. The Retirement Issue and the 2nd Issue continue to be revalued in line with inflation and in addition they have bonuses (4% of purchase price added on the 5th anniversary, 4% of 5th anniversary value added on the 10th anniversary) and annual supplements (paid since 1983–4% of July 1986 value on 1 August 1987, 3% of July 1987 value on 1 August 1988 1.5% of July 1988 value if held until 1st August 1989) all tax free. Taking these additions into account the overall return can be quite attractive. Care should be taken when planning to obtain repayment to ensure that an attractive increment is not missed. For example you could lose out by taking repayment just before the 10th anniversary, or in July just before the annual supplement. At the time of writing annual supplements have been announced only up to 1989.

3   Yearly Plan

This plan was introduced in July 1984 for regular savers after the withdrawal of the index-linked Save As You Earn scheme. It is a regular flexible investment scheme. A person can invest between £20 and £200 a month, in multiples of £5 a month by standing order for 12 months and at the end of that year a Yearly Plan Certificate is issued to the value of the payments plus the interest they have earned in that year. If the Certificate is held for a further four years the maximum guaranteed rate of interest is earned. After the first year, the investor can carry on buying further certificates for as long as the Yearly Plan is on offer by simply continuing the monthly payments. Each year the Savings Certificate Office will inform the investor of the guaranteed rate of interest applying to the next agreement. In this way the investor's saving can build up into a large sum for a major purchase or for retirement. Alternatively the Certificates can be cashed in one at a time to provide an annual income.

The rates of return on offer until 21st July 1988 were are as follows:

Year 1   5.25%
Year 2   7.25%
Year 3   7.25%
Year 4   7.25%
Year 5   7.25%

The 5-year return averages 7% p.a., and at that rate of return £20 and £200 per month will have a value after five years of £326.58 and £3276.2 respectively.

From 22nd July 1988, the rate of return is 7.5% p.a. if 12 payments are made and held for five years.

After the certificate has been held for four years it will earn interest at the General Extension Rate which varies from time to time. The certificate can be cashed before four years, but the return will not be as good as at the end of five years.

Advantages

Regular monthly investments are possible for as little as one year, or from year to year, conveniently made by monthly standing order. The rate of return is guaranteed for a full five year period, whatever happens to interest rates elsewhere. All interest is tax-free. The investor enjoys easy access to the money and complete security of capital. The guaranteed tax-free interest has an appeal to high-rate taxpayers.

Disadvantages

Investors must take into consideration the outlook for inflation, the anticipated trend of interest rates and whether they are able to hold the certificates for the full term.

4   National Savings Income Bonds

These Bonds are attractive to investors who have a minimum of £2000 to invest and who want a reasonably secure income rather than capital growth. Larger purchases and additions to existing holdings are in multiples of £1000 up to a maximum holding of £100 000.

Interest is calculated daily and starts on the date the investment is received. The rate of interest from 1st May 1988 is 9% p.a. but it may vary from time to time. Any change will be widely publicised, giving six week's notice.

The monthly income payments begin six weeks after the purchase of the Bond. They are paid on the fifth day of each month, either into the holder's bank, building society or National Savings Bank account or directly by warrant (like a crossed cheque) to the holder. On the basis of a 9% p.a. rate of interest, the minimum holding of £2000 will produce an annual income of £180 and a monthly average income of £15 (average depending on the number of days in each month). Each additional investment of £1000 adds an average of £7.50 to the monthly income, equivalent to £90 additional annual income. A maximum holding of £100 000 yields an annual income of £9000 and an average monthly income of £750. Interest is paid in full and is taxable.

Almost anyone can buy these Bonds at the post office. Bond holders can have all or part of their holdings repaid within three month's notice. If the Bond is kept for at least a year, interest will be paid in full. If it is cashed within the first year, interest will be paid at half the rate from the date of purchase to the date of repayment. Part encashment is allowed in multiples of £1000, provided at least £2000 is left in the scheme.

Advantages

Income Bonds offer monthly income, a competitive rate of interest, no tax deductions (unlike banks and building societies) and absolute security. It is ideal for those who need regular income from capital (e.g., those who have received redundancy payment or those with low incomes) and non-taxpayers.

Disadvantages

A minimum of £2000 is required to participate in the scheme. Withdrawals within the first year earn half the rate of interest. Interest rate is variable and taxable.

5 Indexed Income Bonds

These bonds protect the investors' income from loss in purchasing power through inflation. Most of the conditions are the same as with the ordinary Income Bonds, except for the following.

The minimum investment is £5000 which may increase in multiples of £1000 to a maximum of £100 000. The bonds guarantee inflation-proofed income for ten years. Interest is paid in full on the 20th of each month and for the first year the rate is 8% p.a. At the end of each year the monthly income is increased in line with the Retail Prices Index. Part encashment of holdings are allowed in multiples of £1000 provided the amount left in the holding does not fall below £5000.

Advantages

Monthly income does not fall in its purchasing power. Interest rates are high and guaranteed. Since interest is paid without tax deduction, they are attractive to non-taxpayers.

Disadvantages

Unlike Index-linked NSCs, these bonds do not provide inflation proofing of capital. A minimum sum of £5000 is required to participate in the scheme.

Note: The Indexed-Income Bonds were withdrawn by the DNS on 28 August 1987. This was due to several reasons, but mainly because the investors began to believe that the government had won the battle against inflation and that the inflation rate will not rise again as dramatically as in the past.

6   National Savings Deposit Bonds

These Bonds are designed for lump sum investment with a view to acquiring capital growth. Interest at 9% p.a. (from 1st May 1988) is calculated on a daily basis and is capitalised (added without tax deductions to the capital value of the Bond) on the anniversary of purchase. The interest rate can change from time to time but any change will be widely publicised, giving six week's notice. Bonds can be bought from most post offices. The minimum purchase is £100. Larger purchases may be made in multiples of £50 to a maximum capital holding limit of £100 000.

A Bond may be cashed in full or in part – minimum withdrawal £50, provided at least £100 in capital value remains – on giving three month's notice in writing. Once a Bond has been held for a full one year, interest is paid on the date it is withdrawn. Bonds withdrawn in whole or in part before the first anniversary earn interest at half the published rate on the amount withdrawn.

Advantages

Premium interest rate is paid in full hence their attraction to investors not subject to income tax. The capital is absolutely safe. Suitable for investors seeking capital growth.

Disadvantages

Although the interest earned is capitalised in full, it is still liable to income tax and must be entered on income tax returns. Interest is paid annually which is not as beneficial a return as the same amount paid at shorter intervals. Since three month's notice is compulsory for withdrawals, the Bonds are not highly liquid.

7 Premium Bonds

The money spent on buying these Bonds is saving, not hoarding, with a spice of gambling, because the money remains safe and intact and the purchaser, who has held the Bond for three months, has the opportunity, if lucky (the chance of a single £1 Bond unit winning a prize in a monthly draw is one in 11 000), of sharing in the weekly and monthly prizes drawn by ERNIE (Electronic Random Number Indicator Equipment). There are three weekly prizes of £100 000, £50 000 and £25 000 each. The monthly prizes include over 170 000 prizes from £50 to £1000, 25 prizes of £5000, 5 prizes of £10 000 and the jackpot of £250 000. Prizes are free of all UK income tax and capital gains tax.

There is a monthly prize fund which is determined by calculating one month's interest at 7% p.a. (from 1 August 1987, the rate may change from time to time) on each eligible Bond. After a Bond has qualified for its first draw it will be included in each succeeding draw until repaid. Even on the death of the holder, a Bond remains eligible for a draw held in the month of his death and in the following twelve calendar months, unless it is repaid earlier. Prize winners will be informed of the good news by the Bonds and Stock Office at their last address. There are thousands of prizes unclaimed because Bond holders have failed to inform the Bonds and Stock Office of a change of address!

Bonds are issued in multiples of five £1 units, subject to a minimum purchase of ten £1 units; no person may hold more than 10 000 £1 units. They can be bought by individual investors from post offices and banks. They can be bought by parents, guardians, or grandparents for children under sixteen. The purchase price of a Bond is repayable in full on application to the Bonds and Stock Office.

Advantages

The Bondholder's capital is absolutely safe and bonds can be encashed in full at any time (liquidity). The more Bonds one holds the better the chance of winning. As prizes are tax free, higher rate taxpayers find them particularly attractive.

Disadvantages

The Bondholder is in effect gambling with the interest on the capital. The Bonds cannot be called an investment because there is no income or capital growth arising from their purchase and they do not provide a hedge against inflation. One pound kept in a Premium Bond since the early 1960s will have a purchasing power of less than 11p in 1988 (but this is true of all unindexed cash or fixed-capital investments).

Building societies

Saving and investing in building society products is, literally, as safe as houses, because between 75 and 80 per cent of their advances are against the security of property which is usually an appreciating asset. It may be argued that building societies, as repositories of the public's savings, are safer than commercial banks: lending against the security of a house is more secure than lending against the security of a business. Two further points add to the safety of building societies: the activities of the building societies are monitored very closely by the relevant government department, the Building Societies Commission, and the great majority of societies are members of the Building Societies Association (BSA), which has entry requirements and is willing to come to the rescue of members in distress. The BSA has a deposit protection scheme, open to members and non-members.

Building societies' products are in keen competition with the products of banks and National Savings, and each building society rigorously competes with the other societies for the public's deposits. There is a large measure of similarity between the features and rates of return of the products of the larger societies. Generally speaking, the range of products of larger societies is wider and the rate of return is slightly lower compared with smaller societies. From the investor's point of view, non-members of BSA and non-participants in the deposit protection scheme of the BSA may legitimately be considered less safe.

A note of caution if investing in building society products: building societies borrow short and lend long. Tax relief on mortgages (see Chapter 5) helps their market, but is not guaranteed for all time. In particular, economic conditions may cause difficulties to arise, e.g. the large number of repossessions during 1986 were due to high unemployment, and similar problems arose during the miners' strike. What happens if investors withdraw their money *en masse* to buy privatisation issues, or if house prices fall and interest rates rise? In addition to these difficulties, there are risks associated with new types of business now being added to their traditional role. In the past, some small societies have run into difficulties.

There are seven main building society products, on which the rates of return and penalties depend upon the length of notice the investors are required to give for withdrawals of their money and the size of deposit. Although each society gives its schemes different names, basically the schemes are similar and are as follows.

1 Deposit accounts

Should a society collapse, the deposit account holders will be paid first. This, coupled with the no notice requirement – therefore no penalty – for instant access, means that the societies offer the lowest rate on their deposit accounts.

Advantages

Usually instant access to funds with no penalties. Top priority in the pecking order in a collapsed society's net assets.

Disadvantages

It is unlikely that a BSA member society would get into serious difficulties but the depositors earn the lowest rate of return. If a society does get into difficulty, there might be some delay before even deposit account holders could withdraw cash. There is a limit imposed on withdrawals of cash.

2 Paid-up Shares

Some societies call them Ordinary Shares. Interest on these is about 0.25% above that paid on deposit accounts. Any amount can be invested and withdrawal terms are similar to deposit accounts. These shares are the main building society investments.

Advantages

A fractionally higher rate is paid than on deposit accounts. Interest is calculated on a daily basis and usually credited on a half-yearly or yearly basis. Paid-up share accounts can be opened with as little as £1. There is usually access to funds without any penalty.

Disadvantages

Interest rate return is lower than available elsewhere, and is paid net of tax; tax deductions cannot be reclaimed by non-taxpayers.

3 Subscription Shares

Sometimes these are also called Monthly Savings Plans, Build-up Shares, etc. and are for regular savers who earn a rate of interest between 1.00 and 1.5% over the Paid-up share rate. Typically the monthly savings range is from £20 to £100, and in some cases, to £250 (double for joint accounts). There is no limit to the amount which can be held. If the investor wishes to keep the interest advantage, he/she should not make more than one (usually) withdrawal or keep a specified minimum sum in the account.

Advantages

Safety with high interest returns. Monthly investment amounts can be varied by arrangement. Interest is earned on a daily basis and credited to the account every six months; thereafter interest itself earns interest which increases the overall return on the investment.

Disadvantages

Lack of liquidity due to very restrictive withdrawal terms. Interest is paid net of tax which cannot be reclaimed.

4   Instant Access Accounts

These are amongst the more recent products of larger building societies. They offer high interest rates with instant access to capital with no loss of interest. These accounts were introduced to compete with the high interest deposit accounts of commercial banks, and virtually replaced the old seven day's notice and 28 day accounts. A minimum balance of £500 is required to open these accounts.

Advantage

The investor has instant access to funds while they are earning very attractive interest rates, much higher than offered by the banks.

Disadvantage

At least £500 is required to open these accounts.

5   Fixed Term Accounts

Sums in excess of £10 000 are deposited for fixed terms in these accounts and in return the building society agrees to pay between 1.5% to 3.5% above the ordinary share rate. Withdrawals can be made without penalty at 90 day's notice. On the other hand, instant withdrawals are available with loss of 90 day's interest.

Advantages

A guaranteed margin over the ordinary share rate is earned. Instant withdrawals are possible.

Disadvantage

While the margin over the ordinary share rate is guaranteed, the ordinary share rate is not: if the ordinary share rate falls then so does the overall rate. (The same is true of interest rates guaranteed to be a few points over the base rates offered by banks.) Investors need to shop around regularly to find the best interest rates and conditions. Interest is paid net of CRT.

6 Fixed Notice Accounts

Larger societies have abolished the seven day and 28 day notice accounts but still offer 90 day notice accounts. The minimum investment required is typically £500. If the balance remains in excess of £5000 instant withdrawals are possible.

Advantage

Safety, along with marginally better rates than offered by banks on savings accounts.

Disadvantage

Instant withdrawals require keeping large balances and early withdrawals are not permitted except at the death of an investor.

7 Save-As-You-Earn (SAYE)

These schemes encourage contractual savings of fixed sums for five years, in the first instance. Anyone over the age of 16 can contract to save from £4 to £20 per month over five years. There is no direct interest return, but at the end of five years the saver gets a bonus of 14 monthly payments, in lieu of interest, which amounts to a compound rate of return of 8.3% p.a. After five years, the SAYE contract may be ended and the capital plus bonus withdrawn. Alternatively, it can be left on deposit for a further two years with no extra payments, to earn a second bonus of 14 monthly payments, which amounts to a saving return of 8.62% over seven years. Savings withdrawn during the first year will be repaid in full but without interest. Savers who withdraw from the scheme after the first year receive compound interest of 6% p.a. instead of a bonus. Where the saver dies before completion of the contract there is compound interest of 8% p.a. Contributions missed may not be made up by paying off arrears, but the contract may be extended by up to six months to complete it. Payments can be deducted, monthly or weekly, from the saver's wages and paid directly to the society. A lump sum SAYE scheme is operated by some building societies which enables a tax advantage to be enjoyed out of a capital sum instead of from regular savings. The scheme works as follows: the investor deposits a lump sum equal to 60 monthly instalments into a special share account. Each month the society transfers a sum equal to one monthly instalment to the SAYE account, while the balance continues to earn interest in its own right. After five years, the saver will have 60 SAYE contributions plus 14 months bonus *plus* the interest earned on the lump sum in the share account. To take advantage of the second bonus the saver simply leaves the money in the SAYE account for another two years.

Advantages

Both bonuses and any interest payments are tax free and therefore, in a modest way, attractive to higher-rate taxpayers. Regular, safe savings with a better rate of return than is available on certain National Savings products. The rate of return is guaranteed for the life of the contract.

Disadvantages

Building societies' own savings schemes may offer better rates of return. If the contract is broken during the first year only the amount paid is returned. If the completed contract savings are withdrawn between the five and seven year period the saver only receives the five year bonus.

Local authorities

Some local authorities, from time to time, invite the public to lend to them directly at a fixed rate of interest over a certain period of time. There are two main types of cash investment offered by the local authorities.

1 Temporary loans

A few local authorities will accept investments for a term of less than one year, on which interest is paid either monthly or at the end of the term. Notice of withdrawal may vary from seven days upwards.

The tax position of these loans depends upon the amounts of deposits and the periods of deposits: for deposits of *less* than 50 000, or for periods of less than seven days, the unreclaimable CRT is deducted from accrued interest. Larger amounts (50 000 or more) deposited for at least seven days receive interest without CRT deduction. Small deposits receive a lower rate than larger ones. The rate paid on the three month's and six month's notice deposits are somewhat lower than those obtainable from finance houses because deposits with local authorities carry a lower degree of risk.

2 Townhall, or 'over-the-counter', bonds

Loans exceeding the one year term are usually mortgage loans to local authorities: these loans are charged against local authorities' assets and revenues.

The terms offered by local authorities on these bonds show considerable variations in the matter of the period of loans, the minimum acceptable amounts (although £500 is fairly common) and the rate of interest. The rate of interest paid on longer term bonds are generally slightly higher than similarly dated local authority stocks quoted on the Stock Exchange (see Chapter 4). These rates are 0.5 – 1% below the banks' base rates depending on the amount to be invested, the period of loan and the trends in interest rates. The rate of interest is fixed for the specified term and paid half-yearly, net of CRT, although some local authorities pay the interest as a lump sum at the end of the fixed term, in which case the rate should be about 0.25–0.5% higher.

Sums invested are locked in for periods of between one and ten years and will be repaid only at the end of the term or on the death of the lender. However, there is a limited secondary market in these loans and there are often arrangements whereby money can be obtained before the expiry of the term on payment of a penalty should an emergency arise. Therefore, mortgage loans should only be entered into if the investor is sure that the capital will not be required during the stated period of the loan. If the rate of interest on a loan exceeds the current rate, then a local authority may be happy to repay before the fixed period to meet some emergency because it could then borrow more cheaply elsewhere.

Advantages

These are low risk investments which pay good rates of return, with no expense initially or on repayment. If interest rates are generally likely to come down, townhall bonds can prove a bargain because the rates are fixed for the full term.

Disadvantage

Capital is locked in for the full period during which general rates may rise. This is a serious disadvantage suffered for a modest additional return.

Others

1 Public Boards

Borrowing by water boards, port authorities, etc. resemble local authority borrowings in so far as security is concerned, but there are others whose security is not quite as risk free. Comparisons with other safer loans are essential before deciding on loans to non-government bodies (see Chapter 4).

2 Offshore Bank Deposits

Most major UK banks have offshore subsidiaries in the Channel Islands and the Isle of Man. Since the banks, building societies and local authorities too now pay interest to investors net of CRT, these offshore deposits are realistic alternatives to investment in National Savings products because they also pay interest in full. UK residents are, of course, liable to income tax on the interest from these deposits.

Summary of cash investments

1   Cash investments are loans to the public and private sector institutions, which, while earning a rate of return, are repayable on demand with or without penalty or at relatively short notice.
2   National Savings' Products, except Deposit Bonds, Income Bonds and Investment Accounts, give a rate of return in full and free of all UK income and capital gains taxes, whereas investment in the products of other deposit-takers produces returns in most cases net of CRT and subject to the Capital Gains Tax. This makes comparisons complicated.
3   A rate of interest paid more frequently is in effect providing a greater return than the same rate paid less frequently (CAR).
4   The investor should carefully balance available rates against potential risks of different investment products.
5   Each investor should keep part of their capital in cash investments as a liquidity cushion to meet unforeseen contingencies.
6   Cash savings schemes not only provide funds for sudden emergencies but also help accumulate sufficient funds for more permanent and worthwhile investments.
7   Cash investments involve no costs, initially or on repayment, and are easy to buy.
8   Cash investments can be started with as little as £1 and increased, in some cases, up to any amount.
9   NSCs, SAYE contracts, fixed term deposits and shares, and Townhall bonds are not cash investments.
10 The disadvantage with cash investments is that they do not grow: the amount of money available can never be greater than the amount originally invested together with the interest earned.
11 Investments with banks, building societies, National Savings, finance houses and local authorities involve no costs, initially or on repayment at maturity.

12 Companies are permitted to invest in the National Savings Banks' Investment Account, but not in Ordinary Account.

13 Building societies often refuse accounts to companies.

14 Clubs and other incorporated bodies may invest in every product described in this chapter, except for certain National Savings products and SAYE contracts.

15 The period of notice for withdrawals and the cash penalty in lieu of notice, are important investment considerations.

Selected questions

The following questions are drawn from or based on questions which were asked in past CIOB Investment examination papers. They have been selected to reinforce understanding of the contents of this chapter. Spend a few minutes jotting down the relevant points before looking at the brief answers provided.

Q1 Describe briefly the differences between savings, investment and speculation.

Q2 Write short notes on the following and indicate the type of investor who would find them most suitable.

(a) A building society share account.

(b) A National Savings Bank Ordinary account.

Q3 Set out the characteristics of local authority mortgages. For what class of investor would they be most suitable?

Q4 Describe the risks involved in holding National Savings Bond Investment accounts, and suggest how these risks may be minimised.

Q5 (a) Describe the characteristics of National Savings Certificates and mention briefly any advantages and disadvantages this type of investment has for different types of investor. (Ignore index-linked issues.)

(b) State briefly the advantages and disadvantages of the current issue (4th issue) of index-linked National Savings Certificates as an investment.

Brief answers

A1 *Saving* refers to the accumulation of surplus income for a specific future objective.

Investment aims at obtaining an income, capital growth and sound value for money.

Speculation is based on expectation of short-term gains resulting from changes in prices/interest rates, and acceptance of a high risk/reward ratio based on a careful examination of available facts.

A2 *A building society share account*: Interest is calculated on a daily basis, credited on a half-yearly basis and paid net of CRT. Not suitable for basic rate and high-rate taxpayers, requiring income and/or a liquid reserve.

A National Savings Bank Ordinary account: Interest is calculated monthly, credited yearly. First £70 p.a. (£140 for married couples) free of all UK taxes. Suitable, in a modest way, for high rate taxpayer. Up to £10,000 can be deposited and up to £ 100 can be withdrawn on any day on demand.

A3 *Local Authority mortgages*: = Townhall bonds = local authority mortgage loans = 'over-the-counter' bonds. They are charged on the authority's assets and revenues. Offered for sale via newspaper advertisements.

Terms simple and straightforward: rate of interest fixed for full term, usually higher than the yield on 2–10 year gilts, interest paid, net of CRT, half yearly. Early withdrawals not allowed, except at death of holder, or in an emergency, with penalties.

Suitable for small investor seeking good yield, low risk but must be prepared to lock up capital for the full term.

A4 *Risks involved in holding National Savings Bank Investment accounts*: Interest rate risk: reduction in income when interest rates fall. Inflation risk: reduction in the purchasing power of capital invested; to some extent high interest in time of high inflation may compensate for the inflationary loss.

Methods for minimisation of risks: Switch to fixed interest investment when the rates are expected to fall. Diversify investment portfolio across investments bearing different kinds of risk.

A5 (a)

- Investment in NSCs guaranteed by the government, absolutely safe.
- Current 34th Issue: No interest, as such, paid, but a fixed, free of all taxes, 7.5% p.a. return added to purchase price, if held for full five years. Tax-free, compounded return can be very high for high rate taxpayers. Certainty and safety make NSCs attractive to all investors. Can be cashed any time: if cashed within one year of purchase, only purchase price is repaid, after that, to minimise early encashment disadvantage, relate withdrawal to the three-month credit period.

(b) Investments in the 4th Issue of Index-linked NSCs, being linked to RPI movements, never falls in value in real terms. Additionally, a 4.04% unindexed bonus is paid if I-LNSC held for full five years. Easily obtained and encashed. Absolutely safe, government-guaranteed. If held during falling RPI, increase on capital is very little.

Specially selected question

The Finance Act 1984 contains provisions which will require a composite rate of tax to be paid to the Inland Revenue in respect of bank interest paid on and from 6th April 1985 to individuals resident in the UK.

(a) What is meant by 'composite rate tax'?

(b) Describe the effects of the introduction of composite rate tax on the following investments: interest-bearing personal accounts with clearing banks; the National Savings Bank; building societies; pension funds. How will this new legislation affect the competitiveness of the interestbearing accounts?

Model answer

(a) Composite rate tax (CRT) is based on an estimate of what investors would pay if they were assessed individually. The rate is fixed annually. Special arrangements exist with the Inland Revenue under which such institutions as are required to deduct CRT at source, before paying interest to investors, pay the amount deducted to the Inland Revenue. Those investors who are liable to the basic rate of tax have no further obligation to pay income tax on incomes which they received net of CRT: interest paid under the scheme is decreed to be income from which income tax at the *basic rate* has been deducted. Clearly higher-rate taxpayers have obligations to pay additional tax. Non-taxpayers, however, cannot reclaim the CRT deductions.

(b) Prior to the implementation of the Finance Act 1984, CRT only applied to interest paid by building societies. After the implementation of this Act, banks are required to pay CRT to the Inland Revenue in respect of interest paid on or after 6th April 1985 on sterling deposits where the interest is due, or ultimately due, to an individual or group of individuals. CRT will not be applied to interest paid by the banks on:

- Term deposits placed before 6.7.84 and maturing after 5.4.85.
- Term deposits for £50 000 or more placed for a period of at least seven days or more.
- All deposits held in Jersey, Guernsey and the Isle of Man whether or not in respect of either a resident or a non-resident.
- Deposits of non-residents who have completed a Declaration Form stating that they are classed as non-residents for tax purposes.

The position of the National Savings Bank is unchanged, i.e. CRT will not apply to interest from the National Savings Bank. Pension funds are outside the CRT scheme, therefore interest payments by them are unaffected.

The competition for deposits between commercial banks and building societies, after the introduction of the CRT scheme, became more even. However, it would seem that there is now a considerable inducement to invest in the National Savings Bank for those investors who are not liable to basic rate income tax. This advantage is strongly emphasised in the advertisement of the National Savings Bank's accounts in the newspapers and on television.

The commercial banks have tried to redress the balance by the introduction of high rate deposit accounts, some with chequebook facilities. The building societies too have met the competition by packaging their extra-income accounts, some with instant liquidity.

Updating

The terms of cash and direct interest-bearing investments change frequently. Therefore, it is essential – especially just before the Investment exams in May and October – to obtain the latest terms of the products of commercial banks (from their branch offices), National Savings (either from large post offices or by ringing (01) 605 9461, or if you have a Prestel set, key *50042#), building societies (from the branches of major societies) and local authorities (by consulting the CIPFA lists at your branch or by telephoning (01) 638 6361 and ordering a copy of the lists).

The Financial Times is an excellent reference source for the current rates on most investment products. *The Investors' Chronicle* and 'Money Box', the BBC's weekly radio programme, will also help keep your knowledge updated. Pay special attention to any *Signpost* article on Investment topics by the CIB chief examiner and/or moderator in *Banking World*.

4 Gilt-edged stocks and other interest-bearing securities

Syllabus coverage

Marketable British Government Securities:
  Fixed, floating/variable rate, convertible and index-linked securities
  Methods of issue
  The gilt-edged market
  The National Savings Stock Register
  The Accrued Income Scheme
Other interest-bearing securities:
  Local authority and public board securities
  Bulldog issues
  Eurobonds
Assessment of gilts:
  Yields
  Yield curves
  Yield gap
  Reverse yield
  Gap anomaly and policy switching

Introduction

Gilt-edged stocks (gilts) are strictly speaking marketable securities issued by the British Government, but the term is sometimes used in a wider sense to include securities of local authorities, public bodies and Commonwealth governments. The name 'gilts' is said to derive from the high quality paper used for the certificates issued to holders of these stocks in earlier times. By inference it now refers to the high quality of the security. A security issued by the British Government is considered to be risk-free as regards the payment of interest and capital in accordance with the terms of issue.

The issue of government stocks is a major method of funding the National Debt. The National Debt as such is said to date from the foundation of the Bank of England in 1694 when William III needed to raise money to fight the French. Over the years the size of the National Debt has grown considerably, particularly in times of war or high budget deficits. The government issues gilts for several reasons: for instance, when it does not wish to finance budget deficits by raising taxes; to control money supply; to replace stocks which have been redeemed.

In August 1987, there were around 115 British government stocks on the market. These include several distinct types arising from the differing financial, economic and political conditions prevailing at the time of issue. The wide range of stocks available, the highly active market with low spreads and commission rates, the ability to deal in large amounts and favourable treatment all combine to make gilts attractive to a wide range of investors, from the private individual to large pension funds and institutions.

Theoretical aspects

Characteristics of British Government stocks

The characteristics which distinguish particular stocks include the coupon, interest payment dates and redemption dates, as well as features such as conversion options, index-linking and tax-exemption for non-residents, while in the past there have been issues with variable interest rates. The main characteristics of gilts are as follows:

Description

The description of the stock consists of the coupon, the name of the stock and the year of repayment.

Name

Stocks are distinguished by names such as Exchequer Stock, Treasury Stock and Funding Loan, in order to differentiate between stocks with identical coupons and repayment years. Some names, such as British Transport Stock, Conversion Stock and War Loan, derive from the circumstances in which they were first issued, whilst words such as Convertible or Index-linked included in the name indicate the nature of the stock.

Coupon

The coupon is the annual rate of interest applicable to £100 nominal stock. For example, 9% Treasury Loan 1994 pays £9 gross interest per annum for every £100 stock (in two equal payments of £4.50 on 17 May and 17 November).

Redemption date

The majority of stocks are redeemable (repayable) on a specified date – 9%

Treasury Loan 1994 is redeemable at par on 17 November 1994. In most cases the redemption date is also an interest payment date so that a full half-year's interest is payable at the same time as the nominal capital value. Some stocks show two redemption dates in order to allow the government the option of redeeming the stock at any time on or between the two dates. For example, 6.75% Treasury Loan 1995–98 is redeemable at par on 1 May 1998 or earlier, all or part, on or at any time after 1 May 1995 on three month's notice from the government. In such cases the government is likely to redeem the stock before the final date if interest rates are lower than the coupon. If interest rates are at the same level as, or higher than, the coupon the stock will probably be allowed to run to its final redemption date.

Undated stocks

There are six stocks which have no final redemption date even where a date is mentioned in the full description, e.g. 2.5% Treasury Stock 1975 or After. Five of these are redeemable at par on three month's notice from the government. Consolidated 2.5% stock is redeemable at par on such notice and in such manner as Parliament may direct, and is therefore the least likely to be redeemed. It is very likely that any of these stocks (except 3.5% Conversion Loan – see below) will be redeemed unless interest rates fall to 4% or lower as their coupons are in the range 2.5% to 4% and the issue terms specify redemption at par.

Classification

Because of a wide variety of redemption dates, coupons and other features, gilts are classified into set groups to aid assessment and comparison. They are divided according to the number of years to redemption into short-dated stocks (shorts) with lives up to five years, 'mediums' from five to fifteen years, 'longs' over fifteen years and irredeemable (undated) having no final redemption date. Before 28 February 1986, only short-dated gilts were quoted at a 'clean' price, i.e. without accrued interest (see below), with accrued interest as a separate item and all other maturities were quoted at a 'composite' price, i.e. including accrued interest (dirty price). Since that date, all gilts are quoted clean with accrued interest added or subtracted separately.

Gilts are also grouped according to the coupon into low-coupons, medium-coupons and high-coupons. These groups could change with time but are approximately 2%–5%, 6%–9%, 9%–15%.

Interest payments

Most stocks pay interest every six months as, for example, 9% Treasury Loan 1994 above. The exception is Consolidated 2.5% Stock (2.5%

Consols) which pays quarterly on 5 January, April, July and October. In most cases interest is paid net of the basic rate of income tax, so that in 1987/88 a holder of £200 9% Treasury Loan 1994 would receive £6.57 on 17 May and 17 November (£200 × 9% ÷ 2 = £9.00 less tax £2.43 at 27%). The redemption date usually falls on an interest payment date, so that a full half-year's interest is paid at the same time as the redemption sum.

Interest payments made without deduction of income tax

There are five situations where interest is paid gross:

1   When the interest payment is £5 per annum or less
2   When the stock is held on the National Savings Stock Register (see below)
3   All interest payments on 3.5% War Loan are paid gross
4   Interest may be paid gross by arrangement with the Bank of England on stocks held by certain tax-exempt investors such as pension funds and charities
5   Interest may be paid gross on exempt stocks held by non-residents (see below).

Taxpayers receiving interest gross under 1, 2, or 3 are obliged to declare the interest on their tax returns and to pay any tax liability in due course.

Sinking funds

A sinking fund provides for the redemption of a stock. Two stocks have sinking funds. 3.5% Conversion Loan is one of the 'undated stocks' and is redeemable at par on three month's notice from the government. If the average daily price of the stock has been below £90 during a half-year (to 1 April or 1 October) a sum of not less than 1% of the amount of stock outstanding at the close of that half-year is set aside in a sinking fund. This is applied during the following half-year in purchasing stock in the market for cancellation. As this stock stands well below £90 the effective rate at which it is being cancelled is nearer 4.5% per annum. As a result, the stock has in effect a redemption date and this is reflected in the higher price and lower yield compared with 3.5% War Loan which has no sinking fund.

Three per cent Redemption Stock 1986–96 has a slightly different type of sinking fund and may be redeemed on or before 1 October 1996 by means of a semi-annual sinking fund. The sinking fund may be used to purchase stock in the market for cancellation or may be invested in approved securities. In 1986 some £29 m of the stock was redeemed out of the sinking fund and cancelled. Otherwise the stock may be redeemed at par on three month's notice from the government. These features and the small amount of stock still in issue are reflected in the market price.

Variable-rate stocks

In the 1970s, a number of variable rate stocks were issued to meet market and economic conditions of the day. They were all short-dated and have now been redeemed. These stocks had the particular characteristic that the rate of interest was variable. Each half-yearly payment was based on the daily average of Treasury Bill Rate over the six month period from the previous ex-dividend date to the ex-dividend date for the payment in question plus a fixed margin of half a point. Thus, if the average Treasury Bill Rate over a period was 10% the interest payment on £100 stock would be £100 × 10.5% ÷ 2 = £5.25.

Index-linked stocks

These were first issued in 1981 to meet the needs of investors for a security which would provide guaranteed protection of both income and capital against inflation. They also broaden the government's source of borrowing and may reduce the cost of servicing that borrowing, especially in times of low inflation. Initially they were restricted to pension funds and life assurance companies in respect of pension business, but since March 1982 they have been available to all investors. In most respects the mechanics are the same as for conventional gilts, but interest payments and repayment of capital at redemption are indexed in line with the Retail Prices Index. Each stock has a nominal 'coupon' and half-yearly interest payments subsequent to the first payment are related to movements in the RPI.

So that the amounts payable to stockholders are known well in advance, indexation is lagged by eight months. Thus the index figure applicable to an interest payment or to repayments of a principal is the figure issued seven months previously in respect of the month before that. For example, the index figure applicable to March 1983 is 323.0 which is the RPI for July 1982, which is eight months before the month of issue.

Convertible stocks

Apart from having all the characteristics of a conventional stock, these stocks give holders the option to convert into a longer-dated stock at times and on terms specified in the prospectus. The conversion dates normally co-incide with the interest payment dates of the two stocks involved. The stock to be converted into may be a new stock (often named 'Conversion Stock') or may be an existing stock. Convertible stocks are usually short or medium dated when first issued. The conversion terms usually become progressively less attractive through the conversion period as in the following example which is unusual in that there is a 'double option': 10.25% Exchequer Convertible Stock 1989 is convertible at the holder's option in whole or in part into either of the following stocks or any combination of both on the following conversion terms:

Conversion date	For every £100 nominal of 10.25% Exchequer Convertible	
	10% Conversion Stock 1996	9.75% Conversion Stock 2006
15 Nov '86	£100	£99
15 May '87	£ 99	£98
15 Nov '87	£ 98	£97
15 May '88	£ 97	£96
15 Nov '88	£ 96	£95

Holders may, of course, ignore the conversion option and let the stock run to its normal redemption date. In the case of 2.5% Index-Linked Treasury Convertible Stock 1999, there was an option to convert in November 1983, May 1984 and November 1984 into 10.25% Conversion Stock 1999 (not an index-linked stock) on the basis of £100 Conversion Stock for every £100 nominal (i.e. not adjusted for inflation) of Convertible Stock. Rather than offering an option to convert to a longer dated stock, this stock offered the unusual option, over a limited period, of converting from an index-linked to a fixed interest stock.

Exempt stocks

A number of stocks, including two index-linked issues, have the provision that capital and interest will be exempt from all UK taxes provided that the beneficial owner is neither domiciled nor ordinarily resident in the UK. Also, interest payments will be exempt from UK income tax provided that the beneficial owner, wherever domiciled, is not ordinarily resident in the UK. These exemptions from inheritance tax and income tax (and any future taxes) may be obtained in appropriate cases upon application to the Inspector of Foreign Dividends. Exempt stocks are identified in SEDOL (Stock Exchange Daily Official List) and on most Stockbrokers' gilt lists.

Registration, transfers, stamp duty

British Government Stocks are registered at the Bank of England or at the Bank of Ireland, Belfast, and are transferable in multiples of one penny free of stamp duty. Certain stocks may also be held as bearer bonds in specified denominations, also free of stamp duty.

Methods of issue of British Government stocks

Offers for sale

Over the years, several methods have been employed for the issue of gilt-edged stock, but the most important is the public offer for sale. Up to 1979, fixed price offers were common, but following the issue of 13.75% Treasury Stock 2000–03 in February 1979, tender offers have been the rule. A rise of four points in long gilt prices between the announcement of this stock and the deadline for applications, with only 15% payable on application, led to heavy oversubscription and pandemonium in Watling Street in the City.

The procedure for an offer for sale is that the Bank of England issues a prospectus and application form giving all the details of the new stock and these are published in major newspapers. With a fixed price issue the price is stated in the prospectus, and is likely to be slightly below par.

Tender offers

For tender offers there is usually a minimum tender price and tenders must be made at the minimum price or at higher prices, usually in multiples of five pence. Applicants enclose the deposit, which must be for a specified amount, with their application forms and these have to be lodged with the Bank of England by a specified time and date. The Treasury decides upon the allotment price, which is not less than the minimum tender price, and allotments are made to those who tendered at or above the allotment price, but all allotments are made at the same price (the allotment price). Those tendering below the allotment price receive no stock. Tenders made at the allotment price may be scaled down, with those above that price being allotted in full. The balance of the purchase money is paid in accordance with the terms of the issue. The normal minimum application for public offers is £100 nominal. Payment is usually spread over a few weeks with a set proportion payable on application and the balance in one or two further calls.

Conversion issues

When holders of convertible stocks exercise their option to convert, the appropriate amount of the relevant conversion stock is issued. The issue terms of a conversion stock are incorporated in the prospectus of the relevant convertible stock.

Issues to the Bank of England

Stock may be issued by the Treasury directly to the Bank of England. Sometimes, if a public offer for sale is not fully subscribed, the balance of the issue will be taken up by the Bank of England. Stock may also be issued to the National Debt Commissioners or held by the Bank of England on behalf of government departments.

Tap stocks

These are usually additional amounts of an existing stock created by the Treasury and issued to the Bank of England at the middle market price on the day of issue. Details are announced in the press. These further 'tranches' of an existing stock rank *pari passu* (equally in all respects) with that stock and application is made for the additional stock to be quoted on the Stock Exchange. The Bank of England is then prepared to sell the tap stock to the public on demand through the normal stock market dealing mechanism. The price at which the Bank of England is prepared to release the tap stock may be adjusted from time to time and in this way the Bank exercises some degree of control over gilt prices. In due course, that particular tranche of stock will be sold out and press comments will indicate that the tap stock 'has been exhausted'. Stock taken up by the Bank of England as the balance of a public offer may also be operated as a tap stock.

Taplet issues

These are simply tap stocks for relatively small amounts. Rather than issuing a tap stock for £1000 million the Treasury might issue, say, two taplets for £200 million each and one for £100 million further as tranches of three existing stocks, followed by further taplets a few weeks later. In this way the authorities achieve greater flexibility with a spread of coupons and redemption dates and finer control over prices.

The auction method

On May 13th 1987 the Treasury issued £1000 million 8% Treasury Stock 1992 by auction on a bid price basis. The first payment was due on May 13th and the balance on June 29th. This was the first 'experimental' issue of a British Government Stock by the auction method, based on a well-established method used to sell US Treasury Bonds. It also marked the first major innovation in the gilt market following the radical changes of Big Bang and the abolition of minimum commissions and single capacity in October 1986 and foreshadowed a move away from the tap and tender system. There were two methods of bidding – the competitive bid and the non-competitive bid. The minimum application was for £1000 nominal of stock and for non-competitive bids the maximum was £100 000. The competitive bid system is more suitable for market makers and large institutions and the non-competitive bid for private investors. For a competitive bid, applicants specify the amount of stock and the price they are prepared to pay and enclose a cheque for the full amount of their bid less £50 per cent. The Treasury decides upon the lowest accepted price and the Bank of England then allocates stock to those who bid at or above that price. Bids made above the lowest accepted price are allotted in full and bids made at that price may be sealed down. Successful competitive bidders pay the prices at which they bid (there is no striking price as with tender offers). In the case of non-competitive bids, applicants specify the nominal amount of stock required and enclose a cheque for £50 per cent of the amount applied for. Successful non-competitive applications are allotted in full at a price equal to the weighted average of the prices at which competitive bids were accepted. If the price is more than £100 successful non-competitive bidders have to pay a further deposit, followed by the £50 call in due course. If the allotment price is less than £100 the balance of the deposit is refunded. It is perhaps easier for private investors to buy the stock in the market rather than bidding. It is also usually possible to buy the stock in the 'grey market', i.e. on an unofficial basis, during the short period between publication of the prospectus and the actual issue date on a 'when issued' basis. Further auctions were announced for September 1987 and January 1988. The former was for an existing stock – 9% Treasury Stock, 2008 – with £60 per cent payable on application. The January auction planned to offer a medium-dated stock.

First interest payment

When a new gilt-edged stock is issued the first interest payment is unlikely to cover a period of exactly six months, so the first interest payment is adjusted to cover the number of days from the date of issue to the first interest payment date. Thus the first interest payment may be greater or less than subsequent half-yearly interest payments. Also, as stocks are frequently issued on a partly-paid basis with calls spread over several weeks, the first interest payment is adjusted to take account of this. The adjustment is based on the proportion of the paid-up amount to the full issue price, which may be above or below par. When a new tranche of an existing stock is offered for sale to the public the first interest payment of the new tranche will be different from the interest payment due on that date on the existing stock, and the new tranche may be only partly paid for several weeks. To distinguish between the old and the new classes of stock, in such an event, the new stock is temporarily designated 'A' stock until it is fully paid and has gone 'ex' and the first interest payment, after which the new tranche ranks *pari passu* with the original stock.

The Gilt-Edged Market

The gilt market was re-structured at the time of the 'Big Bang' in October 1986 and is now based on Gilt-edged Market-makers, Inter-dealer Brokers and Stock Exchange Money Brokers.

Gilt-Edged Market-Makers

These are firms (usually subsidiary companies of major financial groups) registered with the Bank of England, who make a market in gilt-edged stocks. Initially 29 firms were approved, but the number has reduced and it is thought that in time the number of active participants will be even less. By the summer of 1987 the top ten gilt-edged market-makers (also called 'primary dealers') handled 68% of all transactions. They are all members of the Stock Exchange and are subject to its supervision with regard to trading practices and professional standards. In addition, the Bank of England monitors their capital adequacy and risk position. They have various privileges, including direct dealing and borrowing facilities with the Bank of England, borrowing and dealing relationships with Stock Exchange Money Brokers and Inter-dealer Brokers and certain tax exemptions. Gilt-edged Market-makers undertake to make two-way prices in gilts within limits agreed with the Bank of England. They will deal with other Stock Exchange brokers and in some cases directly with investors. Initially, the prices they display on SEAQ (Stock Exchange Automated Quotations) screens will be mid-market prices only, although two-way prices will be supplied to a broker on enquiry. They make their profit from the spread between buying and selling prices, the difference between the cost of holding stocks and the return on these stocks, the skill with which they anticipate price movements and regulate their position in various stocks, and in some cases form issuing derivative securities such as gilt warrants.

Inter-dealer Brokers

Initially six firms were authorised by the Bank of England to act as Inter-dealer Brokers. They deal only with the Gilt-edged Market-makers, not with other Stock Exchange members or the public. They act as intermediaries between the Market-makers by matching bids and offers in gilt-edged stocks so that Market-makers can adjust their positions. In this way the Market-makers trade with each other through the medium of the Inter-Dealer Brokers and retain the anonymity – complete confidentiality is observed. The IDBs do not take up positions in stocks themselves, although they do act as principal to both buyer and seller, rather than agent. They supply price information on screens to the Market-makers, but this is not available to other stockbrokers.

Stock Exchange Money Brokers

Nine firms were authorised by the Bank of England to act in this capacity. They improve the efficiency of the market by lending and borrowing stock for a small charge of around 0.75% per annum. They enable the various participants to balance their books by lending and borrowing stock and cash between the market-makers, major institutions and the discount houses.

The National Savings Stock Register

As an alternative to buying gilts through a stockbroker the Department for National Savings offers a service for buying and selling certain government stocks by post. Application forms and special envelopes are available at most post offices. A purchase may be for a specified nominal amount of stock or to invest a specified sum of money. The purchaser sends the completed application form with a cheque for the amount to be invested plus charges, or, in the case of a specified nominal amount of stock, a blank cheque. In due course the Bonds and Stock Office will send the certificate and a statement of costs. To sell a stock registered on the National Savings Stock Register, the investor sends a completed sale form and the certificate to the Bonds and Stock Office and receives payment of the sale proceeds and a statement in due course.

Commission charges are generally lower than for stock market deals, especially for small transactions, and work out at around 0.4% including VAT. For purchases, the charges (including VAT) are £1 for a consideration up to £250, and £1 plus 50p for every additional £125 (or part) for a consideration over £250. For sales the same rates apply, except that sales under £100 are charged 10p for every £10 (or part). These charges are based on the total net consideration including accrued interest (plus or minus).

All interest payments on stock held on this register are paid gross, which is convenient for non-taxpayers, but of course the interest has to be declared to the Inland Revenue. The choice of stocks is rather limited as only just under half of the quoted Government stocks are available on the NSSR. They do, however, include a number of exempt stocks and index-linked stocks, and new stocks are added from time to time. Investors may sometimes be frustrated in finding that the particular stock to suit their requirements is not on this register. A criticism frequently made about buying stocks in this way is that no price can be specified and that there is a delay between the time the order is sent off and the time of dealing. However, purchase and sale transactions received by the first post are normally transacted on the same day and it is doubtful whether the small investor is usually close enough to the market to be in any more favourable position when dealing through a broker.

The maximum amount which may be invested in only one stock on this register in any one day is £10 000, but there is no limit on the total amount of stock which may be sold on any one day. Stocks may be transferred from one person to another or from the NSSR to the Bank of England register. For transfers from the Bank of England register to the NSSR there is a limit of £5000 on any particular stock per calendar year.

Stock may be purchased in the name of a child but cannot normally be sold until the child reaches seven years of age. Interest on any stock in the sole name of a child under seven will normally be paid into the child's

National Savings Bank Account. Stock cannot be transferred to the Bank of England register until the holder is 18 years of age.

Leaflets giving up-to-date details, including a list of stocks available on the register, may be obtained from most post offices.

Other interest-bearing securities

Apart from British Government Stocks there is a wide variety of interest-bearing stocks and bonds dealt in on the London Stock Exchange. UK local authority stocks and yearling bonds are still regarded as low risk, although not quite in the same class as government stocks. Whilst the yearling bond market is active, the market in longer dated corporation stocks is less important than in the past. As a category, Commonwealth Government and Corporation stocks now have little significance. Most of the outstanding issues are Southern Rhodesia stocks. Any new Commonwealth stocks should be judged in the same way as a foreign stock, taking the political risk into account. Bulldog issues and Eurobonds are two important types of security which have flourished in recent years. There are a number of foreign bonds issued many years ago which are highly speculative and should be treated with great caution. (The distinguishing features of some of these interest-bearing securities are given below. The various interest-bearing stocks of UK companies are dealt with in chapters 2 and 7.)

Corporation stocks

There are a number of quoted local authority stocks having many characteristics in common with British Government stocks. They are charged on the revenues of the local authority and usually rank equally with all other securities issued by that authority. They are free of stamp duty and capital gains tax, dealt on for cash settlement, interest is usually paid half-yearly and gross accrued interest is not included in the market price. There are wide variations in redemption terms and investors should check the terms of issues before buying. The amounts in issue are much smaller than with government stocks, making for poor marketability. In a few cases they are registered at the Bank of England, but more often the registrar is one of the major corporate registrars or the local authority's own finance director. Although these stocks are not guaranteed by the government, it is thought unlikely that the government would allow a local authority to default. There might, however, be problems with high-spending councils and investors could be faced with delays in interest or redemption payments in a worst case. The poor marketability and higher risk compared with government stocks are reflected in a yield of about 0.5% more for comparable stocks. In practice, few of these stocks have been issued in recent years.

Yearling bonds

These are negotiable bonds issued by local authorities and redeemable at par, usually 53 weeks after issue. They are charged on the revenues of the issuing authority and rank equally with other securities of that authority. They are listed on the Stock Exchange and are transferable free of stamp duty in units of £1000 on a common form of transfer. Purchasers pay gross accrued interest in addition to the market price and dealing is for cash settlement. These local authority short term bonds are issued weekly on Tuesdays at par, and the coupon rate and other details are usually published in the press on Wednesdays. Typically, two or three local authorities will issue bonds in any one week for a total amount of, perhaps, £1 million. Investors may ask their broker to apply for bonds at the time of issue, or buy them on the market. Occasionally bonds have been issued for longer periods of up to five years.

Public boards

There are several quoted stocks issued by public boards, such as the Agricultural Mortgage Corporation and the Port of London Authority, with various redemption dates and including some with no fixed redemption dates. They are dealt in for cash settlement, free of stamp duty, with accrued interest payable in addition to the market price. They are not guaranteed by the government and since the collapse of the Mersey Docks and Harbour Board in 1970 they have been regarded with due caution.

Bulldog issues

Following the ending of Exchange Control in 1979, it again became possible for foreign governments and corporations to issue loans denominated in sterling. These are colloquially referred to as 'Bulldog Issues' after the British national symbol. A typical example is the Kingdom of Denmark 13% Loan Stock 2005 of which £75 million was issued at £98 per cent in July 1980 as an obligation of the Kingdom. This stock is redeemable at par on 31 December 2005 or by purchase, tender or private treaty at a price not exceeding 110% of the mid-market quotation. Interest is payable half-yearly on 31 June and 31 December and stock is transferable in multiples of one pence. Bulldog issues are generally exempt from UK stamp duty, dealt in for cash settlement at clean prices with accrued interest accounted for separately and, in many cases, non-residents of the UK may arrange to have interest paid gross.

Eurobonds

These are interest-bearing stocks issued outside the country in whose currency they are denominated. They include fixed and floating rate issues, as well as convertibles and stocks with warrants attached. They are issued denominated in US dollars, Deutsche Marks, Swiss Francs, Yen, Sterling and other currencies. They are usually issued by governments, international institutions or major international companies. Secondary trading is generally carried out by specialist bond dealers, but many of the issues are listed on national stock exchanges, including several on the London Stock Exchange. They are usually in bearer form, interest is payable annually without deduction of income tax, and dealt in for seven day settlement. Marketability is restricted by the relatively small amounts of individual stocks in issue for an international market and because they are lightly held, and it is difficult if not impossible to deal in small amounts of stock.

Derivatives of gilts

Traded options (see Chapter 6) are available in two gilts (as at 1987), a short-dated stock, 11.75% Treasury 1991, and the long-dated 11.75% Treasury 2003–07. On the London International Financial Futures Exchange (LIFFE) there is a futures contract in a 20 year 12% national gilt and a traded option in the long gilt futures contract. In 1987, for the first time warrants on gilt-edged stocks were issued by Gilt-edged Market-makers and discount houses. These are listed on the Stock Exchange and give holders the right to purchase or sell the underlying gilt at a specified price at specified times. An example is the call warrants in 11.75% Treasury Stock 2003–07 issued by Chase Manhattan Gilts Ltd and exercisable from July to December 1987 in units of £100 000.

Practical application

Index-linked stocks

Each stock has a 'base month' and all calculations of interest payments and the amount due on redemption are made with reference to the RPI for the base month – the base index. For any month in which a payment of interest is due, the index rate is equal to the index figure applicable to that month divided by the index figure applicable to the base month. Each interest payment after the first (per £100 nominal of stock) is equal to half the coupon multiplied by the index ratio for the month in which payment is due.

1   *Calculation of interest payments*
Example:
2% Index-Linked Treasury Stock 1996 issued at par on March 27th 1981. Base month July 1980 – Base Index 267.9

Interest Payments		Applicable Index
Sept 81	£0.80 (part year)	
Mar 82	£1.03	297.1 (Jan 81)
Sept 82	£1.15	310.6 (Jul 81)
Mar 83	£1.20	323.0 (Jan 82)

$$\text{Index ratio for month} = \frac{\text{Index figure applicable to month}}{\text{Index figure applicable to base month}}$$

$$\text{Index ratio for March 83} = \frac{323.0}{267.9}$$

$$\text{Interest payment} = £1.00 \text{ (half of 2\% coupon)} \times \frac{323.0}{367.9} = £1.20$$

2   *Calculation of amount due on redemption* The amount due on repayment per £100 nominal of stock is equal to £100 multiplied by the index ratio for the month when repayment is due.

Example:

If we assume that in September 1996 when the above stock is due for repayment the index figure applicable to September 1996 (RPI for January 1996) is 592.0 then:

$$\text{Index ratio for September 1996} = \frac{592.0}{267.9}$$

$$\text{Amount due for repayment} = £100 \times \frac{592.0}{67.9} = £220.97 \text{ per £100 nominal}$$

of stock.

Changes to the index The issue terms of the index-linked stocks contain provisions to cover revision of the index to a new base, non-publication of the index and changes to the basic calculation of the index which might be detrimental to stockholders' interests. The RPI was rebased in January 1987, when it stood at 394.5, and future monthly figures are based on January 1987 = 100.0. Calculations for months after January 1987 therefore require a notional index figure as follows:

Assume index figure for January 1996 is 151.2.

$$\text{The notional index figure will be } 151.2 \times \frac{394.5}{100} = 596.5$$

$$\text{Index ratio for September 1996} = \frac{596.5}{267.9}$$

$$\text{Amount due for repayment} = £100 \times \frac{596.5}{267.9} = £222.65 \text{ per £100}$$

nominal of stock.

As an example of interest payments, the payment due on March 16th 1988 is:

RPI for July 1987 = 101.8

National Index figure = $101.8 \times \dfrac{394.5}{100} = 401.6$

Index ratio for March 1988 = $\dfrac{401.6}{267.9}$

Interest payment due March 16th 1988 = $£1.00 \times \dfrac{401.6}{267.9} = £1.49$ per £100 nominal of stock.

Any index-linked stocks issued with a base month later than December 1986 would not need the calculation of a national index figure unless the RPI were released again.

Dealing in gilts

On receiving instructions from a client to buy or sell a British Government stock, the stockbroker, acting as agent, selects the best price from the SEAQ screen for that particular stock and telephones the Gilt-edged Market-maker to place the order. Prices are quoted for £100 nominal of stock and for all maturities the price quoted is a 'clean' price – accrued interest is not included. Prices are quoted in pounds and 32nds of a pound (not on pounds and pence except in special cases) and the smallest price change is thus £1/32. The stockbroker issues a contract note showing the amount of stock, price, consideration, accrued interest to be added or subtracted, commission, value added tax, time of bargain, date of bargain, settlement date and net cost or proceeds.

Examples:

Purchase of	Bargain date 7/9/1988
	£
£2500 9% Treasury Stock 1994 @ £94 19/32	2364.84
plus 114 days accrued interest	70.27
plus commission £2364.84 @ 1%	23.65
VAT @ 15%	3.55
Total cost for cash settlement	2462.31

Sale of	Bargain date 7/9/1988
	£
£2500 9% Treasury Stock 1994 @ £94 11/32	2358.59
plus 114 days accrued interest	70.27
less Commission £2358.59 @ 1%	23.59
VAT @ 15%	3.54
Total proceeds for cash settlement	2401.73

Settlement date

Gilts are normally dealt in for 'cash settlement' – settlement is due on the business day immediately following the bargain date. It is possible to deal for other settlement dates, for instance for Account Settlement in which case settlement is due on the next Account Day. In this event the price is adjusted appropriately.

Accrued interest

Accrued interest is shown separately from the market price and, in the case of stocks dealt in cum (with) dividend, is the gross amount of interest accrued from the last interest payment date to the settlement date. In the above examples, 9% Treasury Stock, 1994 pays interest on 17 May and 17 November. From 17 May to 7 September (settlement date) is 114 days. Accrued interest on £2500 stock is $114 \div 365 \times 9 \div 100 \times £2500 = £70.27$. The purchaser will receive the full six months' interest payment of £112.50 gross (less tax) on 17 November and so pays for the amount accrued to settlement date. The seller will not receive the November interest payment, but receives the gross accrued interest as part of the sale proceeds.

Most gilts go ex (without) dividend about 37 days before the interest payment date to allow the Bank of England time to prepare interest warrants which are despatched to holders on the register on the ex dividend date. For stocks dealt in ex dividend the accrued interest is calculated from the settlement date to the relative interest payment date and is therefore a negative amount. In the above examples, if the bargains had taken place on 10 May 1988 the amount of accrued interest would have been for minus six days (interest payment date 17 May – settlement date 11 May) that is $6 \div 365 \times 9 \div 100 \times £2500 = $ minus £3.70 giving a total cost for the purchase of £2388.34 and total proceeds for the sale of £2327.76. The purchaser would not receive an interest payment until 17 November and the seller would receive the full interest payment on 17 May.

Commission rates

Minimum commission scales were abolished in October 1986 and commission rates are now negotiable with the stockbroker. In practice, brokers will negotiate rates with institutions and other large customers but have standard rates for private investors. These rates vary from broker to broker and if the private investor is concerned solely with obtaining the most favourable rate of commission it will be necessary to 'shop around'. Commission rates for gilts are generally lower than for equities. Institutions dealing in large amounts will pay a very fine rate, or if dealing direct with a gilt-edged market-maker may pay no commission at all (the market-maker's remuneration comes from the 'turn', i.e. the difference between the selling and buying prices). Typical scales of commission for gilt transactions for a private investor might be:

Broker A on the first £2 500   0.75% Minimum £15
         on the next £13 000   0.115%
         then   0.1%

Broker B on the first £7 000   0.80% Minimum £20
         on the next £18 000   0.25%
         then   0.125%

Broker C on the first £1 000   flat rate £20
         on the next £19 000   0.5%
         then   0.125%

Commission should be charged on the bargain consideration only – not including accrued interest. Value added tax is charged on the broker's commission.

Special ex-dividends

Gilts with more than five years to redemption (except 3.5% War Loan) can be dealt in either cum-dividend or ex-dividend during the three weeks prior to the actual ex-dividend date.

If there is demand for a stock in special ex-dividend form the market price may be slightly higher than the price of the same stock cum-dividend. Purchasers of a stock special ex-dividend will have the appropriate number of days' accrued interest deducted from the consideration, whilst purchasers of the cum-dividend stock would pay accrued interest in addition to the market price. The special ex-dividend facility gives investors more flexibility in timing switches from one stock to another. For example, by selling a stock which has just gone ex-dividend and buying another special ex-dividend (perhaps in order to switch to longer dated) an investor can maintain a regular flow of income and avoid having to wait two or three weeks for the second stock to go ex-dividend.

Settlement

The Talisman (Transfer Accounting Lodgement for Investors, Stock MANagement for Jobbers) system does not apply to gilts and other securities dealt in for cash settlement. The seller of a gilt has to sign a Stock Transfer Form which the broker will send with the contract note. This must be delivered to the broker together with the stock certificate. The broker will then send a cheque for the net proceeds to the seller. In theory settlement is due on the business day following the bargain date but in practice it may take two or three days more before the seller receives a cheque, bearing in mind that each of these steps will take at least a day for the private investor using the postal system. A purchaser must pay the broker immediately on receipt of the contract note. The broker will receive a stock transfer form and stock certificate from the market-maker and will lodge these at the Bank of England for registration. A certificate in the name of the purchaser will be issued in due course (usually a matter of days) and forwarded by the broker.

The Central Gilts Office

In order to avoid the danger of the settlement process grinding to a halt in times of high volumes of trading, the Central Gilts Office was set up in 1986 jointly by the Stock Exchange and the Bank of England. The Office is operated by the Bank of England and consists of a computerised 'book entry' transfer system for settling Stock Exchange transactions in gilts. The Stock Transfer Act 1982 provides the legal basis for 'exempt' transfers, that is computerised transfers without the need for an instrument in writing, and for the non-issue of certificates in respect of such transfers. Initially participation in the system is restricted to gilt-edged market-makers, inter-dealer brokers, Stock Exchange money brokers, discount houses and certain banks and other institutions. Further development may affect a wider range of investors in gilts, but the standard paper-based transfer and certificate system currently runs in parallel.

Taxation

Capital Gains Tax

Since 2 July 1986, gilts (together with qualifying sterling 'corporate' bonds) have been exempt from CGT.

The Accrued Income Scheme

The Finance Act 1985 introduced measures whereby the gross accrued interest received by the seller of an interest-bearing security would be chargeable to tax as income. This undermined the practice of selling stocks full of interest shortly before the ex-dividend date in order to capitalise income, and also eliminated 'bond washing' whereby the purchase of a stock ex-dividend would be matched with a sale cum-dividend to a tax-exempt investor who could reclaim the 'tax' from the Revenue. The Accrued Income Scheme included complex transitional provisions covering the period up to February 1986, but the main provisions apply to transactions after 27 February 1986.

  The provisions apply to gilt-edged securities, loan stocks or similar securities issued by any government, public or local authority in the UK or elsewhere, or by any company or other body. Convertible loan stocks are included, but not ordinary shares, preference shares or convertible preference shares (all of which carry Advance Corporation Tax credits). The provisions apply whether the securities are secured or unsecured, registered or bearer, fixed rate or variable rate, and whether interest is paid on sterling or a foreign currency. Zero-rated bonds are excluded.

Cum-dividend transactions

The seller of an interest-bearing stock is liable to tax on the amount of accrued interest included in the total sale proceeds, whether this is shown as a separate item as in the case of a gilt, or as a memorandum on the contract note as in the case of a company loan stock sold for account settlement. Technically the tax is due on the date of the next interest payment for that stock.

The purchaser of a stock pays for the gross accrued interest as part of the total cost and will receive relief of this amount against the next interest payment. For example, the purchaser of £2500 9% Treasury Stock 1994 (see page 80) on 7 September 1987 has paid £70.27 gross accrued interest and will receive relief to this extent against the interest payment of £112.50 (less tax) payable on 17 November 1987.

	£
Interest payment	112.50
Less relief for accrued interest purchased	70.27
Reduced amount	42.23
Tax deducted on £112.50 @ 27%	30.37
Tax due on £42.23 @ 27%	11.40
Tax overpaid	18.97

Ex-dividend transactions

Where the transaction takes place ex-dividend the accrued interest (a negative amount) is called 'rebate interest'. The seller receives the next interest payment, but the sale proceeds have been reduced by the amount of interest accruing from the settlement date to the interest payment date. The seller receives relief to the extent of the rebate interest and can reclaim the tax overpaid.

	£
Interest payment	112.50
Less relief for rebate interest	3.70
Reduced amount	108.80
Tax deducted on £112.50 @ 27%	30.37
Tax due on £108.80 @ 27%	29.37
Tax overpaid	1.00

The purchaser of a stock 'ex-dividend' does not receive the next interest payment, but the purchase price has been reduced by the amount of rebate interest. The purchaser is liable to tax on this amount.

Multiple transactions of the same stock

Where there are purchase and sale transactions in the same stock in the same interest period the amounts of accrued interest and rebate interest are set off when calculating the amount of any tax liability or claim.

Exemptions

Individuals who hold no more than an aggregate of £5000 nominal of securities covered by the scheme on any day in the year of assessment of in the previous year of assessment are exempted from the provisions. Husband and wife have a total exemption of £5000 for this purpose. Similar exemptions apply to the personal representatives of a deceased person and disabled person's trusts. Non-residents of the UK are also exempt from the scheme. Trustees of a continuing trust or settlement get no exemption.

Objective

The effect of the Accrued Income Scheme is that investors who are liable to tax on income, other than those covered by the exemptions, are liable to tax on the interest during the whole period of their ownership of an interest-bearing security whether this is received as interest payments or in the form of accrued interest on a transfer of ownership.

Assessment of gilts

Yield calculations

Flat yield

The simplest yield calculation is flat yield or interest yield (also known as running yield or current yield). This is the gross annual income expressed as a percentage of market price. The price used is mid-market price (half way between the buying and selling prices) and the clean price is used (ignoring accrued interest). Flat yield is calculated by dividing the coupon by the price and multiplying by 100, i.e. flat yield $\% = \dfrac{\text{coupon}}{\text{market price}} \times 100$.

Thus, in the case of 9% Treasury Stock 1994 priced at £94¾ the flat yield is $9 \div 94\frac{3}{4} \times 100 = 9.50\%$. If the price is £105 the yield is $9 \div 105 \times 100$

= 8.57%. Obviously it is possible to adapt this formula in order to calculate what the price would have to be to give a stated yield. To produce a yield of 10% the price of 9% Treasury Loan 1994 would have to fall to $9 \times 100 \div 10 = £90$.

Flat yields are usually quoted gross in broker/dealers' gilt lists and in the press, but taxpayers can calculate a net yield by multiplying the gross yield by (100 − tax rate) and dividing by 100. For an investor paying tax at 25% the net yield on a stock with a 9% coupon priced at £94$\frac{3}{4}$ would be $9 \div 94\frac{3}{4} \times 100 \times (73) \div 100 = 7.12\%$.

Flat yields can be used to compare one stock with another or with other types of interest-bearing investment such as a bank deposit account. As the flat yield does not take into account the fact that interest payments are received every six months it should be compared with the stated gross annual rate of bank or building society investments rather than with the compounded annualised rate.

Gross redemption yield

Whereas flat yields are concerned only with income, redemption yields take into account any capital gain or loss to redemption in addition to interest receivable. The total price of a stock including accrued interest is the present value of the various interest payments to be received over the life of the stock and of the amount payable on redemption. The redemption yield is the rate of interest at which all of these future payments are discounted in order to arrive at the present value of the stock. Given a particular interest rate for the redemption yield it is possible to calculate the price of a stock, but there is no formula as such to calculate the redemption yield from a stock given the price. Redemption yields are calculated by an iterative process – carrying out a series of calculations at different rates of interest until the resultant present value is as near as possible to the price of the stock. These calculations are usually carried out on a computer and are published by some broker/dealers in daily gilt lists and in the press. For UK gilts and other fixed-interest stocks redemption yields are calculated on a semi-annual basis (because interest payments are made every six months) and then doubled. Some other markets use a different method. Redemption yields are based on the assumption that interest payments are reinvested on receipt at the redemption yield rate of interest. In practice this is hardly ever likely to be possible. It is also assumed that the stock is held to maturity.

Net redemption yield

For non-taxpayers the gross redemption yield is an appropriate measure of the return on a gilt, but for taxpayers it is less useful because it consists of two elements – the capital element which is tax-free, and the income element which is taxable at the investors' marginal rate of tax. Net redemption yields take these taxation features into account and provide a useful indication of the net return of particular stocks at specific tax rates. When selecting gilts for tax-paying investors the net redemption yield, or its derivative – the grossed-up net redemption yield (see below), is the most appropriate means of comparing one stock with another, used in conjunction with the life of the stock. Net redemption yields assume that the relevant tax rates remain unaltered throughout the life of the stock.

Grossed-up net redemption yield

This is simply a net redemption yield grossed up at the taxpayer's marginal rate of tax – the same tax rate as that used to calculate the net redemption yield. It has the effect of grossing up the tax-free element as well as the income element and provides a useful means of comparing a quoted fixed-interest stock with a cash-type investment such as a bank deposit account. It is also called an 'equivalent gross yield'. As an example, the yields on 9% Treasury Loan 1994 on a particular day in September 1987 when the price was £94$\frac{23}{32}$ were:

Gross flat yield	9.50	Tax Rate			
Gross redemption yield	10.03	27%	40%	50%	60%
Net redemption yield		7.52	6.31	5.39	4.46
Grossed-up net redemption yield		10.30	10.52	10.77	11.15

Redemption yields for undated stocks

As undated stocks have no redemption date there is no capital gain or loss to take into account. Gross and net flat yields for these stocks may, however, take into account accrued interest and the semi-annual receipt of income.

Approximate redemption yields

Redemption yields should be treated with caution because of the assumption on which they are based. More sophisticated models may be more useful to the gilt expert, whilst the basic principles of redemption yields are accepted by the general body of investors. There are two methods of calculating approximate redemption yields which are sometimes employed in the classroom to introduce students to redemption yields. The first method takes the number of points to redemption (the difference between redemption price and market price), divides this by the number of years to maturity and adds the result to the flat yield. This produces an approximate gross redemption yield. For example, 6.75% Treasury Stock 1998 priced at £79 and repayable in eleven years' time (as at May 1987):

Points to redemption (100 − 79)	= 21
Years to redemption	= 11
Flat yield 6.75 ÷ 79 × 100	= 8.54%
Add 21 ÷ 11	= 1.91
Approximate gross redemption yield	= 10.45%

Where the price is above par the difference is subtracted from the flat yield. For example: 15.5% Treasury Stock 1998 priced at £131 and redeemable in 21 years' time:

Flat yield	= 11.832
Subtract 31 ÷ 21	= 1.476
Approximate gross redemption yield	= 10.356%

These examples show that if the price is below par (or redemption price if other than par) the flat yield is higher than the coupon and the redemption yield is higher still, whereas if the price is above par the flat yield is lower than the coupon and the redemption yield even lower. This method is only suitable for use in the classroom as it can produce results which are far from accurate.

The second method relies upon published figures for flat and gross redemption yields in order to calculate approximate net redemption yields. Subtract the gross flat yield from the gross redemption yield to find the capital element and add this to the net flat yield at the appropriate tax rate. This can be taken a stage further to produce grossed-up net redemption yields. For example, 6.75% Treasury Stock 1995–98 flat yield 8.52%, gross redemption yield 9.94% on a particular day.

25% taxpayer:	Gross redemption yield	9.94%
	Gross flat yield	8.52%
	Capital element	1.42%
	Net flat yield @ 25% (8.52 × 0.75)	6.39%
	Net redemption yield	7.81%
	Grossed-up net redemption yield (7.81 ÷ 75 × 100)	= 10.41%
40% taxpayer:	Capital element	1.42%
	Net flat yield @ 40% (8.52 × 0.6)	5.11%
	Net redemption yield	6.53%
	Grossed-up net redemption yield (6.53 ÷ 60 × 100)	= 10.88%

This method is useful for studying the effects of net redemption yields and provides a rough guide for selecting gilts according to the investor's tax position, but more accurate yields provided by broker/dealers should be consulted before any actual investment decisions are made.

Gilt prices

The price of a gilt-edged security depends upon the coupon, the redemption date and the general level of interest rates. Other things being equal, all gilts would have virtually the same gross redemption yield, so that if the level of interest rates is 10% the prices of six particular gilts with different lives and coupons might be:

Coupon	Life	Price	Approximate Gross Redemption Yield
3%	15 yrs	£ 46	10%
9%	15 yrs	£ 92	10%
15%	15 yrs	£138	10%
3%	5 yrs	£ 73	10%
9%	5 yrs	£ 96	10%
15%	5 yrs	£119	10%

As the life of the stock reduces the price moves nearer to its repayment value (normally par). This performance characteristic is called 'the pull to maturity'.

There are many other factors affecting gilt prices, however. Stocks which have attractions for particular types of investor may command a slightly higher price for this reason. For example, low coupon short-dated stocks are attractive to high rate tax-payers because they have a large element of tax-free capital appreciation to redemption and they are valued on the basis of the appropriate net redemption yield. As a result they generally have lower gross redemption yields than stocks with higher coupons. Exempt stocks are sought by non-residents. War Loans may have a slightly lower 'redemption' yield than other irredeemables because interest is paid gross and it is also an exempt stock. Banks, building societies and other institutions invest a proportion of their funds in gilts, with an emphasis on short-dated stocks. Interest and capital gains are taxed at the appropriate corporation tax rate, so they are selected on the basis of the relevant net redemption yield. Life assurance companies and pension funds take a longer-term view and invest significantly in long-dated gilts. Pension funds being tax-exempt would select stocks on a gross redemption yield basis and assurance companies on the relevant redemption yield net of corporation tax.

Two of the main factors affecting gilt prices are the level of interest rates and inflation, but more significant is the outlook for interest rates and the prospective inflation rate. The expectation that inflation is to fall over the next year or two has a much greater influence on gilt prices than the latest inflation figures which only describe the historical situation. Gilts are considered to be a risk-free investment in terms of money and security because they are guaranteed by the British Government and (in the case of the fixed interest stocks) the income and capital returns are specified in money terms. They are, however, very vulnerable to inflation risk. An investor knows the amount of income which will be paid each year, but does not know how many loaves of bread that income will purchase. Investors seek a 'real' return from gilts over and above the rate of inflation. With inflation expected to be, say, 4.4% over a future period and the average gross redemption yield on long-dated high-coupon stocks at 9.97% the real yield would be 5.57%. For an investor paying tax at 25% this would produce a net real redemption yield of 4.18%. The inflation outlook has a more marked influence on long-dated stocks, whilst broader interest rate levels have more impact on the shorter end of the market. Interest rates are influenced by the level of interest rates in overseas markets and by the exchange rate, since raising or lowering domestic interest rates is an important means of controlling the exchange rate. Consequently the economic and political factors which impact on the exchange rate may well influence interest rates if the authorities are not prepared to let the exchange rate find its market level.

As interest rates represent the price of money, the supply of and demand for money influences gilt prices. If the institutions are awash with cash, some of which will be invested in gilts, gilt prices will tend to rise. On the other hand, if the supply of gilts is restrained, either because the public sector borrowing requirement is well under control or because it is being met from other sources such as taxation or privatisation issues, then there will be an upward pressure on gilt prices.

Overseas investors can exert a strong influence on gilt prices. They may be attracted by comparatively high interest rates or by a strong economy and political stability. If they anticipate a rise in sterling they will buy gilts and hope to make a profit both from a fall in interest rates and on the exchange rate movement.

Gilt prices are also affected by returns in other financial markets such as the equity market. Following a strong rise in equities investment managers may wish to increase the proportion of their portfolios invested in gilts in order to maintain a strategic balance. A bull market in equities will make gilts look relatively cheap and they may rise in consequence.

Reverse yield gap

The relationship between gilts and equities is measured by the 'reverse yield gap'. This is the difference between the yield on 2.5% Consols (or some other representative stock or index) and the average yield on the Financial Times Actuaries All Share Index. For example, on 14 September 1987 these yields were 9.84% and 3.11% making the reverse yield gap 6.73%. Over a period of time this figure will fluctuate, giving an indication of the cheapness or dearness of gilts compared with equities on a historical basis.

Before the Second World War, the yield gap represented the lower yield on safer fixed interest securities, especially gilts, and higher yield on less safe ordinary shares. However, inflation since the 1950s has *reversed* the yield gap, i.e. the more secure representative government stock giving a higher yield than the average dividend yield on leading ordinary shares. The reverse yield gap illustrates that during long periods of inflation equities offer a better overall protection against inflation than the fixed interest securities, including gilts.

Yield curves

A useful method of examining the interest rate structure of the gilt market is to construct a yield curve (see Fig. 4.1).

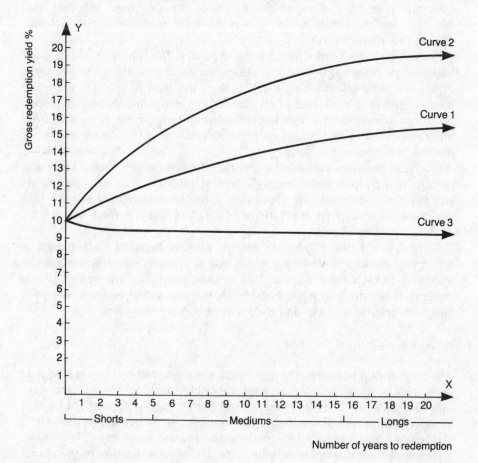

Fig. 4.1 Yield curves

Yield Curve 1

This is a *traditional* money market curve which slopes upwards signifying that, other things being equal, investors investing in mediums and longs require higher yields than those investing in shorts to compensate for higher risks and longer loss of liquidity.

Yield Curve 2

The slope of this curve reflects the expectation that future yields will *rise* and, therefore, that the capital value of lending will fall; hence yields on longs will be much higher than on shorts, not only to compensate for the higher risks but also for the possible capital loss.

Yield Curve 3

If the investors expect that the future yields will *fall*, then long yields will be below short yields in the expectation of earning capital gain; long yields will tend to approximate to the average of expected future yields.

Figure 4.1 is a graph of gross redemption yields on a particular day with the yield plotted against the vertical Y axis and the life of each stock (number of years to redemption) against the horizontal X axis or, more precisely, a curve fitted to the points so plotted. A more sophisticated method, which takes account of the wide range of coupons, is the 'three-dimensional yield curve', in effect three separate graphs for low, medium and high coupon stocks. The normal pattern shows lower yields at the short end, rising towards the medium-dated area and flattening out into the longer end. The theory is that investors require a higher yield on longs to compensate them for a higher risk. Occasionally yields on shorts are much lower than on mediums and longs, producing a steeper curve. This often indicates that interest rates are expected to rise. A curve in which shorts yield more than mediums and longs (negatively sloped) indicates that interest rates are likely to fall. The higher short-term rates are not expected to persist and the lower long-term rates express an optimistic view on inflation. Yield curves need to be used with caution as there are many factors other than the market's expectation of interest rate movements which could affect them, such as a concentration of gilt issues in a particular maturity band.

Gilt and other fixed-interest indices

The Financial Times Actuaries Indices include several fixed-interest indices – 5 year, 5–15 year, over 15 years, irredeemables and All Stocks for conventional gilts, 5 years, over 5 years and All Stocks for index-linked gilts, and Debentures and Loans and Preference Shares for non-government issues. Average gross redemption yields are also published for low, medium and high coupons classified by maturity bands (5, 15, 25 years), irredeemables, index-linked gilts 5 years and over 5 years (at two assumed inflation rates 5% and 10%), Debentures and Loans 5, 15 and 25 years, and average flat yields for preference shares. In addition, *The Financial Times* publishes a Government Securities Index (dating back to 1926) and a Fixed Interest Index.

Other methods of assessment of gilts

Apart from redemption yields, yield curves and indices, there are a number of techniques used by experts in the gilt market to assess the overall market prospects and the relative cheapness or dearness of particular stocks. These techniques are mostly highly sophisticated and call for advanced mathematical skills. They include the concepts of total return, volatility, duration, immunisation theory, price and yield differences and ratios, and price model analysis. Total return is concerned with the return on a gilt over a specific period of, say, one year or three years, as against the whole period to redemption as in the case of redemption yields. It thus includes the theoretical increase in price over that period, but may also include the effect of an across the board change in prices due to a change in interest rate levels. Volatility is concerned with the extent to which the price of a gilt will respond to a change in interest rates. This depends upon the coupon and the term to redemption, so volatility varies from one stock to another. An investor wishing to benefit from a fall in interest rates will look for a gilt with high volatility. Normally this means a long-dated, low coupon stock. Duration is similar to the average life of a stock and its interest payments. Briefly, it is the weighted average of the periods between the purchase of a stock and the receipt of the various payments, including redemption money. Immunisation theory is an attempt to remove uncertainty about the actual rate of return on a stock due to changes in the rate at which income can be reinvested. If the stock is held only until the end of its duration period changes in capital value caused by interest rate movements counterbalance the effect of changes in the reinvestment rate. Price and yield differences and ratios for pairs of stocks are plotted to enable the investor to identify times when a stock is out of line compared with its historic performance, possibly indicating its relative cheapness or dearness.

Switching

Because of the high degree of marketability of most gilts, the low bid/offer spreads, low commission rates, freedom from stamp duty and efficient transfer and settlement procedures, large gilt investors are able to switch between stocks in order to benefit from seemingly minor differences in price or yield. A switch is essentially selling one stock and buying another with the intention of reversing the process within a fairly short time. By contrast, an 'exchange' is selling one stock and buying another with no intention of reversing the transaction. There are basically three types of switch operation – tax switching, anomaly switching and policy switching.

Tax switching

Now that gilts are exempt from capital gains tax, and the accrued income scheme ensures that the holder is taxed on interest covering the whole period of investment, tax switching is less important. There are, however, some institutions such as building societies, banks and insurance companies whose gilt transactions may incur corporation tax on gains, being part of their trading profits. There could, therefore, be occasions when a switch would be worthwhile – for example, to establish a loss to set off against existing gains and reduce the taxable gains for a particular tax year.

Anomaly switching

This is usually carried out between two stocks with similar coupons and maturities – that is stocks with a similar volatility rate – so that an overall movement in interest rates will not ruin the switch by making it impossible to reverse. A switch is carried out when one stock gets out of line – perhaps it becomes too highly priced in relation to similar stocks (this is the 'anomaly') so it is sold and the proceeds reinvested in a similar stock which appears correctly priced. When the first stock falls back into line the switch is reversed and if successful the investor ends up with a larger nominal holding than before the switch, after taking all expenses and interest into account. More complex switches are possible. The proceeds may be split between two stocks whose combined volatilities match the stock sold. A switch may also go through several stages before returning to the original stock.

Policy switching

Policy switching – also called 'view switching' – is when the investor takes a 'view' on the market. If it is expected that interest rates will fall, the investor switches into a long-dated, more volatile, stock to benefit from the increase in prices. If the expectation is fulfilled the investor may then switch back to the shorter-dated stock, and should have increased the nominal amount of the holding.

Assessment of variable rate stocks

The price of a variable-rate (or floating-rate) stock remains fairly close to par as interest payments are directly related to short-term interest rates. If it is expected that interest rates will rise variable rate stocks are more attractive than fixed-interest stocks as capital value will be protected, whilst holders will also benefit from higher interest payments.

Assessment of Convertible Gilts

Convertibles are generally short-dated stocks having an option to convert into a longer-dated stock on specified dates. If interest rates rise it is likely that it would be cheaper to sell the convertible and buy the longer-dated stock in the market. If interest rates have fallen it could be worthwhile to exercise the conversion option rather than letting the convertible stock run to redemption. As each conversion date approaches it is important to calculate the effect of converting the stock.

Examples of Convertible Gilts

1 Take for example the hypothetical case of a 10% Convertible Stock which is redeemable at par in five years' time and which carries the option to convert into a 10% Conversion Stock which is redeemable at par in 15 years' time. Assume that the final opportunity to convert has arrived and that the conversion terms are £100 of the Conversion Stock for every £100 of the Convertible Stock. Assume the market prices and redemption yields are as follows:

	Price	Gross Redemption Yield
10% Convertible Stock	£94	11.7%
10% Conversion Stock	£88	11.7%

The figures show that the conversion would result in an immediate capital loss (£94 − £88) of 6.4%. Conversion would not be worthwhile. If the investor wishes to move into a longer dated stock it would be cheaper to sell the Convertible and reinvest in the Conversion Stock – ignoring expenses this would produce £106.80 nominal stock instead of £100 by converting. In practice the redemption yield on a 5 year stock would probably be rather lower than on a 15 year stock, making conversion that much less attractive and switching in the market that much more attractive. In this example interest rates have *risen* since the Convertible Stock was issued and the investor has benefited by holding the shorter-dated Convertible instead of buying a longer-dated stock.

2 The next example assumes that interest rates have *fallen* since the Convertible was issued:

	Price	Gross Redemption Yield
10% Convertible Stock	{ £108	8.0%
	(£104	9.0%) ex Conversion Rights
10% Conversion Stock	£108	9.0%

The market price of the Convertible is likely to be similar to the Conversion Stock, on the assumption that most holders in this situation will convert. Otherwise, it would be possible to buy at £104 or less, convert and sell at £108. On the assumption of a flat yield curve – in other words that the correct redemption yield for the 5 year Convertible Stock is 9.0% – the market price would be £104. If in practice the price is £108 the difference represents the conversion premium. If the conversion option is not exercised the price will fall to £104, although in practice it might be a little higher than £104 if redemption yields are lower at the short end of the market. Although interest rates have fallen the holder of the Convertible Stock has benefited by being able to convert into the longer-dated stock and has also avoided the risk of rising interest rates during the period in which the Convertible was held.

The basic principle is that it is necessary to ascertain the correct gross redemption yield for both stocks. If the Conversion Stock is already quoted the problem is simplified – otherwise the appropriate redemption yield for (in these examples) a 15 year stock with a 10% coupon has to be calculated. Similarly the appropriate redemption yield for the Convertible Stock without the conversion options is needed – this may well be different from the redemption yield indicated by the market price which may include a conversion premium. If the redemption yield on the convertible is lower than the estimated appropriate redemption yield the investor should consider selling or converting, otherwise the stock may fall in value once the final conversion opportunity has lapsed.

Actual stocks present more complex problems. The conversion terms are likely to be, say, £98 of Conversion Stock for every £100 nominal of Convertible Stock so the prices and yields of the 'convert into' stock have to be adjusted accordingly. There may be a series of conversion opportunities with conversion terms becoming progressively less attractive (this is set off by the advantage of a longer conversion period). There may be a choice of two 'convert into' stocks so that calculations have to be made for both options and a view taken on which stock is more suitable for the investor.

Assessment of index-linked gilts

The capital amount payable on redemption and future interest payments of index-linked gilts depends upon future movements in the rate of inflation as measured by the Retail Prices Index. By making assumptions about the future movements of the RPI, it is possible to calculate assumed interest and redemption payments and from these figures to produce gross and net redemption yields. Gilt edged market-makers usually produce such figures for two assumed inflation rates (say 5% and 7%), in effect the assumption is that this is the average inflation rate over the relevant period. The calculations take place in two stages. The first produces redemption yields in money terms, these are then discounted by the assumed inflation rate to produce redemption yields in real terms. These are the figures which are normally available in broker/dealer gilt lists and in the press. They are useful for selecting the most appropriate index-linked gilt for a particular investor, but do not solve the problem of comparing index-linked and conventional gilts. Some specialist gilt lists show both money and real redemption yields at selected tax rates and projected inflation rates and make comparisons with similarly dated conventional gilts.

The fact that indexation is lagged by eight months' results in the perform-ance of a stock reflecting inflation during the eight months before it was issued, but not reflecting inflation during the eight months immediately preceding redemption. During the last eight months the stock is in effect a fixed-interest stock.

If an interest-linked stock is issued at par with a coupon of, say, 2%, it will provide a real return of 2%. The market may require a higher real return, so the price will fall below par to achieve the return which satisfies investors. In due course, if the RPI increases, both interest payments and the notional redemption value increase, so that even if there is nil inflation for the remainder of the life of the stock, the amount payable on redemp-tion will be above the issue price. Of course, with negative inflation this amount would fall. The market price of the stock reflects the change in the RPI since the base month, together with the market's required real rate of return. It is useful to compare the market price with the movement in the RPI to date. For example, in September 1987 the price of 2% Index-Linked Treasury Stock 1996 was around £125. The RPI had moved from 267.9 (July 1980) to 394.5 (January 1987) an increase of 47.3%, so that if the stock had been redeemed in September 1987 the redemption value would have been £147.25. The market price was 84.89% of this figure. In September the RPI for August 1987 (102.1) was published, so that an investor could calculate that the stock would have been repaid at £150.35 if redemption had been due in April 1988. The market price was 83.14% of this figure.

Selected questions

The following questions are based on questions which were set in past exam-ination papers for the CIB Investment Examination. Jot down the main points that you think should be included in the answers and then compare your notes with the outline answers which follow.

Q1   Write short notes on the following and, in the case of (c) and (d), indicate the type of investor for which they would be most suitable.

(a) Stock Exchange quotations of British Government securities following the introduction of the Accrued Income Scheme in the Finance Act 1985;
(b) Reverse Yield Gap;
(c) Yearling Bonds;
(d) Eurobonds.

Q2 (a) Mr X says he has heard that gilts can be purchased on the National Savings Stock Register. Detail the advantages and disadvantages of this method of buying and holding British Government stocks.

(b) Explain what is meant by the following terms when used by investment commentators:

(i) Grossed-up net redemption yield;

(ii) Sinking fund.

Q3 (a) Which of the following British Government stocks would be the more suitable for each of the types of investor listed below? In each case, show how you arrived at your answer.

		Gross Yields	
	Price	Flat	Redemption
		%	%
3% Treasury Stock, 1992	£80	3.75	8.21
10% Treasury Stock, 1993	£90.50	10.15	10.38

(i) A basic-rate taxpayer;

(ii) An individual paying income tax at 60%;

(iii) An investor who is not liable to tax.

(b) How would you select a British Government stock for an individual investor resident abroad?

Brief answers

A1 (a) Since February 1986, prices quoted clean on all gilts. Accrued interest added to or subtracted from consideration. Accrued interest from last interest payment date to settlement date. Buyer pays for gross accrued interest but receives tax relief against next interest payment. Seller receives gross accrued interest on sale proceeds and is liable for tax on it. Ex-dividend transactions – accrued interest is deducted, buyer is taxed on it, seller gets relief. Measure introduced to clamp down on bond washing. Gilts dealt for account settlement – dirty prices including accrued interest (amount shown as note on contract note).

(b) Difference between gross yield on a long or undated gilt (usually 2.5% Consols) or FT Gilt Index and equities (FT All Share Index). Before 1959 equities yielded more than gilts because of perceived higher risk of equity investment. Since then equities yeild less because of inflation hedge qualities and prospective growth of dividends and capital value. Reverse yield gap fluctuates – can be used to measure relative cheapness/dearness of equities versus gilts.

(c) Yearling bonds are negotiable local authority bonds issued weekly (Tuesdays) in £1000 denominations. Usually one year term, good interest rate. Interest accrues daily, free of stamp duty, Cash settlement, clean prices and accrued interest. Suitable for short term investment.

(d) Eurobonds are fixed or variable interest stocks. US dollars and other currencies. Sold outside country in whose currency they are denominated. Traded on secondary market. Issued by governments and major companies. Often include conversion rights. Bearer certificate, interest paid gross annually. Suitable for investor seeking currency hedge, gross interest, anonymity or high yield (non-resident of UK). Limited marketability, not suitable for small investor.

A2 (a) *Advantages of NSSR*

Interest paid gross – taxpayer need not reclaim. Commission charges low – cheaper than broker/dealers, especially for small amounts. VAT included in charges. Choice of method of payment of dividends, including warrants under £50 encashable at Post Offices. Holders under 18 may transfer stock free of charge to Bank of England register. Stock may be purchased for children under seven years.

Disadvantages

Price may not be specified. Department will not undertake to deal on a particular day so price may have moved. Purchase limit of £10 000 value on any one day for any one stock. Limited choice of stocks on Register.

  (b) (i) Net redemption yield – interest yield net of tax at investor's marginal rate of tax plus (or minus) capital gain (or loss) to maturity expressed as a yield % (net of tax on capital gain if appropriate). The net redemption yield is grossed up at the investor's marginal tax rate. Useful for comparison purposes (e.g. with bank deposit account or other fixed interest stocks). Also called 'equivalent gross yield'.

     (ii) Borrower sets aside regular amount (out of profits) each year to provide for redemption of debenture, loan stock or other interest-bearing security. Redemption then takes place either by drawings, purchase of stock in the market, or by a fund accumulated in other investments. A Stock with a sinking fund enjoys a better market rating.

A3 (a) Calculate approximate net redemption yields for relevant tax rates and select highest in each case:

		27%	60%	nil
3% Treasury	Gross	3.75	3.75	3.75
	tax	1.01	2.25	
	net	2.74	1.50	
(8.21 − 3.75)	profit	4.46	4.46	4.46
	NRY	7.20	5.96	8.21
10% Treasury	Gross	10.15	10.15	10.15
	tax	2.74	6.09	
	net	7.41	4.06	
(10.38 − 10.15)	profit	0.23	0.23	0.23
	NRY	7.64	4.29	10.38

(i) 10% Treasury
(ii) 3% Treasury
(iii) 10% Treasury
(b) Select an exempt gilt (one where the investor may apply to have interest paid gross). Select a stock providing a high gross redemption yield with a maturity date appropriate for the investor's requirements.

Specially selected question

The following information relates to six British Government Stocks on a particular day in September 1987:

Stock	Price £	Accrued Interest £	Yield Interest %	Yield Redemption %
10% Treasury Convertible Stock, 25 Oct. 1990	99 2/32	4.000	10.095	10.340
3% Treasury Stock 13 May 1991	84 14/32	1.052	3.553	7.988
9% Treasury Stock 15 Mar 1992–96	93 14/32	0.074	9.632	10.174
15.5% Treasury Stock 30 Sept 1998	131 8/32 xd	−0.510	11.810	10.623
3.5% War Loan, 1 Jun, 1 Dec	35 30/32	1.045	9.739	9.732
2% Index-Linked Treasury Stock 23 Mar 1992	96 8/32 xd	−0.028	2.126	3.267 * 2.973 #

* Assumed rate of inflation 5%
# Assumed rate of inflation 7%

Outline the main features which are common to all six stocks and describe the special characteristics of each stock, indicating how it would meet the needs of particular types of investor.

Model answer

The features which are common to all six stocks are:
- exemption from stamp duty
- exemption from capital gains tax
- interest and capital guaranteed by British Government
- interest payments every six months
- market prices subject to fluctuation
- dealt in for clean prices with accrued interest as a separate item, subject to the accrued income scheme
- usually for cash settlement

The special characteristics of these stocks and their suitability for particular types of investor are:

10% Treasury Convertible Stock, 1990 is a short-dated stock which may be converted at the holder's option into one or more longer-dated stocks on specified terms at specified dates. It offers a secure high yield. Offers investors an option on the movements in interest rates. If rates rise the investor's capital is protected by the 1990 redemption date. If they fall the investor can benefit by selling or converting into the longer-dated stock. The stock is currently full of interest. (You will not be expected to know the precise conversion terms of this stock, but just to be aware that it is a convertible stock and what this implies.)

3% Treasury Stock, 1991 is a low-coupon short-dated stock. The price is well below par and the tax-free capital gain on maturity produces an attractive net return for high-rate taxpayers.

9% Treasury Stock, 1992–96 is repayable at the borrower's (i.e. the Government's) option on 15/3/92 or 15/3/96 or at any time between these dates. They are more likely to redeem before the final date if interest rates are below 9%. The stock is suitable for a medium-term investor, probably a basic-rate taxpayer, looking for a good yield with a small capital gain. (This is also one of the exempt stocks, but you would not be expected to know this.)

15.5% Treasury Stock, 1998 is a medium-dated high-coupon stock standing well above par. It provides a secure high interest yield but there will be capital loss if held to maturity. It is suitable for gross fund such as a pension fund or a charity (or possibly an individual non-taxpayer) where the gross redemption yield is the principal criterion.

3.5% War Loan is an irredeemable (undated) stock. Interest is paid gross. It is also an 'exempt' stock. It is suitable for non-residents or for investors looking for a fixed income guaranteed for an unlimited period, such as the trustees of an annuity fund.

2% Index-Linked Treasury Stock, 1992 is a short-dated stock. Capital and interest are adjusted in line with the Retail Prices Index. It offers a real rate of return (a real gross redemption yield of 3.267% assuming 5% inflation) and protection against inflation. Redemption value will be well above par and the stock is attractive to high-rate taxpayers and those seeking inflation protection.

Updating

It is necessary to keep up-to-date with any developments in the gilt-edged market. These might involve the dealing and settlement systems, the methods of issue of gilts, or any new types of stock brought to the market. You need to be aware of the current situation of the gilt market in terms of the general levels of interest rates and inflation and the major factors influencing the market. This can be achieved by occasionally reading market reports on the gilt market in *The Financial Times* or other leading newspapers and by checking through an up-to-date list of gilt prices and yields from time to time.

5 Indirect investments and investment in real assets

Introduction

Under *direct* investment, the investors themselves decide which investments to buy or sell, when and how much to buy or sell, and pay the dealing costs, if such costs are involved, in buying and selling investments. They are in control. To carry on direct investment profitably, the investor must possess continuous updated knowledge of the investment market, expertise to know when to buy or sell and large financial resources and to make investments economic and diversified, in order to reduce the risks of putting 'all-eggs in-one-basket'.

Not many private investors, however, possess the requisite expertise, market knowledge and large resources to go for direct investment. And yet all investors can benefit from these requisites, and cheaply, through *indirect* investment. Indirect investment is direct investment, one stage removed: investors buy the investment products of the 'specialised investment institutions' (see below) who, in turn, invest the huge accumulated funds in the most profitable and well diversified investments and closely monitor the performance of these investments through expert managers and sophisticated market information gathering techniques.

In 1982 and 1987 the government has added tax benefit to two schemes, viz. Business Expansion Scheme and Personal Equity Plan, of indirect investments into quoted and unquoted companies. This has led to many specialist funds being set up with the twin objective of making available funds for firms which are not listed on the Stock Exchange and to provide means to investors to benefit from tax-effective investments.

In times of rising inflation and falling confidence in paper currencies investments in property, precious metals, gold coins, chattels (such as, jewellery, objets d'art, antiques) become more desirable. Any person in the street can now have interests in property and other chattels via indirect investment schemes. These investments also have tax benefits: capital gains tax is payable only upon gains which are in excess of the tax-free index-linked threshold.

Finally, many insurance company investment products, in addition to providing income and capital growth to the indirect investor's capital, also provide life assurance cover, for the benefit of the assured's dependents if the assured dies too soon, and for the assured and his/her family if the assured lives a long life.

Theoretical aspects

The number of specialised investment institutions has increased considerably since the 1950s, corresponding with the decline of the direct investor and the rise of institutional investors (see Chapter 9). This trend has to some extent been reversed with the advent of popular and privatisation issues during the last few years. The following are the main institutional investors in the UK.

Investment Trusts (ITs)

ITs are the oldest (in existence since the 1860s) institutions in the group. They were conceived to give the investors of moderate means the same advantage as large investors in reducing their risk by spreading investments over a number of different stocks. The principle is as relevant today as it was then. The growing number of savings schemes introduced by ITs means that they are now easily available to the smallest investor.

Characteristics

An IT is a public limited company whose shares are quoted on the stock exchange. Like any other quoted public limited company, an IT is subject to UK company laws and stock exchange regulations. It has a fixed amount of capital divided into shares which are traded on the stock market. It pays dividends to shareholders out of its investment income. The main difference between an IT and other companies is that its assets are not buildings and premises, plant and machinery and raw materials, but shares in other companies. Therefore an investor, by buying the shares in just one company – an IT company – has a stake in a large number of companies; his or her investment is spread over all the companies in which the IT itself owns shares. As a holder of IT shares, the investor is a part-owner of the IT assets – called its portfolio – and is entitled to a share in its dividends and a say in the way it is run.

The costs of purchasing IT shares and subsequent management charges are low and the discount to asset value at which its shares can generally be purchased mean that the shareholder will have the benefit of additional assets earning increased income. The fixed capital of an IT enables its managers to take a long term view and to make the best possible use of its shareholders' money. The capital gains made on transactions are not distributed in cash to shareholders; instead they are used to build up the portfolio. In this way, its assets grow in value; and since the number of shares is fixed, the asset value per share, increases over the years. However it can go up or down.

Advantages of investing in ITs

1 Their results show that they offer growth both in capital and dividend income. This is because stocks and shares have been an excellent investment – in making money (capital growth) and in beating inflation (the average dividend rate has been higher than the rise in RPI).
2 ITs are not 'trusts' in the legal sense, there is no trust deed limiting their managers' freedom of action. They can invest in any promising opportunity wherever they see it – in quoted and unquoted companies, in property and in domestic and overseas assets. Their freedom to invest in a wide variety of assets results in the diversification of investments, minimising the risk for even the smallest shareholder.
3 If the market price of a share stands at less than its net asset value, the difference in stock market terms is known as the 'discount'. The assets of ITs grow in value as a result of increase in value of the underlying assets. Although the share prices of ITs also increase, they usually stand below the asset value per share. The investors therefore can buy shares in the ITs' assets at a discount (see Practical application below).
4 Unlike any other vehicle for collective investment, an IT, being a public company, can borrow funds to buy assets. If the total assets then grow in value, the shareholders' *net* assets grow proportionately more, because the amount of debt remains unchanged. This is called 'gearing', and it brings

additional capital gains to shareholders. There is a similar effect on income: if the income from an asset rises, then the interest on the borrowed money used to buy that asset takes a smaller proportion of the income. There is, therefore, more left for higher dividends (see Practical application below).

5 The investor buying IT shares, receives expert investment management and constant monitoring of the market at low cost. Average annual management charges, which are deducted from the ITs' income, are only 0.5% of assets. But, additionally, there are initial costs: broker's commission (with VAT) plus government's stamp duty – but on a £2000 investment these should not amount to more than $2\frac{1}{2}\%$ (commission 1.65% + VAT 0.2475% + stamp duty 0.5% = 2.3975% + market maker's turn), even with the abolition of fixed commissions. ITs do not add any management charge to the purchase price (see below).

6 ITs do not have to pay any tax on the gains they make from selling underlying shares, therefore their managers are free to make changes in their portfolios on investment grounds only. But shareholders have to pay capital gains tax if they sell their shares on their total *net* gains plus indexation allowance over the index-linked exemption limit. Shareholders receive dividends net of basic tax rate, and if a shareholder is not liable to the basic rate of tax he or she can use the tax credit, which accompanies the dividend payment, to claim a refund from the tax authorities.

7 Direct investments, particularly overseas investments, create administrative and tax problems. Shareholders in ITs have these problems removed from their shoulders: it is obviously much easier to deal with a single investment than with many.

Disadvantages of investing in ITs

1 Gearing in an IT is a double-edged sword: while prices of the shares it owns increase, the value of its portfolio will increase more quickly, despite the need to repay loans; but if prices of shares it owns fall, it may be left with heavy liabilities in terms of fixed interest loans, which would leave less for shareholders. Thus the share prices of highly geared ITs fluctuate more than the market as a whole (see below).

2 Investors in IT shares have, in effect, to pay the stamp duty and commission (plus VAT) twice: once for their purchase of IT shares, and the other paid by the IT company for IT purchases of shares in other companies.

3 Another factor which affects the prices of IT shares is the net asset value of an IT. The net asset value is the net market value of the investments the IT owns. It changes day by day as the underlying assets change in value. If the market rating turns against the IT, its shareholders may incur loss even when the underlying assets increase in value.

4 The shares in smaller ITs (not many) are not always easily marketable, hence there is usually a wide spread between their buying and selling prices.

Types of ITs

Split-Capital Trusts

These ITs, introduced in the mid-1960s, have their share capital split from the beginning into two classes: one class provides income, and those investors who want income from investment (e.g. low income households) buy the income shares; the other class promises capital growth, and investors who would rather get the promised capital growth than income (e.g. high rate taxpayers) buy the capital shares. The date when the IT would be wound up is fixed at its inception – say 20 years. Until then the income shareholders get most of the income earned by the IT, the capital shareholders get very little or no dividend. But when the IT is wound up, the income shareholders only get back an amount agreed in advance when the IT was launched; the capital shareholders get all the rest of the IT's assets. The price of income shares (plus yield) rises over the years and declines as wind-up-date approaches. Therefore care is needed to sell before then in order to crystalise capital gain.

ITs with 'B' shares

These were also introduced in the 1960s as another method of giving shareholders a choice between income and capital returns. 'B' shareholders receive no dividend, instead they receive a regular scrip (free) issue of 'B' shares, the value of which is equivalent to the *actual* cash dividend paid to the ordinary shareholders. Therefore 'B' shares have no special attraction to basic rate taxpayers and of course they are disadvantageous to the non taxpayer. Since 1975, the receipts of scrip issues have been made assessable as income liable to higher rate tax. Most 'B' shares on issue may be converted into ordinary shares.

'Limited life' Trusts

Before 1981 the only ITs with a limited life were the majority of the Split-Capital Trusts. Recently, however a few 'conventional', mostly newly-formed, ITs have adopted a limited life structure. This gives the opportunity to the shareholders from time to time, annually, or every five years, to decide if they wish to continue.

Savings schemes offered by ITs

A number of ITs' managements have established savings schemes for investors. These schemes offer the following three broad methods of investing in ITs.

Dividend reinvestment

Existing shareholders of an IT may have their dividends used to buy more shares in that IT.

Regular savings

Any investor can invest a monthly sum in the purchase of shares of whichever IT he or she chooses; most of these schemes accept as little as £25 per month.

Occasional investments

Most schemes will accept 'one-off' contributions, usually of £250 minimum, for investment.

The advantage to investors in using these savings schemes is that they do not have to find their own stockbrokers to deal for them and, especially for people investing small amounts, their dealing costs are lower than if they dealt directly with a stockbroker or an agent.

Unit Trusts (UTs)

UTs are another form of collective investment which provides investors with simple, indirect access to the stock market and professional investment management. By purchasing units in a UT, investors pool their money in a fund which is run by professional managers who invest the fund in a very wide selection of the UK or overseas companies' shares (the range of assets in which 'authorised' UTs may invest is being widened), or in safe securities like British government stocks.

Units in a fund can be bought from the UT group, or through agents like banks, solicitors, stockbrokers and others. Each UT has a minimum investment, ranging from as little as £100 to as much as £2500, but it is usually around £500. The units can be sold by unitholders by sending back the unit certificate, which they received when they purchased the units, to the UT group. After giving appropriate instructions to the managers directly, or through an agent, the certificates have to be renounced. UT managers must buy back the units if investors wish to sell them.

Each UT quotes two prices. The higher of the two is the 'offer' price, at which the investors can buy units. The offer price is based on the current market (offer) price of shares in the fund plus dealing expenses and the initial charge UT groups make for managing investors' money. The 'bid' price is the lower of the two prices; this is the price per unit which the investors will receive when they sell their units.

Managers of each UT have to calculate their unit prices according to a formula laid down by the Department of Trade and Industry. Under the formula, at the time of writing (a new system is being discussed), the spread between the offer and bid prices can be as wide as 12%, usually it is around 5 to 7% (see below). Both the offer and the bid prices are usually calculated daily, and held for 24 hours. The wider the spread between the two prices, the more the unit price will have to rise before the investors start to make a profit on their unitholding. The new system which is being discussed will deal with forward pricing problems. See Practical application below.

The investors pay two fees for having their money managed by a UT group: an initial charge and an annual management levy. Since 1979 there is no fixed scale of UT management fees but the initial charge set by trust deed is usually 5% plus VAT (whether VAT is charged on the initial fee depends on whether new or reissued units are involved) which is included in the offer price. The annual levy can vary, but is usually between $\frac{3}{4}$ and 1%, (plus VAT), on the value of the trust portfolio which is normally deducted from the income earned by the trust. Generally speaking annual management levies are higher on trusts which invest in overseas shares or in highly specialised investment areas.

UT groups also make a 'rounding up' charge on the offer (buying) price of units, and a 'rounding down' charge on the bid (selling) price, this avoids unit prices being quoted in awkward fractions. The rounding charge cannot be more than 1.25p or 1%, whichever is smaller. The managers of a UT group can deal in the units of the group at a profit: buying them back from investors and subsequently selling them at a profit to new buyers.

Investors can calculate how much their units are worth – by looking up their UT in one of the leading national newspapers – i.e. *The Financial Times, The Times, The Telegraph* – for the latest bid price, and multiplying the bid price with the number of units they own, as shown in their unit certificate.

UTs themselves do not have to pay capital gains tax on any profit they make on their investments within the fund. Investors receive the income from their unitholding net of the basic rate tax (25% for 1988/89), with a tax credit. The income received, and the tax paid, must be declared by investors on their tax returns. However, non-taxpayers can reclaim the tax deduction from the Inland Revenue, basic rate taxpayers have no further tax to pay and higher rate taxpayers have to pay additional tax. Any capital gain plus indexation allowance, on the sale of units which is in excess of the index-linked tax-free limit (£5000 of gains for the tax year 1988/89) will be subject to the marginal rate of tax of the investor.

Advantages in investing in UTs

1 Investors can achieve a much wider spread of risk than most could secure out of their own resources. Most UTs divide investors' cash between 50 and

100 shares. A UT cannot invest more than $7\frac{1}{2}\%$ of its money in any one share; this avoids the 'all-eggs in one-basket' type of risk.

2   Investors buy professional investment management at a 'reasonable' cost. The 5% initial charge is high, but this cost benefit arises from small holdings which avoid a high minimum fee. Decisions, and all the associated paperwork, about which company or industry to back, and when to buy and sell shares or whether to accept a rights issue (i.e. issues of new shares to existing shareholders at a price usually lower than the market price) are taken by managers who have access to detailed research from their own research departments and from a large number of stockbrokers.

3   Those investors who do not have a lump sum can acquire a holding of units through regular, flexible savings schemes offered by many UT groups. This is a useful facility enabling investors to build up a stake in shares painlessly over the years.

4   Over the years, a UT should provide investors with growth in capital value and growth in income. Many UTs have produced capital growth and income performances which have outstripped inflation, and have given better returns (when both capital and income growth are taken into consideration) than savings which involve no risk of capital loss, such as the national savings and government gilt stocks. Due to short term market fluctuations, investments in units of UTs should be seen as longer-term investments.

5   Virtually all UT groups offer the 'share exchange schemes' which enable investors to convert most shares into units at little or no cost. UT managers like these schemes because they provide them with a means of attracting new money into their funds; they may be able to take the share into one of their own trusts.

6   Many UT groups offer regular savings linked to life assurance plans. These plans continue with agreed regular investments in a UT with some life assurance protection for the saver and his or her family.

7   Investors requiring regular or additional income can join UTs 'withdrawal plans'. Under this plan, income received from the investor's UT earnings is topped up by selling some of the investor's units on a regular basis.

8   There are legal restrictions on the maximum deviation allowed between unit prices and the underlying net-asset value of the fund, and the managers ensure that this deviation is as little as possible. This means that the units are highly marketable at the bid price, which gives liquidity to investment.

Disadvantages of investing in UTs

1   The cost of dealing in UTs is high. The investor pays a rather high initial charge and the annual levy. These charges are on top of the commissions (with VAT) and stamp duties paid by the UTs on their purchases. The purchase or sale prices of units will include an initial management charge

and a 'rounding up' (or 'rounding down') element to arrive at *inclusive* buying or selling prices. The effect of these charges, on average, is to add about 9% to the purchase price and deduct about 3% from the sale proceeds of a unit.

2   Being 'open-ended' funds, the UTs are not allowed to borrow for their traditional business activities, therefore cannot benefit from the gearing effects. (Back to back loans, however, are allowed for insolvency hedging.)

3   Authorised UTs, i.e. those approved by the DTI, must not invest more than $7\frac{1}{2}\%$ of their money in one firm, must not hold more than 10% of the shares of one firm, and must not invest more than 5% of their money in securities not listed on the stock exchanges – this constrains their investment activities.

4   UTs invest most of their money in shares quoted on the stock exchanges, which means investing in the performance of companies. If the companies perform badly the unit prices will go down, and so will the value of unit-holders' investments.

Types of authorised UTs

Although all UTs operate in the same way, yet they invest in a wide variety of industries in different stock markets throughout the world. The diversity of investment by different UTs means that investors with very different priorities can find a UT which will meet their needs. The diversity of invest-ment can be seen from the following main categories or *authorised* UTs.

Equity Income Funds

These UTs cater for the investors whose main need is for maximum income. These UTs therefore concentrate on buying shares in companies that are likely to give a high yield. In order to minimise the risk the managers also invest in gilts and fixed interest stocks including preference shares.

Capital Growth Funds

The emphasis in these funds is on a rising unit price for investors whose main aim is capital growth. This category will include UTs which invest entirely in the shares of small companies at home and abroad, or in recovery shares. The prices of units of specialist UTs can be particularly volatile, because short-term gains and losses, especially in UTs which invest in just one or two industries, are likely to be very dramatic. The investor must accept a high risk/reward ratio.

General Funds

These UTs are for investors who want steady growth in both income and capital. The investment in these UTs is broadly-based in mainly UK shares covering several industries. Some general funds are called 'rainbow-funds' because they allow investors to select what proportions of their savings should go into different funds, colour-coded by their type.

Financial and Property Funds

These UTs invest in the shares of financial institutions like banks and insurance companies, and in the shares of property companies: UTs are not allowed to invest directly in property, *but this is changing* (see below).

Commodity and Energy Funds

These UTs concentrate on the shares of companies producing raw materials, oils, gold, mining and other primary commodities: UTs are not allowed to invest in actual commodities. The unit prices of these funds are very volatile, because the prices of commodities tend to rise and fall quite quickly. These are very speculative investments.

Investment Trust Units

These UTs, by investing in the shares of investment trust companies, achieve a much wider diversification of their investments because the ITs themselves invest in a wide range of shares, or rather because individual ITs may be rather specialised.

Gilt and Fixed Interest Funds

These invest in government securities and public companies' bonds, with the obective to produce a high and secure income for investors. A few gilt funds concentrate on capital appreciation rather than income, these are known as Gilt and Fixed Interest Growth Trusts.

Unit Portfolio Managed Fund

Most management companies have several UTs under their management. Since 1985, several management groups have offered these managed funds ('funds of funds') which are permitted to invest in any UT (before 1987, they could invest in only four sub funds), giving a choice currently of 1050 funds run by more than 130 management groups. These Funds involve a double layer of investment supervision, for which the groups are permitted to make two sets of annual levies, but only one initial charge. The advantage of these managed funds is that switches can be made among the underlying funds without incurring capital gains tax, which could arise if an individual investor switched funds at profit which exceeded the annual tax free threshold.

Money Market Funds

This type of UT was authorised by the DTI during 1987. They invest in cash (including foreign currency), i.e. deposits with, and loans to, banks and building societies and certain other 'authorised' (under the 1987 Banking Act) institutions, gilts, bank and building society debt instruments (e.g. certificates of deposit). Essentially the funds are highly liquid, since at least 75% must remain in cash as assets repayable within two weeks. These funds are seen as a natural complement to Equity Funds.

The inclusion of foreign currency under 'cash', effectively means that a manager could run a Money Market Fund as a pure Currency Fund, earning a return not on interest, but on the far more volatile exchange rate movement of currencies, which are as yet not available to authorised UTs.

UTs with foreign 'flavour'

(a) *North American Trusts* These invest in American and Canadian companies. Some offer a general spread of the US shares, others invest in more specialised areas like US recovery stock, US smaller companies or in companies concerned with new technological developments.

(b) *European Trusts* These invest in companies in a number of different European countries. Some UTs in this category concentrate exclusively on French, German, Spanish or Scandinavian shares.

(c) *Far Eastern Trusts* Investment here can either be in a spread of companies in Japan, Hong Kong, Malaysia, Singapore, Australia and New Zealand, usually aimed at capital growth, or concentrated on individual stock markets in the region, like Hong Kong, Singapore, Malaysia.

(d) *Japanese Trusts* The bulk of their portfolios will be invested in Japan, either in a general spread of shares or in specific sectors of the Japanese market, such as smaller companies, technology stocks and recovery situations.

(e) *Australian Trusts* They invest in a spread of Australian companies and occasionally in British companies whose interests are mainly in Australasia.

(f) *International Income Trusts* Some of these UTs invest in a broad spread of international markets, while others concentrate exclusively on America, Japan, Europe or the Far East. All the funds are designed to provide an above-average income, as well as some capital appreciation.

Investment Trusts and Unit Trusts compared and contrasted

Some people think that the unit and investment trusts are one and the same thing, but while there are some similarities between the two types of institutions, there are also important differences between them.

Similarities

1   Both are vehicles for collective indirect investment.
2   Both are managed funds, with in-built diversification of investment.
3   The tax treatment of income and gains in both is the same.
4   Investment in both should be seen as long-term, for full benefits.
5   Value of investments in both can go up or go down in line with the value of their underlying assets.

Dissimilarities

Investment Trusts	Authorised Unit Trusts
1 Public limited companies whose shares can be bought and sold on the stock exchange. Cannot market own shares, therefore do not benefit financially from own share dealings.	1 Legal 'Trusts', with trust deeds and trustees, in which units can be bought and sold directly or through agents, from and to the trusts' managers. Can benefit from unit dealings.
2 The share capital is fixed by law – 'closed-end' funds.	2 The funds are open-ended; units bought and sold increase and decrease the fund sizes respectively.
3 Share prices fluctuate with changes in supply and demand and do not necessarily have any relation to the value of underlying assets.	3 Unit prices are fixed by the managers within a range laid down by the DTI, and are based directly on the value of the underlying portfolio.
4 Shares can usually be bought at a discount of their underlying net asset value.	4 Units are bought at their underlying net asset value.
5 Can borrow additional funds to enjoy the potential benefits of gearing.	5 Limited in their ability to borrow.
6 Freedom to invest in a wide variety of assets including, for example, property, commodities.	6 Are generally limited to investing in the shares of quoted companies and the British government securities.
7 Cannot advertise and market own shares, therefore do not benefit financially from share dealings, but avoid advertising and marketing costs.	7 Free to advertise and commission agents to market units and make profit on unit dealings.
8 Average Annual management charges are about 0.5% of the assets under management; there is no 'initial' charge.	8 The annual management levy is normally between 0.75 and 1%, which is additional to an initial charge of about 5%.

Unauthorised Unit Trusts (UUTs)

These trusts are not authorised by the DTI, and therefore cannot advertise their products in any way, but the details of their products can be supplied to professional investment advisers. There are three main categories of UUTs: house funds, property funds and offshore funds.

House funds

These in-house funds are set up by the stockbrokers, banks and other investment houses for the benefit of their own customers. Investors who, even on the advice of their investment advisers, invest in these funds should realize that they are not afforded the same protection as with authorised UTs. The Financial Services Act requires all investment advisers to disclose to their customers any connection between themselves and the in-house funds which they recommend.

Property funds

These funds invest directly in property, and are designed for and available to tax-exempt investors, such as the pension funds and charities. For the tax-exempt investors investment in these UTs is more profitable than investment in the shares of property companies and in property bonds, because investment in property UUTs, unlike the other two, is free from corporation tax.

All property UUTs can borrow from the banks up to a certain percentage – usually 20 to 50% – of the value of the fund, which provides them with the means for long-term gearing.

Offshore funds

These funds are established outside the UK – the location is chosen on account of the favourable tax treatment of investment income. They are often run on the authorised Unit Trust lines by the UK investment management group and may accept money from the UK investors. Investments in these funds are high risk, therefore there are severe restrictions on the marketing of offshore funds in the UK. These risks may largely be overcome by staying with funds which are backed by large UK institutions.

Until recently the chief attraction for the UK investor of these funds was their 'exemption' from capital gains tax. They were not exempt from CGT for UK residents, but there was the problem of 'roll up' of income, their distributor status etc. However, this attraction has now been eliminated. For UK investors there is now no great incentive to invest in these funds because the UK authorised managed UTs and ITs provide world-wide spread of investments.

To the non-resident and non-domiciled investors, however, these funds do provide certain tax advantages.

There are several kinds of offshore funds, including Commodities Fund

-- investing in actual commodities, and not in commodity shares; Gold Fund – investing in gold metal and gold coins, and not in gold shares; USM Funds – wholly invested in unlisted securities; and currency funds – which may invest in the deposits of major or minor currencies, or in a combination of currencies at the discretion of fund managers.

Currency Funds are actively managed and switches are made frequently to keep the Fund liquid. Most Funds invest on an overnight to three-month basis. Charges on these Funds are much lower than on the conventional authorised managed funds. Small businesses can hold investments in Currency Funds to hedge the exchange rate risks on their currency commitments. Investors in the Currency Funds must be willing to accept a high risk/reward ratio because the currency exchange rate movements in relation to sterling can be very volatile.

Exempt UTs

These UTs are only open for investments from tax-exempt investors. Charities and pension funds are exempt from either the UK income tax or capital gains tax. Note that non-taxpaying individuals are not classed as 'tax-exempt', and therefore are not eligible to invest in exempt UTs. These trusts are liable to income tax but the exempt investor will be able to reclaim payment. There are both exempt unauthorised (e.g. Property UTs) and exempt authorised UTs in operation.

New types of unit trusts

Draft regulations were announced in November 1987 for new types of UT which may be offered in 1988. Since these new UTs are potentially much more risky, most UT managers would like them to be called something other than UTs. See Practical application.

1 *Money funds* will invest in cash or near cash instruments.
2 *Futures, options and commodity funds* To reduce risks there will be lower limits on the proportion that must be kept in these funds in cash or near cash.
3 *Mixed funds* These will invest in at least three of the following seven sectors: equities, government securities, debt instruments, property, options, futures and commodities.
4 *Property funds* These will be allowed to invest directly in industrial, commercial and residential property. No property may account for more than 15% of the fund at the time it is acquired. For example, an office block costing £2 million could only be purchased by a fund with assets in excess of £14 million.

Insurance and investment

Only those insurance schemes which give back a monetary rate of return to policyholders, whether or not the event insured against occurs, may be classed as investment schemes.

The value of insurance-linked investments which are directly linked to the prices of stocks and shares, like any other stock market investment, can go up or down according to the price movements in underlying securities. Insurance companies selling their life-linked investments will want to know the age of the insured investors and also their state of health. Non-declaration of a relevant fact, even though not asked by the insurance company, could make the policy invalid.

The investor can buy a regular payment policy – which is like a regular savings scheme with a UT or an IT – or a single premium policy/bond. Insurance companies deduct management charges from the increase in value of investors' policies.

Advantages and disadvantages of investing in insurance products

The main insurance investment products are discussed below individually, but, overall, the following advantages and disadvantages arise from investments in insurance products.

Advantages

1 The investor is guaranteed a future return at a *known* date, i.e. on maturity of policy or earlier death of policyholder: the former is a vehicle for savings and the latter provides for the next of kin and is a device for paying off outstanding debts (e.g. mortgage).
2 Capital invested will be repaid in full and, with some products (e.g. index-linked bonds) it will be protected against inflation.
3 Investment advertisements are officially regulated and provide some protection for investors.
4 Apart from commission paid to intermediaries, there are no extra charges in buying and selling insurance investments. With unit-linked products the expenses are included in the spread between the 'offer' and 'bid' prices.
5 They provide the prospects of capital gains, and, with certain products (e.g. income bonds), income payments are guaranteed.
6 The investor can take a modest income out of his or her investment-linked insurance policy with no obligation to pay the basic rate of tax on it; this is accounted for by the companies at their special rate (see below).
7 If a regular payments policy is kept up till maturity or for 10 years, any gain from it, with some provisos, is not assessed for income tax, and does not affect age income relief (see below).

8 Life assurance companies pay tax on dividends at basic rate, and on other income at 35% (they do not pay the higher rate Corporation Tax), the higher rate taxpayer can 'roll up' incomes over a long period, paying tax when the single premium policy is encashed.
9 Tax burden can be reduced by claiming 'top-slicing' relief (see below).
10 Capital gains tax is not normally charged on gains made from life insurance investments, but life company is liable for CGT.

Disadvantages

1 The terms and conditions of insurance products seem to have a very large amount of 'small print' which nevertheless must be understood fully, without relying too much on the sales talk, in order to avoid any snags later on.
2 Insurance-linked investments are mainly designed as long-term investments, early encashments usually suffer heavy financial penalties.
3 The management charges are not standardised; the investor needs to shop around for the lowest charges.
4 Although 'switching' (see below) facilities are usually available, in some cases switching charges may be high.
5 There is a history of failures of off-shore companies offering insurance-linked investments!

Insurance investment products

There are two main categories of insurance products: the conventional products that provide protection for the investor's family, with or without a bonus at maturity or earlier death; the other category is investment schemes first and foremost, with a small element of life cover.

1 Conventional schemes

(a) *Term insurance* The insured pays fixed premiums for a fixed period and the sum assured by the life office (insurance company) is payable only on death before the term ends. If the insured survives beyond the fixed term, he/she gets back nothing. Term policies can be bought cheaply, depending upon the age and state of health of the insured and the length of the term.

(b) *Whole life* The insured pay agreed premiums throughout their lives or until they reach an advanced age. The sum assured is payable on death; however, the insured can surrender the policy after a few years; the cash-in, or surrender, value received will depend upon how long the policy was held. The capital growth may be as little as 2%, even with bonuses.

(c) *Endowment policies* Both the term and whole life policies can hardly be regarded as investments, but endowment policies contain a very substantial investment element. Premiums are paid over a fixed period, and the company pays back a guaranteed lump sum at maturity or earlier death. Endowment policies can be 'with' or 'without' profit; if 'without' profit, then the amount to be paid back is fixed in advance. It is cheaper than 'with profit' policy. The life companies generally estimate profits conservatively, therefore 'with profit' policies are much the better investment of the two, despite higher premiums.

With-profit policies guarantee a smaller lump sum but add regular bonuses – the 'reversionary' bonuses – to the investment. Reversionary bonuses once given cannot be taken back. Over the years the bonuses have steadily increased. In addition, there may also be a 'terminal' bonus at maturity of the policy. Terminal bonuses tend to be volatile. The life companies generally invest premium income in a balanced portfolio which usually includes substantial elements of gilt-edged securities and equities. The size of bonuses depends on the success of the company's investment performance. There are, however, government regulations about the valuation of the life companies' assets and how bonuses are arrived at.

Policies need not be maintained throughout the whole term. The holder nearly always has the option of 'surrender' or 'conversion to a paid-up policy', i.e. freeze its value at the current level without paying any further premiums. However, these options are usually available on terms that bear harshly on the policyholder, therefore conventional life contracts should be entered into after due consideration and for long-terms.

(d) *Variable life policies*   These are new innovations in the insurance industry and may be considered as 'half-way-house' between the 'conventional' and investment insurance products. Policyholders can vary the protection and savings elements in their policies according to their family needs and income. Perhaps early on they may prefer the less expensive combination of more protection and less savings and, later on, want a greater element of saving than protection. They may increase the premium in line with inflation, so that their return is index-linked. The in-built flexibility of these policies means that investors do not have constantly to take out new or different policies.

2   Investment-linked policies

(a) *Unit-linked policies*   The underlying principle of these policies is the same as that underlying the UT schemes, i.e. collective investment, diversification, comparatively low costs; except that with the insurance unit-linked policies there is some life cover for the policyholder and a guaranteed death payment.

Units of these policies are bought at offer price and sold at the prevailing bid price. The spread between the two prices covers management charges. In addition, the insurance managers deduct from the premiums an annual management charge of between 0.75–1% of the value of investment.

The proportion of the policyholder's premiums that is used to buy units, usually 90–95%, depends on his/her age at commencement, the length of the period of policy and the assured lump sum at maturity or earlier death. For investors over 60 life covered assured is less, therefore a much larger proportion of the premium is used in buying additional units. The longer the policy is kept the lower the charges in proportion to its value, and vice versa. There may be a minimum unit holding required, say 10 to 200 units, or a minimum regular payment, say £20. The pound/cost (see Practical application) averaging averages out some of the stock exchange investment risks. Investing in units does away with the problem of timing – when to buy and, especially, when to sell.

There are two types of schemes, the fixed period policy and the open-ended policy, i.e. until the policyholder decides to surrender it.

Advantages

1 If the main objective is not the maximum protection of the dependents in the event of a would-be participant's premature death, then unit-linked insurance polices are a satisfactory means of building up a stake in equities, plus some life assurance.
2 There is a guaranteed death payment which is normally in excess of the minimum requirements for obtaining the pre-14 March 1984 life assurance tax relief (see below).
3 On maturity or surrender no loss can accrue to the policy holders' capital, i.e. they cannot receive less than the total amount paid in premiums.
4 On the death of a fixed term policy holder during the currency of the fixed term, the next of kin will receive all the units bought till then, plus cash equal to the remaining premiums that would have been paid had the policy holder survived the full term.

Disadvantages

1 The removal of life assurance relief (see below) has tilted the tax advantage in favour of UT schemes. Whereas the unit-linked insurance funds are liable to CGT, the UTs are exempt, as is the individual investor in UT schemes – provided his or her realised gains do not exceed the annual tax-free ceiling.
2 The benefits of gains during the currency of a conventional with-profit endowment policy would have been periodically consolidated by means of reversionary bonuses, with the lump sum payable on death or maturity. No such consolidation of gains takes place with unit-linked insurance. Indeed, despite the guaranteed sum payable at death, the actual sum realised from the sale of units, should the death of the policyholder occur, might prove disappointing if the stock markets were at a low ebb at the vital time. Also,

the markets may be low at maturity or surrender and the policyholder may receive less than he or she had anticipated.

3 Before all benefits related to the value of the units are paid out, the managers may make deductions to cover the tax on the insurance company's realised gains.

(b) *Insurance-linked single premium bonds.* Such a bond is a lump sum life policy bond linked to a unit fund and the bond's value is measured by the performance of the fund. The minimum single premium is often £1000. Usually the units purchased are of the accumulating type whose value is increased by the income accruing from the underlying investments in the fund. The units can be bought in a fund of the investor's choosing, from amongst a wide variety of funds, viz, property, equity, fixed interest, international, offshore, 'managed' and money funds. Some switching facility between funds is available. No annual interest or dividend is paid to bondholders. Although the bonds aim at capital growth, and are therefore attractive to higher-rate taxpayers, bondholders can take out up to 5% of the bond value annually, tax free. The life insurance element is usually of limited value. The bonds are bought and surrendered through the management companies in much the same way as in unit trusts, and the management charge structures are similar.

One of the liveliest topics in the personal finance world these days is whether investment bonds or unit trusts are the better product for the private investor.

The case for UTs against unitised insurance bonds

1 Bond funds are able to invest directly in property and run managed funds. The Financial Services Act 1986 will give UTs the freedom to invest directly in property and all the other forms of investment which were hitherto open only to the unitised insurance company funds.

2 UTs pay no CGT on the profits made from buying and selling shares within the UTs. The bond's underlying fund is subject to CGT on realised gains and will have to make an allowance of 10–20% for the prospective liability on the realisation of those gains, which are at present only 'paper' gains since the relevant assets have not been sold. As a result the UTs often perform better than a bond invested in the same shares.

3 Investors can switch units between the different types of unitised funds without incurring any personal liability to CGT, whereas switching between UTs is a disposal for CGT purposes. However an individual, during the fiscal year of 1987/1988, can take up to £6600 worth of gains (£5000 for 1988/89) before incurring any CGT liability. As most UTs give a big discount to investors on the initial 5 to 6% charge if they switch between UTs within the same group, the 'lower switching charges' on bonds cease to be a major argument in favouring bonds.

4   Higher-rate taxpaying bond holders can defer encashment of their bonds until retirement when they would probably be liable to pay basic rate tax. But this is true of many people who after retirement pay only the basic rate of tax and are therefore able to avoid higher rate tax altogether.

5   The higher-rate taxpayer who invests in an income UT will have to pay higher rate tax on all dividends paid out by the UT. But most higher-rate taxpayers go for a low-yielding growth UT and obtain income by cashing in their profits up to a maximum of £6600 (£5000 for 1988/89) within the tax-free CGT exemption. This effectively produces a tax-free income.

6   Even the insurance companies which have a vested interest in promoting bonds admit that for most people UTs are a better bet. This is one of the reasons why most of the insurance companies have now launched UTs themselves, and are now just as anxious to sell units as unitised bonds.

7   There is a potential liability for higher rate income tax on the investor cashing in an insurance bond or taking out more than 5% per annum, whereas the UT investor is subject only to CGT. On the other hand no higher rate tax liability arises until a bond is cashed in whereas a UT investor may be assessed on the dividends that he or she receives.

This analysis indicates that UTs are a better bet for those who are investing for capital growth. Smaller investors may well not have capital gains in excess of £5000 annual exemption, whereas they would suffer a deduction for capital gains if they invested via a bond.

The case for unitised insurance bonds against UTs

1   The typical 'entry fee' (i.e. bid/offer spread) to a UT is $6\frac{1}{2}\%$ to 7%, which means that the UT has to increase by at least 7% for the investor to break-even, let alone move into profit. With a bond, and particlarly if an investor is able to take advantage of a pre-launch offer which can often significantly reduce the initial charge, the 'entry fee' can be reduced to zero for the larger investor or only 2% to 3% for the average investor. This means that the costs of getting into an investment bond are typically considerably less than for a UT.

2   With a UT an investor is totally exposed to the vagaries of the stock market. If the market takes a down turn the investor must either sit tight and hope for the best, or come out of the UT and put his or her money on cash deposit until market conditions improve and then buy back and incur another $6\frac{1}{2}\%$ to $7\frac{1}{2}\%$ cost. It is therefore a very expensive process to go in and out and in again with UTs. With bonds, and particularly with managed bonds (see below), the investor can move out of equity markets when they start falling and can switch partially or wholly into cash, gilts or property. Such switches in the managed funds are almost always available completely free of charge – irrespective of the number of switches that are made.

3   Many investors require income. Dividends from a UT (irrespective of

whether income or accumulation units are selected) are grossed up (the amount of gross income available per £100 invested) and taxed at the investor's higher rate of tax: in a bond fund, the dividends are deemed to be the income of the fund and are not taxable directly in investor's hands.

4   The 5% withdrawal facility is extremely valuable.

5   Unlike a UT, no annual tax return is necessary, unless a chargeable event has arisen. Paperwork is kept to a minimum, while a known level monthly income can conveniently be taken.

6   Age allowance is an extra personal allowance worth up to, in 1987/1988, £237 to a married couple where one of them is aged 65–79, and £283 where one is 80 or over. Age allowance is lost progressively once gross income exceeds £9800 (1987/88) and the advantage disappears completely once gross income exceeds £11 120 (aged 65–79) or £11 375 (aged 80 or over). For 1988/89 rates see pages 255 and 256. It is worth noting that between the income levels above the effective marginal rate of tax (i.e. the loss of age allowance at £2 for every £3 of income on the one hand, plus the tax at 27% which now has to be paid) becomes a huge 45%. Unlike UTs, bond investment can help investors to keep the age allowance in their pockets. In a bond the first 5% of the original investment taken each year is regarded as repayment of capital, not income, and does not count at all in calculating income for age allowance purposes. Any amount in excess of 5% is not grossed up – so that a total of 8% per annum from a £10 000 bond investment would only count as £300 for age allowance calculations. Whereas if one were to receive 8% net from a UT, then this figure would be grossed up so that the same £10 000 investment would actually count as £1096 for age allowance purposes. (Indeed, precisely the same reasoning applies when comparing bond investment to building society and bank deposits.)

7   Investors can add to their bonds at any time, often from as little as £100. By adopting this approach investors can obtain significant tax advantages because in assessing any higher rate tax due on the profit arising from additional investment, the additional investment is deemed to have been made on the date the bond originally became effective. The profit can be 'top sliced' (see below) over a longer period than it has actually been made (and tax liability reduced).

In conclusion it might be said that, depending on individual circumstances and investment requirements, for a basic rate taxpayer the UT will probably be more tax efficient than the insurance bond. Insurance managed bonds may be a sensible precaution against a 'bear' (falling) stock market, as these funds have some defensive quality. If the circumstances permit, a balanced and carefully constructed portfolio should include both UTs and bonds. However, this area of investment is fraught with technical complication and frequently changing legislation hence professional investment advice should be sought.

Types of insurance-linked bonds

These bonds are not stock exchange securities but are actively marketed to the private investment sector, for which they are solely designed. There is a wide variety from which the investors can choose. Individual management groups offer their own range of funds, covering equity, property, fixed interest securities, cash deposits or a combination of these in managed funds. Switching between funds under a management group is allowed, often on attractive terms, to investors. The decision to switch is entirely that of the investors or their advisers, the management company gives no advice as to the timing of switching and into which fund to switch. The following are the principal types of bonds.

1   Equity bonds

These bonds are linked to an equity fund (frequently a UT, under the same management group) invested in ordinary shares. Apart from a modest life assurance element and different tax treatment of income and gains, there is little difference between an equity bond and a conventional UT.

2   Property bonds

By buying a property bond the investor is acquiring interest in commercial (office blocks, industrial estates) or agricultural and forestry property companies. The two main problems with these bonds are liquidity and valuation. Property is less readily marketable than are stock exchange securities, therefore most property funds maintain a high element of liquidity to meet withdrawals, which dilutes the 'property' interest to some extent. Property is difficult to value precisely, unlike stocks and shares, therefore the value of property bonds is linked to the estimated, not real, market value of underlying properties. These bonds can therefore be bought at appreciable discounts to their estimated net asset values.

3   Fixed interest bonds

These take advantage of fixed interest investment such as the gilt stocks, local authority issues, fixed term deposits with banks and building societies. Since the income received by the fund is effectively converted into capital, higher rate taxpayers find these bonds attractive. On the other hand direct investment in gilt stocks will yield fixed returns plus CGT advantages. However, bonds give professional active management on a daily basis.

4   Cash deposit bonds

These bonds are invested in cash or near cash deposits, so they are known as money or convertible bonds. They are temporary investments, and the interest received by the fund is effectively converted into capital, hence their attraction to higher rate taxpayers. If investors believe that property or equity markets will fall they can switch from property and equity to cash within the same management group, and switch back when they believe that property and/or equity values will rise.

5 Managed bonds

These bonds are also known as flexible or three-way funds because the investment in a single bond is a mixture of property, equity and fixed-interest stocks, and the managers have absolute discretion as to the split between the three investment sectors. The investor, in buying a managed bond at once obtains an interest in a diversified range of holdings. The fund managers have flexibility in readjusting the amount committed to each segment from time to time according to their judgement of the outlook in the three sectors. However, their flexibility is constrained by the practical difficulties, say, of acquiring and disposing of property quickly, but they can invest new funds in those areas that currently appear to offer the best prospects for investors. This flexibility can be offset at times when the outflow of funds exceeds the inflow. Managed funds are designed for cautious investors who do not wish to be actively involved in the management of their capital.

6 Annuity

An 'annuity' is an annual allowance or income, and the annuitant is the person who receives the annual income. An annuity contract is an insurance linked investment and is in a sense the opposite of a life assurance contract: in a life assurance contract the assured pays fixed amount premiums in return for a lump sum at death; in an annuity contract, the annuitant pays a lump sum to a life insurance company and the life office agrees a fixed sum as soon as the contract is signed (immediate annuity) or until the death of the annuitant, or until the arrival of a fixed date (temporary annuity), but if the annuitant dies before that fixed date, the remaining payments are made to his next of kin. A common practice is for the husband to take out a joint annuity contract with his wife, so that the life office continues annual payments until the death of both the annuitant and his wife. Joint annuities create additional obligations for the life office, therefore the annual payments by the life office are less under joint annuities than under a straightforward annuity for one life. Women are expected to live longer than men, therefore the annuity rates offered to them are less attractive.

The underlying principle of all types of annuities is the same, i.e. conversion of capital into income. And one of the main attractions of annuities emanates from this principle: a proportion of the annual payment is regarded as being a return of capital and therefore not taxable, except when an annuity is bought under the terms of a will, in which case the total amount of each payment is liable to tax in full.

A major disadvantage of annuities is that the annuitants can never get their capital used for the purchase of the annuity back, nor can they bequeath it to their heirs. Therefore it would be a better strategy to commit only a part of one's capital to the purchase of an annuity at retirement, thereby retaining some flexibility in one's financial arrangements. The older the annuity the larger will be the annual payment.

Another drawback of annuities is that the annual amount's purchasing power is subject to inflationary loss. To overcome this drawback, schemes are now available which link the annuity payments to the performance of a portfolio of equity or property.

Another variant of the annuity contracts is the 'home income scheme'. Under this scheme the annuitant mortgages his/her house, obtaining the tax relief up to his/her marginal rate on the interest. With the amount raised, he/she purchases an annuity, the annual payments from which exceed the net annual interest costs, thus increasing his/her income. The main disadvantage of this scheme is that the annuitant sacrifices a substantial amount of capital in return for income which is relatively modest. Home income scheme is only available to the elderly, and can be a useful, albeit expensive, way of supplementing an inadequate pension. The amount of annuity payments depend upon the age and sex of the annuitant, the amount of the lump sum paid, and the interest rate at the time of purchase of annuity.

7   Guaranteed income bonds

These life company bonds in return for a lump sum (the minimum is usually £1000) immediately provide a guaranteed high income for a fixed term of years. At the end of the term, the life office will repay in full the lump sum to the bondholder, or alternatively, convert the capital into a deferred annuity for life.

The life company divides the lump sum into two parts, one part to be invested to produce immediate annuity payments, and the second part to produce cash for the repayment of capital at the end of the term or for the deferred annuity.

A larger proportion of the income received from the temporary annuity is regarded as return of capital and therefore not taxable. The exact size of this proportion is dependent upon the age and sex of the bondholder. The remaining smaller proportion of the annuity income will be paid net of the basic rate of tax.

The bondholder can withdraw the capital invested during the currency of the term, but the deduction from this capital will be progressively more the earlier the withdrawal. If the bondholder dies before the term has ended, most life companies pay the full amount invested to the bondholder's next of kin.

The main advantages of these bonds are high, safe and tax-effective income return, and the return of capital in full. These bonds can be purchased by any one except the very young and the very old. The disadvantage is that there is no capital growth and inflation reduces the real value of the annuities. To mitigate this drawback the bondholder, if he expects the inflation rate to continue rising and causing interest rates to rise, could choose a short term, so that at the end of the term he could reinvest his capital at higher rates.

8   Guaranteed growth bonds

These bonds differ from the income bonds in that the growth bonds have a 'growth option', which simply involves reinvestment of the income during the fixed investment term. After the fixed term, like the income bond, the purchaser has the option of taking a deferred annuity or a lump sum in cash. Again, as with income bonds, it is beneficial to take the cash option because the tax free element relates only to the original purchase price. At maturity, the 'overall gain' will be liable for higher rates of tax. In the case of income bonds this gain will consist of the difference between the cash proceeds and the part of the original purchase price allocated to provide the alternative benefits of deferred annuity or return of lump sum in cash. With growth bonds the 'gain' will be the compounded interest return. In all other respects guaranteed income and growth bonds are largely similar, with the same advantages and drawbacks.

Friendly society investment products

Before the creation of the welfare state, mutual self-help societies – the friendly societies – were often a poor family's only insurance against impoverishment should its breadwinner fall ill, become too old to work or die. The advent of National Insurance (1911) and the National Health Service (1946) diminished the need for this self-help, and the subsequent fiscal legislation has further eroded the tax attraction of the friendly societies' investment products. Nowadays their products are increasingly overlooked, even though they are safe long-term investments offering tax-free returns; in some cases, the fund itself is tax-exempt.

Current legislation recognises three forms of friendly societies' schemes: tax exempt, mixed status and taxable. Typically a tax-exempt scheme operates as follows. Monthly (£9) or annually (£100) contributions are made for 10 years. All monies are invested in a narrow-ranged fund; which may be unitised, in which case the unit prices may rise as well as fall. The front-end charges are generally high: about £65 or pro rata, in addition to a 5%

bid-to-offer spread, with an on-going fund charge of 0.75% a year, and about 30p a month on premiums paid other than annually. The death benefit is a fixed sum or the current value of units, whichever is higher. After 10 years, investors may take the tax-free proceeds either as a lump sum or income, or have it accumulate with or without further contributions.

The restrictions imposed on tax-exempt business have forced many societies to offer hybrid schemes in their search for cost effective premium levels. Many impose a minimum premium of about £20 per month, of which only £9 gets tax-exempt status, and is invested in the society's own tax-exempt fund. The balance is usually invested outside the society (usually in building societies' or banks' leading unit trust fund's products). Returns are tax-free provided policies are held for a minimum of $7\frac{1}{2}$ years. Old societies are able to offer products outside the usual range of whole life and endowment business.

Advantages

1   The main advantage of investing in friendly society products is that the returns are completely exempt from all taxes in the hands of policyholders.
2   They provide insurance cover for the family of the policyholder in the event of the policyholder's death.

Disadvantages

1   Investment business of friendly societies is subject to the requirements of the Trustee Investments Act, 1961. This Act restricts the areas of activity by forbidding societies direct investment overseas, or investments in unitised (on the Stock Exchange) securities, futures or traded options (see below). Also, 50% of the receipts must be in 'narrow range' investments such as gilts, local authority loans and other fixed interest securities, including convertible UK loan stock. Although some societies achieve a broader range of investment by investing the other 50% of receipts in equities directly or through a UT, others invest it wholly in building society products, because the friendly societies are able to obtain building society interest payments gross by making a claim to the tax authorities.
2   The amount of investment is restricted by law. Friendly societies are able to write a restricted amount of life and endowment business whereby the underlying fund is exempt from income tax, corporation tax and CGT, thus boosting the returns to investors. However, policyholders are allowed to invest a maximum of £100 a year (or £9 a month, or £2 a week) in life contracts, and up to £156 a year in an annuity. Investors must be over 18 to initiate a policy in their own right; married couples may each invest £100 a year. Contracts are written to run for a minimum of 10 years. There are heavy penalties for encashment before $7\frac{1}{2}$ years are over; the investor may receive no more than the annual premiums paid, with no interest. There are

even harsher penalties for encashment during the first two years; some policies pay back nothing at all in the first two years.

3 Investments in friendly society products are not protected under the Policyholders' Protection Act of 1975, and therefore policies are purchased without the statutory 10-day cooling-off period during which the policy-holder has a right to cancel a contract without prejudice. It also means that should a society go bankrupt, the policyholders cannot receive 90% of the anticipated value of their policies. Societies are supervised by the Chief Registrar of Friendly Societies.

Investments through pensions schemes

For a person to become a personal pension plan (PPP) holder, one of the following conditions must apply in his/her case:

1 He/she is self-employed.
2 If employed, his/her employer does not operate a pension scheme.
3 He/she has enough freelance earnings outside his/her regular job to make such a plan worthwhile.
4 He/she has two or more jobs and at least one has no pension scheme.
5 He/she is aged between 19 and 65 next birthday.

The self-employed and those who are not members of a pension scheme have to rely on the State Scheme for pension. For the self-employed, the State Scheme provides only a minimum basic pension. For the employed, there is an additional earnings related benefit, but the full rate of earnings related pension will not come into force until 1998 and only then if 20 years' contributions have been paid. Thus the State pension will not be sufficient for many, particularly the self-employed and higher paid employees, to enable them to maintain their standard of living in retirement.

Prospective PPP holders must state when they intend to retire, and this must be within the ages of 60 to 75 unless their job has a fixed early retire-ment date. However, they do not have to retire on that date, they can draw pension benefits any time from the age of 60 to 75, even while continuing to work. If they have to retire because of ill-health, they can immediately draw benefits, even before the age of 60, but the benefits will be lower than if they stayed the course at least to the age of 60. They can choose to have a level pension of a fixed amount, or a pension increasing at a selected percentage annually.

All premiums are payable for the PPP holder's lifetime but, in addition, they can choose a pension guaranteed for a minimum term of five years, or ten years, or their lifetime, and continuing for the lifetime of their spouse should they die first.

The exact amount of the pension will depend on the bid value of the units in the Plan when they decide to draw their benefits and the pension rate applicable to their age at that time for the type of pension selected (see below).

Advantages of PPP

There are many plans on offer by insurance companies, banks and other financial institutions. Broadly the terms and conditions, and advantages and disadvantages of various plans are similar. The following advantages and disadvantages relate to most PPPs.

1   All contributions qualify for income tax relief at the highest rates of tax payable on planholders' earned income.
2   The income and capital gains from the investment of contributions – regular or single premium – accumulate free of UK taxes for the planholders' benefit.
3   Part of the retirement benefits may be taken as a cash sum, entirely free of tax.
4   There is usually a wide choice of benefits, including one which increases each year to combat inflation.
5   In most plans, contributions can be increased, decreased or even suspended thus enabling the planholder to vary their annual outlay according to changing financial circumstances.
6   Contributions can be invested in a choice of professionally managed investment funds with the flexibility to vary the amount invested between the chosen funds, and of switching accumulated investment between funds.

Disadvantages

1   With some plans if the contributions cannot be continued before reaching the selected retirement age, the planholder cannot claim a refund of contributions; they remain frozen in the plan until retirement.
2   PPPs linked to stock exchange securities suffer from the risks of such securities.
3   Although the pressure to sell PPPs is intense, the investor needs to compare relative advantages of a PPP and, say, an endowment with profit policy, coupled with some other savings policy.

Additional Voluntary Contributions (AVC) Schemes

An employee who is in a company pension scheme for at least five years can top this up with AVSs so long as these remain below the maximum of 15% of his or her earnings. Income tax relief is available on AVCs. AVC funds operated by many companies are given the same concessions as are given to regular pension funds, so that the rate of return is higher than in other ordinary investments. The personal pension scene is changing fast, thanks to the Finance (No. 2) Act 1987 and the Social Security Act 1986. The changes in legislation offer significant opportunities for the establishment of highly tax-effective new personal pension schemes and the extension of the existing pension arrangements. The features of the new Personal Pension Schemes are given under the Practical application section of this chapter (see below). Note that the investment in personal pensions at the time of writing is probably the best and safest investment in terms of returns available in the market.

Recent indirect investment schemes

There are a number of investment areas which have significant tax benefits, some of which have been discussed above. In recent years, the government has given big tax incentives to private investors to enter the realm of risk investment. However, investment should never be made solely for tax reasons and before proceeding investors should take more time evaluating the prospects of tax-free efficient investments, or seek specific advice. The following two tax-efficient schemes have been officially launched during the past five years.

1   Business Expansion Scheme (BES)

BES was enacted in the 1983 Budget, and was designed to promote investment by private individuals in the shares of unquoted companies.

By investing in the shares of 'eligible' companies under the BES and holding them for five years, an investor and the spouse may obtain full tax relief at their marginal tax rate on investment of up to £40 000 per annum. To qualify as an eligible company under the BES, its shares must not be quoted on the stock exchange or the unlisted securities market (USM), and it must carry on 'qualifying' trade, such as manufacturing, wholesaling, retailing, research and development.

A higher-rate taxpayer may find investing through the BES advantageous. Provided the investor retains the shares for five years, relief for the cost of acquiring them is given at the top rates of income tax. Furthermore, he or she is exempt from CGT on BES shares purchased after 18 March 1986 (see below). The annual £40 000 limit applies per married couple.

The relief is available to 'outside' investors (i.e. who are not directors, partners or employers or their blood relatives of the eligible company) who do not own more than 30% of the total shares of the company, and who are investing a minimum of £500 in the company's shares. They can invest directly, or indirectly through an approved investment fund – if invested through an approved fund the £500 minimum does not apply.

The disadvantages to investors under the BES are that (a) they are subject to more than usual risk of losing capital, and (b) should the company cease to qualify within three years, or cease to trade, then the investors will not only lose all the tax relief claimed but also may have to repay it to the Inland Revenue.

The 1988/89 Budget and the BES

The Budget introduced three changes to the Scheme:

(a) After 15th March 1988, the amount of finance a BES company can raise in any 12-month period is limited to £500 000, *except* where the finance is raised for ship chartering or for the provision of private rental housing; in which case the limit is £5 million, and where a company had issued a prospectus before 15th March 1988, and the shares themselves were issued before 6th April 1988, a limit of £1 million will apply. The reason for imposing a limit on the company (as opposed to the investor), where none has previously existed, is to direct finance towards smaller companies. Until this limitation, the prospectus issues had dominated the market, frequently raising £5 million or more for indivdiual BES companies. The authorities believe that, following the rapid growth in recent years, the venture capital industry is now able to supply the needs of 'prospectus issues' without resort to the BES. It may be argued that, broadly speaking, smaller companies carry a somewhat greater risk than larger 'prospectus' companies. Therefore, it is now even more important that, in every case, investment should be based on an assessment of the individual company's prospects.

(b) The small investor is allowed to spread the risk by subscribing for the shares in a number of BES companies, via Inland Revenue approved funds, without being bound, as previously, to invest a minimum of £500 in any one company. Such funds will stay open for a limited period of time.

(c) The authorities intend to use the BES as the main thrust to create rented accommodation. Income tax relief will be granted from summer 1988 for investment in companies which buy or build unoccupied property for letting under 'assured tenancies', which will become available towards the end of 1988. The investors can expect an indirect interest in a stream of income which will grow over the years, increasing the capital value of share-holding in property, or portfolio of property companies; additionally, the shares on disposal will not attract CGT.

2 Personal Equity Plan (PEP)

PEPs were introduced on 1 January 1987 to encourage greater personal share ownership by way of tax relief. Any UK resident, aged at least 18 years, can invest up to £3000 in one PEP in any one year (£6000 for married couples), by lump sum or by instalments. In subsequent years £3000 can again be invested, but in different plans. Qualifying investments are defined as ordinary shares of UK registered companies quoted on the stock exchange or dealt in on the USM, including investment in UTs, ITs and cash. Up to £540 (£45 per month) can be invested in a unit or investment trust.

Provided that the plan has been in operation for one complete calendar year, gains made from selling shares within a plan or withdrawals of capital from a plan, are free of CGT. In addition, dividends and their tax credits and interest on cash (up to the permitted limit) are free of income tax if reinvested in the PEP.

A number of investment managers are offering these plans and, in choosing a PEP, investors will need to make the normal comparisons regarding management charges, investment policy etc. In the short term the tax benefits may be minimal and will to some extent be offset by management charges, but a taxpayer who invests the maximum amount for a number of years could build up a sizeable tax-free fund. The planholders are not eligible to attend or vote at meetings of companies in which their fund is invested.

PEPs are likely to be of particular interest to higher rate taxpayers and individuals who exceed their tax-free CGT limit (see below). However, PEPs may also have attractions for smaller investors, not least because they can shift the responsibility for the paperwork involved to the PEP manager.

If, during the qualifying period, any shares or cash are withdrawn the plan will come to an end and the investor will become liable to all income tax and CGT on gains which arose before the plan became void. The qualifying period varies in length from 12–24 months and ends on 31 December in the year following the calendar year in which the investment was made. For instance, the money invested at any time during 1987 will have to remain in the PEP until the beginning of 1989. Once the qualifying period has passed, the investor may withdraw cash or shares from the plan without loss of tax relief previously granted.

Investment in house and other property purchases

In due time, UT managers will take advantage of the regulations made under the Financial Services Act 1986 to invest directly in property. Until then there are four main ways of investing in property: direct purchase (with or without a mortgage); direct purchase of 'timesharing'; purchase of property company shares; and purchase of property bonds.

Direct purchase of houses

Many people purchase houses to make homes in, without much caring that in buying a house they are probably making the largest investment of their lives. Over a period of years, the return on capital used in buying a house could be 300 to 400%.

Advantages

1   If the house purchase is mainly financed through a mortgage loan, then the mortgagor (the house buyer) can obtain tax relief on interest on loans of up to £30 000.
2   There is no commitment to CGT on the sale of an owner-occupier house (see below). The income tax and CGT benefits are given by the authorities to encourage the UK population to become a property-owning democracy. (Just as the BES and PEP schemes are designed to attract the UK population to become a share-owning democracy.)
3   Owning a house adds an extra dimension to the owner – man of property, which gives him a psychological boost.
4   House prices usually at least keep pace with inflation, thus making them an ideal hedge against inflation loss. Also in times of inflation, which is always present to a greater or lesser degree, the real value of the outstanding mortgage tends to reduce.
5   Matching assets with liabilities is a recognized method of reducing risk. A house purchaser is matching his asset (the house) with his liability (the outstanding mortgage).
6   If the house is let, the rent is fixed and often paid in advance, besides rent is a 'prior' charge on income or profit of the tenant.
7   House insurance can safeguard against physical damage to the house, thereby providing security of capital.

Disadvantages

For owner-occupation
1   Houses cannot be valued, like stocks and shares, on a day-to-day basis. House owners simply make *estimates* of what their houses are worth. The real value is what they will get when they actually sell their houses. If the house has a short leasehold, then it is declining in value asset.
2   The owners suffer a certain degree of lack of liquidity because houses are normally very illiquid, although a house deed is generally acceptable as a good security by lenders.
3   Maintenance and repair costs are not covered by house insurance, and these can be quite expensive and ought to be added to the purchase price to estimate the capital gain. On the other hand, 'enjoyment' of living in the house, free of rent and tax, may be set against the maintenance and repair costs and rates.
For letting
1   There is no tax relief on mortgage loan, and there is liability to CGT on selling but offset by indexation allowance.
2   If tenants do not pay rent, and do not keep property in good repair, they may not be evicted without costly litigation.

3 If rents are 'fixed' then the landlord cannot benefit from the housing shortage.
4 The sheer size of a single transaction in proportion to one's income generally precludes diversification of investment.
For holidays
1 No tax relief on buying and liability to CGT on selling.
2 Insufficient usage, therefore wastage if capital is invested in buying and insuring a holiday home.
3 If rented for some part of the year, then all the problems associated with letting may arise.

On balance, investment in a house by a private investor, except for owner-occupation, is not very attractive. The following are the four main methods of buying one's own house, from which the most beneficial method, taking account of the circumstances of the purchaser, inflationery expectations, housing situation and the level of interest rates, may be chosen.

Repayment mortgage

The mortgagor contracts to pay the mortgagee equated annual payments. Since the interest on mortgage loans is paid first, the interest element will be much larger in annual instalments during the early years of repayment and, in later years, annual payments will largely repay capital borrowed. In order to protect his interests, the mortgagee would probably insist on mortgage protection policy on the life of the mortgagor. This is a relatively cheap method of simply buying a house, but with no investment income, and is suitable for those who wish to hold the house for the average life of a mortgage – approximately seven years – because the actual net cost is much lower.

Endowment mortgage

This method is more expensive than the repayment method. It requires the mortgagor to pay equated annual instalments which repay the interest due only, albeit usually at a higher rate. The additional payment is invested by an insurance company or bank to produce over the period of mortgage a sum equal to the amount of the loan. Therefore a matured straightforward endowment mortgage policy, which also provides life cover for the mortgagor, will extinguish the mortgage debt. The advantage is that the first time house buyers with low income pay smaller annual instalments, but it too produces no investment income. Therefore a 'with-profit' endowment mortgage policy may be taken out which, in addition to providing a life cover, will also yield a surplus sum after repayment of the loan at maturity. This method is a more expensive method of buying a house but it does produce an investment return. Suitable for those with permanent and sufficient means.

Low-cost endowment mortgage

It is a half-way house between a repayment mortgage and a with-profit endowment mortgage. Under this method the mortgagor takes out a with-profit endowment policy for, say, 35 to 40% of the mortgage loan *and* a decreasing term insurance for the rest. Suitable for longer mortgage periods (25 years or longer) and for those with low incomes.

Loanback

With this method the house buyer is in effect borrowing money from his own personal pension fund managed by a life company. The interest payments by the investor will go to his pension fund, and not the life company, but the life company will deduct a management charge from the interest received. That deduction is a 'loss' to the investor, who will also receive less from the fund at retirement, unless he or she pays back the money borrowed from the fund before retiring. Although the investor's interest payments go into the fund, yet the fund would have earned more interest had the amount remained in the company's fund. The company will require security, e.g. the house deed, for the loan.

The investor, via a loanback, is taking advantage of the tax concessions that allow him to backdate contributions to his pension fund.

Recently there have been proposals whereby those on lower incomes can have a reduced system of repayments in return for sharing some of the profit on disposals with the lenders of the mortgage.

Direct purchase of timeshare

If a person does not wish to buy a holiday house, they can buy a timesharing contract by paying a lump sum for the right to have a particular week's or fortnight's holiday in a luxury apartment each year, for up to 80 years in England and Wales, but in perpetuity in Scotland and Spain. A management company looks after the maintenance and repairs for which the timesharers pay an annual sum which generally increases in line with inflation, and also covers insurance charges for the contents of the apartment. There are swapping agencies who will normally find someone in Britain or overseas to swap with someone else. Although timesharing is basically a way of organising holidays it can produce an investment income. For example, the timesharer or the managers can let an apartment at a good rent: the rent and the purchase price will depend upon which particular week or weeks during a year have been bought: it costs more in season than off season. Secondly, the timesharers can sell their week(s) often with some capital gain.

The drawbacks are that the annual charge for maintenance etc. could rise too high. When the timeshare is bought VAT is paid but when it is sold VAT cannot be reclaimed unless the seller is VAT registered. After a few years the quality of maintenance and repairs may not be maintained. There is the British Property Timeshare Association which does protect time-sharers' interests. Although the law governing timeshare contracts is very stringent in the UK, it is not so overseas. It is therefore essential to take advice and to deal with a reputable firm with a reputable trustee (e.g. a bank or insurance company).

Indirect investment in property

Purchase of shares in property companies

With a small outlay and without any skilled knowledge, an investor can acquire a well-diversified portfolio of prime properties, commercial and residential, for rental income and development gains in the UK and else-where, by purchasing shares in the larger property companies. The special attraction of these shares is their higher level of gearing, which means that any increase in the value of the company's assets leads to a more than proportionate increase in the value of ordinary shares of the company. But gearing is a double-edged sword. Excessive borrowing, especially in times of high interest rates, means that shares may have very low earnings and shareholders receive low dividends relative to the company assets. Gearing contributes to the extreme volatility of property company shares.

Purchase of property bonds

Although technically these bonds are single premium life policies and are subject to Insurance Companies Acts, in effect, they are property unit trusts. The authorised UTs invest indirectly in property by investing in property company shares. Exempt UTs can invest directly in property, but exempt UTs are not open for investment to the general public.

The following table compares the strengths and weaknesses of shares in property companies and property bonds as alternative methods of investing in 'bricks and mortar' or real estate.

Shares in property companies	Property bonds
1 Due to gearing, share values fluctuate violently, which means that investors can make large capital gains or losses depending on their need for cash and the state of the property market at the time.	1 Bonds have no gearing therefore bond values are comparatively stable, offering a sound investment to investors.
2 Shares provide no life cover to shareholders.	2 Being insurance policies, bonds always provide an element of life cover to bondholders.

Shares in property companies	Property bonds
3 Property companies pay dividends.	3 Bonds pay no dividends, but withdrawal schemes are available which provide a higher potential income stream than dividends.
4 Property companies pay corporation tax at 35% on income and shareholders are liable for higher rates of tax and also CGT on gains from share sales.	4 Bond incomes are taxed at life assurance fund rates of 35%. However, bondholders pay neither income tax nor CGT unless they are liable to higher rates of tax in the year they sell bonds, but even this liability can be deferred or reduced by top slicing arrangement. (See below).
5 Property companies have greater freedom in purchase and development of properties whenever they think the time is opportune.	5 Property bonds are constrained by the extent of the net inflow of funds.
6 Shareholders may enjoy a windfall gain if their company becomes the target of a takeover bid.	6 No such windfall profits for bondholders because takeover bids are irrelevant to non stock market securities.

Investment in woodlands

The UK produces only 10% of its total timber requirements and therefore demand for home produced timber is likely to be maintained provided that it remains competitively priced. In order to encourage home production of timber and to reduce imports, the government, until March 1988, gave generous grants and income tax relief towards the production of timber. Under the 1988/89 Budget tax changes, a more specifically 'targeted' assistance will be given to encourage timber production with a better balance between broad-leaved trees and conifers.

Otherwise, under the 1988/89 Budget provisions, commercial woodlands have been removed completely from the tax system, and it will not be possible to claim expenditure on planting and maintaining trees as a tax deduction against other income, and the sale proceeds of timber will not be charged to tax. These changes took effect from 15th March 1988, subject to a transitional period to enable existing occupiers to obtain relief until 1993. Thus, other than for existing occupiers – and then only until April 1993 – investment in woodlands has now disappeared from the list of tax saving possibilities.

Investment in precious metals and other chattels

Gold and gold coins

From time immemorial gold has been a symbol and measure of wealth and has enjoyed universal marketability. Due to these reasons, whenever an acute crisis of confidence in paper currencies and in paper currency denominated financial assets occurs, people turn to gold as the repository of their wealth. No wonder it has become the haven for investment funds.

The removal of exchange controls in the UK in 1979 means that the people in this country can freely buy gold as an investment. There are two main ways in which a private investor can invest in gold.

1 *By buying gold bars* However, buying gold bars is beyond the means of most small investors. But most investors can buy full value gold coins, such as the South African Krugerrand and the Canadian Maples; the British Sovereigns and half Sovereigns, the investor's items, have not been struck since 1982, as collectors' items they are struck with an annual limit of 12 500 each. Investors can also buy gold jewellery. However, in buying jewellery they are paying not only for the gold but also for the craftsman's and middleman's charges. With gold coins the craftsman's mark-up is very low, especially so with Krugerrands, therefore the prices of gold coins is more broadly in line with gold metal prices. Hence investing in gold coins is the nearest thing to investing in gold bars.

In October 1987, the Royal Mint issued a new gold coin, Britannia, in four sizes: 1 oz – with a legal tender value of £100; $\frac{1}{2}$ oz – with a face value of £50; $\frac{1}{4}$ oz – value £25; and 1/10th oz – the 'baby Britannia', value £10. It is available from Britannia Building Society, banks and bullion dealers.

The progressive freezing out of Krugerrand coins has opened up the world's coin trade. The Royal Mint hopes that Britannia may capture more than 5% of the world bullion market. It is meant to replace gold sovereigns as an investment item.

Britannias are unlikely to be used as legal tender and their value will reflect the world price of gold. The bulk of sales are likely to be for investment purposes – investment advisers have traditionally advised that between 5% and 10% of a portfolio should be held in gold. However, Britannia's investment value is considerably reduced by the 15% VAT charged on bullion coins. The gold sovereigns that are in existence are unlikely to rival Britannia because of their peculiar weight of 0.2354 ounces.

As a general rule, the profit realised on the disposal of gold coins is treated as income and taxed accordingly. If investors wish to avoid paying income tax on disposal gains they must hold gold coins or jewellery as long-term assets, and show their purchases on their income tax returns and keep receipts of the prices paid, then capital gain on disposal may only be liable to CGT. VAT is payable on gold coin purchases from the UK coin dealers, but VAT can be avoided by buying and *storing* coins with a dealer based in the Channel Islands; the coins should not be imported into the UK. The *drawbacks* of investing in gold coins are that they produce no returns in terms of interest or dividend, they are generally bought to make capital gains. The supply of gold is dependent upon natural factors and political factors, therefore the prices of gold and gold coins are subject to very sharp fluctuations. Storage and insurance costs reduce the capital gain on disposal. In times of high interest rates investment in gold coins is particularly unattractive.

2 *By buying shares in gold mining companies, or shares in funds specialising in gold shares*. The fluctuating nature of gold supply, and therefore of its price, makes gold shares speculative and risky. However, over a period of time, and in return for accepting an above average risk, the gold shareholders tend to get higher than normal yields, which raises the value of their shares. It should be noted however that gold mines are wasting assets.

Other chattels

Chattels are defined for tax purposes as tangible, moveable goods. They include antiques, wine, rare stamps and coins, paintings, china, jewellery, first editions, carpets and so on. Sometimes chattels are also called 'alternative investments'. Investment in chattels has certain problems, e.g. more expensive storage and insurance costs, difficult valuations, expensive commissions, no dividend or interest returns and price falls (and increases) can be spectacular.

The main attraction of investing in chattels and objets d'art is high value appreciation. On their disposal the treatment of gains for CGT purposes is different from most other gains. On disposal, where the sale proceeds of an individual item, per person, are below £3000 they are exempt from CGT. This means that a chattel jointly owned by husband and wife has CGT exemption of just under £6000, which is about £1000 *more* than the 1988/89 CGT free limit.

Investment in chattels is a highly specialised area and expert knowledge of the chattels chosen for investment is essential, not only to detect fakes and forgeries, but also to estimate values correctly in order to calculate commissions correctly. It is a high risk/reward investment area, not suitable for middle of the road small investors.

Practical application

Investment Trusts

Cost of buying shares in ITs

UK residents are subject to the following expenses when buying IT shares (indeed shares in any quoted company).

1 *Government transfer stamp duty* This is payable on a purchase of ordinary shares, preference shares and convertible loan stocks at a rate of $\frac{1}{2}\%$.

2 *Stockbrokers' commission* Since 27 October 1986, all commissions are now open to negotiation. Assuming no change in commissions charged on small bargains in shares, the commission rate is as follows:

Bargain Value (consideration)	Commission	
less than £300	at discretion of stockbroker	
£300–£606	£18	*Note*: a minimum commission
£607–£7000	£1.65%	of £20 or more is now quite common

On larger bargains, commission is at reducing rate.

3 *VAT* on commission, at standard rate, currently 15%

Example

Assuming the above transfer stamp duty, commission and VAT rates, the total costs on the purchase of IT ordinary shares costing £2000 are as follows:

Consideration for share purchase		2000.00
Stamp duty at $\frac{1}{2}$%		10.00
Stockbroker's commission @ 1.65%	33.00	
+ VAT @ 15%	4.95	37.95
Total cost to investor purchasing £2000 IT shares =		£2047.95

On a sale bargain similar expenses would arise, except that no stamp duty would be payable.

Therefore, the total receipt by an investor selling £2000 IT shares would be equal to £2000 less £37.95 = £1962.05 (less the market makers turn, i.e. spread between buying and selling prices).

Taxation

1 *The liability of the individual*

(a) *Capital gains tax (CGT)* The holder of IT, or any other type of company shares is liable to CGT (or obtains relief from losses) on gains in excess of the index-linked tax-free ceiling, which for 1987/88 is £6600, but £5000 for 1988/89. (For this purpose, net gains of spouses are aggregated and treated as one.)

Example

If the net gains in 1987/88 are £7000, the CGT liability will be calculated as follows:

Net gains	7000
Less exemption limit	6600
Chargeable gains	400
CGT @ 30% on chargeable gain =	120

(b) *Income tax* The IT shareholder, either ordinary or preference, receives his dividend, net of basic rate of tax, accompanied by an income tax credit. The net result is that a shareholder liable to tax at the basic rate will, in practice, have no further tax to pay. If he is not liable to the basic rate of income tax, he will be able to recover the tax deducted by sending the income tax credit to the Inland Revenue. If he is subject to higher rates of tax, he will have an additional tax liability.

The IT debenture or loan stockholder, likewise, receives his interest payment less income tax at the basic rate with a certificate of tax deducted. If he is a non-tax payer he can claim a refund of the tax deducted; the basic rate taxpayer has, in practice, no further tax liability; and the higher rate taxpayer has to pay additional tax.

The positions of non-resident IT shareholders and stockholders depend on their status and the double taxation agreement between the government of UK and the governments of their own countries: tax is normally deducted only once and in one country.

2   *The liability of ITs*

(a) *Capital gains* ITs are, under the Finance Act 1980, exempt from tax on capital gains after 31 March 1980. Capital gains made by an IT cannot be distributed to shareholders in the form of dividends, under its Memorandum and Article of Association, and the gains are therefore retained in full for reinvestment.

The tax exemption applies to an 'approved' IT. To obtain approved status (under the Corporation Taxes Act 1970, as amended by the Finance Act 1972) an IT must be resident in the UK, listed on the Stock Exchange and derive its income wholly or mainly from shares and securities. It must not invest more than 15% of its assets in any one company, except in another IT, nor can it retain more than 15% of its income from shares and securities. Any surplus arising from the realisation of investments must not be distributed as dividend to its shareholders.

(b) *Revenue* The revenue of ITs is subdivided into '*franked*' and '*unfranked*' income.

Franked income is made up of the ordinary and preference dividends together with associated tax credits received by the IT from holdings in the UK companies which have themselves paid corporation tax on their own profits. The franked income does not bear a second layer of tax and can be distributed in fact to IT shareholders as dividend.

Unfranked income includes all the dividends received from foreign investments, plus any interest and underwriting commission. This income is subject to corporation tax, *after* deductions of payments by the IT; such as debenture interest, overseas loan interest and management expenses. Against this tax liability can be set withholding taxes (most double taxation agreements provide for a 15% withholding tax on dividends by foreign governments) on income received from abroad and the advance corporation tax (all companies pay dividends to shareholders net of basic-rate income tax, but at the same time make a payment of advance corporation tax (ACT) to the Inland Revenue; ACT has always been set at the same rate as the basic rate of income tax), if any, paid on dividends distributed to the IT's own shareholders out of unfranked income.

The liability to corporation tax will therefore depend on the structure of the individual IT, on its investment policy and, within these limits, on the ability of the managers in offsetting tax. In many cases corporation tax is substantially reduced or even eliminated. This widens the appeal of such ITs to such institutions as have tax exempt status, such as pension funds and charities.

Useful statistics relating to ITs

1 *Net asset value (NAV)* The NAV of an IT, like any other public company, is the total value of all its assets at current market value *minus* the value of the 'prior charges' against its assets, i.e. its preference shares and debenture or loan stocks. The prior charges can be deducted either at their nominal value or their market value. (The AITC – The Association of Investment Trust Companies – use the nominal value basis in their monthly 'Investment Trust Table'.) Care should be taken to ensure that the NAVs used for comparative purposes have been calculated on a uniform basis. The NAV is usually expressed as an amount per ordinary share, calculated according to the following formula:

$$\frac{\text{Total current value of assets} - \text{all prior charges}}{\text{total ordinary shares}} = \text{NAV per ordinary share}$$

NAV is a widely used statistic in the IT sector because the fluctuation of each IT's NAV reflects the performance of the underlying portfolio.

2 *Discount/Premium* The difference between the market price of an IT's ordinary shares and the NAV per share is either a discount or a premium. If the share price is *less* than the NAV per share, the shares are said to stand at a discount; if the reverse is the case, the shares stand at a premium. The discount or premium is usually expressed as a percentage of the NAV. Formula:

$$\frac{\text{the larger market price of share and NAV} - \text{the smaller of the two}}{\text{Total ordinary shares}} \times 100$$

For example, if an IT's NAV is 125p per share and the market price of its ordinary share is 100p, the discount is 20%, i.e.

$$\frac{(125 - 100) \times 100.}{125}$$

Conversely, if the NAV is 120p and the market price is 132p, premium is 12p or 10%, i.e.

$$\frac{(132 - 120) \times 100}{120}$$

3 *Dividends* The ability of ITs to distribute dividends to shareholders is limited, like other companies, by the amount of available profits or distributable reserves, but, unlike other companies, there are some factors peculiar to approved ITs, viz, they are required to distribute nearly all their net income as dividends and they must not distribute capital gains as dividends.

4 *Gearing* As a public company, an IT is free to borrow money or raise various forms of finance in addition to its ordinary shares. These include preference shares, debentures, unsecured loan stocks, convertible loan stocks and foreign currency loans, whose prior entitlements to annual income and to capital repayment is unrelated to the performance of the IT's underlying portfolio. Funds raised in these ways provide the IT with its gearing. Gearing affects both capital and income.

(a) *The capital effect* If the stocks in which the IT funds are invested rise in value, the gains generated on behalf of the ordinary shareholders are magnified or geared. For example, assume the following capital structure of an IT:

£4 000 000 5% Debenture stock (5 years)	£4 000 000
6 000 000 £1 Ordinary shares	£6 000 000
Total portfolio	£10 000 000

Assume further that the whole portfolio of the IT is invested in equities which *double* in value, and the debenture stock is paid in full at the end of year 5, the capital effect will be as follows:

	Year 1	Year 5
Value of portfolio	£10 000 000	£20 000 000
Less Debenture stock	£ 4 000 000	£ 4 000 000
Assets attributable to 6 000 000 ordinary shareholders	£ 6 000 000	£16 000 000
NAV per ordinary share	£1	£2.67

Thus, while the portfolio has increased by 100%, the assets attributable to each ordinary shareholder has risen from £1 to £2.67, a capital gain of 167%.

On the other hand, if the stocks fall in value, then the fall on the NAV of the ordinary shares is similarly magnified or geared: gearing can work in either direction. The gearing effect can often be mitigated when it is un-favourable – when the market is falling; by investing in fixed-interest secu-rities, or by holding cash in bank or building society deposits.

(b) *The income effect* Income gearing exaggerates the effect for ordin-ary shareholders of dividend movements in the IT's underlying portfolio of investments after the interest payment on borrowing, especially if at a fixed rate, has been made.

For example: assume the above capital structure of an IT, and further assume, for simplicity's sake, that dividends include the tax credit, but ignore any other taxation effects. If in Year 1 the portfolio is invested to yield 6% but by Year 5 the income received has doubled, the income effect of gearing will be as follows:

	Year 1	Year 5
Income from the portfolio	£600 000	£1 200 000
Less Debenture interest:		
£4 000 000 @ 5%	£200 000	£ 200 000
Gross income attributable to		
6 000 000 ordinary shares	£400 000	£1 000 000
Attributable amount per share	6.7p	16.7p

Thus, while the income from the portfolio has risen by 100%, the amount available for distribution as dividend to the IT's ordinary shareholders has risen by 150%.

5 *How best to make comparisons between individual ITs* Total return statistics enable the investor to make comparisons between individual ITs with different investment and dividend policies.

There are two main bases on which the total return statistics are computed, but in both cases it is assumed that the dividends received by shareholders net of basic rate income tax are reinvested in the assets of the IT. The first is calculated on the *NAV performance* of the IT, and the dividends are 'reinvested' in the *assets* of the IT at NAV. The second is calculated on the *share price performance* of the IT, and the dividends are 'reinvested' in the *shares* of the IT at the then market price.

Unit Trusts

Calculation of UT prices

The current formulae by which UT managers calculate both the price at which investors buy ('offer') and sell ('bid') the units are laid down by the DTI and supervised by an independent trustee. The following example explains how the offer and bid prices are calculated:

Assume the value of underlying investments in the UT fund is £50 *million* and the number of units in issue is *100 million*.

(a) *Offer Price Calculation (DTI formula)*

	Value £	Pence Per Unit
Value of Investment (at buying price)	50 000 000	50.0000
Plus		
Stock Exchange Commission etc (0.3%)	150 000	0.1500
Stamp Duty (0.5%)	250 000	0.2500
	50 400 000	50.4000
Unit Trust Instrument Duty (0.25%)	126 000	0.1260
	50 526 000	50.5260
Accrued Income	140 000	0.1400
	50 666 000	50.6660
Management Charge (5%)	2 533 300	2.5333
	53 199 300	53.1993
Rounding Adjustment		0.4007
DTI Offer Price		53.6p

(b) *Bid Price Calculation (DTI Formula)*

	Fund Value £	Pence Per Unit
Value of Investments (at selling price)	49 000 000	49.0000
Less		
Stock Exchange Commission etc (0.3%)	147 000	0.1470
	48 853 000	48.8530
Plus		
Accrued Income	140 000	0.1400
	48 993 000	48.9930
Rounding Adjustment		0.4930
DTI Bid Price		48.5p

In effect, the DTI pricing formulae establish the highest 'offer' price which can be paid by an incoming investor and the lowest 'bid' price payable to an outgoing investor. The explanation of the DTI offer and bid prices is that in the above hypothetical UT, where the share portfolio is valued at £50 million and there are 100 million units in issue, it follows that each unit represents 50p worth of investment. But the price paid by an investor must also take account of any income which has already been received by the fund (i.e. Accrued Income) and should also include a share of UT's expenses and the managers' initial charge. Hence the offer price, in the above example is not 50p, but 53.6p.

When the units are eventually sold, the outgoing investor will be entitled to receive, not 50p but a price equivalent to a share of the underlying investments in the fund, *plus* any accrued income, *minus* the stock exchange commission. In the calculation of both the prices, a rounding adjustment is made to avoid awkward fractions.

The 'spread' (difference) between the DTI offer and bid prices is typically around 11 or 12% (as shown in the above example). However the UT managers usually quote a spread of 6 to 7%. The reason that they are able to do this is that they are constantly dealing in units and so are in a position to match sales with purchases, thus avoiding the full stock exchange dealing costs allowed for in the price calculations.

When there are more buyers of units than sellers, the managers have to create new units to meet the demand, and, when the reverse is the case, the surplus units are usually liquidated (although the managers may hold on to them in anticipation of future demand). One of the rules which is designed to protect existing unit holders' interests, is that new units must be created at the 'DTI offer price' and old units liquidated at the 'DTI bid price'. This ensures that the assets of the UT are not diluted by incoming investors buying in cheaply or outgoing investors receiving more than their fair share when they sell.

Forward pricing of Units: new recommendations

For the last 40 years, the UT industry has been regulated by the DTI under the Prevention of Fraud (Investments) Act 1958 (the PFI Act). The Financial Services Act 1986 (the FSA) provides for the regulation of the UT Industry under a successor regime to the PFI Act, under which regulation making powers may be delegated to the Securities and Investment Board (SIB) by the DTI (see Chapter 10). The SIB will be responsible for monitoring the industry, but it is the DTI which will lay down the rules for that monitoring.

The SIB published *draft* rules for controlling the industry at the beginning of October 1987. Its recommendations, *inter alia*, included that (a) buyers and sellers of units should trade on a 'forward pricing' system, under which prices would be determined *after* the deal order rather than on a historic basis; (b) the administration charges and fees for deals should be quoted separately from the price of units; and (c) the settlement times should be tightened.

1 *Forward pricing of Units: SIB Proposal.* At present, deals effected by the manager with the trustee (the creation and cancellation of units) are done at prices which reflect the value of the fund at its last valuation. In theory, this means that, according to the current pricing formula, the value of any unit should be unaffected by the creation or cancellation of any other units. For a typical fund invested in UK securities, the prices which will

govern today's dealings will be based on a revaluation of the fund reflecting the prices of the securities in the fund at some time during the previous day. In many cases, particularly for funds invested overseas, the prices for units are slower to reflect changes in the markets for the underlying assets. This means that whenever units are created or cancelled, the prices at which such transactions are effected will not reflect the true current value of the underlying net assets, to the extent that there has been a movement in market prices since the fund was revalued. The objective of achieving equity between incoming, outgoing and continuing unitholders may therefore be frustrated when there is a significant market volatility. The fact that unit prices are based on an out of date valuation of the fund opens up opportunities for professional market operators and managers to profit at the expense of other unitholders because they can effect transactions on the basis of current information not yet reflected in unit prices. This is, SIB believes, clearly contrary to the best interests of unitholders and should be prevented.

Therefore SIB proposes that all dealings in units should be at the next price to be calculated after an order is taken, a procedure known as *forward pricing* (FP). FP would mean that all creations and calculations of units would be at prices which achieve equity between incoming, outgoing and continuing unitholders in the fund. It will also remove the opportunity for either investors or the manager to deal in units on the basis of information about movements in value of the underlying assets of the fund which is not yet reflected in the prices of units. FP will result in *prices published* in newspapers which give historic information about recent dealing prices rather than prices at which the manager is prepared to deal. This will not, on its own, indicate where the prices lie within the range permitted to the manager by the formula. Therefore SIB proposes to require the manager to place a symbol against the relevant prices in newspapers to indicate whether they have been calculated on a full *offer*, *bid* or *intermediate* price basis, i.e. their positions within the permitted range. SIB suggests that letters *O B I* might be used for this purpose: *O* and *B* applying to bands at the respective ends of the permitted range.

In effect FP formula, *if implemented*, will mean that the prices at which dealing takes place will not be known until they are circulated after the close of business. At this point, the managers will be required to balance repurchases against sales of units and calculate the net number of units that will need to be created or destroyed.

The management company will be permitted to continue to run a 'box' of units already created to iron out small daily swings from net redemptions to net sales and vice versa. However, the management company will be prohibited from backdating the creation or destruction of units. This will remove an important source of extra revenue for some management companies which have backdated the creation of units by up to one week – very profitable in a bull market!

2 The management charges are to be shown separately on the contract note from the unit prices. The rounding adjustment of the lesser of 1.25p or 1% is to be abolished.
3 The information regarding the balance of repurchases against sales of units and the number of units to be created and destroyed should be reported to the trustee within two hours.

The Unit Trust Association (UTA) has vigorously objected to the SIB's FP formula on the grounds that it is unworkable and would mislead a public used to dealing on the basis of *known* prices, i.e. prices fixed on the previous day and published in the morning newspapers. SIB admits that the main drawback of the FP proposal would be that investors could not know the *precise* price at which the deals would be effected at the time they gave a purchase or sale order, however, it believes that this disadvantage would be outweighed by the benefits to investors, after some transitional operational difficulties for managers and trustees have been overcome, as can be seen in the USA mutual fund industry where the FP system operates successfully. Nevertheless, the UTA, as well as expressing strong objections to the SIB, also expressed its concern direct to the DTI. The DTI has responded by emphasising that changes are necessary to resolve certain areas of potential abuse in the present *historic pricing* system – a contention the UTA accepts – and FP is one method of protecting investors. The DTI has, however, agreed to an extra consultation period. At the time of writing, the DTI intends to complete the consultation process by early January 1988 and to produce its *final* set of rules by the second half of February 1988. The final rules, whatever form they may take, shall become operative in April 1988. The final rules were not, in fact, implemented until 1st July 1988 when FP became operational.

Pound/Cost Averaging (P/CA)

The regular investments of a fixed sum in a UT scheme, as opposed to the regular purchase of the same number of units, brings in the benefits of P/CA to the investor, i.e. the average price paid for units is lower than the average unit price over the savings period because the regular investment buys more units when the unit price is low, and fewer when it is high. This advantage of P/CA arises from the difference between the *harmonic mean* and the *arithmetic mean*, as shown in the following example:

Suppose an investor invests regularly £20 per month in a UT scheme. The price of units fluctuates: 50p during the first month; 100p in the second month; and 200p in the third month. The arithmetic mean of the three prices is 116.67p $\frac{(50 + 100 + 200)}{3}$, but the harmonic mean is only 0.86p, as calculated below:

	Price (p)	Regular sum invested (£)	Units purchased
First month	50	20	40
Second month	100	20	20
Third month	200	20	10
		60	70

The harmonic mean $= \dfrac{60}{70} = £0.86$, considerably lower than the arithmetic mean.

The greatest advantage of P/CA is obtained over a long savings period – say, 10 to 20 years – and especially when the unit price is fluctuating, as it normally would over a long period (assuming there is no persistent downward trend in unit price fluctuation). The P/CA advantage is another reason why regular investments in UT schemes should be kept up over long periods.

Taxation

The tax treatment of the incomes and gains received by UT managers and unitholders is basically similar to that accorded to the incomes and gains received by IT managers and IT shareholders (see above). Unlike the ITs, the UTs are not required to distribute all their available income to unitholders, although in practice they do distribute it. The reason for this is that the Inland Revenue treats income held or distributed as taxable income for the financial year in which it is received by the UT.

Accumulation units and Income units

Accumulation units are designed for investors wanting capital growth only; with these units any income derived from the UT's underlying investments is automatically reinvested, increasing the value of each unit, without having to pay a further initial management charge. Reinvested income is subject to tax, and the higher-rate taxpayer must pay the additional tax due.

Income units or distribution units, while increasing with capital growth, split off any income and pay it out to unitholders twice a year. Should a unitholder want his income to be reinvested to buy more units, he can ask the managers to do so – but this is a less efficient route to capital growth than the automatic reinvestment carried out by accumulation units since the latter (i.e. accumulation units) does not involve paying the initial charge.

Insurance

Top-slicing

Insurance companies enjoy certain tax concessions which can be passed on to bondholders. Investment bonds are technically single-premium life assurance policies, they are exempt from CGT and basic rate of income tax in the hands of the investor, the only tax consideration being the possibility of a tax liability to higher-rate taxpayers when they encash the bonds. This liability is calculated on a 'top slicing' basis, but the investor can claim top-slicing relief, which may be calculated in the following way:

1   Total gross gain = sum received on encashment + any income taken during the life of the bond – bond purchase price.
2   Average annual gross gain = Gross capital gain ÷ the number of complete years the bond was held. (The average capital gain is treated as if it were the 'top slice' of the bondholder's income in the year of encashment.)
3   Tax liability on average gain = Average capital gain × (marginal rate of tax − minus the basic rate of tax).
4   Total tax liability = Tax liability on average gain × the number of years the bond was held.

Example
Investor X buys an investment bond for £15 000, takes an income of £500 a year for 10 years, and then encashes the bond for £20 000. His marginal rate of tax is 40% and the basic rate is 25%.

1   Total gross gain = £20 000 + 5000 (10 × 500) − £15 000 = £10 000
2   Average annual gross gain = £10 000 ÷ 10 (years) = £1000 p.a.
3   Tax liability on average gain = 1000 × (40% − 25%) = £150
4   Total tax liability = £150 × 10 = £1500

If X delayed the encashment until he retired, i.e. when his marginal tax rate fell to the basic rate, he would avoid paying higher rate tax.

Top-slicing benefit to insurance bondholders

Insurance bondholders enjoy tax benefits over unitholders in UT schemes. Suppose, Z invested £1000 in 1977 in a Managed Bond, which was worth £4000 in 1986. In 1986, Z made an additional investment of £50 000 in the Japan Fund, which in 1987 was worth £75 000, and the Managed Fund holding grew to £5 000 in 1987. Z is deemed to have invested £51 000 in 1977, and earned a profit of £29 000 (£4000 + £25 000) *over 10 years*. If Z encashes the bond in 1987, to assess any liability to higher tax £2900 only $\left(\dfrac{£29\ 000}{10\ \text{years}}\right)$ is added to his income, rather than £25 000 (which would have been the case if he were to have encashed a *new* bond after one year). In a UT, Z would have had to pay the CGT on the whole profit.

Partial surrender of single premium bonds

For *basic* rate taxpayers there is no problem if their receipts from the partial surrenders *exceed* the cumulative 5% p.a. withdrawal allowance, i.e. no income is payable on the excess amount withdrawn. However, if the excess amount *plus* the investor's taxable income moves into a higher tax band, then the investor will be liable to higher rate tax.

Example

Y investor has a taxable income of £17 500 in 1986/87:

Y bought a single premium insurance bond for £60 000 five years ago.

Y withdrew £30 000, on a partial surrender

Y enjoys a tax-free allowance of 5% p.a., therefore the tax-free allowance for five years=

$5 \times 5\% = 25\%$ of £60 000 = £15 000

Net taxable partial surrender value:

£30 000 − £15 000 = £15 000.

Average annual slice (for top slicing):

£15 000 ÷ 5 = £3000

1987/88 Income Tax Bands

£	%
0–17 900 –	27
17 901–20 400 –	40
20 401–25 400 –	45

Tax rate	Portion of slice £	Tax liability £
27%	400	108
40%	2 501	1 000.40
45%	101	45.45
	£3 000	£1 153.95

Average percentage rate tax £3000 (the slice) =

$$\frac{1\ 153.95}{3000} \times 100\% = 38.47\%$$

Tax rate applied to gain = Average tax rate on slice − basic tax rate = 38.47% − 27% = 11.47%

Tax payable on gain = £15 000 × 11.47% = £1720.5

When Y eventually encashes the bond, Y can obtain a credit for £1720.5, and use the tax credit to reduce the *higher* tax liabilities. Basic rate taxpayers, however, get no credit for the tax paid. The strategy therefore should be to buy several low priced bonds; all equalling to one large priced bond which the investor wished to buy. Then surrender some of the bonds; thus, while utilising the 5% withdrawal allowance, not getting caught in the partial surrender rules.

Qualifying policies

If a unit-linked life policy was taken out after 1 April 1976 but before 14 March 1984, it may be 'qualified' for the tax relief on premiums. The rules for a policy to be a qualifying policy are complex but the following basic criteria must be met.

1 Premiums must be payable annually or more frequently for at least 10 years and must be fairly evenly spread over the period.
2 For fixed term endowment policies: the sum assured must not be less than 75% of the premium payable over the full term, but if the assured is over 55 years old at the commencement date the percentage is reduced by 2% for each year above 55.
3 For open-ended whole life policies: the sum payable on death must not be less than 75% of the total premiums on assumption that the policyholder dies when he reaches the age of 75 years.

The holder of a qualifying policy obtains a relief of 15% of gross premium up to a maximum of £1500 or 1/6th of his income for tax purposes for the fiscal year, whichever is greater. The policyholder pays a premium net of 15% tax relief to the life company, and the life company recovers the 15% from the tax authorities. The following example illustrates the advantage enjoyed by a holder of a qualifying policy.

Y has taken out a 10 year qualifying policy in 1983 with monthly premiums of £20, 94% of the premiums are invested in units.

	£ p
Total gross annual premium (12 × £20)	= 240.00
Total net annual premium paid by Y (£240 less 15% tax relief)	= 214.00
Total investment in units (94% of £240)	= 225.60

Thus, Y obtains units costing £225.60 for an outlay of £214 in addition to a 'free' life insurance cover.

However, if Y were to surrender (an open-ended policy) or discontinue or convert to a paid-up policy (a fixed-term policy) *within* ten years of the commencement date, he would receive the money value of the accumulated units at the prevailing bid price minus *CGT* from the life company, but he may find himself being assessed for income tax at a higher rate on the excess value of the units over the premiums paid.

Furthermore, any early surrender, discontinuance or conversion to a paid-up policy within the first four years will mean that the tax authorities will 'clawback' some or all of the tax relief. The clawback works as follows:

Time of surrender	clawback rate	maximum clawback
Within two years or less	15%	surrender value less 85%
Between two and three years	10%	surrender value less 90%
Between three and four years	5%	surrender value less 95%

Suppose, in the previous example, Y surrenders his policy after $2\frac{1}{2}$ years, having paid £510 net premium (£600 gross), and the net surrender value of his policy is, say £545.

Basic clawback (@ 10% of £600)	= £60
Maximum clawback (£545 − (£600 − £60)=	£5
Y receives (£545 − £5)	= £540

On 22nd January 1988, the Inland Revenue announced that after 25th February 1988 it will no longer certify certain life policies which may be converted or restructured as 'qualifying' for tax relief purposes. At the time of writing, many life assurance policies are sold on the express under-standing that their terms may be altered at or before their maturity date. These alterations can convert a policy from 'whole life' (payable only on the death of the assured) to 'endowment' (the sum assured is payable either at the end of a specified period or on the earlier death of the assured).

So far, such alterations have been regarded as variations of an *existing* contract rather than the creation of a new contract. However, the legal advice recently obtained by the Inland Revenue has suggested that under contract law changes of this kind almost invariably result in the original contract being rescinded and the creation of a *new* contract which is likely to be 'non-qualifying'.

The policies concerned are 10-year endowment policies which are converted on maturity to whole-life plans, with a 'peppercorn' premium of perhaps £10 a year. This keeps the policy in force while investors can draw off a regular income from them with no further tax to pay. These policies are known as Maximum Investment Plans and include unit-linked and with-profits policies.

Owing to the way in which life policy investments are taxed, these policies are not particularly appealing to the basic rate taxpayers, or those who will become basic rate taxpayers in 10 years' time, but they can be a useful way for higher rate taxpayers to build up capital over a period of years and then have freedom to take out an income without attracting higher rate tax. The loss of 'qualifying' status of these policies means that higher rate taxpayers will have to pay an extra charge if they withdraw income from such policies. Basic rate taxpayers would not be affected, and the straightforward endowment or whole-life policy, which provides a tax-free cash sum on maturity or death, is not affected either.

No policy *already* in existence or completed *before* 25th February 1988 will be affected.

Guaranteed income bonds

An investor, aged 65, had bought a guaranteed income bond for £10 000; £7000 of which was allocated by the life company to provide for the temporary annuity for 10 years, and £3000 for either a deferred annuity for life or the return of capital, after the 10 year term.

Suppose the investor has received since commencement an annuity, payable for 10 years of £950.00 (gross) (in half-yearly instalments of £470).
Of the £950, £700 is the return of capital therefore bears no tax. The remaining £250 will bear tax @ 27%

$$= \frac{£37.50}{}$$

Net annuity = $\underline{£912.50}$

After the 10 year term, the investor has a choice of either taking a deferred annuity of, say, £1250 for life or of taking £10 000 in cash. If he takes the deferred annuity option, then he will continue to receive the net annuity, calculated in the manner shown above with adjustment for the prevailing basic rate of tax, for the rest of his life.

If he chooses the cash option then the tax treatment will be that he will have a liability for higher rates of tax on £7000 (£10 000 – the purchase price *minus* £3000 allocated to provide for the alternative benefits).

The choice of taking cash will probably be more beneficial because the investor can then purchase a new bond with a greater proportion of the annuity being classed as return of capital therefore not taxable.

Personal Pension Plan

PPP's legal position

The PPP is a retirement annuity contract approved by the Inland Revenue under the Income and Corporation Taxes Act 1970 as amended. A PPP cannot be surrendered, or assigned, or used as security for a loan, or sold, or otherwise disposed of at any time; it must be used to provide a pension with the exception of the amount which is permitted to be commuted (i.e. taken as a lump sum) for cash or the benefit payable on premature death.

Income tax relief on contributions

A prospective PPP holder is entitled, in any fiscal year, to contribute a percentage of his 'net relevant earnings' in that year, and to set off the whole of the contribution against his earnings in order to obtain tax relief from both basic and higher rate tax. 'Net relevant earnings' is the total of a planholder's net earnings from non-pensionable employment or business. The maximum percentage of net relevant earnings which may be contributed and be eligible for tax relief is shown in the table below.

If born in	Maximum percentage
1934 or later	$17\frac{1}{2}$
1916–1933	20
1914 or 1915	21
1912 or 1913	24
1911	$26\frac{1}{2}$

Tax exemption of pension funds

Pension funds are not liable to UK taxes on income and capital gains, therefore by investing in a pension fund the investor can accumulate greater benefits than if he invested via direct investment. The following table illustrates this by comparing the projected value of a net contribution of £1000 into a pension fund growing at 10% p.a. compound net of charges with direct investment each year of £1000 returning 10% p.a. compound, the income of direct investment being subject to income tax in the hands of the investor. The example assumes that growth is entirely income rather than capital.

£1000 net invested each year for:	Accumulated Investment			
	27% Taxpayer		50% Taxpayer	
	Direct investment £	Pension fund £	Direct investment £	Pension fund £
5 years	6 271	9 559	5 802	13 431
10 years	15 067	24 892	13 207	35 062
15 years	27 421	49 525	22 657	69 899
20 years	44 789	89 136	34 719	126 005
25 years	69 220	152 869	50 113	216 364
30 years	103 606	255 250	69 761	361 887

Under the current legislation arrangements can be made for any lump sum benefit payable on death before retirement to be held for the beneficiaries of the planholder, normally free of *Inheritance Tax*.

Contributions to and benefits from PPP

Suppose B, aged 40 next birthday, with taxable earnings of £15 000, plans to retire on his 65th birthday. Assuming that his earnings increase by 5% p.a., he will be earning at retirement a little over £50 000 p.a. B purchases a PPP by making regular annual contributions of £2000. What will be his total net outlay?

Regular annual contributions	£2000
Less income tax relief at an assumed average rate of 27%	540
Net outlay per annum	£1 460
Total net outlay on B's 65th birthday (£1460 × 26 years)	£37 960

B's retirement benefits, shown below, are based on assumed annual compound growth rate of 10% and 12%, made up of reinvested income and capital gains less management charges and on a premium rate of 13.195%.

Value of B's Retirement Fund	Based on assumed annual compound growth rate of:	
	10%	12%
The projected fund value at the selected retirement date of 65 is:	£207 522	£284 714
B can choose, as retirement benefit,		
either an annual pension of	£27 383	37 568
or, a maximum tax free cash sum of	£63 842	£87 589
plus an annual pension of	£18 959	£26 011

In addition to the regular contributions for retirement benefit, B may contribute an additional single contribution in respect of previous years and claim tax relief against the current year's earnings, provided that the maximum contribution is also paid for the current year.

Personal Pension Schemes (PPS)

A PPS is essentially an arrangement offered by a pension provider to individuals to provide benefit on death or retirement. When the PPS is 'appropriate' it may be used to contract out of the State Earnings-Related Pension Scheme (SERPS), (see below).

The Inland Revenue accepts the following as pension providers for the purpose of establishing a PPS: insurance companies, banks, building societies, unit trusts and friendly societies.

PPS became available from 1 July 1988 to:

(a) *Employees*, who are currently in an occupational scheme which provides *only* death-in-service benefits in respect of those employees.

(b) *Self-employed*. They may make payments concurrently to a PPS and to an existing retirement annuity provided that the combined payments do not exceed the following relevant contribution limits:

Age attained at commencement of tax year	*% of earnings*
51–55	20
56–60	22.5
61 or more	27.5

Contributions to PPS contracts will attract tax relief at the individual's highest rate. The self-employed will continue to obtain tax relief by making a claim to the Inland Revenue after the end of the income tax year in which the contributions are paid. In the case of employees, where an employer contributes, the combined contribution must not exceed the above limits; and the employer's contributions will qualify as a business expense. Employees will pay contributions net of basic rate tax and the pension provider will claim the tax deducted from the Inland Revenue. If they are higher rate taxpayers the employers will receive the balance of tax relief by reclaim or through their PAYE coding. Unused relief may be carried forward for up to six tax years to set against any contributions paid in excess of the limits referred to above. Contributions may also be related back to the previous two tax years. The 'carry forward' and 'carry back' provisions will only be available in respect of contributions made by the member.

Contracting out of SERPS

Employees may choose to contract out of SERPS by arranging for 'minimum contributions' to be paid to an Appropriate Personal Pension Scheme (APPS). Minimum contributions will normally amount to the rebate part of the National Insurance contributions of both the employer and the employee. The NI rebate for the tax year 1987/88 amounts to 6.25% of 'band earnings', i.e. between the lower and upper earnings limits (£39–£295 weekly). For the tax years 1988/89 to 1992/93 the rebate will be 5.8% of band earnings.

In addition to the NI rebate, a member of an APPS may qualify for an incentive payment of 2% of band earnings which will be payable for each of the tax years from 6 April 1988 to 5 April 1993. The NI rebate and incentive payment, where applicable, will be paid by the Department of Health and Social Security together with tax relief at the basic rate on the member's part of the rebate.

Payments will be made direct to the pension provider as a lump sum following the end of tax year.

Thus the minimum contributions for the tax years 1987/88 and 1988/89, will be as follows:

	1987/88 %	1988/89 %
NI rebate: employer	4.10	3.80
employee	2.15	2.00
Tax relief on employer's rebate (at basic rate tax)	0.80	0.74
Incentive	2.00	2.00
	9.05	8.54

This assumes basic rate tax of 27%. Any tax relief at the higher rates will be claimed by the individual through his tax return.

Minimum contributions are in addition to the contribution limits outlined above.

Benefits from PPS

1 Except in relation to the tax free cash, benefits from a PPS will be dependent only on the level of contributions paid and the return on investment. Benefits can be taken at any time from age 50 onwards (but not later than age 75). The tax free lump sum will, in respect of each scheme, be the lower of:

(a) 25% of the fund and
(b) £150 000.

If the member wishes to take the lump sum, payment must be made not later than the date on which the annuity is purchased.

2 Where the PPS is used to contract out of SERPS, benefits must be split between those attributable to the investment of minimum contributions and those bought by other contributions (if any).

The benefits bought by minimum contributions are referred to as 'projected rights' and will take the following forms:

(a) A personal pension payable at state pension age (or later by agreement) the rate for which must take no account of sex or marital status.

(b) A spouse's pension payable at half the rate applicable to the personal pension.

(c) Escalation on pensions in line with the cost of living but with a maximum of 3% p.a.

1 *Variable AVCs* Employers will be able to vary the amount and timing of AVC payments. The requirement for regular contributions payable for at least five years is being removed. The increased flexibility as to amount and timing of contributions will give employees greater control over the amount of tax relief obtained in any year. However, relief will still only be allowable on contributions up to 15% of remuneration. These provisos took effect in relation to contributions paid on or after 6 April 1987.

2 *Free-standing AVCs* From 26 October 1987, members of occupational schemes will be able to make their own arrangements to pay AVCs, i.e. completely separate from their employer's scheme. Contributions will be paid net of basic rate tax with the balance of relief in the case of higher rate tax being regained by reclaim or coding. The pension provider will have to reclaim the basic rate tax element from the Inland Revenue.

AVC Schemes will operate on a money-purchase basis and will be available only to members of an occupational scheme in respect of whom pension benefits are being provided under the scheme. Twenty per cent directors will not be able to become members of such schemes.

Benefit under the AVC scheme will be aggregated with those of the employer's scheme for the purposes of Inland Revenue limits. Any over-funding which might result will cause the benefit under the employer's scheme to be reduced. It is proposed to minimise the risk of overfunding by requiring the employer's scheme and the AVC scheme to exchange information periodically.

Recent indirect investment schemes

BES relief

Suppose C, a 60% taxpayer (1987/88 tax year) invests £10 000 in a spread of BES Investments. Some fail but eventually, after five years, C is able to sell his remaining investments for £16 000. Although the actual growth in value of C's portfolio of BES Investments is only a modest 60% over the five year period, C has in fact *quadrupled* his money since (a) his net cost after tax relief was only £4000 (£10 000 less 60% relief) and (b) he is not subject to CGT on the disposal.

For BES shares issued before 6th October in any year of assessment it is possible to carry back up to half of the relief to the previous year, subject to a maximum of £5000. The £40 000 applies to the relief available against the *income* of any one year, rather than to the amount subscribed for BES shares in the year. Suppose X, a top-rate taxpayer, subscribed £45 000 in 1988/89 and claimed full relief spread over 1988/89 and 1987/88. For X, the amount carried back will obtain relief at 60% rather than 40%.

PEP relief

PEPs are an effective tax shelter for individuals who normally exceed the annual exemption limits for CGT because they can redeploy part of their investments within a PEP. Exemption from income tax is another attraction for higher-rate taxpayers, who can for example use a PEP to shelter the higher yielding part of an equity portfolio. However, typical initial charges 1%–5%, and 1%–2% annually thereafter will absorb much of the benefit. Nevertheless over the longer term a PEP investment of £2400 (raised to £3000 in 1988/89 Budget) could accumulate to a substantial sum.

For example, D, a taxpaying investor, invests £2400 p.a. in January each year in a PEP. The net return on his investment (i.e. gross dividends plus capital appreciation less management charges) is 15% p.a. compound. At the end of 10 years, D will have a tax free fund worth in excess of £56 000.

Investment in house and other property purchase

Mortgage interest relief for owner occupiers

Interest paid on the first £30 000 borrowed to buy a house is considered by the Inland Revenue as an 'outgoing' eligible for tax relief. Suppose the prevailing mortgage rate is 13% p.a., and E, a basic rate taxpayer, buys a house costing £20 000. The actual rate of interest he will pay to the mortgagee (building society or bank which makes the loan) can be worked out according to the following formula:

$$\frac{\text{Rate of interest quoted by mortgagee} \times 100 - \text{mortgage marginal rate of tax}}{100}$$

Therefore, the actual rate of interest paid by E on £20 000 loan is, not 13% p.a. but, 9.49% p.a. $\frac{(13 \times 100 - 27)}{100}$ i.e. a saving of £705 (£2600 – @ 13% less £1895 – @ 9.4%).

It follows therefore that the higher the marginal rate of tax of the mortgagor the better off he would be. For example, the actual rate of interest for a 60% taxpayer, in the above example, would be 5.2% p.a. giving a saving of £1560.

Apart from owner occupation, there are two more conditions to mortgage interest relief: (i) the loan must be specific to property and must run for at least twelve months, unless interest is paid in the UK to a bank, stockbroker or discount house. (ii) Purchasers must normally move into the property within twelve months, otherwise any relief may be withdrawn.

Relief extends to properties purchased by members of approved co-operative housing associations, self-build societies, local authority tenant purchase schemes and, with some conditions, a houseboat or a caravan.

Interest payments on qualifying loans within the MIRAS scheme (Mortgage Interest Relief at Source) are made net of basic rate-tax, thus benefiting non-taxpayers as well. Higher rate taxpayers need to reclaim the balance above basic rate from the Inland Revenue. Married couples are allowed only one £30 000 upper limit. If, however, a couple are not man and wife, separate limits used to apply and the relief was allocated between the two according to the proportion of interest each pays. From August 1988, mortgage tax relief will be restricted to £30 000 no matter how many people are buying the house or flat. This is meant to shop unmarried couples getting more tax relief than married couples.

Absence from a main residence for more than a year may result in the loss of tax relief. If, however, an employer requires the owner to live away from home, relief is available for a period of four years and after that it stops until the owner returns. The relief would not be lost if the property was sold within the four year period.

2 As the population increases and the society becomes better off, the demand for houses exceeds their supply – more so in areas of high employment. The housing shortages generate capital gain. Suppose E sells his house after five years for £40 000, he will have no liability to CGT on the gain of £20 000. Using this amount and taking a mortgage of £30 000, E could buy a more desirable house for, say, £50 000, while obtaining the tax relief on interest over £30 000. By such 'trading up', E can continue to increase the value of his investment, so long as he has other sources of income to continue paying the actual mortgage interest on loans, and he keeps the house in owner-occupation for residential purposes only. E would lose tax relief if he rented the house or used it as business premises.

Selected questions

The indirect investment areas are of extreme importance to students of Investment. It is highly likely that at least one question is asked in the question paper from this section. The following questions have been selected to give you an idea of the type of questions that have been asked in the past from this area of the syllabus. See if you can answer them before looking at the brief answers given below.

Q1 You have been asked to put forward proposals for setting up an entirely new unit trust management group. List eight types of unit trusts, and, in each case, give the investment objectives and indicate the main selling points. What facilities, such as regular savings schemes, would you also recommend? Restrict your answer to authorised unit trusts.

Q2 (a) The advice often given to an investor who wishes to invest prudently is 'to spread the risk'. What does this mean?

(b) Briefly describe the various types of investment which would meet the objective of spreading the risk.

(c) Taking into consideration your replies to (a) and (b) above, prepare a scheme of investment showing types of investment for a customer who:
  (i) has £20 000 to invest; and
  (ii) requires that his capital should provide him with an immediate overall return before tax of approximately 7% with reasonable emphasis on protecting both income and capital against inflation.

Q3 In assessing the merits of a life assurance policy it is helpful to disentangle three of the main features – life cover, investment, taxation. Discuss the relative importance of these factors for the following major types of policy:
  (a) a managed bond;
  (b) a mortgage protection policy;
  (c) a regular premium with profits endowment policy;
  (d) a guaranteed income bond.

Q4 Write short notes on the following, and indicate the type of investor for whom they would be most suitable:
(a) Business Expansion Scheme;
(b) money funds;
(c) annuities;
(d) offshore funds.

Q5 (a) What are the advantages and disadvantages of immovable property as an investment?

(b) Describe the two types of investment which enable the small investor to invest indirectly in immovable property.

Brief answers

A1 *Proposals for a new unit trust management group*

(a) *Gilt fund* – a portfolio of gilts. Subject to inflation and interest risks. Objective: steady high income and some capital growth.

(b) *Equity income fund* – a portfolio of smaller UK companies' shares, yielding more than average. Objective: income and growth.

(c) *Capital fund* – consisting of UK and overseas equities, with above average growth prospects. Objective: capital appreciation, suitable for higher-rate taxpayers.

(d) *Balanced fund* – investing in shares of leading UK companies, lower risk. Objective: reasonable income and some capital growth, for a new investor taking a long-term view.

(e) *Recovery fund* – investing in UK companies about to recover profitability. Higher risk/reward ratio. Objective: above average capital growth, suitable for adventurous investors.

(f) *USA fund* – a balanced portfolio in leading US companies. Objective: capital growth with modest income, for higher-rate taxpayers.

(g) *Financial and property fund* – investing in shares of leading UK financial institutions and property companies. Objective: switching, to benefit from the 'ups' and neutralise the 'downs' of property market.

(h) *High technology fund* – specialising in new technology companies. Objective: good growth projections, higher than average risk reduced by diversification, for the more sophisticated investor who already has a traditional portfolio.

Main selling points: expert and active management; convenience; switching facility; local contracts.

Facilities recommended: share exchange scheme; insurance-linked scheme; monthly income packages; withdrawal plans; accumulation units and switching between funds at favourable rates; regular saving schemes.

A2 (a) *'Spreading the risk'* – The investor's equity stake does not consist entirely of the shares of one company, and is spread among first class companies engaged in various spheres of activity – this avoids the 'all-eggs-in-one-basket' type of risk. Many investors either lack resources or expertise for directly spreading the risk. Indirect investment via, e.g. unit and investment trust, provides the spreading of risk cheaply, conveniently and professionally.

(b) *Unit trusts* – by purchasing units in a UT, the investor obtains advantages of collective investment spread over a wide selection of the UK and overseas companies' shares. Switching facility provides defensive mechanism. *Investment trusts* – by buying shares of an IT company, the investor reduces investment risk by spreading investment over a number of different stocks and shares, including property, fixed interest securities and cash investments.

Unit-linked insurance bonds – based on the same principles as UTs and ITs: regular premiums (or a single premium) buy units in a bond sold by an insurance company which spreads the risk and opportunities for growth of capital and income over a wide range of stocks and shares, plus a modest life cover.

Friendly society products – These are insurance policies issued by friendly societies, and at maturity the proceeds are free of all taxes in the hands of policyholders. There are heavy penalties for early withdrawals. These investments are not protected by the Policyholders Protection Act 1975.

Property bonds – They are insurance bonds (usually single premium but sometimes regular premiums) which invest directly in property. They are *not* UTs, property companies or ITs. Like other insurance bonds they are run on a unitised basis. Precise valuation is difficult. To meet withdrawals equity is maintained because property is not quickly sold. There is some life cover for bondholders.

National Savings investments – These investments are not subject to equity bond securities, because all forms of national savings are in effect loans to the government, therefore capital and income are absolutely safe, without applying the 'spreading of risk' principle.

(c) Immediate return of £1400 required (7% of £20 000) before tax. This may be achieved by investing 50% in fixed-interest securities (e.g. NSCS, high-yielding gilts) and the remaining 50% is invested in equity based investments (e.g. UTs, ITs, friendly societies).

A3 (a) *Managed bonds* – life cover is trivial, investment is the main element. Insurance company pays tax on income and capital gains, no further tax liability to basic rate taxpayers. Higher-rate taxpayers may defer the higher rates to a later date, when they will probably have lower incomes.

(b) *Mortgaged protection policy* – life cover is the main element, investment element is negligible. Sum assured is only payable, tax free, on death of the assured during the term of the policy. Tax relief on premiums apply only to policies taken out before March 1984 Budget.

(c) *Regular premium with profits endowment policy* – life cover and investment element are probably equally important. Premium relief now applies only to pre-March 1984 policies. Insurance company pays tax on income at rates lower than the high-rate taxpayers, and on capital gains, therefore still advantageous to high-rate taxpayers.

(d) *Guaranteed income bond* – investment is important, and bond gives a high-yield. The original investment is guaranteed. Insurance company is taxed on income and gains, and higher-rate taxpayer may benefit from 'top-slicing'. No special tax benefit for the basic-rate taxpayer unless premium relief applies.

A4 (a) *Business Expansion Scheme* – investors get tax concessions if they invest as outsiders in certain unquoted companies, either directly or through an approved fund. Provided the shares are retained for five years, relief for the cost of acquiring them is given at the top rates of the investor's income tax, on investment of up to £40 000 per married couple, per tax year. Furthermore, the investor is exempt from CGT on BES shares bought after 18 March 1986.

The rules as to which companies qualify for BES relief are complex, but broadly the eligible company must carry on a qualifying trade, such as wholesaling, retailing, manufacturing, research and development. The higher-rate taxpayers find BES investment very attractive. However, should the company cease to qualify within three years, or cease to trade, investors will not only lose all the tax relief claimed but also may have to repay it to the Inland Revenue. BES investments are subject to more than usual risk of loss of capital.

(b) *Money funds* two types: high interest accounts with an 'authorised' institution, under the 1987 Banking Act, or money-market funds invested in identifiable low risk assets. Interest is paid gross, the minimum investment is fairly low (£1000–£2500), and a cheque book is usually included. Suitable for small investors, particularly the non-taxpaying investors, who usually want safe and high income returns from investment.

(c) *Annuities* – guaranteed annual payments, other than interest payments, continuing for life unless otherwise restricted. They are usually associated with an insurance policy under which the annuitant pays a capital sum to an insurance company in exchange for regular annual payments for the remainder of the annuitant's life or for a fixed period. Annual payments consist partly of capital, partly of income. Annuities provide a high fixed return but because of inflation they are only suitable for elderly people. Rates depend on the age of annuitant at the time an annuity is taken out. Rates are higher for elderly people. Through Home Income Plans they can be used to unlock insurance tied up in a house. They can also be linked on a fixed term with other types of insurance.

(d) *Offshore funds* – open-ended investment vehicles, such as unauthorised UTs or IT companies based outside the UK; for example in the Channel Islands, where nearly all the major UK investment houses and bankers have offices, offering a range of managed funds, such as commodities, gold, USM, currency. Originally, the offshore funds were aimed at expatriates, i.e. those investors who live or work abroad but wish to leave their investment in a tax-efficient yet stable environment. Nowadays these funds are designed as much for the UK investor as the expatriate.

Until recently with these funds there was the problem of roll up of income and their distributor status etc, which gave some benefit to UK investors. However, these problems have now been eliminated. For non-resident investors these funds do provide certain tax advantages, but no great advantage or disadvantage to the mainland investors.

A5 (a) *Advantages of property as an investment*:
- a tangible investment having an emotional appeal;
- investor has control over it;
- prices are less volatile than with equities;
- acts as an inflation hedge over the longer term;
- a good yield is possible;
- with owner occupied residential property: tax relief on mortgage interest and no CGT on gains when sold.

Disadvantages of property as an investment:
- dealing expenses (surveyors, solicitors) and administration costs (letting, rent collecting, repairs, insurance, ground rent) are high;
- financial standing of tenants and the nature of the locality may produce problems;
- the investment is highly illiquid;
- diversification requires large scale investment.

(b) *Two methods of investing in immovable property by the small investor*:
(i) *Property company shares*   bought and sold on the stockmarket like shares in any other quoted company. The company owns and administers properties, and may also develop or trade in them. The shareholder receives dividends and hopes for growth of income and capital value. He has the benefit of expert management, diversification and, usually, of gearing. The share price usually stands at a significant discount to the underlying asset value.
(ii) *Property bonds*   are single premium bonds issued by life assurance companies with their special taxation characteristics. They are run on a unitised basis and invest directly in properties. Expert management and diversification are provided. Problems of valuation and liquidity may arise.

Specially selected question

One of the liveliest topics in the personal finance world in recent years is whether investment bonds or unit trusts are the better investment vehicles for the private investor. In view of this, the following question has been selected for special emphasis.

The competing attractions of authorised unit-trusts and single premium investment bonds have long been debated by financial writers and planners.

(a) Describe the similarities between these two types of investment.

(b) Describe the taxation differences. How do these affect the individual investor?

(c) What other differences are there between the two types of investment?

Model answer

(a) The *similarities* between authorised unit trusts (UTs) and single premium investment bonds (Bonds):

  (i) They are both open-ended, i.e. have no maximum capital.

 (ii) Both offer small savers (£500–£1000) a spread of investments that are managed on a full time basis by managers of a financial institution.

(iii) Unit prices in both cases reflect performance of underlying investments.

(iv) Both have an initial charge and an annual charge deducted automatically.

(b) The effects of *taxation differences* between UTs and Bonds upon individual investor:

  (i) *Capital Gains Tax (CGT)*:

With UTs – The investor is almost in the same position as he would be if investing directly, i.e. the liability to CGT is of the holder *not* UT group. UT is also exempt on switching. Holder can make real (i.e. after adjustment for inflation) gains of up to £5000 (1988/89) per year tax free.

With Bonds – CGT is the responsibility of the life company who issued the Bond, *not* of the investor. Therefore the investor cannot make use of his £5000 a year exemption. Life companies make deductions in the unit price as they go along for tax payable on both realised (at 30%) and unrealised (of usually between 15% and 25%) gains. Many life companies use UTs as the underlying vehicle for their range of equity-linked funds – this allows CGT liability to be deferred in active wheeling and dealing.

 (ii) *Income Tax (I/Tax)*:

With UTs – Dividends received by the unit holders are franked income (i.e. net of basic rate of tax, for 1988/89 – 25%). Non-taxpayers can reclaim the tax; basic rate taxpayers have no further tax liability; higher-rate taxpayers must declare and pay extra tax due. Unfranked income received by the UTs from any other source, except gilts, is taxed at Corporation Tax rates (35% in 1988/89). Income from gilts, by concession, is taxed at 25% as long as the UT concerned invests solely in gilts.

With Bonds – I/Tax varies according to the status of Bondholder.

For basic rate taxpayer: life companies, like other companies, pay I/Tax at 35%. Corporation Tax is charged on unfranked income, while franked income is taxed effectively at 25%.

For higher-rate taxpayer: when a higher-rate taxpayer encashes the Bond, top-slicing takes place.

All Bondholders enjoy withdrawal facilities of 5% p.a. for 20 years – cumulative allowance – which counts as withdrawal of capital, therefore free of tax.

(c) *Other differences* between UTs and bonds:
 (i) Technically a Bond is a life assurance policy but with a minimal life cover.
 (ii) UTs can invest in equities, cash (under the regulations of 1986 Financial Services Act), gilts and other fixed interest securities. Bonds can invest in 'real' property as well as the above, and can have a specialist cash fund (UTs will be able to do this soon).
 (iii) Unitholders can sell one unit (at lower bid price) and buy another unit (at higher offer price) – the spread between the two prices is typically $6\frac{1}{2}\%$. Some UTs give discounts on switching but rarely more than one or two per cent. Bondholders switch on a bid basis, and sometimes pay no extra charge for switching, sometimes pay a flat fee of £10 of £15 per switch. Thus switching is comparatively advantageous to active bondholders.

Updating

In order to keep abreast with changes in the products and practices of, and effects of tax changes on, the financial institutions mentioned in this chapter, you must regularly and carefully study the financial pages of the *Financial Times, The Daily Telegraph, The Times* and other serious national dailies. For specific updating read: the *Fact Sheets* and other publications of The Association of Investment Trust Companies, especially their 'More For Your Money'; the publications of the Unit Trust Association, especially their 'Everything You Need To Know About Unit Trusts'. (Both the AITC and UTA have kindly supplied some of the material used in this chapter.) The *Financial Times* publishes an annual, *Self-Employed Pensions Handbook*, which has exhaustive factual information and performance tables of various pension schemes. Read the literature on your own bank's investment schemes on offer and compare them with those of other banks and insurance companies. Above all, you must not miss any *Signpost* articles on Investment in *Banking World*. The Chartered Institute of Bankers' *Examiners Reports* and *Updating Notes* are absolutely essential learning aids.

6 The Stock Exchange and other securities markets

Syllabus Coverage

The Stock Exchange:
  Antecedents of the 'Big Bang'
  Developments since the 'Big Bang'
  Organisation and procedures
  Function of members
  SEAQ
The dealing system in registered and bearer securities:
  Contracts, settlements, carry-over transactions
  Transfer of securities: marking names, depository receipts etc.
  Commission charges, 'bed-and-breakfast' arrangements
  Stamp duty and reserve tax
  'Listing' requirements and the continuing obligations of 'listed' firms.
The significance of Unlisted Securities Market
The Third Market
Dealings under Rule 535(2)
Over-the-Counter market
Conventional and traded options markets

Introduction

The London Stock Exchange (SE) has long served the needs of government, industry and investors in providing the central market place for listed securities. It provides a channel through which the savings of the personal and institutional sectors can reach those who need finance. When companies and the government wish to raise capital by issuing securities the SE provides investors with a place to trade in those securities confidently and with safety, in what is called the 'secondary market'. In addition to being a central market place for government stocks (gilts) and company securities (shares and fixed interest stocks), it is also the market place for a number of other investment instruments, such as traded options on equities and currencies.

Under the influence of new technology the 'market floor' of the SE is now the automated quotation television screen located in brokers' offices – anywhere in the UK and overseas, but connected to the central SE computers in London. The same market price information which used to be found only on the market floor is now used by brokers all over the world to conclude deals over the telephone, and through computer systems, on behalf of their clients.

While the new technology has changed the market floor, the protection for investors who use SE member firms for their investment business has not changed. SE member firms still agree to uphold certain rules governing their relations with their clients and other market users. These rules and regulations are set by the Council of SE, which also administers and enforces these rules and standards of professional conduct.

This practitioner-led framework has a long history of effective and respected self-regulation, which is now being adapted to accommodate changes, ensuing from the deregulation of the financial services industry (the 'Big Bang'), in the nature of SE membership and to the new legal requirements of the Financial Services Act.

Out of this adaptation to the changes under the new regulatory framework, two bodies have arisen: the International Stock Exchange of the United Kingdom and the Republic of Ireland to supervise the operation of the market place and the activities of investment business in four markets: the Domestic Equity Market (which will cover the 'listed' market, for well-established companies with full 'listing', the unlisted securities market, for smaller less matured companies and the third market, for the smallest companies), the Gilt-edged Market, the Traded Options Market, and the Foreign Equities Market.

The second body is The Securities Association, which is the Self-Regulating Organization and is responsible for the supervision of the investment relations between its authorised members and their clients.

Theoretical aspects

The Stock Exchange

1   *The antecedents of the 'Big Bang'*
The abolition of the exchange controls in 1979 was the beginning which culminated in the deregulation of the entire UK financial services industry, colloquially called 'The Big Bang'. It made it easier for the UK savings institutions to invest their money in overseas markets. This exposed the SE member firms to competition, for the first time, from overseas brokers, particularly those based in New York and Tokyo. This competition was not only for foreign companies' securities but also for the major UK companies' securities which were traded on the overseas markets. The UK institutional fund managers now had a choice and increasingly they were choosing,

because of lower costs and greater flexibility, to invest through foreign brokers. By comparison with the major overseas brokers, the SE member firms were relatively small and lacked the capital necessary to trade in very large volumes. Thus there was growing pressure for the London firms to become somehow more competitive.

The pressure for change came from another direction as well. In 1976 the Restrictive Practices Act was extended to cover services industries too with the result that the SE was obliged to register its rule book with the Office of Fair Trading (OFT). The OFT considered the SE rule to be restrictive of trade in three main areas: the operation of a scale of minimum commission, separation of capacity between broker and jobber, and the restriction on membership. In 1978, the government took the SE to the Restrictive Trade Practices Court. The case threatened sudden change in the SE rules with no chance of orderly transition. Finally in 1983, the SE and the government reached an out-of-court agreement: the case against the SE in the Restrictive Practices Court was dropped and in return the SE undertook to abolish its system of minimum commission by the end of 1986. This agreement acted as the catalyst that led to other major changes. From March 1986, SE member firms could be owned 100% by a single outside corporation; previously non-members could own up to 29.9% in a SE member firm. Many firms were bought by UK and overseas banks and securities firms, which thereby became direct members of the SE; and with adequate capital base were ready to compete in the international securities markets. The new ownership rules led to a further change in the voting rights of SE members; their rights were vested in the member firm (now mainly limited companies rather than partnerships as previously) and not with the individual member as had been the case for nearly 200 years.

Collectively all these changes came to be known as the 'Big Bang', which took place on 27 October 1986.

2 Developments since the Big Bang

With the abolition of the scales of minimum commissions, members are free to negotiate commissions with their clients, and the clients can shop around for the lowest commissions and the best service.

The scrapping of the separation of member firms into brokers and jobbers meant that firms simply became broker/dealers are able to act as either agency brokers representing clients in the market or principals, buying and selling securities on their own account. Firms were also permitted to act as market-makers committed to making firm buying and selling prices at all times. The Financial Services Act 1986 heralded a new regulatory system for the entire financial services industry in the country, and especially for the City. Under the Act, all investment business in the UK had to be authorised and supervised. The Securities Investment Board (SIB) now oversees the whole UK investment community with self-regulating organisations (SROs), setting conduct of business rules for their members and Recognized Investment Exchanges (RIEs) running the markets on which that business is conducted. The SE member firms are covered by a single SRO, viz. The Securities Association, and a single RIE, viz. The International Stock Exchange of the United Kingdom and the Republic of Ireland (see Chapter 10, for more details).

SE organisation and procedures

The Council of SE is the governing body of the SE, presiding over the activities of the market. Since June 1987, it has 25 members, and between a quarter and a third are drawn from outside interests – this is a practice common on leading overseas markets, where close links with users of the market are considered as vital. The remainder of the Council membership is a balanced representation from within the market. The Council members set rules, administer and enforce standards, as well as govern the activities of the SE staff.

The Council is assisted in its work by a number of standing committees. Member firms can gain influence through their participation in these important standing committees, who oversee more than 2500 employees who run the SE services and computer systems through which SE member firms conduct their business. Other standing committees are devoted to setting and enforcing the market rules, as well as disciplining any members found to be in breach of those rules. The Council is thus able to devote more of its time to matters of general policy and in ensuring the maintenance of high standards of regulation.

Functions of members

There are four types of member firms:

1 *Broker/dealers* They are able to act as follows:

(a) Agency brokers representing clients, in a single capacity, in the market and obtain the best price available for them from market-makers.

Such broker/dealers always follow the'best execution rule', and this protects the interests of their clients. This rule implies that the broker/dealers can act as principals provided the price quoted to their clients is as good as or better than the best price available from a market-maker. Acting simply as agency brokers, they will look up the prices quoted on the SEAQ (see below) and will deal with those market-makers who are offering the best price.

(b) Broker/dealers acting, in dual capacity, as agency brokers and as principals buying and selling shares on their own account, by quoting a two-way price.

2 *Market-makers* Firms are permitted to register as market-makers committed to making firm buying and selling prices at all times in specific securities. They are granted the privileges previously enjoyed by jobbers,

such as the ability to borrow at favourable terms. The market-makers in gilts are known as Gilt-edged Market Makers (GEMMs).

3 *Inter-Dealer Brokers (IDBs)* They belong to a specialist category of firm in the gilt-edged market. One market-maker may find itself holding an uncomfortably large amount of a particular stock that another market maker is desperate to buy. Neither, however, will be willing to 'expose its books' by publicly acknowledging its position. IDBs offer to both GEMMs the ability to 'unwind' such positions anonymously, by posting bids and offers for large amounts of stock on the IDB dealing screens. The business must be transacted with a strict Code of Conduct and Dealing. In particular, there is a limit to the credit risks to which IDBs can be exposed and they may deal only to match buying and selling orders placed by GEMMs (see also Chapter 4).

4 *Stock Exchange Money Brokers (SEMBs)* These specialist firms can arrange for GEMMs to 'borrow' stock to satisfy immediate demands, to be returned at a later date. The stock comes from approved institutions (for the most part insurance companies or pension funds), for whom the facility is a useful extra source of income (see also Chapter 4). There are nine recognised SEMBs, who must be individual companies, separate from market-making firms. SEMBs are crucial to market- makers' confidence in their ability to settle – and thus the market's confidence in maintaining cash flow in the gilt market.

In whatever capacity member firms choose to act they are obliged to trade at the best possible price for their clients at all times. High standards of investor protection are provided by a well-established complaints procedure, discipline and enforcement arrangements as well as a compensation fund (see Chapter 10).

SE member firms undergo rigorous admission procedures, and their employees who deal with the public (called 'Registered Representatives') are required to have certain qualifications, usually obtained by taking examinations set by the SE.

The Stock Exchange Automated Quotations System (SEAQ)

This is a computerised information system run by the SE. It provides screen-based information on the state of the market and dealings to broker/dealers, both in their offices and on the trading floor, and to major investing institutions or other subscribers to the system. Information is fed through the established TOPIC system to the TOPIC terminals. (TOPIC = Teletext Output of Price Information by Computer system, is the SE's own videotex terminal network.) There are three different levels of service for SEAQ users.

Level 1 This is called the Investor Service, meant for the investing institutions which are not members of the SE. It displays the best bid and offer prices for each security on the database. For Alpha Stocks (see below) it also gives the number of transactions reported in the last five minutes and the total turnover for the day.

Level 2 This is the Delivery Service for the members of SE. For each quoted security the various competing market-makers' prices are displayed with the number of shares for which the quotation is valid. The best quote, in the case of Alpha and Beta (see below) stocks, are in a yellow band.

Level 3 This is available only to market-makers and allows than to update their prices and input trading information, i.e. the prices at which they are prepared to trade, and the volume for which these prices are binding. Levels 1 and 2 are available to all investors, both in the UK and overseas, who wish to subscribe to them.

Stock classification

The securities traded on the SE are classified according to the level of investor interest in them and hence the level of information which is required to be displayed on the SEAQ system to serve the needs of the market. This classification is not a reflection of the quality of the company as an enterprise or as an investment, but simply the degree of interest it arouses among investors. As investor interest changes, so does a security's SEAQ classification.

For the effective operation of SEAQ, securities are classified into four grades, Alpha, Beta, Gamma and Delta.

1 *Alpha Securities* These are the largest and most liquid stocks in the market. All stocks in the Financial Times 100 Share Index (see Chapter 9) are classified as Alpha securities, as are an increasing number of UK shares with an international following. Prices shown on SEAQ in these securities are firm in the size displayed to all other member firms. Transactions are reported within five minutes of their taking place and details are displayed both on TOPIC and the next day in SE's Daily Official List (SEDOL) (see Chapter 9) under 'Business Done'. Most Alpha stocks will have 10 or more competing market-makers.

2 *Beta securities* These are the next 500 to 600 most actively traded securities. The price display and trade reporting obligations for member firms are the same as for Alpha securities but trade details are not published in real-time on SEAQ. They are, however, shown the next day in the Daily Official List. There will be fewer market-makers in each stock, generally between six and twelve.

3 *Gamma securities* These are of smaller companies. There are about 1500 Gamma stocks, most of the Unlisted Securities Market (see below) and most of the Third Market (see below) stocks fall into this category. The number of market-makers per share will be between two and five. Prices

on SEAQ may be firm or indicative. The market-makers indicate their intentions in this respect on the screen display.

4 *Delta securities* These securities are largely illiquid stocks with very few market makers, probably one per share. An index is maintained on TOPIC to allow firms to identify market-makers prepared to deal in them, and the indicative mid-prices are displayed on TOPIC screens.

SEAQ International

The 24-hour trading has arrived. The equity trading day starts in Tokyo, moves to London after Far Eastern markets close, and the daily cycle is completed in New York and the North American markets. To deal with the requirements of international 24-hour trading, the SE has introduced an electronic screen system for non-UK equities (SEAQ system is for the UK securities) displaying quotes from competing market-makers, viz. SEAQ International. Its growing reputation is based on a highly effective marriage of the SE's long experience in securities trading and its pioneering work on screen-based trading.

International equities have now become highly accessible to investors of all type – from the large international institution handling a wide portfolio of funds for major clients, to the domestic managed fund with its own particular needs. Effective communication is the key to the success of the international market of today. The SEAQ International service provides today's serious investor with highly competitive and dynamic prices on leading stocks in all the important global regions. A firm quotes dealing system that is both straightforward and precise gives the investor an immediate 'fix' on the true market prices of the international stocks with no complications or added costs or charges. Prices are quoted on a strictly net basis.

The Dealing and Transfer System

In registered securities

For Alpha and Beta securities the SEAQ will show a firm two-way price for each market-maker and the number of shares (the size) for which the quotation is valid. The best bid and offer price is highlighted by a yellow strip. For Gamma securities each market-maker's indicative two-way price and size is shown. For Delta stocks no prices are shown, just a list of the market-makers registered for that stock.

For the Alpha and Beta securities the broker/dealer calls up on the SEAQ screen the page displaying the relevant security, selects the market-maker showing the best bid or offer price as appropriate and telephones that market-maker to place the order. The market-maker is committed to the price and size displayed. For larger or smaller sizes the broker/dealer will have to make an enquiry as to the price. For Gamma securities the prices and sizes displayed are indicative only and the broker/dealer again has to enquire as to a firm price. For Delta stocks no prices are displayed and enquiry by telephone is necessary.

For all four categories of security the market-maker must enter the price and the number of shares dealt into the computer within five minutes of the transaction being executed. All trades are published in the next day's Stock Exchange Daily Official List. In the case of Alpha stocks trades are published immediately on SEAQ.

The *dealing costs* include broker's commission charges on both buying and selling deeds, basic-rate VAT on commission charges, government stamp duty at 0.5% on virtually on all purchases, but not on sales (the main exceptions exempt from stamp duty are British government stocks and Eurobonds) and Contract Levy on contracts with a value over £1000 of 80p for equities and 50p for gilts (exceptions to Contract Levy payment are unit trust, offshore and overseas funds, and insurance and property bonds).

After carrying out the client's instructions, the broker will send the client a *Contract Note*, showing full details of the transaction including the time the deal was struck (see Practical aspects below). If the broker carried out a purchase bargain for the client, the broker will register the purchase and the new owner with the company or any other body concerned and will send the client in due course a certificate evidencing ownership. In the case of sales bargains, the client will receive from the broker, usually along with the Contract Note, a transfer form which the client must sign and return along with the covering certificate to the broker, for onward transmission by the broker to the company or any other body concerned so that the seller's name is removed from the holder's register.

Bearer securities

Bearer securities are non-registered securities, therefore the name of the holder is not recorded in the company's or any other issuing body's share/stockholders' register. Dealing in bearer securities via a broker is largely similar to dealing in registered securities, i.e. dealing costs are mostly the same. The difference lies in the transfer of bearer securities. The ownership certificates of bearer certificates do not include the holder's name and there is no transfer form, therefore their ownership is transferable by mere physical delivery to the buyer, either directly by the seller or through a broker, requiring no other transfer document. Since there is no transfer form therefore there is no transfer stamp duty to pay (but stamp duty is paid on the original issue of the bearer securities). The risk of losing and of forgery of unnamed bearer securities is high, therefore these securities should be carefully guarded. Often the bearer securities are deposited with a bank for safe custody.

Note that it is *not* essential for a transfer of ownership of registered or non-registered securities to be a SE transaction. Non-SE transactions in registered securities need a stock transfer form, but not a Talisman transfer form (see below) – in a takeover, for example, ownership is transferred using a form of acceptance and transfer.

Most of the bearer securities are foreign, however, a few major UK companies have issued bearer shares, and certain British government stocks are in bearer bond form. With bearer securities the financial press needs to be monitored for announcements of dividend, new issues, meetings and company reports. The main problem arises with the payment of interests and dividends, because there is no register of holders the company or some other issuing body cannot send off warrants for amounts due to holders of bearer securities. It is up to the holders to spot the announcement in the financial press informing holders which numbered coupons from the certificate to detach, and when and how to submit them and from whom to claim payments. Payments are normally made by the company registrars or paying agents. The last coupon on the certificate is usually larger than the rest, called the talon, and it can be exchanged by the holder for a new sheet of coupons.

Marking names

The shares of US and Canadian companies are registered securities, but their share certificates have a form of transfer (unlike the normal UK companies' share certificates) on the reverse. If this form is signed by the registered holder without completing the name of the transferer the certificate becomes a quasi-bearer certificate. In order to reduce the time and cost involved in dealing with US and Canadian securities held in the UK it is customary for them to be registered in the name of an institution recognisd by the SE, and endorsed in blank. These institutions are known as 'recognised marking names'. Dividends are paid to them and must be claimed from them by the owner. The term arises from the practice of 'marking' the certificate to show that the dividend has been paid, but nowadays marking as such only occurs when there is a change of ownership. Shares registered in good marking names command a higher price than those in an individual's name. The recognition by the SE to banks and its member firms as marking names is in return for an undertaking to pay interest and dividend when claimed by beneficiaries at the approved rate of exchange.

Depository receipts

Many investors use depositories (not to be confused with 'marking names'), such as brokers, banks, solicitors, as custodians of their bearer securities. Depositories only accept those bearer securities for safe-keeping which are delivered in reasonable condition, i.e. not badly torn or the wordings on them materially obliterated, due to the risk of forgery. For the securities accepted for custody the depositories issue depository receipts. If the owners of the deposited securities wish to sell them all they have to do is to withdraw them and deliver them to the buyers directly or via a broker.

In 1970, a *Bearer Deposit Receipt Scheme* was introduced to avoid lost rights of owners caused by the extreme delay which was due to the registrar of companies in Australia and the UK sending information and documents by sea mail. Under the Scheme shares in many Australian companies may now be deposited with certain Australian banks (depository banks) and registered in the name of the depository's nominee company. In London, bearer deposit receipts may be issued against the depository receipts issued for the deposited securities, and pass as any other securities. Thus buying and selling do not involve the share certificates changing hands; the holder of the deposit receipt owns the shares represented by the receipts and held by the nominee. Similar arrangements have been introduced in many other countries.

SE settlement and transfer procedure

After the broker/dealer has carried out the, say, 'buy' instructions of a customer and has issued the Contract Note to the customer, then the SE system by which the securities are paid for and transferred into the customer's name begins to operate.

1 *For cash settlement*

Bargains in certain securities are on a cash basis, i.e. the payment is due the day after the bargain is struck. These securities include all securities traded in the gilt-edged market, (viz. the stocks of British government, local authorities, public corporation, public boards, Commonwealth and Irish government), new issues (in renounceable form), most unit trusts and some foreign securities (for delivery abroad).

Under certain circumstances payment for gilt-edged securities can be delayed, e.g. switching investments in equity which are for the 'Account' (see below) into a gilt-edged security. The transfer procedure is similar to transfer of securities which are for 'Account' settlement.

2 *For Account settlement*

This covers all normal dealings in registered shares and industrial fixed interest stocks. (See Practical aspects below).

The settlement procedure is through the SE's computerised settlement system, known as *TALISMAN* (Transfer Accounting, Lodging for Investors and Stock Management for jobbers). Briefly the Talisman works as follows: All SE member firms are required to report details of their bargains to the Checking system each day. The Checking system validates these details and produces overnight reports for each member firm which provide details of matched and unmatched bargains; only matched bargains are passed on to Talisman where they form the basis of settlement. Selling member firms acting as agents deposit their client's stock at any one of the nine Talisman offices in major UK cities and three overseas offices (Melbourne, Sydney and Johannesburg). The stock is then transferred into the SE's nominee company, known as *SEPON Ltd* (Stock Exchange Pool Nominee Ltd), which protects the sellers' interests until settlement takes place. The physical stock is then sent to the appropriate registrar for registration out of the seller's name and into Sepon. All stock in the process of settlement is held uncertificated in Sepon. This custody of stock in Sepon is the basis of Talisman.

Settlement of sold bargains is achieved by transferring the ownership of stock, by book-entry, within Talisman. Every member firm who acts as principal has a trading account within Talisman for every security it deals in. Principals may hold stock in their trading account and give instructions to withdraw it or use it to settle bargains when they have in turn sold stock. Principals' sold bargains awaiting apportionment are placed in a queue. Stock in the trading account is apportioned to all principal sold bargains by book entry transfer until either no stock is left or all outstanding bargains have been fulfilled. In the case of a bargain where stock is due to be delivered to a client a Talisman Bought Transfer is prepared showing the details of the buying client. This is sent to the registrar who then registers stock out of Sepon and into the buyer's name. Certificates are produced by registrars and issued to member firms for onward transmission to their clients. All payments due to and from each member firm are netted into one figure for each firm's code (see Practical aspects below).

Bargains in South African and Australian registered securities between member firms may also be settled through Talisman in the same way as those in the UK securities. The Stock Against Payment Service allows UK firms to settle with overseas brokers and clients to receive or make payment for physical stock overseas. A Depository Service (for Australia only) is also available for clients who do not wish to take physical delivery of stock. Change of ownership between the depository participants and the dealing member firm is effected the same day by a book entry transfer (see Depository receipts, above).

Bulls and bears

These are speculators, as distinct from investors, in the stock market. A bull buys in the hope of selling for a higher price before the end of the 'Account' (see below). A 'stale bull' buys shares in anticipation of a short-term rise which fails to occur. A stale bull who lacks cash and does not wish to sell at a loss may be able to *carry the bargain over* into the next account by a 'cash and new' deal (this method has almost replaced 'contango' – see below). Many bankers will not allow 'cash and new' deals over more than two accounts and may require a cash deposit as security.

A bear is the opposite of a bull and sells shares he does not own. A bear who owns the shares that he sells, in anticipation of a fall, is known as a 'covered bear'. There is a theoretical unlimited loss for an uncovered bear. A 'bullish market' denotes a rising market, generally due to optimism in the economy, and is typified by buying. A 'bearish market' is a falling market, typified by selling, because the investors have become pessimistic about some aspect of the economy, and are taking cover (or taking gains) under the safety of cash.

Contango

This a method of carrying a stock market transaction over to the next account. Shares are sold for settlement on the normal Account Day (see below), and immediately repurchased on settlement on the following Account Day. The sale and purchase are carried out at the same price (making-up price) which is based on the price ruling at the close of the business on the last day of the Account. The charge for this privilege is called 'contango'.

New time

This refers to deals carried out on the last two dealing days of an Account, which can be for settlement as though they had been done in the next Account. 'Dealing in new time' is slightly more expensive than dealing in the normal manner, due to the privilege of the extended settlement time.

'Bed and Breakfast' (B and B) arrangements

This is a stock market dealing device which enables the holder to sell shares just before the close of the business one day and repurchase them immediately the next day, at a fractionally higher cost, in order to establish capital gains or losses and yet effectively retain the share. Originally the motive was to avoid CGT. This popular ploy was made obsolete by the operation of indexation in 1982. However, since the 1985/86 Budget, 'B and B' transactions have been permitted so long as they are at 'arms length', i.e. the sale and repurchase are spread over two SE account periods. Although stamp duty is now payable on 'B and B' transactions, the broker/dealer may normally charge only one lot of commission, and the market-maker's turn is also reduced.

Buying-In and Selling-Out

If the broker cannot obtain delivery of shares purchased on behalf of a customer, the broker may apply to the SE's Buying-In and Selling-Out Department (BISO) which will attempt to buy an equivalent amount of the security in the market. The original deal will be cancelled and the seller will have to pay any difference. Usually the mere threat to report to BISO is sufficient to persuade the seller to produce the share certificate and signed stock transfer form. Thus actual appeals to BISO are uncommon.

Selling-Out occurs with non-Talisman stocks. If the seller has not received a name for delivery and settlement by the Thursday before settlement day (see below), the seller's broker can apply to BISO for the shares to be sold in the market, which BISO will attempt to do. The BISO deal supersedes the original deal, and if the BISO selling price is below the original price, the original purchaser has to pay the difference to the seller.

SE listing requirements and continuing obligations of 'listed' firms

The admission of the shares and debentures of companies to full listing on the SE is governed and regulated by (a) the Stock Exchange Listing Regulations 1984, (b) the Admission Directive – a part of the UK law, and (c) the Stock Exchange's Admission of Securities to Listing, 1984, as amended from time to time. Since the SE's own requirements exceed that of the Admission Directive, and impose heavier obligations on listed companies than the Admission Directive, they are accepted adequate and valid by the UK law.

Listing particulars (formerly called 'prospectus')

(a) A statement that the listing particulars have been submitted with the Registrar of Joint Stock Companies and that an application has been made for the admission of the securities to the SE Offical List.

(b) The name of the issuing house acting as the sponsor.

(c) Details of the capital structure of the company and the price of the shares being issued.

(d) Names and addresses of directors, secretary, bankers, solicitors, auditors and brokers.

(e) The history, growth analysis and description of the company plus well researched statements of the projected developments.

(f) The details of directors' functions, other relevant business interests, age and activities.

(g) The statement of working capital, which should be adequate.

(h) Its balance sheets for the past five years, interim figures covering the last six months and its profits, dividends and earnings per share and future prospects.

(i) Accountant's report analysing its balance sheets and trends over the past five years.

(j) Statutory and general information concerning share capital history, memorandum and articles of association, material contracts, subsidiary companies, directors' interests, substantial shareholders in the company, directors' duties and service agreements and of such persons as exercise control over the company and their proportionate voting rights.

(k) At least 25% of the issued capital must be made available to the general public, and the total market capitalisation must be at least £700 000.

(l) The sponsoring broker and normally two market-makers must support the listing application, the particulars of which must be published in at least two leading newspapers.

(m) All the relevant documents must be deposited with the Stock Exchange Quotation Department for formal approval.

Continuing obligations

After the Quotation Department has granted full listing to the applicant company, it must then join in the 'continuing obligations' incumbent upon all fully listed companies, in order to retain its listing.

(a) It must inform the Quotation Department at once of any information relevant to investors' appraisal of it.

(b) It must issue two-way proxy voting forms.

(c) It must send all appropriate circulars and announcements to shareholders.

(d) It must issue six-monthly interim reports.

(e) It must promptly register stocks and shares and issue certificates to new owners.

(f) It must obtain existing shareholders' permission to any issue of additional equity capital, if it is not issued to existing members.

Prospective investors in a company 'going public', i.e. seeking full listing on the SE, can obtain extremely useful information about the company from the listing requirements. For instance, the good standing and reputation of sponsors, e.g. the issuing house, broker/dealer, who stake their reputation when they undertake to sponsor a candidate company for listing. Indeed, because of their sponsorship a company's quest for subscription of capital from the general public is more likely to be successful.

The investors can judge for themselves whether it would be worthwhile investing in the company's shares by studying its track record (normally it is the private companies or partnerships seeking to achieve access to new equity capital, greater prestige with customers and creditors and easier access to loans, which seek listing on the Stock Exchange), history, past years' balance sheets and accounts, accountants' reports, profit forecasts and comments on future prospects and reasons for the share issue. A knowledge of the background of the directors is very helpful too, because management is an important ingredient of a company's success. Their contribution in the track record of the company, their reputation in other companies, their own track record, and material contracts relating to their service agreements are all pointers to the success or otherwise of the new issue. Other listing conditions which the investors need to study with care are underwriting arrangements (in the case of the issue not being subscribed to at least the level of minimum capital), the terms of offer for sale (if that is the method the company is choosing in going 'public') which should be in line with other companies in the same field, details of the company's capital structure, asset value of the shares, and profit-sharing arrangements.

Unlisted Securities Market (USM)

The USM was launched in November 1980 to bring the capital raising and other facilities of the SE within reach of private businesses which had not previously considered going public. Over 600 private business firms have been granted listing on the USM.

The owners of a successful private business often find that the paper wealth of their shares is not always reflected by their living standards. Even if all spare cash is not required for the company's expansion plans, there is reluctance to incur higher taxes and national insurance on increased dividends/salaries. Going public is one solution to this dilemma and its commonest form is obtaining a listing on the USM. As a result the owners can realise part of their holdings with the gain subject only to relatively low rates of CGT, without surrendering control of the company.

Although the USM has been a success in attracting private firms to it in large numbers, it has underperformed the main market due to its over-weighting in oil exploration and high technology stocks.

The *main advantages* of obtaining a USM quotation include:

(a) A source of new capital both at the issue and later.
(b) The opportunity to expand by acquisition for shares.
(c) Cash for vendor shareholders.
(d) Publicity, particularly for a consumer orientated product.
(e) Enhancement of the status of the company.
(f) Providing a quotation for employees shares/options (see below).

The *main disadvantages* include:

(a) Public scrutiny – the need to justify price sensitive matters and results and to end perks sometimes enjoyed in private companies.
(b) Costs – these can be high, particularly for smaller issues, these typically range from £80 000 for an 'introduction', to $1–2\frac{1}{2}\%$ of the total market capitalisation on a 'placing' or 'offer for sale' (see below).
(c) Time element – in a small company the key personnel will be heavily engaged in preparing the prospectus for about three months prior to the issue.

(d) Takeover risk – it is small in most cases since for a USM listing (see below) only 10% of the capital of the company needs to be made available to the public, but a listing can be used as a strategic step towards inviting an attractive offer.

(e) Continuing obligations to outside shareholders and pressure to perform.

The USM listing requirements

These are not quite as strict and stringent as those with full listing, and include:

(a) Only 10% of the ordinary issued capital must normally be in public's hands when dealing starts.

(b) The company must have been trading for at least three years, and the trading results must support the projected marked capitalisation.

(c) Latest audited figures presented must not be more than nine months old.

(d) Not less than 25% of the amount placed should be offered to the market-makers to ensure a wider spread of shares to the public.

(e) The company must prepare a new issues particulars card for inclusion in the Extel Ltd USM Service.

(f) One box advertisement should be made in at least one leading daily newspaper.

(g) It must maintain an adequate and continuing disclosure of its affairs.

A company will be considered an unsuitable candidate for listing on the USM if it has a poor trading record; is a one man business; has queries over management, labour problems or a record of legal or accounting problems, or has a short-life product/service; is subject to major uncertain future events (e.g. litigation or unresolved tax liabilities) or is involved in un-severable private activities.

Methods of entry to the USM

There are three main methods of obtaining a USM listing (for details, see Chapter 2):

1 *Introduction* It is the cheapest method available if no new money is being raised and where 10% of the equity is already held by the public, hence no prospectus is required by the Companies Acts.

2 *Offer for sale* Either at a fixed price or as a tender offer when the shares will be priced by the market; this method is obligatory for issues of £3 million or capitalisation over £15 million.

3 *Placing* The shares are placed with institutions on the day of the issue; this method is cheaper and more common than offer for sale.

Comparison between full listing and USM listing requirements

	USM	Full listing
Minimum trading record	3 years	5 years
Minimum equity for the public	10%	25%
Audited accounts prepared within	9 months	6 months
Accountants' report required if	New share issue	Always
Minimum expected value	No minimum	£700 000
Minimum advertising	1 small box in one national daily newspaper.	Prospectus in two national daily newspapers.

Obligations after USM entry

These are outlined in the *general undertaking* the directors are required to give to the SE after entry to the USM. They must:

(a) provide details of dividends, results, changes in capital structure, the drawing or redemption of securities, material acquisition or realisation of assets, directors' dealing in shares, changes in directors and any purchase by the company of its own shares;

(b) issue accounts within six months of the year;

(c) publish a half yearly report within six months;

(d) get shareholders' consent before issuing option or convertible loan stock;

(e) register all share transfers and issue share certificates.

The reasons for the success of the USM

Companies are attracted to the USM because:

(a) the requirements are less onerous than for full quotation;

(b) the costs are lower than for full quotation;

(c) the owners of the company do not have to part with as much of the equity as under full listing, to enter the market;

(d) it enables owners to raise cash by disposing of some of their shares;

(e) it puts a value on the shares for tax purposes;

(f) the company is able to raise cash for expansion;

(g) it provides a means of motivating employees through share-participation schemes.

Special characteristics of shares dealt on the USM and their relevance to prospective investors

(a) The USM companies include a large proportion of small companies in new, fast-growing business, including areas of new technology as well as traditional activities.

(b) The risk of failure may be higher with newer and smaller companies in new areas, hence a cautious approach is needed.

(c) The amount of equity in public hands is limited, which may affect marketability.

(d) The share prices can be more volatile.

The Third Market

The SE Rule 535 covers all possible dealing in company securities. It has four sub-sections:

535(1) — for dealing in securities listed on SEDOL, USM and Third Market.

535(2) — covers dealing in securities not listed on any market.

535(3) — deals with securities of companies engaged solely in mineral exploration.

535(4) — for securities quoted on overseas securities markets.

The Third Market is covered by Rule 535(1), and was launched on 26 January 1987 by the International Stock Exchange to provide a market for the securities of young companies and other companies which are traded off-market and for which no Stock Exchange Market previously existed. This market is primarily intended for companies incorporated in the UK (usually excluding the Isle of Man and the Channel Islands).

Third Market candidates must be:

(a) companies which have not yet begun trading, but which can demonstrate a well researched project or product which has a reasonable prospect of significant revenues within, say, 12 months;

(b) companies whose securities are traded off-market, i.e. on the Over-The-Counter market (see below) by a licensed dealer firm or a firm that has recently become a member of the SE;

(c) companies which have been trading continuously for one year and show through their annual audited accounts significant revenue flows.

(d) companies which have been established for some years but only had one year's commercial trading success, which can be demonstrated from their audited accounts; and

(e) companies whose securities are already traded off-market under SE Rule 535(3), i.e. mineral exploration companies.

A company will not normally qualify for admission to the Third Market if the following activities represent more than 10% of its profits or turnover:

(a) holding of cash or 'near-cash' assets;

(b) holding of minority interests in other companies; and

(c) holdings of or dealings in investment, property and commodities.

Admission procedures and requirements

These are simpler and less exacting than those for the other two markets covered under Rule 535(1), and are as follows.

(a) Applicant companies must be sponsored by a SE member firm. The sponsor will guide the company through the admission process and will be responsible, following admission, for supervising the production of circulars and other documents and the release of results and other significant new items, and ensuring that the ownership of the company's securities is always sufficiently well spread to permit a reasonably liquid market in its shares to be maintained. The sponsor will appoint lawyers and reporting accountants for the company.

(b) The companies and their sponsors must comply with the relevant classes of the Companies Acts and the Financial Services Act.

(c) There must be at least three directors.

(d) Applicant company must initially supply its sponsor with the following information:

  (i) a statement of its objectives and trading experience;

  (ii) either audited accounts for at least one year, or a comprehensive demonstration that the well-researched project or product will produce sufficient income in a reasonably short time;

  (iii) any recent circular to shareholders and any published capital raising documents; and

  (iv) any other data which the sponsor may consider relevant.

(e) The required documents must be lodged with Quotation Department of the SE.

(f) The company should send an appropriate circular to shareholders.

(g) The details of an company must be circulated by Extel.

On the completion of the above procedures and requirements, the Council of SE will admit the company to the Third Market, and will inform SE members that dealing may begin. Companies thus admitted might with the passage of time graduate to the USM or to a full SE quotation.

Continuing obligations of companies admitted to the Third Market

(a) To notify sponsors of any information necessary to enable share-holders and the public to appraise the position of the company;

(b) To provide a level of disclosure which the sponsors may seek and which may be additional to that required by law.

The cost of coming to the Third Market is kept down; the SE waiving the initial and annual fees and requiring only one advertisement in a national daily newspaper.

Third Market companies will usually be either Gamma or Delta stocks and dealing in them will be settled through the Talisman. Normally there will be at least two market-makers to deal in shares, but a member firm may be permitted to set up as an accredited dealer or matching broker in them. Thus the Third Market enables young companies to raise new equity capital and to have existing shares traded and settled in a properly constructed and disciplined market.

Risks to prospective investors in the Third Market companies

The risk element will be significantly higher because the information on young companies will be comparatively little to judge the quality of their management. However, broker/dealers are required under the Financial Services Act to demonstrate to the clients that an investment in the Third Market stock is suitable for their needs. Broker/dealers can neither recommend nor buy Third Market stocks unless such stock is explicity mentioned in the customer agreement letter.

Dealings under Rule 535(2)

Since the securities whose dealing is covered under this sub-section of Rule 535 are not listed on any stock exchange, they have not been subjected to the strict scrutiny and stringent listing requirements.

However, the SE, after a satisfactory result of the examination of their most recently published accounts, permits *ad hoc* transactions in their shares.

Regular dealing is not allowed. The bargains are carried by broker/dealers in the normal way but, due to the much higher risk element in investing in such shares, the broker/dealers are required to mark the Contract Notes to say that this security is not listed on any stock exchange. Nevertheless, the transactions are subject to SE rules and therefore enjoy the protection of the SE Protection Fund.

The Over-The-Counter (OTC) Market

This market is a securities market operating *outside* the SE, having no trading floor, and with deals taking place by telephone. In the UK the OTC market had grown by 1986 to comprise some 40 licensed securities dealers making a market in the securities of some 150 companies. The dealers set their own requirements for including a company in the market and there are no formal regulations, although a prospectus would be required under the Companies Acts prior to a sale to the public. Some companies in the market were sufficiently active to support two-way business but a large number of OTC stocks have very poor marketability, with dealing in them being extremely difficult, if not impossible. Prices of some of the more active stocks may be advertised by their sponsors in the press.

Following the Big Bang, licensed security dealers were eligible to become members of the SE and it was envisaged that some OTC companies might move out to the Third Market. An alternative course of action which received serious consideration was the possibility of setting up a separate 'Recognised Investment Exchange' to comply with the Financial Services Act, 1986, for the OTC firms.

The so-called '*Grey Market*' became quite active when the Bank of England, when introducing the auction system of issuing gilts, allowed trading to take place on a 'when issued', but before allocation, basis. The recent popular privatisation issues gave the dealers in this market some publicity. Several OTC firms were actively involved in the Grey Market, but which at present has shrunk to just one firm providing the Grey Market (dealing usually free of commission, but with a wider spread in the bid and offer prices) in selected securities.

Conventional and Traded Options

Options appeared on the UK investment scene in 1958. Basically, they entitle the holder to buy (call option) or sell (put option) within a fixed period of time, at a pre-arranged price, known as the exercise or striking price. Options allow the investors to take a very big position in leading shares at a very low stake. If the underlying share price does not rise above (calls) or fall below (puts) the prearranged price, the option is rendered worthless, and the optionholder loses the stake money plus dealing expenses. Options can be conventional or traded. Whereas, with conventional options, the holders can exercise this right to buy or sell the underlying shares, with traded options the holder, in addition to conventional option rights, can trade their *right* to buy or sell before the expiry date. The normal period for conventional options is three months (a period covering no more than seven settlement days after the setting up of the contract although one month options can be arranged at less cost), but the period for traded options is in series of three, six and nine months.

Conventional options

1   Call options

The *exercise price* is more or less in line with the market bid price at the time the option is bought. Call options are therefore of interest to investors who expect a *rise* in price of the underlying share during the option period.

2 Put options

The exercise price is more or less in line with the market *offer* price of the underlying share at the time the option is taken out. These options are of interest to investors who anticipate a *fall* in the share price during the option period.

3 Double options

These entitle the holders to *buy* or *sell* the underlying share depending upon which way its price moved. The exercise price is usually in line with the middle of the bid and offered prices of the underlying share. These are probably of interest to cautious investors, but they would lose out if the middle price did not move much either way, and they have to pay twice the cost of single call or put option for a double option.

The *purchase price* of the option (not to be confused with the bid, offer or offer price of the share or the option exercise price) depends on three main factors: (a) the market price (bid, offer or mid) of the share, (b) the marketability of the share, and (c) the volatility of the share. The purchase price is usually lower for a stable share and higher for one that is volatile. Normally, most option purchase prices tend to range between 5% to 15% of the share market price.

In addition to paying the option purchase price, the buyer also pays the dealing costs: broker's commission, calculated on full exercise price (not the option purchase price) plus VAT on Commission plus 0.5% stamp duty, payable if and when the option is exercised. Options are treated as cash bargains and the payment is due on the next working day after the bargain. The details are given in the Contract Note issued by the broker to the client. *The Financial Times* publishes the representative call option rates (see Practical aspects below).

Traded Options (TOs)

Like the conventional options, TOs can be either Call TOs or Put TOs. Call TOs entitle the holder to *buy* the underlying shares, or sell the right to buy them during their lifespan, quite independently of the shares to which they relate. Put TOs, similarly entitle the holder to *sell* either the underlying share, or quite independently of the shares, sell the right to sell the shares during their lifetimes. Hence the name 'traded options'.

In TOs the minimum indivisible unit in which an investor may deal is one 'Contract'; and a contract in UK shares (because of lower prices; average price is less than £5) normally represents an option on 1000 shares of the underlying security. A contract for a few British and most foreign companies, due to the high price of their shares, represents an option on 100 shares. The purchase price of a TO is known as the 'Premium', and is quoted in terms of an option of a *single* share of the underlying security, not for the Contract as a whole. Premiums are mainly determined by the market forces of supply and demand (see below). All the call TOs on a particular underlying security are known as a 'Class'. Put TOs on the same securities have a separate class. Within a class, all those options which have the same expiry date and exercise price are known as a 'Series'. The date on which the option's life ends, and therefore the last day on which the option may be exercised is known as the 'Expiry Date'. The price at which the holder is entitled to buy (call TO) or sell (put TO) the underlying security is known as the 'Exercise Price'. This price should not be confused with premium or the underlying securities market bid and offer prices.

Expiry dates are fixed at three-monthly intervals, producing three possible cycles in a year:

January–April–July–October
February–May–August–November
March–June–September–December.

The TOs on the shares of a company are introduced by the SE, and are allocated permanently to one of the above cycles, therefore their expiry dates will occur in the same months. TOs have a maximum life of nine months, so at any time of the year three of these specific expiry dates will be quoted by the broker, and will always be stated on clients' Contract Notes. For example, in January there will be BP TOs with expiry dates in April, July and October. When the April expiry date is reached April options will cease to exist and February options will be introduced, so there will then be May, August and November options available, and so on. The precise date on which TOs for a particular month will expire is announced by the SE.

Exercise prices are fixed by the SE as follows: from 50p to 140p (inclusive) at intervals of 10p, from 140p to 300p (inclusive) at intervals of 20p, from 300p to 500p (inclusive) at intervals of 30p, and above 500p the scale rises at intervals of 50p.

The rates of commission charged on TO transactions are:

Commission		*Option Money*
£1.30 per option contract and	*plus*	Up to £5000 2.5% (min. £20)
(0.75 FTSE charge)		on next £5000 1.5%
		on the excess 1.0%

The commission charged on TO transactions is higher in percentage terms than that charged on the purchase and sale of the underlying shares and on conventional option transactions. However, the sums of money involved in TO bargains are very small by comparison, therefore the overall 'dealing expenses' are substantially lower for TOs than for shares. When the exercise price of a call TO is below the current price of the underlying security, the difference between the two prices represents the 'Intrinsic Value' of the option. If the reverse is the case then the option has no intrinsic value, but has 'Time Value' until the expiry date. A call TO with intrinsic value is said to be 'In-the-Money' Option. A call TO with an exercise price above the current price of the underlying security is said to be 'Out-of-the-Money' Option. An investor who buys a TO contract makes an 'Opening Purchase' and becomes the holder of that contract. When the holder of a TO sells it in the market in order to close his position, the transaction is known as a 'Closing Sale'.

When a holder exercises his/her call TO, an 'Assignment Notice' is issued to a writer (see below) of an option contract in the same series of options, instructing the writer to deliver the underlying security to the exercisor. The actual operation of delivering the share is handled by the brokers of the two clients through the normal SE settlement system. The exercisor instructs his broker to submit an 'Exercise Notice' on the exercisor's behalf to London Options Clearing House (LOCH) – a wholly owned company of the SE. LOCH, by a computerised random selection process, will select a writer (an investor) in the same series of the underlying security and issue the writer an assignment notice. The writer is then obliged to deliver the appropriate number of the underlying security to his broker for the exercisor, and will receive in return the sum of exercise price multiplied by the number of shares, *minus* dealing expenses (see below).

Factors which cause option prices to move

1 The market price of the underlying security

Since all options give the right to purchase underlying shares, therefore a rise or fall in the share price will make the option more or less valuable respectively, and consequently the premium will rise or fall. However, the relationship between the share price and premium is not exact. For instance, if an option is very far out-of-the-money then a modest rise in share price might leave the premium unchanged.

2 Supply of the demand for options

When markets are rising, there is a greater demand for call options, but the supply of writers (investors) who are willing to write options is scarce, hence premiums rise and the options become more expensive in relation to underlying shares. The reverse happens when markets are pessimistic and falling.

3 Time value

The passage of time works in favour of the writers but against the buyers of options. Unless the share price rises above the exercise price, then the buyer of an out-of-the-money option will lose his premium at the expiry of the option's lifespan. The out-of-the-money option nearer to the exercise date will have low premiums.

4 Volatility

A share with a volatile price history will tend to outperform others when the market is rising, therefore the greater the volatility of a share the higher the premium in a rising market. However, in a falling market a volatile share will underperform others, therefore its premium will be low in bearish markets. Generally speaking, buyers of call options tend to be optimists and expect that the market will rise, and therefore are usually willing to pay higher premiums for options on volatile shares than on stable ones.

5 Dividends

Option holders, unlike shareholders, are not entitled to the dividends declared on the underlying shares. Therefore the option premium of an underlying share which is soon to go 'ex-div' will be lower than the option premium on a 'cum div.' share; this is because when a share goes ex-div, its market price falls.

6 Interest rates

When interest rates are high, call option premiums tend to increase, because the investor can take a big position in the underlying security at a comparatively small outlay, and can invest the rest of his investment capital at high rates of interest.

Writing of call options

The investor who decides to *sell* a TO which he does not already own is called 'Writer' of a TO contract. The buyer of a TO pays the premium; the writer of the option receives the premium and, in return, incurs the liability (in the case of a call option) to supply shares to a holder who exercises an option contract, on receipt of an Assignment Notice from LOCH. Normally exercise occurs only with options which are in-the-money. Just as a holder can close his/her position at any time by selling the option in the market, so can the writer of a TO close his/her position by buying it back in the market. 'Opening Sale' implies that the writer of a TO has written a TO contract. 'Closing Purchase' means that the writer of the TO contract has subsequently repurchased it in the market in order to close his position.

Dealing arrangements in the Traded Options market

1 Investors who wish to deal in the TOs market should contact a broker

for advice on dealing procedures, commissions and any 'Margins' required. Margin is the collateral which all writers (but not buyers) of TOs must lodge with the broker (see below).

2   Clients instructing brokers to deal on their behalf must give them the following information:

   (a) the number of contracts to be bought (each contract is an indivisible 1000 share unit);

   (b) the underlying security and whether the TO is call or put (known as the 'Class');

   (c) the expiry month and expiry price (known as the 'Series');

   (d) whether the order will be an open or close position (i.e. to buy or sell); and

   (e) whether it is to be entered as a Public Limit Order, either good till cancelled (GTC) or good for the day (GD). Clients can control the price at which they are prepared to purchase or sell options, if such a price cannot currently be achieved in the market. The broker is instructed to register a public limit order with the SE. The client's order will be held until cancelled or executed.

3   Writers of TOs must lodge collateral against written options with LOCH, know as the 'Margin', and may be provided in a wide variety of forms, such as ordinary shares, gilts, Treasury bills or in cash.

4   Pay option premium before 10 am on the business day following the purchase.

5   The broker will issue Contract Notes to clients with details of the bargains made.

6   The market in each option class is made by market-makers and brokers trading openly with each other between 9.05 am to 3.40 pm on the floor of SE, and no off-floor or out of hours dealings are permitted.

7   A broker with a client order will come into the market and see on the TOPIC screens the price of the underlying security, the latest premium quotations of all the option series currently listed, the premium at which the most recent bargain was done and, for each series, the prices and sizes of the Public Limit Orders.

8   Dealing is by 'open outcry' audible to the whole 'Crowd', i.e. brokers and market makers must ask for and make prices in voices which can be heard by all brokers and market-makers. Once the bargain is agreed, the TOPIC price displays are than altered to show the last trades made. Dealing slips are filled by all parties, officially time stamped and placed in special boxes around the floor. These slips are collected and their information is put into the SE bargain matching system.

9   For each class a 'Board of Officials' is responsible to the SE for the orderly conduct of trading, for ensuring that Public Limit Orders take precedence over business at the specified price and for displaying price information on the TOPIC system. At the commencement of business each

of the Board of Official personnel call over in rotation the prices of the series in each class until all possible Public Limit Orders have been executed and a trading level is established.

10 All bargains, except currency options, are registered and settled at the LOCH, which acts as a registrar for all open contracts on behalf of the SE. When a holder exercises a contract, LOCH, by a computerised random selection process, selects a writer of a contract in the same series to deliver or receive the shares. For currency options, the functions of LOCH are performed by the International Commodities Clearing House.

Currently, investors can deal in TOs on the shares of 60 large, listed companies on the SE.

Practical aspects

The effects of new technology on the equity market

The new technology connected with share dealing that was introduced as part of the Big Bang has performed according to specification, even though the number of bargains has risen from 30 000 a day to 104 000; and the system was originally designed to cope with up to 70 000 transactions a day. The SEAQ technology coped well during the week of the financial whirl-wind beginning on Monday 19 October 1987. However, enforcing the best execution rule was impossible during that week because the telephone system was jammed with calls. A new telephone system was installed to cope with the higher volume of business.

The new technology has, however, changed the nature of the business transacted; from being an *order* or *client driven market* to a *price driven market*. At its peak, 50% of the volume of trade was between different market-makers, and a sale of only 50 000 shares between nervous market-makers has been known to drive the market down!

Market-making still tends to be concentrated in the hands of old jobbing firms, even though they may now be a part of financial conglomerates. Now that the old style partnerships, with the attendant unlimited liability, have been replaced by limited liability companies, their attitude to risk has become much more relaxed. SEAQ system is going to be upgraded to allow markets to be made in transactions of up to 10 million shares at a time. Another development that has occurred is the sale of a whole institutional portfolio of shares to the market-maker offering the highest price.

One of the biggest, and perhaps unfortunate, changes resulting from the introduction of the SEAQ technology has been the loss of human contact experienced by the brokers and jobbers in the pre-Big Bang period. A screen-based dealing system means that dealers may be located anywhere and currently can be found all over London and as far away as Cardiff and

Glasgow. The lack of personal contact does sometimes present difficulties in ironing out settlement problems.

While the commission paid by institutions fell after Big Bang, they have recovered and, as in the case of private clients, are now for the most part higher than before Big Bang. What brought about this reversal was the practice by brokers with profitable new issues and placings to confine their allocation to clients who paid full, as distinct from negotiated, commissions.

The new International Stock Exchange (ISE) is currently functioning well.

Had the Big Bang and the consequent changes it caused in the structure of the SE not occurred, the ISE could easily have become a backwater dealing only in Beta, Gamma and Delta stocks while the ISE financial houses that make up the International Securities Regulatory Organization (ISRO) creamed off the trading in the Alpha and international stocks. By merging with its competitors, the SE has prevented this and the extent of the change can be seen from the composition of the membership of its standing committees, all of which now contain Japanese and American members.

The ISE is trying to remain amongst the leaders in the application of technology. The successful introduction of SEAQ was only the first step. During 1988 two new facilities may be introduced:

1 *Blox (Block Order Exposure System)*. This will display large purchase or sales orders to institutions. This large block computer dealing facility will assist the market-making process. Those with blocks of, say, £150 000 in Alpha securities and who wish to place them can enter the information on the TOPIC page and the prospective buyers can see, from bids and offers displayed, whether they would be negotiating over the telephone.

2 *SEAF (SEAQ Automatic Execution Facility)* This facility will permit automatic execution at the touch of a button in transactions up to 1000 shares at the '*touch*' or best prices shown on the yellow strip on the SEAQ screen. There will be automatic checking and feeding of the required information into 'Talisman' (see below). Since 70% of bargains are for 1000 shares or less, this will give dealers more time to concentrate on the larger more complex bargains, perhaps those displayed by BLOX. In 1989, the ISE hopes to introduce a new settlement system: TAURUS (Transfer and AUtomated Registration of Uncertified Stock). This system will reduce the flow of paper through the settlement system by allowing a book entry style of settlement of transactions.

Contract Note (C/N)

Its *contents* include: the name and address of the broker/dealer; the name of the client; the C/N number and other reference numbers; whether the transaction is a purchase or a sale; whether the broker/dealer is acting as a principal and/or agent; the bargain date; the time of the deal; the number of shares or amount of stock; the name of the security and the SEDOL (see below) number; price; consideration; commission; VAT; stamp duty; contract levy; total cost or proceeds; settlement date; the days and the amount of accrued interest (if relevant); and possibly the commission rates.

The following examples of C/Ns illustrate the cost calculations for Bought and Sold transactions.

Example 1
Bought on behalf of A, broker/dealer acting as A's *agent*:
532 Hillsdown Holdings PLC 10p ordinary shares.

	£ p
Price 348p	
Consideration	1851.36
*Commission	30.55
	£ p
VAT at 15%	4.58
Transfer stamp	9.50
Contract Levy	.80
Total	£1896.79

* Commission breakdown: £1851.36 @ 1.65%

Example 2
Bought on behalf of B, broker/dealer acting as *principal*:
700 Royal Insurance PLC 25p shares

	£ p
Price 552p	
Consideration	3864.00
*Commission	63.76
Transfer Stamp	20.00
Contract Levy	.80
Total	£3948.56

*Commission breakdown: £3864 @ 1.65%
Note: In this example the commission charge is deemed to be a 'mark up' because the broker/dealer has acted as principal and is therefore not subject to VAT, but stamp duty is charged on £3927.76, the total of consideration plus 'commission'.

Example 3
Sold on A's behalf, broker/dealer acting as A's *agent*:
5000 TSB Group PLC 25p ordinary shares

	£ p
Price 142½p	
Consideration	7125.00
*Commission	105.63
VAT at 15%	15.84
Contract Levy	.80
Total	£7002.73

Commission breakdown: £7000 @ 1.5%
£ 125 @ 0.5%

Note: No transfer stamp is payable on sold bargains.
Commission and VAT are *deducted* in sold bargains.

Example 4
Sold on A's behalf, broker/dealer acting as A's *agent*
Bargain date: 17 February 1988
For Settlement: 29 February 1988
£1 000 Hanson Trust PLC 10% Convertible Unsecured Loan Stock, 2007–12

Price £147 × d	£ p
Consideration	1470.00
Commission (minimum)	25.00
VAT at 15%	3.75
Contract Levy	.80
	£1440.45

Including – 10 days accrued interest £2.74.
Note: Accrued interest is included in the price with the days and amount shown as a separate note. As the stock is ex-dividend the calculation is minus 10 days (from the pay date 19 February to 29 February).

Value Added Tax (VAT)

VAT at the standard rate is payable on the broker/dealer's commission. If the transaction is carried out with the broker/dealer's own market-making operation or if the broker/dealer is otherwise acting as principal the commission is not subject to VAT. This is because in such cases commission is deemed by H.M. Customs and Excise to be a mark-up. In these cases where the broker/dealer is acting as principal stamp duty or SDRT (Stamp Duty Reserve Tax – see below) is charged on the full consideration including commission or mark-up. Principals sometimes show commission as a separate item and sometimes just provide a net price.

Stamp duty (or transfer Stamp)

Since 27 October 1986 stamp duty has been payable on purchases of shares, including preference shares and convertible loan stocks at the rate of 50p per £100 or part of £100 of the consideration. Purchases of gilts and most loan stocks are exempt unless it is the first transfer of the bearer instrument in the UK or another instrument is used to transfer title. Purchases by a charity are exempt from stamp duty.

Stamp Duty Reserve Tax

This tax came into effect on 27 October 1986. The rates are the same as for stamp duty. Basically, the tax applies to transactions which would be liable to stamp duty but would otherwise escape because there is no transfer form or other instrument to be stamped. These include the purchase of shares which are sold again during the same Stock Exchange account, renounceable letters of allotment or acceptance, shares registered in the name of a nominee acting for both buyer and seller, and shares resold before being transferred into the buyer's name.

The Contract Levy

The name of this levy has been changed twice. First it was called the CSI Levy, to finance the Council for Securities Industry, therefore it contributed towards shareholder protection. Its second name was PTM Levy, to finance The Panel on Takeovers and Mergers. It thus represented the contribution made by investors for the protection provided by the Panel's activities. PTM Levy was charged at 60p on all transactions of £5000 or over. Its current name is Contract Levy. From 11 January 1988 contracts with a value of over £1000 attract a levy of 80p for equities and 50p for gilts. Up to that date only bargains of over £5000 attracted this levy, which funds the Panel on Takeovers and Mergers and the Securities and Investment Board.

The Stock Exchange Account and Settlement System

The SE year is divided into a series of Accounts which are usually of two weeks duration, with occasional Accounts of approximately three weeks at holiday times. All non-cash transactions are due for settlement on Account Day, which is the second Monday after the end of the Account. Dealing for the next Account is allowed on the last two days of an Account. Such deals are said to be for the *new Account* or for *new time*.

Sales or repurchases following a purchase or sale in the same Account period are known as closing bargains. Such bargains, at the discretion of broker/dealer, may be free of commission charges. Similar transactions in gilt-edged securities within 28 days are considered closing bargains and may, at the discretion of the dealer/broker, be free of commission charges. The transfer and settlement procedure begins when the stock is transferred from the seller by means of a Talisman sold transfer form into Sepon, who act as trustees of the stock for the seller until the Account or Settlement Day, and for the purchases thereafter. The Talisman Centre keeps separate accounts for each market-maker. On Account Day the buyer pays the broker/dealer. On the same day the Talisman Centre transfers the stock into the market maker's buying account and the selling broker/dealer receives payment from the Talisman Centre on the market-maker's behalf.

Registration details of the purchase will have been lodged with the Centre before the Account Day, and the stock is then transferred out of Sepon's name into the purchaser's name by means of a Talisman bought-transfer. When this transfer is registered legal title passes to the purchaser. The company registrar prepares a certificate in the purchaser's name and this is forwarded in due course via the centre and broker/dealer to the purchaser, who does *not* sign a transfer form.

Conventional Options

Example: Call option
Suppose X, an investor, has £2000 to invest. X anticipates that the price Y PLC share will rise from its current *bid* price of 100p to 150p in the near future. The 3-month exercise price is 100p and the option purchase price is 20p. X can:

(1) Buy outright 2000 shares with his £2000.
(2) Take out a call option on £2000 shares for £400, (ignoring costs) and invest the balance £1600 at, say, 6% for three months.
(3) Take a very big position in Y shares by taking out a call option in 10000 shares by staking his £2000.

Suppose:

(a) Y share bid price *rises* to 150p, as X anticipated:
Under (a) X makes a realisable profit of £1000 (2000 × .50)
Under (b) X makes a realisable profit of £600 (£1000 − £400) by exercising the option *plus* interest £24 (6% for three months on £1600). X may retain the shares in expectation of a further rise in price; should it *not* happen X has to pay out £2000 to take up shares.
Under (c) makes a realisable profit of £3000 (by calling 10 000 shares and selling them at 50p per share *less* £2000 option price). Under (a) and (b), X may retain the shares in expectation of a further rise in price. Under (c), to retain 10 000 shares X would need an additional sum of £10 000.
(b) Y share bid price in fact *falls* to, say, 50p:
Under (a), X makes a realisable loss £1000, or X may retain his purchase of 2000 shares in the hope of recovery in the bid price.
Under (b), X loses £400, by not exercising the call option, *less* £24 interest.
Under (c), X loses the £2000 option purchase price.

If X anticipated a *fall* in the *offer* price, other things remaining the same, X can take out a *put* option, and the calculations will show profit or loss in each case.

If X took out a *double* option, then the realisable profit will be *reduced* by the double option price cost and the loss will be *increased* by the double option price cost.

Traded options

Example: Traded Call Option
Shares of Y PLC stand at 290p. X, the investor, anticipate that the shares are likely to rise in a few weeks. X buys a call option contract in Y PLC January 300 series. X's broker carries out X's instructions at, say, 14p. Ignoring dealing expenses, the cost to X is £140 (1000 shares × 14p). Before the expiry date, Y PLC share price rises to 320p, therefore the option would also rise, perhaps to, say, 28p. X sells the option contract for a 100% profit without ever actually owning the underlying shares. X can of course acquire Y PLC shares by exercising his option, by instructing his broker to issue an 'Exercise Notice' and the share will be delivered to him in return for payment of the exercise price of the option *plus* the appropriate dealing expenses.

Intrinsic Value and Time Value

Example:
Suppose the Table of Z PLC option prices at the beginning of November is as follows:

Z *PLC*: Share price 254p   Option Price (p)

Exercise Price (p)	January	April	July
240	30	38	42
260	17	23	27
280	8	13	17
300	2	8	11

Option purchase price = 28p

With January 240 option, Z PLC shares are worth 14p (254p − 240p). The 14p represents the *Intrinsic Value* of the Option. The balance of 14p (28p − 14p) is the *Time Value*, and represents the amount which buyers are prepared to pay in the hope that the share price will rise during the next three months. With July 240 options, the premium is 42p, and the intrinsic value is 14p (254p − 240p), as it is in January 240 option, but the time value is 26p (40p − 14p), much higher than in January 240 options. This is due to the fact that the July options have a life of nine months ahead of them, and the chances of share prices rising substantially during nine months are correspondingly greater. With January, July and April 260 option, there is no intrinsic value because the exercise price is 4p higher than the market price of Z PLC shares (260p − 254p). Therefore the premiums of 17p, 23p and 27p represent purely time value which progressively grows larger as the lifespan of the option increases.

Writing of call TOs

An investor is attracted to write call options on a share when he/she anticipates that the share price will fall or remain unchanged.

Example

Suppose A holds 4000 Z PLC shares which are currently priced at 295p, and
carry a premium of 20p per share. A feels certain that Z shares are unlikely
to rise in price for sometime. A writes 4 contracts on Z shares, costing £800
(ignoring dealing expenses). Exercise price = 300p

Assuming that A does not close his option position by a closing purchase,
there are three possible outcomes for A:

1   The share price rises to 300p and the holders exercise their options. A
will receive 320p (exercise price 300p plus 20p premium) against the current
price of 295p: a gain of £200.

2   At the expiry date the share price is 297p. Option holders are unlikely
to exercise their options, and A therefore will make a pure profit of £800
(20p per share on 4000 shares).

3   The share price falls to 280p, A will still make a pure profit of £200 (20p
premium less (295p − 280p) = 5p on 4000 shares). However, if the share
price falls to 270p, A will suffer a loss of £200 (295p less 20p premium =
275p − 270p = 5p per share on 4000 shares), but A will still be better off
than if he had held the shares without writing the options; a paper loss of
£1000 (295p less 270p × 4000 shares).

If the Z share price rises to say 340p than A will suffer a loss of £800
(340p less 300p + 20p = 20p per share on 4000 shares). A's profit will be
reduced, penny for penny, by any rise in the share price above 300p exercise
price and, above 320p A will be facing a pure loss, assuming A has written
the 4 contracts without owning 4000 Z shares.

Margin on written options which must be lodged by option writers

Formula for calculating the margin:

20% of the value of the underlying security *plus* the amount by which the
option is in-the-money, *or minus* the amount by which the option is out-of-
the-money.

Example:

Suppose:

A has written 5 contracts in Z shares

Z shares stand at 300p and there is an out-of-the-money element of 5p per
share.

Margin Calculation:

20% of 300p	=	60p
less Out-of-the-money element	=	10p
Margin required	=	50p
Margin per contract 50p × 1000	=	£500
Margin for five contracts 5 × £500	=	£2500

A must lodge £2500 through his/her broker in cash or in ordinary shares and other acceptable assets. Margins are recalculated daily, and A may be required to lodge margin in excess of £2500.

Selected questions

The de-regulation of the London Stock Exchange in 1986 introduced major changes in the market-making and dealing systems for securities. The questions asked in this topic of the CIB Investment syllabus require up-to-date knowledge of the new system, especially with regard to market-making and dealing in equities and gilts. Briefly answer the following questions before comparing your answers with those given below.

Q1 The revolution in the Stock Exchange in London, sometimes known as the 'Big Bang', has been discussed at length in the financial press. Describe the main changes proposed to the rules and regulations and outline how these changes are likely to affect the operations of the Stock Exchange in London.

Q2 In April 1978 the Stock Exchange introduced a new type of option, known as the traded option. What are 'traded options' and how do they work?

Q3 Write short notes on three of the following:
   (a) ex-dividend and cum-dividend;
   (b) marking names;
   (c) buying in and selling out;
   (d) the Stock Exchange account system.

Q4 (a) A customer asks you to instruct a firm of stockbrokers to purchase 1000 British Petroleum 25p ordinary shares on his behalf. The shares are purchased at 325p. Outline the Stock Exchange procedure by which the shares are paid for and transferred into your customer's name.

   (b) What are the essential differences from a shareholder's point of view between holding registered shares in a company and holding bearer shares?

Brief answers

A1 *Main changes proposed to the Stock Exchange (SE) rules and regulations:*

- Outside groups should be allowed to own 100% of the SE broking and jobbing member firms in which they have already acquired interests.
- Single capacity dealing system should end and be replaced by a dual capacity dealing system.
- Fixed commissions should become negotiable.
- A Competing Market-Maker System for dealing in equities required.
- To open membership of SE to those who wish to deal in gilt-edged securities. To produce flexibility and close control by the SE and the Bank of England, four types of member firms to be involved in the gilt market: broker/dealers; market-makers; inter-dealer brokers; money brokers.
- More and rigorous regard to investor protection.

The effect of these proposed changes on the operations of SE:

- Issue of rules on conflicts of investment advice and agency broking, principal fund management, market making, corporate finance, underwriting and banking. Compulsory disclosure of internal barriers between areas of activity which could cause a potential conflict of interest.
- The Compensation Fund, with certain modifications, to continue.
- A more flexible exemption policy for qualifications of SE membership.
- Acceptance of the creation of Securities Investment Board, under a new Financial Services Act.
- Acceptance of the 'Big Bang' day on 27 October 1986.

A2 *Traded Options (TOs) are of two types:*

- 'Calls' (COs) give the holder the right to *buy*, and 'Puts' (POs) to *sell* linked shares.
- Both COs and POs can be sold independently of the linked shares, during their lifespan.
- All COs on a particular security are a 'Class'; POs on the same security form a separate class.
- The life of an option ends on its 'expiry date' – the last day on which it can be exercised.
- Within a class, all options with the same expiry date and 'exercise price' are known as a 'Series'. Expiry dates are fixed at three-monthly intervals.
- The price at which a CO holder has the right to buy (a PO holder, to sell) is called the 'exercise price', and is fixed by the Stock Exchange.
- TOs minimum unit of trading is 1000 shares, called a 'contract'.
- The price at which a TO can be bought is called the 'premium', determined by market forces.

A Call Option transaction

- Suppose, at the beginning of May, Company X shares stand at 290p.
- Exercise price is 300p.
- Y, an investor, expects them to rise over the next few weeks.
- Y buys one July 300 call option contract at, say, 14p (£140) from his broker.

- Y now has the right to buy 1000 X shares at 300p each at anytime until expiry date in July.
- Y does not have to exercise his CO; he can trade it if X share price rises above 300p, and take the gain.
- Suppose X share price rises to 320p before expiry date, the premium will also rise to, say, 28p, and Y could then sell the CO contract for a 100% profit, less dealing costs, without ever actually owning X shares. Of course, Y can buy X shares at 14p and hold them, by instructing the broker to issue an 'Exercise Notice', and 1000 X share certificate will be delivered to Y in return for payment of exercise price (£140) *plus* the appropriate dealing expenses.
- If X share price does not rise beyond 300p, Y will lose the premium *plus* costs.
- When exercise price is below the underlying share price, Y is 'In-the-Money'. If the reverse is the case, Y is 'Out-of-the-Money'.
- A Put Option transaction works largely in the same way, except that Y *sells*.

A3 (a) *Ex-dividend and cum-dividend (Ex-div. and cum-div.)*

- A company pays dividends to its shareholders who are registered on the *record* date, i.e. when its books are closed.
- The SE appoints a date, sometime before the dividend payment date, when shares go ex-dividend. Xd date is first day of the two-week Account.
- On the Xd day, share price will fall to adjust; investors buying shares on or after Xd date are *not* entitled to dividend; which is retained by the seller.
- Share sold before Xd date, are 'Cum-div'; buyer, not seller, is entitled to dividend.
- Record Date is the company's concern, Xd date (usually before Record Date) is SE's concern.
- Government's gilt stocks are normally dealt on cash basis, therefore are quoted ex-div. on the day books are closed, i.e. the record date and the Xd date are the same. Exceptions: 37 days (or the next business day) before the interest payment date. 'Mediums' and 'longs' (other than War Loan) may also be dealt in 'Special ex-div.' during the three weeks before the ex-div. date.

(b) *Marking names*

- To reduce time and cost in dealing with US and Canadian securities held in the UK, it is customary for them to be registered in the name of an institution recognised by the SE, and endorsed in blank. These institutions are known as recognised 'Marking names'.
- Dividends are paid to them and must be claimed by the owner.
- Share registered in good marking names command a higher price than those in individual's name.

(c) *Buying-in and Selling-out*

- If the purchaser of a security cannot obtain delivery he may apply to the Buying-in and Selling-out Department of the SE which will attempt to buy an equivalent amount of security. The original deal will be cancelled and the seller will pay the difference.
- Selling-out occurs when no name is received for delivery and settlement, and only applies to non-Talisman securities.

(d) *The Stock Exchange account system*

- The SE year is divided into a series of Accounts which are normally of two-week duration, with occasional Accounts of approximately three weeks at holiday times.
- All non-cash transactions are due for settlement on Account Day, which is the second Monday after the end of the Account. Dealing for the next Account is allowed on the last two days of an Account.

A4 (a) *Transfer procedure*

- Stock transferred from vendor via Talisman Transfer Form into Sepon Ltd.
- Stock registered by BP in the name of Sepon, as trustee of the stock for seller till Account Day, and of the purchaser thereafter.
- Talisman Centre (TC) keeps accounts for each dealer in equities.
- Registration details of the purchaser lodged with TC before Account Day.
- On Account Day, purchaser pays the broker.
- The same day stock transferred by TC into dealer's buying account, and the selling broker receives payment from TC on the dealer's behalf.
- Stock transferred out of Sepon's name into purchaser's name via a Talisman bought transfer.
- When this transfer is registered the legal title passes to purchaser.
- BP registrar prepares share certificate in purchaser's name, and forwards it throught TC.

(b) *Essential difference between holding registered shares in a company and holding bearer shares from shareholders' point of view*

- With registered shares – ownership is recorded in the company's register and is transformed by means of a transfer form (not necessarily via the Stock Exchange) which incurs stamp duty; dividends are paid direct to shareholder or to his bank account; company reports, notices of meetings, rights and slip issues are sent direct. If share certificate is lost, a duplicate can be obtained.
- With bearer shares – the name of the shareholder is not recorded in the company register, ownership passes by mere delivery of the certificate (therefore greater risk of loss), there is no transfer form therefore no transfer duty, although transfer duty is paid on the original issue of share. Dividends are collected by delivering coupons to a paying agent and it is necessary to watch the press for announcements of dividends, new issues, meetings and company reports.

Specially selected question

1 Outline the market-making and dealing systems for securities quoted on the London Stock Exchange following de-regulation ('The Big Bang').
2 What changes have taken place in the London Stock Exchange's rules and regulations affecting buying and selling costs? Explain how these changes affect both the personal investor and the institutional investor.

Model answer

1 *Equities:*
The traditional single capacity system has been replaced by a dual capacity system. This system is known as the Competing Market-Maker system, and is modelled on the lines of the United States National Association of Securities Dealers Automated Quotations System (NASDAQ). The CMM system ensures considerable flexibility in moving from single to dual capacity. For example, broker/dealers can combine functions of brokers and jobbers or continue to act in one capacity, i.e. acting as either agency brokers representing clients in the markets or principals, buying and selling shares on their own account. Broker/dealers are also permitted to register as market-makers committed to making firm buying and selling prices at all times in shares in which they have chosen to deal. Market makers display their prices through the Stock Exchange Automated Quotations system (SEAQ). For purposes of display on SEAQ the 3800 (approximately) securities traded on the Stock Exchange are divided into four separate categories, Alpha, Beta, Gamma and Delta, according to the level of investor interest in the share and hence the level of information which is required to be displayed on the SEAQ system to serve the needs of the market. Nearly 95% of business is now conducted off-floor over the telephone on the basis of quotes displayed on the Exchange's own Teletext Output of Price Information Computer system (TOPIC) network. Broker/dealers can competitively deal in shares in which they do not act as market makers.
Gilts The Bank of England, instead of dealing with the seven jobbers who formerly dealt in gilts, now deals with 22 Stock Exchange member firms as its nominated Gilt-edged Market Makers (GEMMs). A GEMM's must make continuous and effective two-way prices, on demand to other Stock Exchange member firms and to outside investors known directly to it. The gilt market works on 'cash' settlement, and the GEMMs' task of ensuring next day delivery of the stock is eased by the existence of Stock Exchange Money Brokers (SEMBs). SEMBs arrange for GEMMs to 'borrow' stock to satisfy immediate demands, to be repaid at a later date.
In today's gilt-edged market there is another specialist category of firm, the Inter-Dealer Broker (IDB). If a GEMM finds itself holding an uncomfortably large amount of a particular stock that another GEMM is

desperate to buy, but neither is willing to 'expose its book' by publicly acknowledging its position, then IDBs offer them the ability to 'unwind' their positions anonymously, by posting bids and offers for large amounts of stock on the IDB dealing screens.

The Bank of England will continue to issue gilt stocks by tender and tap methods, particularly the tap method. A third method of issuing gilts, the auction method, was tried for a few months. The experiment however was not very successful, and was put in abeyance.

2   The fixed commissions have been replaced by negotiated commissions which are subject to competition. Large institutions can negotiate fees as low as 0.2% dependent upon the size of guaranteed business. The stamp duty has been haived by the government to 0.5%. VAT on commission is payable. In fact, in house market-makers might not charge commission by quoting an all-in price, so the VAT will not be payable.

Most banks have negotiated special rates and share of commission. Rates already vary for small investors, either the same as before (1.65%) or slightly cheaper. Minimum commission is generally higher (say £20) than before. Cheaper dealing services are available but these offer no advice.

Since January 1988 contracts with a value of over £1000 will attract a Contract Levy of 80p for equities and 50p for gilts. Up till then bargains of over £5000 had attracted this levy and only on equity bargains. The money raised from this levy goes towards financing the Panel on Takeovers and Mergers and the Securities Investment Board.

Market-makers make turn on bid and offer prices, and can afford low commission rates on high turnovers, therefore overall costs ought to be lower for larger investors. Additional services such as research might have to be charged separately.

The small investors, it seems, are facing more problems since the 'Big Bang', and a number of firms who had previously publicised cheap 'no frills' dealing costs are having to revise or withdraw their terms.

Updating

The three main sources of updating this topic are: the material available from the information section of the Stock Exchange, the financial press and the CIB chief *examiners' reports*. The 'Signpost' articles in *Banking World* are also very helpful in this connection. You will need to be very alert to pick out changes as they occur, as the Big Bang changes and the Financial Services Act become fully operational.

7 Practice of investment (I) Investment considerations and ratios

Syllabus coverage

Considerations:
  Safety
  Liquidity
  Marketability
  Flexibility
  Risks and returns.
Factors affecting movements in security prices
Analysis and assessment of company securities:
  Corporate debt and interest cover
  Dividends and earning yields
  P/E ratios
  Dividend cover
  Priority percentages.
Company affairs:
  Financial and operational gearing
  Cash flow
  Net asset value
  Quality of management
  Economic and other factors affecting company affairs
Technical analysis of company affairs:
  Charts
  Filters etc.
Corporation Tax
Advance Corporation Tax and the investors

Introduction

The sellers of investment products, like sellers of any other products, package and promote their products, within the confines of the law, in such a way as to create the maximum impact on the potential buyers, i.e. the investing public. Although most investment products have prominently emphasised benefits for the investors, most of them have drawbacks too –

indeed, under certain circumstances outright disadvantages. While investment planning is a subjective issue, nevertheless investment practice provides certain objective criteria, which may be used to examine the benefits and drawbacks to establish the suitability or otherwise of various investment products on sale.

In this and the next two chapters we shall study the main objective criteria of investment practice, with a view to their usage as the tools of investment as bases for comparison among different investment products, and investment portfolio construction.

In this chapter we shall look at the investment considerations and ratios criteria in connection mainly with company securities.

Theoretical aspects

Investment considerations

The two *basic* objectives of all investments are: increase in capital invested and/or increase in income from the invested capital. However the satisfactory achievement of these objectives presupposes, for almost all investors, the presence of *wider*, nonetheless crucial, investment considerations, viz: *safety* of capital and income; availability of *liquid* funds to meet urgent and unforseen expenditures; the ease with which the investment products can be *marketed*, i.e. cashed; the *flexibility* in increasing, decreasing and switching investments, at no or negligible cost; and the *rates* of *return* provided by investment products and whether these returns would retain their purchasing power.

1   Safety

Safety of investment is a vital consideration, but for low income households and most pensioners it is an absolute necessity. Safety, by and large, depends on the creditworthiness of the investment-taking institutions. For instance, there's not much likelihood of the UK government defaulting on its debt obligations, therefore investment in gilts and National Savings products, both in terms of repayment of capital and the levels of returns they produce, can be considered absolutely safe, and may be used as a standard for measuring safety in investment products of other financial institutions. However, not all investments, even in gilts and National Savings products, provide safety against the inflationary loss in value in real terms, in both capital and income, and against a rise in the level of interest rates.

Next on the safety ladder are the fixed interest investments with local authorities, public corporations, banks, building societies and insurance companies. The unitised investments, e.g. unit trusts, unit-linked life insurance and pension schemes, are mainly in the shares of private sector companies, therefore the value of the units can go up or down in line with the stock market fluctuations. Hence the safety element in unitised investments is relative. The same is true with the products of investment trusts. However, the safety element in unitised and investment trust investments is greater than in the direct investment in shares of quoted companies because, unlike direct investment in individual company shares, unitised and investment trust investments are diversified over a wide range of companies in different sectors of the economy, which means that the risk to safety is widely spread too and therefore minimised. Speculative investments have the least degree of safety of capital and income, and these should be avoided by investors who cannot afford the loss of capital and/or income.

2 Liquidity

A liquid investment can be converted into cash without delay, difficulty and no, or negligible, financial loss. There is a liquidity spectrum on which, at the one end, there are absolutely liquid financial assets, such as sight and other instantly withdrawable deposits, with no risk of financial loss, with banks and building societies. And at the other extreme, there are highly illiquid investments, such as investments in property, chattels and fixed long-term investments: it is both difficult and costly to encash such investments. In between these two extremes of liquid and illiquid investments, there are other investments with varying degree of liquidity, such as 7-day, 30-day, 90-day notice deposits with banks' and building societies, which may be withdrawn without notice but by accepting the loss of interest on the amount withdrawn in lieu of the notice period. Investments in the stocks and shares of blue chip companies and gilts can be encashed fairly easily but involve dealing and other costs. Unit trust investments may be withdrawn without dealing costs. Except for the cash investments, the timing of encashments is important. If an investment, especially a longer term investment, is encashed at the wrong time – when its market price is low, or when better prospects are on the horizon, assuming of course that its liquidation is possible – a sizeable loss may be incurred. A part of any investor's portfolio should be in liquid investments – in bank or building society short notice deposit accounts – otherwise the investor would find it difficult and costly to meet urgent unforseen contingencies. Borrowing is an alternative to encashing investments, but borrowing involves interest payment costs.

What proportion of a portfolio should be in cash investments would depend on each investor's security of income and employment, immediate commitment and his/her own view of the markets for different types of longer term investments. The important point is that each portfolio should have an *adequate* liquidity cushion.

3 Marketability

This investment consideration is allied to liquidity consideration. Marketability of an investment asset implies the ease with which its holder can obtain the highest price for it that any buyer is willing to pay. This is basically dependent on the efficiency of the market organisation and information dissemination, the largeness of supply of the asset, the level of transaction costs, the number of investors wishing to buy and sell it during any given period of time, and a low degree of uncertainty attaching to the price of the asset.

Broadly speaking, if the above elements are present then the marketability of the investment product will be good and the transaction costs in finding the highest bidder for the asset will be small. Conversely, the absence of the above market elements will result in a narrow marketability and therefore higher transaction costs.

Viewed from the above criteria, the Stock Exchange in the UK is highly organised, and much of the UK financial press, especially *The Financial Times*, provides excellent information dissemination on gilts, quoted company shares and stocks, unit trusts, overseas securities and insurance investment products.

The need for marketability arises from the need for liquidity, not only to meet a contingency but also, perhaps, to realise funds so as to place them in a more beneficial investment when it is thought correct to do so.

4 Flexibility

Flexibility has two meanings:

(a) Investors *can* readily dispose of their holding of investments when they so wish, i.e. their capital is not 'locked-in' for specific periods, as it might be if they held fixed term bonds and certificates of local authorities, private companies, insurance companies, banks and building societies, and National Savings and the central government.

(b) The investors *can* increase or decrease their investment in an investment product, and *can* also switch between various products of the same financial institution. Flexible endowment policies permit repayment to investors at the end of the part of the term (say 10 years for a 20 year policy), or the investors may continue investing until the end of the term. Flexible pension plans offered by some companies allow investors to vary the amount of contribution each year to some extent and to miss contributions (up to a limit) without penalty. Regular savings schemes offered by some unit trusts, banks, building societies and other institutions also permit the same kind of flexibility. Unit and investment trusts allow switching, in some cases free of cost, between various products within the same fund.

5 Risks

Risk in investment is uncertainty, present to some degree, for one reason or another, in most types of investment. It concerns the future behaviour of a share or portfolio. An objective measure of risk is *variability in price*. The greater variability of return on a particular share or portfolio, provided that investment decisions are sensibly made, may produce greater profitability, otherwise it would not attract investors. Variability can be of two types.

(a) *Market variability (or risk)* This is the variability in the rate of return of a share or portfolio caused by the fluctuations on the stock market. The extent to which a share or portfolio is sensitive to upward and downward movements in the market determines whether it is an 'aggressive' or 'defensive' share or portfolio. The greater the degree of independence from the market fluctuations the more defensive the investment or portfolio will be.

(b) *Residual variability (risk)* This is the variability of the share or portfolio independent of any stock market changes. Whereas the residual risk can be eliminated by diversification (swings and roundabouts), market risk cannot be eliminated by diversification and therefore has to be compensated through increased return. Hence the greater the market risk in an investment the more profitable, on average, it could prove to be: the high risk/high reward ratio syndrome. Risk in investment can also be classified in other ways.

A (i) *General risks*

These result from adverse movements in interest rates, inflation rate, currency rates and political conditions. They are called 'general risks' because they affect, to a greater or lesser degree, all sectors of the business world.

(ii) *Specific risks*

These relate to:

- a particular *sector* of business, and result for example from adverse movements in demand for that sector's products, due to successful foreign competition against domestic goods, rising operating and production costs;
- an individual *company*, and result from falling profits, inefficient management, lost contracts and takeover bids.

B An *individual company's risks* may be further subdivided:

(i) *Business risks*

These arise from changes

- in demand, mainly caused by changes in tastes, competitors' lower cost, new products, recession or
- in supply, chiefly caused by new methods of production, rising labour and raw material costs.

Business risks may be reduced by a company via diversification of business activity.

(ii) *Financial risks*

These are associated with a company's main affairs:

- *gearing ratio* – this ratio measures the proportion of the company's long-term borrowed funds to its overall capital. A high gearing ratio makes the earnings available to shareholders much more volatile (see Practical aspects, below).
- *liquidity* – this ratio measures the proportion of the company's short-term ('current') assets to its liabilities. It gives an indication of the liquidity available to meet current commitments (see below).

  The more highly geared and the more illiquid the company, the greater the financial risks to investors, causing fluctuations in shareholders' returns and to probability of liquidation of the company.
- *risk and safety* – the 'risk' and 'safety' as investment considerations are inter-related: risk avoidance increases safety. There are two kinds of risk in this connection:

Investors' capital which may suffer short-term fluctuations in values, and may be lost in part or altogether.

Investors' income which may not be paid, or may at least be unreliable. Income risk may also point to capital risk: the company which has difficulties in paying interest and dividends is most probably incurring losses, which may threaten the capital invested in it.

Risk avoidance is an important and underlying theme of all sound and stable investment practice. Although some investors are happy to accept a high risk/high reward ratio, most other investors would probably wish to *control risk exposure* to their portfolio by taking the following steps:

- Maintain adequate liquidity in their portfolio to meet expected and unexpected contingencies without having to sell or cash in illiquid investments, or to borrow.
- Ensure appropriate diversification, either through direct investment or, in the case of small investors, via unit and investment trust products, to spread the risk.
- Watch for the major changes in the direction of price movements, and buy investments as near to the bottom of the market as possible and sell as near the top of the market as possible. 'Take the gain, and cut the losses' is a sound investment principle.
- Hold high risk/high reward investments only up to such a percentage of the total portfolio as can be lost, if things go wrong completely, without causing financial difficulties.
- Keep a balance between investments in equities and fixed interest securities, to mitigate risks arising from falling stock market prices or changing interest rates.
- In times of rising inflation rate, other things being equal, ensure adequate index-linked investments in the portfolio.

- Avoid investment dependence upon the fortunes of a single country, a single industry or a single currency.
- Buy shares of companies which are involved in relatively stable industries (e.g. food industry vs drilling for oil), and of companies that have adequate liquidity and are not too highly geared.

6   Returns

Just as workers are worthy of their hire, so too are investors worthy of returns on their investments. Investment returns related to both capital and income are rewards for taking risk and for parting with liquidity, therefore returns must be commensurate with the level of risk undertaken and the length of the loss of liquidity. If this were not the case, many people would not bother to invest. Returns in the hands of investors are significantly influenced by (a) whether they are taxed (and at what rate) or are taxfree, and (b) how often they are received (monthly, quarterly, half-yearly, yearly or at the end of a specific term). Obviously tax-free, frequently received returns are the most effective inducements for the investing public.

If neither the equity nor the fixed-interest markets appear attractive (as when the yield curve is downward sloping), cash investments provide a high return compared with other investments. By 'going liquid', to a large degree at such times, personal investors would be ready and able to opt for higher returns when the equity and/or fixed-interest markets show definite signs of becoming attractive.

Factors affecting movements in security prices

The following factors affect the *whole* securities market. Although the factors affecting security prices have been separately identified below, these factors *interact* to produce movement in prices.

The rate of inflation

The rate of inflation has direct and indirect effects on security prices.

1   Direct effects

If the rate of inflation exceeds both the interest yield and redemption yield of fixed interest securities, then the real return on these securities, i.e. the inflation rate *minus* the interest yield, or the yield to redemption, is negative. This will cause the demand, and therefore prices, of fixed interest securities, to fall. Index-linking of the fixed interest securities will protect their purchasing power against the influence of inflation. The falling inflation rate causes fixed interest securities to yield a high real rate of return, leading to an increase both in their demand and prices.

An outward sign of inflation in the economy is an increase in the general price level. A general rise in prices tends to increase the the profitability of companies, leading to increased rates of dividend being distributed. This makes investment in shares attractive, causing the share prices to rise generally. Since the unitised investments tend to have shares mainly as their underlying assets, the bid and offer prices of units rise.

2 Indirect effects

Rising inflation increasingly undermines the confidence in money, leading to increase in wages, unemployment and, if the domestic inflation rate is higher than the inflation rates in countries of the trading partners, may create a balance of payments deficit. To counter this, the government may introduce deflationary monetary and fiscal measures, such as higher interest rates, higher taxes, reduction in public spending. Rising interest rates and falling demand will reduce the rates of return from both the existing fixed interest securities and equity, causing their demand and therefore their prices, to fall. Direct and indirect effects of inflation can appear to be contradictory and the interactive effect depends on the way inflation starts.

Interest rates

An increase (or decrease) in the interest rates causes capital loss (or gain) in the value of *existing* fixed interest securities. Thus the market prices of existing fixed interest securities are inversely related to the level of interest rates. High interest rates increase the demand, therefore prices, of *new* fixed interest securities.

High interest rates increase borrowing costs of companies and may reduce demand for their products. Company profitability, and therefore dividends, tend to fall, causing a fall in share prices. Low interest rates tend to increase share prices.

Government controls

If the government is unsympathetic towards investors, it may take measures to reduce investment incomes. For example, it may raise the corporation tax on company profits, particularly when profits are rising, and thereby reduce the ability of companies to distribute higher rate dividends. This will depress the demand, therefore prices, of company shares. The government may put ceilings on interest rates, thereby reducing the interest yield and capital gain on fixed interest securities and causing their price to fall. The nationalisation of private industry will exclude the private shareholders' opportunity to earn dividends.

Political events at home and abroad:

The 'privatisation' process in the UK during the 1980s by creating opportunities of quick and fairly certain gains (although there have been exceptions), has stimulated wider share ownership generally, giving a boost to the share prices as a whole. The reduction of income and corporation taxes, coupled with the reduction in public sector borrowing, has released very large supplies of cash to the private sector, much of which has gone towards making the industry and commerce more profitable which in turn increased the demand for stocks and shares.

OPEC (the Organisation of Petroleum Exporting Countries) by restricting the supply of oil during the 1970s, caused the oil prices to rise to very high levels, thus boosting the incomes of oil-producing companies and consequently increasing the demand and price of their shares; whereas the oil-using industries suffered a recession, and the prices of their securities fell. In 1987, the precarious position of the US economy – massive domestic budget and international trade deficits – and the genuine fears of a world-wide economic slump if the US administration opted for a protectionist policy, led to 'Black Monday' on 19 October, when the world stock markets fell by around 40% in a couple of days. The prices of company securities across the board fell heavily. However, gilt prices rose as the investors ran for cover under the safe and fixed interest return of gilts.

The political risks in some countries are greater than in others. Some countries, their governments spurred by nationalistic fervour, may legislate against non-resident investors, use tax policies to the detriment of overseas investors, manipulate exchange rates to the disadvantage of foreign capital and nationalise or confiscate foreign companies and their assets. These considerations are bound to affect the security prices of some overseas investments.

Taxation changes

Any change in taxation, whether on corporate or personal incomes and gains, which leaves more of the investment income and gain in the hands of investors is bound to increase demand, therefore prices, of all better quality investments, be they government stocks or private sector companies' stocks and shares.

General uncertainty

When people perceive a rising tide of general uncertainty, political and economic, they tend to encash their investments. People feel more secure with cash-in-hand than with even the most remunerative investments in times of acute general uncertainty. Thus political and economic uncertainty depress security prices in general.

Levels of unemployment

A high level of employment in a country broadly means that there is a greater amount of spending and saving activity by the public. Higher spending by the public increases the profitability of companies and leads to greater demand and higher prices of company shares. Increased savings can result in increased investment of all types, which will raise all security prices. A low level of investment will imply the opposite and hence can result in lower security prices.

The level of money supply

The rate of increase in the money supply and the level of interest rates are closely connected. Amongst various views in this connection, the monetarists believe that increases in money supply will increase expenditure, some of the new money being used to buy goods and services, which increases expenditure directly, and some being invested in safe securities, such as first-class fixed-interest bonds, which increases expenditure indirectly. Increased purchase of bonds increase the market prices of bonds but lower interest rates (the level of interest rates is inversely related to the level of fixed interest securities); lower interest rates increase capital investments and consumption expenditure. A larger than expected increase in money supply figures tends to increase bond prices due to lower interest rates, and therefore higher returns on existing fixed interest securities.

The balance of payments position

A rising balance of payments surplus points to a healthy domestic economy which, in turn, implies *lower* inflation rate, interest rates and costs of production and *higher* industrial growth and output rate – as compared to the similar aspects in the economies of the trading partners. A strong balance of payments position is therefore associated with high bond and share prices. On the other hand, a weak balance of payments position, categorised by the increasing deficits, often leads to the introduction of deflationary policies by the authorities to correct the balance of payments position. Deflationary policies (higher interest and taxation rates, lower government expenditure) cause lower profitability in the company sector, and hence cause a fall in the bond and share prices.

The following special factors affect the prices of the existing securities of *specific* companies. However, all the separately identified factors below *interact* to produce movements in prices.

The exchange rate

A fall in the external exchange value of the domestic currency means that one unit of a foreign currency will buy more of the domestic currency, and therefore more of the domestic products priced in terms of domestic currency. Hence the demand for domestic goods will increase abroad. Those domestic companies which can benefit from the competitive price advantage by selling more abroad either directly or through their overseas subsidiaries will find that their profitability and their share prices will rise. On the other hand, those domestic companies which depend heavily for their profits upon imported goods or raw materials will find that their profitability and share prices will fall. Bond prices may also fall in the anticipation of higher yields, due to high interest rates, required to defend a weaker currency. A rise in the external exchange value of the domestic currency normally has a short term and a longer term effect on the prices of securities. In the short term, the strong domestic currency means a healthy economy and strong balance of payments surplus position, consequently, profitability and shares prices will rise. In the longer run, a high domestic exchange rate may lead to a weak balance of payments position, which will depress both the profitability and the share prices of those companies which are dependent on export earnings. Low interest rates which are generally associated with strong currencies, will cause the yields and bond prices to remain high.

Costs of production

Increase in costs of production is normally expected to reduce profitability, and vice versa. Therefore those companies in an industry whose comparative production costs are higher than their competitor companies' costs, will have to raise prices of their products to recoup higher costs. Their sales revenue will fall, as will profitability and share prices.

Takeovers

A takeover bid is a method by which one company (the bidding company) tries to obtain the ownership and control of another company (the target company) by acquiring a majority of the target company's voting share capital. To achieve its objective, the bidding company, unless it is a rescue operation, makes a generous offer to the shareholders of the target company and this often causes the price of target company shares to rise well above the price they are being currently traded on the Stock Exchange. If the bid is contested by the target company's directors, or if a second bidding company appears on the scene, then the share price of the target company may rise to a very high level (see Chapter 10).

Change of fashion

A change in fashion towards or away from a company's products, may favourably or unfavourably, affect its sales, and therefore its profits and the price of its shares.

Comments in the media

In free countries, the power of the media (the press, radio and television) over the public's thinking and attitudes is considerable. The ordinary investors read and react to media comments. If the media comment is that a particular company's shares are 'cheap' or 'expensive', it often significantly affects the public's demand for that share, pushing up or down its price quite considerably.

Anticipation and announcement of company trading results

For the average investor, the annual report and accounts are the major source of primary information of a company's trading results, and to a limited extent, persuade the investors whether or not to buy its shares. If the actual announcement of company results confirms the expectations of the investors then the demand for its shares may rise (or fall), leading to an increase (or decrease) in the share price on the stock market.

Analysis and assessment of company securities

We shall now study the *fundamental* and *technical* analyses (see below) for ordinary shares and the assessment of company loan stocks and shares. Through fundamental analysis, we can determine whether it would be prudent to invest in company's stocks and shares. Fundamental analysis involves the study of balance sheets, profit and loss accounts and management over a period in the assessment of ordinary shares. It is the way in which the majority of investors, or their advisers (analysts), assess the value and potential of shares. The function of fundamental analysts is to endeavour to determine whether a share is a bargain in relation to its *intrinsic worth* (true worth). To achieve this the analyst attempts to assess the company's future profits over a period and to predict future dividends and then compare these and the company's prospects with competitor companies and the market as a whole. The following investment ratios assist us in assessing the intrinsic worth of company securities.

Interest cover

Interest payable by a company is a prior charge on its profits, and it would be in very serious difficulties if it is unable to service its interest payments. By calculating the interest cover (see Practical aspects below) prospective investors can find out whether the company can safely service its loan interest payments.

Dividend yield

The calculation of the gross dividend yield (see below) enables comparison with the gross yields of other shares and investments in order to decide whether to hold on to the shares or to sell them.

Earnings yield

Adequate earnings are essential if a company is to continue trading as a going concern. Earnings represent the net profit of the company, and can either be distributed as dividends or retained as reserves within the company. If paid out as increasing dividends, then the dividend yield will rise, leading to a rise in the price of the shares. If earnings are retained, then the reserves will increase, along with a corresponding increase in the net asset value per share (see below), leading to an increase in share prices. Thus an increase in the earnings of a company leads to an increase in the price of its shares. Earnings yield is calculated from earnings per share (see below).

Price/earning ratio

The 'earnings' of a company are its profits after tax and preference dividends. The P/E ratio expresses the market price of the shares of the company as a multiple of the last published net earnings per share of the company for a given trading period. P/E ratios are quoted in *The Financial Times*, financial journals and in the financial columns of other newspapers. P/E ratios, as yardsticks of performance of companies, are mainly used to compare the share ratings of companies in the same or related industries. Sectors with the best current growth prospects have relatively high P/E ratios and low dividend yields. Low P/E ratios indicate sluggish performance (see below).

Dividend cover

This usually means the number of times the declared annual dividend on share capital of a company is covered by its available earnings for that year. A high dividend cover normally suggests that the dividend is not only safe but also that there is scope for the dividend to be increased. A dividend cover figure of less than one generally implies that the profits of the year are insufficient in themselves to pay the declared annual dividend, and the company has had to draw upon the retained profits from previous years, i.e. reserves, to make up the payment. Therefore for investors a low dividend cover or uncovered dividend is less attractive than a high dividend cover. A high dividend cover is often coupled with a low yield, and vice versa. Dividend cover is given for Ordinary Shares in the *Financial Times London Share Information Service* which is used as one of the measures of the potential of the company concerned (see below).

Priority percentages

These are of two kinds

1 *Capital Priority Percentages (CPPs)* These show what percentage of the available assets of the company belong to which class of loan stockholder and shareholder, in accordance with their legal priority rankings. The higher the overall capital cover for a particular class of lender and shareholder the greater the security of that class's capital invested in the company (see below).
2 *Income Priority Percentages (IPPs)* These show the proportions of profits of the companies absorbed by various classes of its loan stockholders (in interest payments) and shareholders (in dividend distributions), in their respective legal pecking order. Like the CPPs, the higher the IPPs the greater the safety of returns on capital invested in the company. IPPs are a better way of showing the relative claims on profits of loan interest preference and ordinary dividends than interest and dividend covers.

In addition to the usage of the above investment ratios under fundamental analysis, the following aspects of Company Affairs are also considered in the valuation of companies' shares.

Gearing

The term 'gearing' denotes the relationship between a company's creditors and its ordinary shareholders. There are two main types of gearing ratio.
1 *Capital (or Financial) gearing ratios (CGRs)* The CGRs show the proportion of funds supplied by the creditors as compared with those from the equity of the company. These ratios can be expressed in terms of book value (from the balance sheet) or by using the market value of the quoted securities; the second method is more realistic. Preference shares are included in the fixed interest capital because they must be paid before any dividend payment to the ordinary shareholders. CGRs show the ability of the company to repay loans in the event of liquidation. Broadly speaking CGR

should not exceed 0.5, in so far as the safety of the lenders' capital is concerned (see below).

2 *Income (Operational) gearing ratios (IGRs)* The IGRs measure directly the ability of the company to meet its fixed interest commitments, therefore they are connected with the interest cover and income priority percentages. Broadly speaking, the IGR of a company should not be less than 2:1. IGR is a useful yardstick for lenders, not investors, in deciding whether it would be safe to lend to the company (see below).

The significance of gearing of a company is considerable to its ordinary shareholders. A 'high gearing' means that a large proportion of the company's profits is required to meet in full the fixed interest commitments, leaving a smaller proportion of profits for distribution as dividends to ordinary shareholders. Therefore, the ordinary shareholders in highly geared companies should benefit more in periods of rising profits and suffer more in periods of falling profits. Hence shares in highly geared companies tend to become more volatile, compared with 'low geared' company shares, i.e. the companies which have a low proportion of fixed interest borrowing to ordinary shares. Provided that a company's profit record is sound, a measure of operational and financial gearings is desirable because it will assist in increasing earnings per share. However, high gearing is a cause for concern, both for the creditors and investors, in a company with fluctuatory profits.

Cash flow

It is usually equivalent to retained (undistributed) profits from the previous years plus depreciation for the replacement of fixed assets when they become obsolete. Thus cash flow represents the funds for use within a company which are generated by its own internal operations. These funds are available to it for ploughing back, i.e. for expansion, without borrowing or raising new capital. A company with adequate cash flow, effectively used, will enjoy increasing profitability for the greater benefit of its ordinary shareholders.

Net Asset Value (NAV)

It is the value of assets available, on liquidation, to the ordinary shareholders, after the loan stockholders and preference shareholders have been redeemed at par.

NAV is less important than earnings because it is only realised on liquidation, but it is more significant if a takeover bid is likely. If earnings fall, the NAV acts as a support to the share price. A steady upward trend in NAV per share is a healthy sign. The value is based on figures on the balance sheet date (*book value*) when stocks may have been abnormally high (or low) and the figures should be treated with caution. NAV can also be calculated on the *break-up* value of assets (i.e. actual realisable value) and on the current or *replacement cost* (i.e. value of assets as a 'going-concern'). It is important to consider the basis of NAV valuation (see below). Buildings may be undervalued, investments shown at cost rather than market value. factories and machinery at a 'going-concern' valuation. When the NAV is above the share price it may be an indication that the assets are not being used efficiently, perhaps due to economic depression or poor management. The relationship of NAV to the share price also depends upon the nature of the business. Capital intensive industries will have a relatively high NAV, while service industries such as advertising, where the most important 'asset' is people (not shown in the balance sheet) will have low NAVs.

Quality of managements

Management is an intangible factor and much more difficult to assess except on the basis of the company's trading results over a number of years. If a company's rate of growth consistently outperforms other companies in the same field this is almost certainly due to superior quality of management. Management thus has a very important influence on the share rating, and therefore share price; and is probably of more significance than even the earnings and net asset value.

The ability to recognise changing circumstances and adjust policy accordingly is the principal growth factor in the best companies. Management changes may therefore be an important early indicator of a change in the profitability of a company and consequently in its market rating.

Technical analysis of company affairs

Technical analysts base their decisions for buying and selling of shares on price movements as reflected in graphs and charts, e.g. line charts, bar charts, point and figure charts.

Share price movements can be divided into three main kinds:

1 Tertiary movements – day to day movements.
2 Secondary movements – movements over a period of weeks and months.
3 Primary movements – long term movements.

Analysis of these movements, either for individual shares or the market, enable analysts to give advice on correct times to buy and sell. Interest in this type of advice is increasing but its accuracy is not infallible.

Line charts

These are graphs which show the progress of an individual share, or of a share market index, over a required period of time.

There are two main ways of constructing line charts.

1   By plotting the closing share price daily along the Y axis and the time period along the X axis. When the daily price points are joined, a Tertiary Line Chart results, which is used to show a minor price movement lasting just a few days.
2   By plotting the weekly or monthly or longer moving averages on graphs, and by joining them, Secondary and Primary Line Charts result, which show longer term trends.

Line charts give signals of the upward/downward movements of the share price (see p. 233), hence suggest the time to buy and sell shares.

Bar charts

These graphs are produced by charting daily the highest and the lowest prices of the share, joining the two prices by a vertical bar to indicate the range of price movement, and by a horizontal bar across the vertical bar to indicate the closing price. Bar charts produce 'head and shoulders' and 'neckline' patterns, signalling the upward and downward price movements (see p. 234).

Point and figure charts

On these graphs closing prices are along the Y axis: rising prices by a vertical column of 'X's and falling prices by a vertical column of 'Os' next to the X column. In order to keep small price changes separate from directional changes, up or down, by a fixed amount (say 3p) are indicated by a shift to a new column. Although there is a horizontal time axis nothing is recorded on it, because these charts emphasise price movements but no regular time intervals (see p. 235).

The Random Walk Hypothesis (RWH)

In an *efficient* market share prices *already* reflect all the information that can be obtained from studying share price movements. Therefore, according to RWH, competition between buyers and sellers on best terms will determine market prices and, at any point in time, share prices are just as likely to move up or down, i.e. the prices follow a random walk, despite what the technical analysis may show. Hence, without special knowledge about a company, the industry in which it operates and the economy as a whole, where this knowledge is *not* reflected in market prices, it is unlikely that performance of one portfolio will be better than another in the long run.

The Efficient Market Hypothesis (EMH)

The EMH follows from the RWH. It states that in an efficient share market, the current prices have already taken account of all the information available to buyers and sellers. The EMH takes three forms.

1 *The weak form of EMH* Since the current share price has already taken account of all *available* information conveyed by the technical analysis charts, therefore such charts cannot help predict the future share price. This form of EMH seeks to expose the weakness of technical analysis.

2 *The semi-strong form of EMH*. This claims that not only the *past* but also the *current* information concerning a share is available to buyers and sellers, and therefore reflected in the current price (thanks largely to the availability of efficient fundamental and technical analyses!). Therefore investors following a buy-hold-sell strategy on the recommendation of the financial press tipsters or stockbroker newsletters are unlikely to outperform the market index *in the long run*.

3 *The strong form of EMH*. This states that not only *publicly* available information but also *privately* (insider) known information of leading companies is available to buyers and sellers and are already discounted for in the current share prices of the leading companies, i.e. the leading shares are already priced on their *intrinsic* worth. Therefore, as stated by the RWH, the leading share prices will move in a random manner. It may be concluded, therefore that both the EMH and RWH claim that sticking a pin at random in *The Financial Times* (or any other leading financial publication) may be as good a method as any in deciding which share to buy or sell. The best that investors could do would be to invest roughly equal amounts in all the leading shares, which are all priced at their respective intrinsic values, and hope for the best.

The Hatch System

This is an automatic system of trading in shares, designed to *filter* out minor price movements. The shares are sold if the price falls more than a *set percentage* (say 10%) below the purchase price. At the end of a fixed period (say one month) a new selling price is set 10% below the current market price provided the current market price is above the purchase price or the previous month's price. If these rules trigger off a sale, then a new purchase price is set at 10% above the sale price, and reset each month until a new purchase has been triggered.

A point of importance is of setting buying or selling limits only on *regular set dates*, because if the selling limit is changed every day it will only become effective if the price falls by a full 10% in *one* day. Another crucial point is the determination of the *set percentages*: if they are set too high investors would lose out on most price rises and suffer on most of the price falls; if they are set too low, the frequent dealing costs will absorb most of the potential profits.

The *filter methods* – like those used in the Hatch System – are designed to assist investors to sell off such shares as are likely to cause sizeable losses and to purchase those shares which possess a good likelihood of sizeable gains.

Line pattern

A line pattern, on the technical analysis charts, emerges when the buying and selling activity is evenly matched, say within 4%, for a time. The line pattern will move sideways, until the buyers *or* the sellers gain the upper hand, then there will be a sharp price breakaway up or down. The longer the line pattern moves sideways the sharper will be the breakaway price rise or fall. According to the line theory, the buyers should buy as soon as the breakaway price rise occurs, and the sellers should sell as soon as the breakaway price fall occurs (see p. 236).

Triangle pattern

The chart shows that when the equally matched forces of buying and selling face each other, the resistance prices, moving sideways, come closer, thus forming a triangle, until one or the other gives way and the strong breakaway price movement occurs against the loser. That is the time to buy or sell shares (see p. 236).

Line and triangle patterns may emerge either for a share index or for an individual share.

Corporation Tax (CT)

Corporation Tax is the taxation of the profits, incomes and chargeable gains of companies resident in the UK or trading in the UK through a branch or agency. In the latter case only the profits earned in the UK are taxable. CT is charged for an annual accounting period which usually coincides with the period for which the company prepares its annual accounts. The period cannot exceed 12 months. When the annual accounting period of a company does not coincide with the UK financial year: 1 April to 31 March, its trading results must be apportioned on a time basis and this will assume significance when there is a change in the CT rate.

In the assessment of the CT liability of a company, deductions are allowed for expenditure incurred in acquiring plant, machinery, industrial buildings and similar assets by the company. However, unlike individuals, companies do not enjoy the free CGT allowance on gains from disposals.

There are two CT rates: the full rate and the smaller companies' rate. The full rate for 1988/89 is 35%. It has been steadily reduced from 52% since 1983, to offset the phasing out of the initial year allowances and the withdrawal of stock relief. The CT rate for the smaller companies for 1988/89 is 25%. A company is deemed 'smaller' if its profits do not exceed £100 000. If its profits exceed £100 000 but not £500 000, a marginal relief at the rate of 1/50th is available, calculated by subtracting from the CT liability at the full rate a fraction of the difference between the actual profit figure and £500 000 (see Practical application).

Advance Corporation Tax (ACT)

ACT is a pre-payment of the mainstream CT bill of a company. Companies are required to pay ACT to the Inland Revenue on their 'qualifying distributions' made after April 1973. Qualifying distributions include dividends on shares, benefits provided to shareholders and other advantages. Non-qualifying distributions include bonus debentures, bonus redeemable shares and the like which carry a future potential claim on the company's profits. On non-qualifying distributions no ACT is payable by the company.

The qualifying distributions are paid in full without income tax deductions by the company. However, the company must make a payment of ACT at the 1988/89 rate of 25/75ths, to the Inland Revenue. The ACT payment, being a pre-payment of the company's CT bill, can be offset against the company's CT liability for the period during which the distribution is made; the CT liability is only ascertained when the company submits its annual accounts to the Inland Revenue. ACT may also be offset against CT on capital gains arising on disposals after 16 March 1988.

There is a limit to the amount of ACT which a company can offset against its mainstream CT liability. The limit is the ACT amount which would be paid on a full distribution of a company's income before the deduction of any tax. In computing the full distribution, account is taken of the notional ACT payable (see below).

If any ACT payment is not absorbed by the mainstream CT payable for the accounting period, the unrelieved 'surplus' ACT can be carried back or forward, and set off against past or future CT liability of the company. Shareholders receiving dividend distribution also receive a tax credit certificate which is equal, in 1988/89, to 25/75ths of the distribution. The amount of the credit must be added to the amount of the dividend to establish the total income of the shareholders for income tax purposes. If a shareholder is not liable to income tax at the basic rate, he/she can claim the repayment of the tax credit from the Inland Revenue. Basic rate income tax-paying shareholders have no further tax liability on the dividend income received. Higher rate taxpayers will pay additional tax in excess of the basic rate of currently, 25%.

The recipients of the non-qualifying distributions get no tax credits at the basic rate, and are not liable to such tax on such distributions, but are liable to higher rate tax over the basic rate on the actual value of the non-qualifying distributions.

Franked payments

The ACT returns by companies to the Inland Revenue must show for the relevant accounting period the 'franked payments', i.e. a qualifying distribution made by them together with the relevant ACT (see below).

Franked investment income

A company's franked investment income is received from UK resident companies, and the amount is included in the relevant tax credits (see below). The ACT returns must show for the relevant accounting period the franked investment income of companies. In computing the ACT payable, companies may deduct tax credits on receipts of franked investment income during the relevant accounting period.

Practical aspects

Gearing ratio

It indicates the extent of debt/equity ratio, i.e. the proportion of borrowing to *shareholders' funds (i.e. the total assets of the company minus* total liabilities):
Formula: Gearing ratio = (Preference share capital + Loan capital) ÷ (Ordinary share capital reserves).
Example: Gearing ratio = (£55 000 + £345 000) ÷ (£350 000 + £200 000) = 0.72
Ordinary shareholders may be better off investing in a company with a large gearing; but *not* greater than one. The effect of greater-than-one gearing in bad years of profitability is particularly harsh on the ordinary shareholders. But high gearing in high profitability years can be beneficial both to the company (because the cost of interest payable will be less than the nominal rate of borrowing due to tax considerations) and to the ordinary shareholders (the company needs only to make an overall trading return in excess of the nominal interest rate to make gearing worthwhile).

Liquidity

The liquidity ratio of a company may be tested by two methods:
1 *Current ratio*
Formula: Current assets ÷ Current liabilities = Current ratio

Example: £400 000 ÷ £150 000 = £2.6

This ratio indicates a company's ability to pay its debts as they fall due. A current ratio of around two is normally considered healthy for most companies.

2 *Liquid ratio*

Formula: Current assets − Stock ÷ Current liabilities = Liquidity ratio

Example: £400 000 − £100 000 ÷ £150 000 = 2

A liquidity ratio of around 1.5 may be considered safe for most companies. Liquidity ratio is a better test of a company's liquidity. The investor should look for the change in the trend rather than the one-off ratio figures of the ratios and should find out reasons for the change.

Interest cover

Formula: Interest cover = (Profits before tax + Interest payable) ÷ Interest payable

Example: Interest cover = (£10 000 000 + £500 000) ÷ £500 000 = 21 times

This means that profits could fall to one-twenty-oneth of £10 000 000 (£476 190.47) before the company would have to meet its interest commitment out of its capital. Therefore the larger the interest cover the greater the safety of loanstock interest payment to the company loan stockholders.

Dividend yield

It is the amount of gross income receivable per £100 invested in the shares at that market price:

Formula: Dividend yield = Gross dividend × 100 ÷ share price

Example: (a) Dividend yield = 5p × 100 ÷ 45p = 11.1%

Example: (b) Dividend yield = 10p × 100 ÷ 90p = 11.1%.

The following formula will convert net dividend per share into dividend yield per share:

Net dividend ÷ (100 − basic rate of income tax) × 100 ÷ share price

Example: 175p ÷ (100 − 25) × 100 ÷ 70p = 3.14%

Companies deduct the Advance Corporation Tax (ACT) from the gross dividend and send it to the Inland Revenue. The ACT rate is equal to the current basic rate of income tax (see below).

Earnings yield

There are three separate ways of defining earnings.

1 *Nil earnings*

This definition assumes that no dividend is paid, even if one is actually paid. Nil earnings therefore simply equal to net profits *less* preference dividend, i.e. net profits available to ordinary shareholders:

Formula: Net profits − preference dividend = Earnings (nil basis)

Example: £10 million − £500 000 = £9 500 000 (nil basis)

Earnings per share (EPS) on nil basis:

Formula: Earnings (nil basis) ÷ number of ordinary shares

Example: EPS (nil basis) = £9 500 000 ÷ 10 000 000 = 9.5

2 *Net earnings*

This takes into account net dividends and retained profits:

Formula: Dividends − Advance Corporation Tax (ACT) + Retained profits = Earnings (Net basis).

Example: £500 000 − £166 666.65 $\left(500\ 000 \times \dfrac{25}{75}\right)$ + £90 000 = £423 333.35 (Net basis).

Formula: EPS (Net basis) = Earnings (net basis) ÷ number of ordinary shares.

Example: EPS (Net basis) = £405 068.5 ÷ 100 000 = 4.05

In most cases, 'Nil' and 'Net' bases will produce the same earnings. In cases where dividends are 'excessive', i.e. above 25/35 of the Corporation Tax bill, the company will incur unrelieved ACT, which will be deducted from the retained profits, and therefore, the net earnings will be less than the nil earnings.

3 *Full earnings (maximum distribution)*

Under this definition of earnings, dividend cover and earnings yield are calculated by reference to the maximum gross ordinary dividend a company *could* have paid to shareholders:

Formula: Nil earnings + ACT × net dividends = Earnings (full basis)

Example: £50 000 + (25 ÷ 75 × £12 000) = £53 999.99

EPS (full basis) can be found by dividing full earnings by the number of ordinary shares.

After the report of the Accounting Standard Committee during the 1970s, earnings are defined as profits *after* taxation, minority interests (e.g. employees' shares, shares held outside the company) and preference dividend but *before* extraordinary items, e.g. items in the profit and loss account which are outside the ordinary business of the company and dilution of earnings caused by increase in company's ordinary share due to the issue of convertible loan stock. If all profits are used in this way, then no Corporation Tax is due, i.e. earnings are *nil*. But if some of the profits are used to pay a dividend then the basic rate of income tax, as Advance Corporation Tax, is payable, i.e. Profits *minus* ACT on profits distributed as dividends = *net* earnings. (*The Financial Times* bases its Price/Earnings ratio on net earnings, but if the difference between net and nil earnings is more than 10%, the P/E ratio is given in brackets.)

However, there is no universally agreed definition of what constitutes earnings and this has made P/E ratio, especially since the imputation system of Corporation Tax in 1970 (see below), a less satisfactory yardstick.

Price/Earnings (P/E) ratios

Formula: Market price per share ÷ Earnings per ordinary share = P/E
ratio
Example: 200p ÷ 23.5 = 8.51 times
A P/E ratio of less than five is considered low : low expectations of growth
in earnings in the forseeable future have led to the sales of the share,
causing its price to fall. A P/E ratio in excess of 15 indicates considerable
optimism for the growth in earnings, causing the share price to rise. This
would be the case with growth shares and recovery shares, both of which
have a higher P/E ratio but lower dividend yield.

Dividend cover

Formula: Net profits after tax ÷ Dividend payable = Dividend Cover.
Preference dividend cover = Profits after tax ÷ Preference
Dividend
Examples: Profits after tax = £10 000; Preference dividend = £500.
Ordinary dividend = £3800; Retained profits = £5700.
Preference dividend cover = £10 000 ÷ £500 = 20 times
Ordinary dividend cover = £10 000 − £500 ÷ £3800 = 2.5 times.

In the case of Preference dividend cover, earnings per share is 20 times
greater than the net preference dividend per share, hence the preference
shareholders can rest assured that their dividends are safe. With Ordinary
dividend cover, net EPs is 2.5 times the ordinary share dividend per share,
this is not a high cover, and can be a cause for concern but for the large
proportion of net profits transferred to reserves; and the reserves belong to
ordinary shareholders.

In many respects dividend cover can be a misleading yardstick. Income
priority percentages (see below) are a better way of showing relative claims
on profits of loan interest, preference and ordinary dividends.

Priority percentages

1 *Capital Priority Percentages* see Question 3 and Answer 3 below.
2 *Income Priority Percentages* at the end of this chapter.

Gearing

1 *Capital Gearing Ratio (CGR)*
Formula: Loan capital + Preference share − cash ÷ Shareholders' funds
+ loans − cash − intangible = CGR

Example: (£100 000 + £75 000 − £5000) ÷ (£600 000 + £100 000 − £5000
  − £5000 (goodwill)) = 0.24
  CGR gives lenders some indication of the protection of their
  loans.
  Normally a 25% CGR is low, 100% is neutral and 150% highly
  geared.
2. *Income Gearing Ratio (IGR)*
This calculates the number of times the fixed *interest* on loan stocks is
covered by the total available profits.
Formula: Profits before interest and tax ÷ Gross interest payments = IGR.
Example: £13 560 ÷ £2475 = 5.4 times.

Cash Flows

These are saved up funds of the company, which are available for expansion
and replacement of fixed assets.
Formula: Net retained profits + Depreciation = Cash flow.
Example: £105 000 + £7500 = £112 500

Net Asset Value (NAV)

This shows, in three different ways, the value of a company's assets to its
ordinary shareholders, expressed in per share terms.
1. *NAV, as per Book Value, per ordinary share*
Formula: Balance sheet value of total assets − (Loan stock + Preference
  shares) ÷ Number of issued ordinary shares = NAV
Example: £4 million − (£200 000 + £250 000) ÷ 3 million = £1.18 per share
NAV, as per book value, can be misleading because the book values of
assets is unlikely to bear much relation to their current values.
2. *NAV, as per Breakup Value, per ordinary share*.
This measures NAV per share from the *actually realised value* of total assets
(e.g. premises, plant and machinery and debtors) on a liquidation.
Formula: Actually realised value of tangible and current assets − (Loans
  and preference share) ÷ Number of shares = NAV.
Example: £3 million − (£200 000 + £250 000) ÷ 3 million = 85p NAV
This calculation has relevance only in an actual liquidation situation.
3. *NAV, on Replacement or Current Cost Value, per share*.
This method evaluates the assets of a company, neither at book value nor
on a liquidation but on a 'going concern' basis.
Formula: Replacement cost of assets − (Loans + Preference share) ÷
  Number of issued ordinary shares = NAV
Example: £5 million − (£200 000 + £250 000) ÷ 3 million = £1.51 per
  share.
  Share analysts prefer to use this method in evaluating the NAV
  of sound going concerns.

Technical analysis

Whereas the fundamental analysts base their interpretations, in their rating of companies, solely on the *pattern* of past share prices, the technical analysts (also known as 'Chartists') believe that the patterns of past share prices are *indicative and predictive* of future share prices, therefore use their various charts in giving advice on when to buy or sell shares.

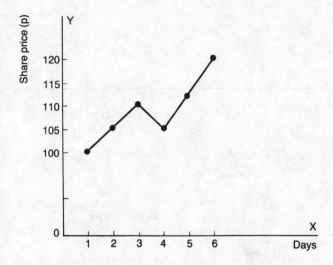

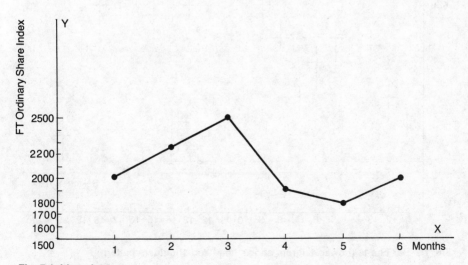

Fig. 7.1 Line charts

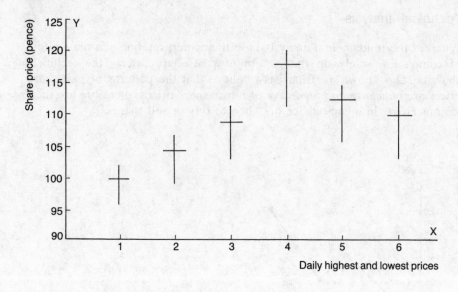

Daily highest and lowest prices

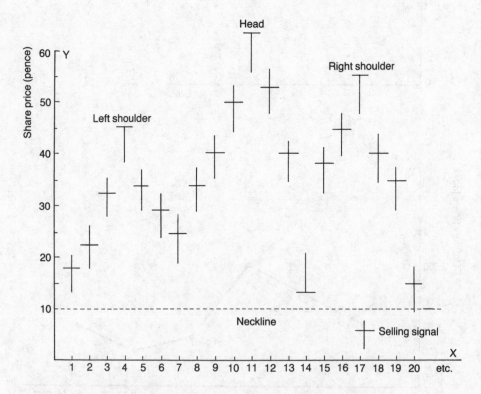

Fig. 7.2 Bar charts (Lower diagram shows head and shoulders pattern)

The 'head and shoulders' pattern emerges when the share prices rise very quickly (e.g. takeover bid rumour) then fall back quickly due to investors selling and taking the profit (the left shoulder), the price rises sharply (take-over bid confirmed) and reaches a high level (the head), falls again (profit taking) but then rallies (bid offer increased) and rises, more profit taking (and withdrawal of the bid offer) causes the price to fall sharply (the right shoulder) and if it falls below the neckline it is a signal to investors to sell their shares.

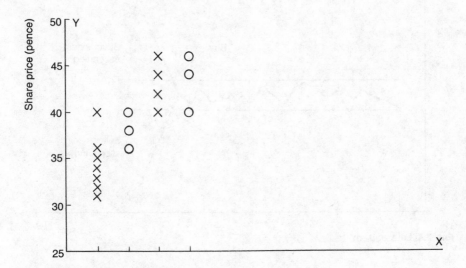

Fig. 7.3 Points and figures chart

Corporation Tax (CT)

1   The CT liability of a smaller company which prepared its annual accounts on 30 September, for 1986/87 and 1987/88 assessment.

Example: Profits till 30 September = £90 000 (less than £100 000).
Six months' (till 31 March 1987) CT liability at 1986/87 rate, 29%
= $\frac{1}{2}$ × £90 000 × 29% = £13 050
Six months' (till 30 September 1987) CT liability at 1987/88 rate
27% = $\frac{1}{2}$ × £90 00 × 27%   = £12 150
Total CT liability (£13 050 + £12 150)   = £25 200

2   The CT liability of a smaller company with profits in excess of £100 000 for the year ending on 31 March 1988.

Example: Profits for the year 1987/88 = £190 000

CT at the full ratio of 35% = £190 000 × 35%   = £66 500

Less marginal relief on:

£500 000 − £190 000 = £310 000 × $\dfrac{1}{50\text{th}}$ = £6200

Total CT liability   = £60 300

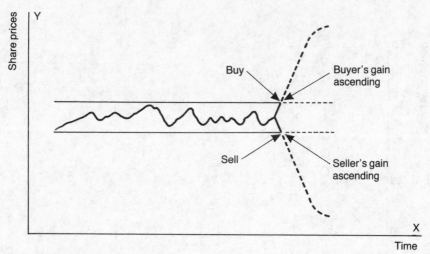

Fig. 7.4 Line pattern

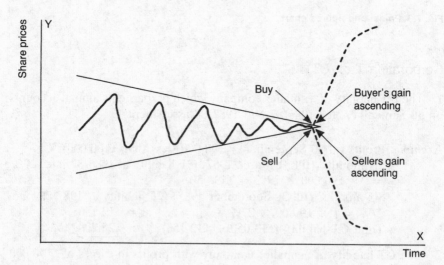

Fig. 7.5 Triangle pattern

Advance Corporation Tax (ACT)

1 *The limit of ACT which may be set against its mainstream CT liability.*
Suppose a company makes adjusted revenue profits of £500 000 before tax
for the year ending 31 March 1988.

The maximum set off limit for $\text{ACT} = \text{£500 000} \times \dfrac{27}{73} = \text{£135 000}$

If the company distributed £400 000 it would pay

$\text{ACT} = \text{£400 000} \times \dfrac{27}{73} = \text{£108 000}$

and its entire profit would be absorbed. After the end of its account year,
it would be assessed as follows:

Mainstream CT liability on £500 000 = £5 000 000 × 35% = £175 000
Less £108 000 ACT already paid, therefore the net amount payable =
£175 000 − £108 000 = £67 000.
2 *Franked payment by a company*
Qualifying distribution = £5000
equals franked payment of £5000 + £5000 × 27/73 = £6350
3 *Franked investment income of a company*
£10 000 dividend received by a company = a franked investment income of
£11 367.98 (£10 000 + £10 000 × 27 ÷ 73).

Selected questions

Attempt to answer the following questions from the knowledge gained from
the text in this chapter, before looking at the brief answers given below.
Q1 What are the main factors which cause changes in the market prices
of ordinary shares? Distinguish between those factors which affect the share
price of a particular company and those which affect the market as a
whole.
Q2 How is each of the following calculated and what is its significance
to the investor?
   (a) Liquidity ratio
   (b) Asset value
   (c) Dividend cover
   (d) P/E ratio.
Q3 The capital structure of Herbert Clay PLC, a long established brick-
making company, is as follows:
£375 000 7½% Debenture Stock 1988/91
£530 000 5¼% (net) Cumulative Preference £1 shares
1 200 000 Ordinary stock units of 50p each

The profit after debenture stock interest and corporation tax for the year ended 31 December 1984 was £225 937.

A dividend of 9.8 per ordinary stock unit has been paid.

Required:

Calculate the income priority percentages showing the cost of interest and dividend, the capital priority percentage and the overall cover for each class of stock or shares.

Q4 In assessing the ordinary shares of a quoted public company, what importance would you attach to the following factors:

(a) Earnings

(b) Net Asset Value

(c) Management?

Q5 With help from your bank, your customer, Mr Trendsetter, has made a number of successful applications for new shares in companies which have been privatised from the public sector. This has resulted in his having an increasing interest in direct investment in companies quoted on the stock market. He is, however, bothered by some of the jargon used in the assessment of shares. Explain the following terms to your customer:

(a) technical analysts

(b) net asset value

(c) fundamental analysis

(d) head and shoulders pattern

(e) break-up value

(f) random walk theory

Q6 (a) Describe briefly the use of 'filter' rules with reference to the 'Hatch' system.

(b) Distinguish between line charts, bar charts and point-and-figure charts.

(c) Describe the following chart patterns commonly identified by technical analysts and say how they are usually interpreted:

(i) line;

(ii) head and shoulders.

A1 *Principal factors affecting the share prices of individual companies*: increase/decrease in the dividend, rise/fall in profits, change in NAV, management change, introduction of new products, discovery of new drug/mineral deposit, good/bad harvest, natural disaster, health scares, adverse/favourable comment by press or brokers, presence of large buyer/seller of shares and a takeover bid.

Principal factors affecting the market as a whole: increase/decrease in interest rates, increase/decrease in consumer spending, exchange rate fluctuations, changes in balance of payments, relative inflation rate, level of industrial production, tax changes, fiscal measures, government spending, control over industry, nationalisation/privatisation, dividend control, credit restrictions, wage freezes, general industrial strife and foreign government action.

A2 (a) *Liquidity ratio* – indicates company's *true* liquidity. It is calculated from figures in the balance sheet.
Formula: (Current assets − stock) ÷ current liabilities.
A ratio of 1.0 in normal times is regarded fairly safe. The *trend* of the ratio is more important than one-off ratios.

(b) *Asset value* – it is the value of assets available on liquidation to the ordinary shareholders, after the loan stockholders and preference shareholders have been redeemed at par. NAV per share when compared with the market value per share indicates if the company can be a target for a takeover bid. Three methods of calculating NAV from information in the balance sheet:

(i) $$\frac{\text{(Book (balance sheet) value of ordinary share capital + Reserves)} - \text{Goodwill}}{\text{number of ordinary shares}}$$

(ii) $$\frac{\text{(Market value of ordinary share capital + Reserves)} - \text{Goodwill}}{\text{number of ordinary shares.}}$$

(iii) At current or replacement cost basis.

The third formula values assets on a 'going concern' basis, also known as 'break-up' value, and is commonly used to evaluate a business by share analysts.

(c) *Dividend cover* indicates the number of times the total dividend for a year could have been paid from the net profit of the company for that year, if the net profit is distributed in full to shareholders. It is calculated from the figures in the profit and loss account of the company by the following formula: net profit after tax ÷ dividends payable, or net earnings per share ÷ dividend payable per share. A high cover suggests that the dividend is safe. If it is less than one, then reserves will be used to make up the dividend payment.

(d) *P/E ratio* – Price/Earnings ratio is based on the current expectations of future earnings of the company based on past earnings and reflected in the market price of ordinary shares.
Formula: Market price of the share ÷ earnings per share.
P/E ratios are used to compare the share rating of companies in the same or related industries.

A3 Profits available for interest and dividends:

profits after debenture interest and tax	£225 937
Add back net cost of debenture interest	£ 14 063
Available profits	£240 000

Capital priority percentages and cover on the assumption that the asset value equates with the disclosed issued capital.

	Priority percentage	Overall cover
£375 000 – Debenture stock	0–24.9	4 times
£530 000 – Preference shares	24.9–60.1	1.7 times
£600 000 – Ordinary stock	60.1–100	1 time
£1 505 000		

Income priority percentages

	Cost interest dividend	Priority percentage	Overall or cover
£375 000 7½% Debenture stock 1988/91 (1)	£14 063	0–5.86	17.07 times
£530 000 5¼% Cumulative Pref. share £1	£27 825	5.86–17.45	5.73 times
£1 200 000 ordinary shares, 50p each (2)	£17 600	17.45–66.45	1.50 times
Retained profits	£85 512	33.55	

(1)   After deduction of Corporation Tax of 50% (in 1987/88), the deduction for Corporation Tax will be at 35%.

(2)   Dividend of 9.8 per Stock Unit (gross 14p). In 1987/88, the basic rate of 25% will be used to obtain the gross value per Stock Unit.

A4   (a) *Earnings* are a tangible and inportant factor. Growth in earnings influences share price and protects the dividend. Trend of earnings should be followed over a number of years. An upward trend, in excess of the rate of inflation is desirable. Comparisons of the rate of earnings with other companies helps performance assessment of the company. Earnings should be related to capital employed and assets employed. Earnings are available for equity holders and may be paid out in full or may be ploughed back, in part or in full, in the company. Capital growth depends on growth of earnings; if they are retained the capital of the company is enhanced, if paid as dividend market rating in shares improves.

(b) *Net asset value* is more significant if a takeover bid or liquidation is likely. If earnings fall NAV supports the share price. A steady upward trend in NAV is a healthy sign. NAV should be treated with care, because figures are based on the balance sheet date when stocks may be abnormally high or low. *Basis* of NAV is important. When NAV is above the share price it means inefficient usage of assets. Capital intensive industries have relatively higher NAV than service industries.

(c) *Management* – although an intangible factor, therefore difficult to assess, yet very important for share rating. It is the management essentially which leads the company consistently to outperform other companies in the same field, because good management adjusts policy quickly to changed circumstances. Management change affects profitability therefore the market rating of the company.

A5   (a) *Technical analysts* base their decisions for buying and selling of shares on price movements reflected in graphs and charts, e.g. line, bar, point and figure charts.

Analysis of the price movements enables analysts to advise on the correct time to buy and sell. Their advice is not infallible.

(b) *Net asset value* – – the value of assets that are available, where a majority stake is held or in liquidation, to the equity holders. It can be calculated on the book value of the assets, on break-up value, on current or replacement cost. It can be a factor in assessing the value of a company in fundamental analysis.

(c) *Fundamental analysis* – involves the study of balance sheets, profit and loss accounts, management, in the assessment or ordinary shares.

(d) *Head and shoulders pattern* – technical analysts use a chart to predict the future trend of shares under this method. A chart shows steep rises and falls in share prices, the support level for following prices and and the test of the support level. The pattern is usually a prelude to a large fall.

(e) *Break-up value* – useful in liquidation when assets (e.g. plant and machinery, stocks, debtors) fail to reach their book value. On occasions, land and building may be worth more than the book value; it has some relevance to fundamental analysis.

(f) *Random walk theory* – states that in an efficient market, the market forces will determine market prices of shares, therefore prices may rise or fall in a random manner, and therefore without special knowledge about a company, the performance of one portfolio is unlikely to be better than another in the long run. Sticking a pin in the paper may be as good a method as any.

A6 (a) *The Hatch System* – an automatic system of trading in shares, designed to filter out minor price movements, by selling shares if the price falls below a certain percentage below the purchase price. After a fixed time period a new selling price is set below the current market price provided the current price is above the purchase price or the previous month's fixed period. If this triggers off a sale, a new purchase price is set at the fixed percentage above the sale price, and reset in each fixed period until a new purchase price has been triggered.

(b) *Line chart* – a line drawn through the daily closing prices of a share, or possibly through the weekly average prices.

Bar chart – shows the highest and the lowest prices for a week or other period joined by a vertical bar. The closing price for the period is indicated by a horizontal bar on the vertical bar. Bar charts are more popular in America in conjunction with volume figures. The other types of bar chart are frequently used in company reports, showing a series of profit figures, dividend etc. by columns of varying heights.

Point-and-figure chart – has no time scale. A rising share price is represented by a vertical column of 'Xs', and a falling price by a vertical column of 'Os' next to the X's column. The year and month are shown in place of an X or O on the first dealing day of each month. For clarity a change of direction is only shown if the price changes by a fixed amount (say, 3p) or more.

(c) (i) *Line pattern* – a chart pattern where the price moves sideways within a narrow trading range, indicating that buyers and sellers are evenly matched. When a breakout occurs either upwards or downwards this is a buy or sell signal. The longer the period of consolidation, the greater the rise or fall.

(ii) *Head and shoulders pattern* – emerges by a price rise due to buying pressure forming a left 'shoulder' on a reaction falling to the 'neckline'. Further buying carries the price to a higher level to form the 'head'. Some investors then take profits and price falls back to neckline drawn through these two low points. If a reaction to a final upsurge penetrates the neckline a sell signal is registered.

Specially selected question

The following question has been selected because it seeks the essential and basic knowledge of calculating the investment ratios. Answer it, and then check your calculations with those given below.

The issued capital of AZ Ltd consists of 5 000 000 ordinary shares of 25p each, fully paid. In the last financial year pre-tax profits, all earned in the UK, were £840 000. Corporation tax was at the rate of 52%, basic rate tax 30% and advance corporation tax 3/7ths. A dividend of 14% net was paid on the ordinary shares. The current share price is 80p.

(a) Calculate:
 (i) dividend yield;
 (ii) earnings yield (full basis);
 (iii) price/earnings ratio (nil basis);
 (iv) dividend cover.
 (Show how you arrived at your answer.)

(b) What might an investor deduce about a share with a relatively high price/earnings ratio?

Model answer

(a) (i) Dividend yield

$$= \text{Rate of Dividend } (gross) \times \frac{\text{nominal price of share}}{\text{market price of share}}$$

$$= 14 \times (100 \div 70) \times (25 \div 80)$$

$$= \underline{\underline{6.25\%}}$$

(ii) Pre-tax profits $\qquad$ = £840 000
Corporation tax @ 52% = £436 800

Profits available $\qquad$ = £403 200

Largest possible distribution *plus* related ACT

$$= £\ 403\ 200\ \times \frac{100}{70} = £576\ 000$$

$$\text{Earnings yield} = \frac{\text{Full earnings per share}}{\text{share price}} \times 100$$

$$= \frac{£576\ 000}{£5\ 000\ 000} \div £0.80 \times 100$$

$$= \frac{11.52}{80} \times 100$$

$$= 14.4\%$$

(iii) Earnings if no distribution is made = £403 200

$$\text{Price/Earnings ratio} = \frac{\text{Price per share}}{\text{Earnings per share}}$$

$$= £0.80 \div \frac{£403\ 200}{5\ 000\ 000}$$

$$= \frac{80}{8.064}$$

$$= 9.92$$

(iv) Cost of dividend = 14% × 25p × 5 000 000 = £175 000
Profits available for dividend = £403 200

$$\text{Dividend Cover} = \frac{\text{Profits available for dividend}}{\text{Cost of Dividend}}$$

$$= \frac{£403\ 200}{£175\ 000}$$

$$= 2.304 \text{ times}$$

(*Note*: In 1988/89, 'AZ Ltd' will be called 'AZ PLC', the Corporation Tax rate will be 35% and the basic rate tax 25%.)

(b) A high price/earnings ratio implies that earnings are expected to grow at an above-average rate or that earnings have fallen and the share price has not fully adjusted to this, perhaps because recovery is expected.

Updating

The most appropriate sources are the financial press and journals. The CIB *Examiners' Reports* and '*Signpost*' articles in *Banking World* will help you to understand the required and updated knowledge you are expected to possess to pass the CIB Investment question paper.

8 Practice of investment (II) Investment portfolio construction

Syllabus coverage

Identifying the needs and requirements of various types of investor:
   Individuals (taxpayers, non-taxpayers, employed, unemployed, retired,
     self-employed, minors, non-residents)
   Trusts
   Family trusts, charitable trusts, pension funds
   Companies
   Charities
Taxation of investment income and capital:
   Income tax
   Capital gains tax
   Inheritance tax
   Portfolio planning, management and review
   Portfolio diversification:
   Company and sector spread
   Overseas investments
Importance of 'timing' in buying, selling and 'switching'.

Introduction

In this chapter we shall apply the knowledge gained from the earlier chapters in order to plan and construct investment portfolio for various types of customer with varying investment objectives. Portfolio planning and construction are accorded a very high degree of importance in the CIB Investment examination papers. It is essential therefore that the portfolio planning techniques and allied matters are thoroughly understood. Starting from May 1988, the Investment examination papers will *state* certain standard tax information. Such information will relate to income tax and Capital Gains Tax rates, and any allowances associated with them; and the Corporation Tax and Advanced Corporation Tax rates. However you are expected to study and learn the *principles* of taxation in relation to investment.

In this chapter you will study the techniques of portfolio planning, management and review, and taxation as related to investment incomes of various levels of taxpayer.

Theoretical aspects

Investment is not an exact science. In many cases of portfolio planning, there is no *one* correct answer. There are situations where a successful investor for capital growth, whose tax rate may be high or low, may produce an investment portfolio where the tax liability is completely outweighed by the successful growth of the investment. The risk involved and the investment 'climate' must be carefully assessed; e.g. when interest rates are outstripping inflation, even a higher rate taxpayer may be better off concentrating on income than capital, and when interest rates are low capital growth, after taxation, may be more important even to a basic rate taxpayer; it can be creamed off and used as income. Efficient tax planning requires constant reassessment.

Investment policy should never ignore the impact of taxation whether one is talking about Income Tax, Capital Gains Tax or Inheritance Tax, but the importance of taxation must always be a matter of opinion. Every individual's needs should be strictly defined in an objective way but a subjective element almost always creeps in.

There will always be some risk in investment and the customer should always be made aware of the degree of this. The real value of the safest investment can be eroded by inflation or changes in interest rates and this is what makes wide diversity of choice so important. Prudent management and good timing of purchases and sales play a vital part.

When preparing a portfolio of investments you should bear in mind that the customer needs to *understand* it. It must be set out neatly and clearly and display all the essential requirements for ease of comprehension by the customer. For instance, if a certain income is required, show precisely what each investment will produce and total the column of income figures. Show a knowledge of yields obtainable both in the UK and elsewhere in the world for equity based and fixed-interest investments and, if relevant, be prepared to explain the different yields. Explain the type of investment you select, e.g. a short- or long-dated government stock, a debenture stock or a preference share, etc. – don't just write in the answer, 'a fixed-interest investment giving 10% gross yield'. Show you are aware which sections of industry are prospering and give reasons for your choice. Most importantly, show the customer your originality of mind and decisiveness of thought – make your answer vital, understandable and interesting.

Practical application

Identifying the needs and requirements of investors

Individuals

The more details of the circumstances of your customers you possess, the more able you would be able to assist them with investment needs and problems. The only way to obtain such details is by closely (without giving offence) questioning them. If you are able to generate confidence in them that you are genuinely interested in their material welfare, you are more likely to obtain the information you need. Make sure that you treat with utmost care the information entrusted to you in confidence.

Questions, such as the following, should be asked and answered at the first interview with the customer.

(a) *Personal details* – name and address; age of self (and spouse); marital status; state of health of self (and spouse); dependents (children's ages, relatives); insurance covers (life, property); and whether resident of UK.

(b) *Occupational details* – (if both self and spouse are earning members of the family, then occupational details of both are relevant and should be obtained) salary; length of employment; nature of occupation (permanent, temporary); pension rights; car or other allowances; and if self-employed – nature of business, position in the business (partner, director, sole proprietor), financial state of the business.

(c) *Financial details* – residential house (wholly owned, mortgaged amount outstanding – how much, for how long, to whom and how often?); state of repair of the house; lease position (freehold or leasehold – length of lease remaining); any other incomes (interest, dividend, royalties, rents etc.); contractual financial commitments (hire purchase, borrowings, school fees, covenants); other expenses in the near future (car purchase or repairs, house decoration etc.); and tax position.

(d) *Existing investments* – value, company and sector diversification; does it need tidying up before rebuilding?

(e) *Investment objectives* – safe, steady, regular income to supplement current income or to build up capital; income growth; capital growth; income and capital growth; attitude to risk; preferred investment products; time horizons (short, medium, long terms); and the size of the sum (lump sum or regular savings) available for investment.

From the information ascertained from replies to the above questions, a pattern of investment needs and requirements will emerge. Although the patterns for various groups of investor will be different, broadly speaking there may be basic similarities in the pattern of investors in the same tax group/band.

Taxpayers

The tax position of an investor is one of the most important considerations in his/her choice of investment, because the effect of taxation upon investment returns can be considerable. The two taxes that most affect the investment selection in portfolio planning are Income Tax and Capital Gains Tax.

Among the taxpayers, the broad division is between the basic rate taxpayers and higher rate taxpayers. It is safe to say that taxpayers in both groups wish to pay no tax or as little tax as possible, without infringing the tax laws. Tax avoidance, *not* tax evasion, should be one of the main objectives of portfolio construction.

(a) *Basic rate taxpayers' needs:*
- Easy access to cash *plus* best return from cash investments.
- Highest tax-free return investments.
- Highest net income – when interest rates are expected to rise/fall.
- Protection of the value of income and capital.
- Highest net income and capital growth – in longer terms.
- Avoidance of CGT on capital gains.
- Pension income.

(b) *Higher rate taxpayers' needs:*
- Capital growth is more important than income.
- Easy access to cash *plus* best return from cash investments.
- Maximum capital growth with maximum tax savings.
- Protection of capital's real value (i.e. against inflation) *plus* tax free capital growth.
- Investments with the higher capital returns, free of CGT.
- The avoidance of CGT, on gains beyond tax-free threshold.
- Higher net pension payments for the self-employed/employed.

Non-taxpayers

Needs:
- Easy access to cash with no tax commitments.
- Higher gross return investments – in the short and long terms.
- Higher net return investments where tax paid can be reclaimed.
- Investments free of CGT.
- Higher gross pension payments, with no tax liability.

Employed persons

Needs (appropriately includes the taxpayers' and non-taxpayers' investment needs):
- Highest net income to supplement earned income.
- Availability of funds if made redundant.
- Access to funds in times of temporary loss of earnings.
- Increased pension payments.

Unemployed persons

Needs:
- The most tax-effective way in which redundancy payment can be invested to provide for day-to-day living expenses, mortgage payments and other expenses, and to supplement unemployment benefit receipts.

Retired persons

Needs:
- Safety of capital, in money terms and in real terms.
- Easy and regular access to cash, to supplement old-age payments.
- Tax free transfer of capital between the spouses, on the death of either.
- Tax free gifts to children and grandchildren.
- Outright lifetime gifts, wedding gifts, bequests to charity – not attracting tax liability from the donors or donees.
- Adequate income flow until death to meet living expenses.
- Availability of funds to pay for nursing house/old people's home fees and expenses and funeral expenses.

Self-employed persons

Needs (appropriately including the taxpayers' and non-taxpayers' investment needs):
- Investment income to provide for pension, and for such expenditure as cannot legitimately be met from profits or earnings.

Minors

(a) Special features: A minor is a person who has not attained the age of 18 years. For tax purposes, a minor is a single tax-paying person, with a single person's tax relief. A minor's income arising from money given by a parent, is deemed to be the income of the parent and liable to tax accordingly. However, a minor's income arising from money given by a grandparent, uncle or aunt or any person other than a parent is deemed to be the income of the minor, and liable to tax as such. However the changes in the 1988/89 Budget should be borne in mind. (see below)
(b) Needs:
- If investment is made by a parent, it must be tax efficient for the parent's marginal rate of income tax.
- If investment is made by the minor or by another person other than a parent, it must be tax efficient for a tax-paying single person.
- Access to cash, easy and tax efficient.
- Highest gross investment income in the longer term to build up capital.

Non-residents

(a) Special features:
- Not liable to CGT on investment capital gains;
- Exempt from stamp duty on share purchases;
- Liable to income tax on income arising in the UK;

- Eligible to receive bank, building society interest gross after filling the Declaration Form;
- Eligible to obtain some gilts on which interest will be paid gross.
  (b) Needs:
- Guaranteed maximum income, net of all UK taxes;
- Some UK investments, if return to UK is planned, with capital growth orientation.

Trusts

Family trusts

Special features

These will arise under the terms of a will, from the statutory provisions of intestacy and by an inter-vivos settlement deed. In all these cases the express provisions written in the will or settlement deed or the statutory provisions is the case of an intestacy, must be observed. Express provisions which are restrictive, however, can be widened by using the powers contained on the Trustee Investments Act 1961 (TIA). TIA provisions are in themselves somewhat restrictive and where the widest investment powers are desirable they can often be obtained by agreement among all of the beneficiaries if this is practicable or by application for an order from the court. However the legal aspects of investment powers can be complicated and difficult and in those situations which are not straightforward legal advice should be obtained.

In all of the aforementioned types of family trust, trustees have a duty to act responsibly and in the manner of a prudent business person and to cater fairly for the respective interests of all the beneficiaries whether they are entitled to income or capital or both. Generally trustees should obtain and follow professional advice unless the trustees are themselves professionals.

Where the investment powers of trustees were restricted to statutory powers or there were no investment powers expressed in the settlement or will, only those investments specified in the Trustee Act 1925 (in Scotland, the Trusts (Scotland) Act 1921) could be purchased. These were mainly fixed interest investments in the form of gilt-edged stocks. A main exemption to this was the additional powers given to trustees under the Settled Land Act 1925 enabling them in certain circumstances to purchase land and buildings and also to spend capital on alterations and improvements. To meet changing requirements the Trustee Investments Act 1961 was brought in. Trustees do not have to operate the provisions of the Act but the investment power contained in the Act usefully widens the scope for investment, particularly in equities. To accomplish this it is necessary to divide the trust fund into two equal parts called narrower range and wider range. Where trustees are given specific powers to retain or acquire investments not allowed under the TIA such investments can be retained in a third range, called special range. Investments authorised under the TIA are as follows:

(a) Narrower range investments:

Without advice as defined in section 6(4) of the Act:

- National Savings Certificates and their Northern Ireland counterparts.
- Deposits with the National Savings Bank, ordinary deposits with Trustee Savings Bank and deposits with banks and bank departments.
- National Savings Income Bond and Deposit Bonds.

With advice a trustee may invest in:

- Other fixed interest securities issued by the governments of the UK or the Isle of Man, and Treasury bills;
- Securities, the interest on which is guaranteed by the government of the UK;
- Fixed-interest securities issued in the UK by public authorities or nationalised industries;
- Fixed-interest securities issued in the UK by the government of an overseas Commonwealth territory or by any public or local authority within such Territory, and registered in the UK;
- Fixed-interest securities issued in the UK by the International Bank for Reconstruction and Development and the Inter-American Development Bank and registered in the UK.
- Debentures registered and issued in the UK by a company incorporated in the UK (debentures include for this purpose debenture stocks, whether charged on specific assets or not and loan stocks).
- Stocks of the Bank of Ireland.
- Debentures issued by the Agricultural Mortgage Corporation PLC and its Scottish equivalent;
- Loans to local authorities in the UK and certain other authorities;
- Debentures guaranteed and preference stocks of water boards which have paid a dividend on their ordinary shares of at least 5% per annum in each of the ten years preceding the investment.
- Investment accounts with a Trustee Savings Bank.
- Building society deposit accounts (the societies must be designated under section 1 of the House Purchase and Housing Act 1959 generally referred to as having 'trustee status').
- Mortgages of property in England, Wales or Northern Ireland which is freehold or leasehold with sixty years or more unexpired and loans on hereditable security in Scotland.
- Perpetual rent–charges on land in England, Wales or Northern Ireland for farm rents issuing out of such land, and for duties of ground annuals in Scotland.

(b) Wider range investments:

With advice a trustee may invest in:

- Any securities issued in the UK not being narrower-range investments by a company incorporated in the UK and which are registered in the UK;

- Shares in building societies of which the deposits qualify as narrower-range investments;
- Authorised unit trusts.

Securities of companies, both shares and debentures, must meet four criteria to qualify as investments under the Act:

- They must be securities of a fully listed company;
- Any shares must be fully paid except for new issues to be paid up within nine months;
- The company must have a paid up share capital of at least £1 million.
- The company must have paid a dividend on all classes of share capital in each of the five years preceding the investment.

As already mentioned the powers given under the TIA are not completely unfettered. There is an inability to invest in freehold or leasehold land or buildings and trustees are not allowed to invest in insurance based products. Overseas companies registered abroad are not allowed. Criticisms have also been made against the criteria referred to above. A company with a paid up capital of £1 million is now quite small. The requirement concerning payments of dividends does not stipulate maintenance or increase of dividends and a company could still be authorised as a wider-range investment if dividends were consecutively falling or paid out of diminishing reserves.

The division of a trust fund under the requirements of the TIA 1961 requires care:

(a) Special range Property – in the absence of any special powers in the trust investment to return or postpone sale or acquire particular types of investment, there can be no Special-range part of the trust fund when division of the fund takes place. However if a special power of investment exists investments may be retrieved or acquired in the Special-range. If authorised Special range investments are purchased, including rights issues, the cost can be met by sale if necessary of investment from the narrower and wider-range.

(b) Narrower-range (NR) and Wider-range (WR) Property – trust funds to be divided under the TIA where no or restricted powers exist, mainly with the objective of buying or retaining equities in the trust funds must be set up initially with NR and WR funds of equal value. Once these funds have been set up there can be no reversal of the decision. Investments on the NR are restricted to authorised NR investments whether they are transferred in from existing investments in the trust fund when division takes place or are purchased. In the WR, investments can comprise both WR and NR investments transferred into the WR fund from the existing trust fund when division takes place or are purchased. Unauthorised investments may not be held in either the NR or WR but must be sold and reinvested in suitable investments, authorised under the TIA. Subsequent proceeds of sale of Special Range investments, which cannot be re-invested in the Special

Range as no power to do so exists in the trust investment, must be divided equally between the NR and WR parts for authorised re-investment.

Transfers between NR and WR can only be made by compensating transfers of equal value. Any additions such as rights issues or bonus issues are accrued to the part of the fund which holds the existing investments. Funds introduced to the trust fund must be divided equally between NR and WR. Capital paid out of the fund can be taken from NR, WR or SR and no compensating adjustment is necessary.

After division NR and WR parts will not remain equal in value for long. Differing rates of growth, the effect of inflation withdrawals from different parts of the fund, all contribute to this.

The need for proper professional advice cannot be stressed too highly and if there is any doubt in the mind of trustees about this, legal guidance should be obtained. If a trustee, who acts in a fiduciary capacity, does not maintain the highest standards, he/she can be personally liable for loss occurring.

The Trustee Act 1925, although amended by the TIA 1961, still remains in force for a number of important statutory powers. These include:

(a) The purchase and retention of bearer securities if authorised, provided they were registered.

(b) Powers and duties of lending trust funds on mortgages.

(c) Authorisation to trustees to concur in schemes of arrangement for the reconstruction, amalgamation or take-over of a company.

(d) Authorisation to exercise any conditional or preferential right to subscribe for any securities which may be offered in respect of an authorised holding.

All the aforementioned matters can be complicated and, if necessary, legal advice should be obtained.

Needs:

Different types of family trust have investment needs for investment purposes as follows:

(a) Bare trusts – funds held in these trusts usually consist of incomes held for absolutely entitled beneficiaries (often minors) subject to their obtaining a specified age. As the beneficiary is eventually entitled to both capital and income apart from investing according to the emphasis, required on the need for capital or income tax considerations are a feature and 'Minors' on page 250 should be referred to.

(b) Interest in possession trusts – these arise under the terms of settlements or probably most often under will trusts. Beneficiaries usually are entitled to income or capital but not both. The trustee has a duty to preserve a balance between the differing interests and needs of those beneficiaries who require income and a continued growth of income, against the beneficiaries who eventually inherit the capital which they naturally wish to grow as much as possible, and this can lead to conflict. The trustee therefore has to follow a firm and delicate path in order to maintain a proper balance in pursuing an investment policy. The provisions of the trust investment should be carefully borne in mind and, where appropriate, any enlargement of investment powers necessary to enhance the interests of the beneficiaries should be adopted whether by statutory or other means.

Generally the interests of beneficiaries can be achieved by maintaining a balance between fixed interest securities and equities or equity based investments such as unit trusts.

From 1988/89 trust income will bear tax at 25%. The annual exemption limit for capital gains tax will be at a rate equivalent to the basic rate of income tax.

(c) Discretionary Trusts – in such a trust discretion is given to the trustees as to which of a wide class of beneficiaries will benefit either in the form of income or capital or both. Consequently investment policy has to be flexible particularly as beneficiaries do not have a predetermined right to income and usually no right to capital either. The trust will normally include investment powers to accumulate income and advance capital. Accumulated income will be taxed from 1988/89 at 35% (10% above basic rate) and when distributed will suffer tax at the marginal rate of the beneficiary. The trust funds are liable to inheritance tax once every ten years and the tax is levied at the lifetime rates which are half the rates applied at death. Capital Gains Tax is dealt with as for an interest in possession trust.

(d) Accumulation and Maintenance Trusts – these are flexible trusts for the benefit of minor children who can be in existence or unborn when the settlement is created. Income can be used for the maintenance, education or advancement of minor beneficiaries. If the capital put into this type of trust comes from other than the parent (see 'Minors' on page 250) tax can be recovered on behalf of the minor up to the amount of the personal allowance. Accumulated income is taxed as accumulated income is treated in discretionary trusts. However there are inheritance tax advantages over discretionary trusts as the ten-yearly lifetime inheritance tax charge is not applicable. Funds put into most types of trust are subject to lifetime inheritance tax at the time of the gift by the settlor but this does not apply to accumulation and maintenance trusts and trusts for the disabled. Investment policy must be flexible, bearing in mind the need for income and the expected duration of the trust.

Charitable trusts – Charities

Special features:
A charity fund/trust can be set up provided its organisers satisfy the Charity Commissioners that it will serve at least one of the following causes:
- Advancement of education
- Advancement of religion

- Relief of poverty
- Any other cause beneficial to the community.

Unlike personal trusts which must come to an end eventually (the Rule against Perpetuities effectively limits their 'life' to around 100 years), charitable trusts may go on indefinitely.

Registered charities are exempt from the UK income tax and CGT. Charitable trusts are managed by trustees and, if the powers conferred upon them by the deed are inadequate, they may take advantage of the Trustee Investments Act 1961.

Needs:

- Highest growth element and the highest redemption yield from investments, within the constraints of the current demand for liquidity.
- Investments where distributions are made gross of tax, or where the charities can reclaim the Advance Corporation Tax deductions (e.g. certain unit trusts and collective investment and management through the Collective Investment Scheme, allowed under the Charities Act 1960).
- Donations under a deed of covenant of more than three years so that the charities may reclaim tax at the basic rate.

Pension funds

Pension funds are among the largest investors in the UK and are controlled by the trustees who are usually appointed by the employers, although in a minority of cases employees have a say in their appointment. Trustees often appoint professional investment managers to carry out the investment policies subject to guidelines laid down by the trustees. Pension funds are approved by the Inland Revenue as exempt from all forms of taxation although if benefits are deemed excessive the fund may only be granted partial exemption. Contributions are allowable for tax relief. Investment powers are usually very wide and if they are at all limited powers can easily be widened. The actuary appointed to the fund usually lays down the desired annual return.

Needs:

Beneficiaries or members of the fund are interested in the total return from both capital and income. There has to be an element of liquidity in the fund to meet the pensions paid and the way in which this is achieved depends on the reserves of the fund, its size and the number of pensioners. In a typical fund the proportion of investment in each type of security could be 20% in gilt-edged, 10% in property and 70% in equities (30% overseas).

Taxation of investment income and capital

The tax position of an investor is one of the most crucial considerations in the choice of investments and in formulating an investment portfolio policy.

This is because the effect of taxation on investment capital and income can be quite considerable. There are three main taxes which directly affect the investors; viz. Income Tax, Capital Gains Tax and Inheritance Tax. It is therefore vital that you understand the application of these three taxes in some detail.

Income Tax (IT)

Income received by persons from all sources is taxed, after the deduction of approved allowances, at the taxpayer's marginal IT rate.

A person's marginal rate of income tax is the rate of tax he/she pays on the highest band (marginal band) of his/her taxable income. The IT rates and allowances are subject to alteration by the Chancellor of the Exchequer for each year which runs from 6 April to the following 5 April. Anyone (including an infant) who is resident or domiciled in the UK or who has income which comes from the UK, is liable to IT.

IT is a tax on income from earnings – wages, salaries, fees, pensions, investments (interests, dividends, rents) and from other sources – received by individuals, unincorporated businesses (sole traders, partnerships) and trusts.

The tax rate bands in 1987/88 and 1988/89 on the taxable income of individuals are given below.

1987–88 taxable income (£)	Rate of tax %	1988–89 taxable income (£)	Rate of tax %
Up to 17 900	27	Up to 19 300	25
17 901–20 400	40	Over 19 300	40
20 401–25 400	45		
25 401–33 300	50		
33 301–41 200	55		
Over 41 200	60		

The main personal *IT reliefs* for 1987/88 and 1988/89 are given below. When the appropriate relief *plus* the 'allowable outgoings' (see below) are offset against the total gross income, the amount of taxable income results.

	1987/88(£)	1988/89(£)
(a) Single person	2 425	2 605 (+180)
(b) Married man	3 795	4 095 (+300)
* (c) Wife's earned income allowance	2 425	2 605 (+180)
(d) Additional personal allowance	1 370	1 490 (+120)
(e) Single age allowance (65–79)	2 960	3 180 (+220)
(f) Married age allowance (65–79)	4 675	5 035 (+360)
(g) Single age allowance (80 and over)	3 070	3 310 (+240)
(h) Married age allowance (80 and over)	4 845	5 205 (+360)
** (i) Age allowance income limit	9 800	10 600 (+800)

* This is the maximum.

** Age allowance is reduced down to personal allowance levels by £1 for £1 of excess income over £10 600 in 1988/89, £9800 in 1987/88.

Allowable outgoings

These mainly include mortgage interest, pension subscriptions, payments under deeds of covenant (not on new covenants made after 15 March 1988 except to charities), and certain payments in connection with employment or self-employment. No tax relief on home improvements is allowed *after* 6 April 1988.

Under certain circumstances, where a couple have substantial joint earnings, it may be advantageous for them to be assessed separately, i.e. wife's earning election, as shown in the following examples.

Example 1   IT liability calculation – jointly assessed, no election (1988/89)

	£	£
Earned income:		
Husband		25 000
Wife		15 000
Investment income		
(husband and wife)		5 000
		45 000
Deduct:		
Married man's allowance	4 095	
Wife's earned income allowance	2 605	
Mortgage interest (gross)	3 900	
Outgoings	250	10 850
Taxable income		34 150

Tax payable:
at 25% on £19 300 = 4 825
at 40% on £14 850 = 5 940   £10 765

Net income (£45 000 − £10 765) = £34 235

Example 2   IT liability calculation – separately assessed – with election (1988/89)

	£	£
Earned income:		25 000
Investment income		
(husband and wife)		5 000

	£	£
Deduct:		
Single person's allowance	2 605	
Outgoings, paid by husband	4 150	6 700
Husband's taxable income		23 245
Tax payable at 25% on £19 300	4 825	
Tax payable at 40% on £3 945	1 578	6 403
Husband's net income (£30 000 − £6403)		£23 597
Wife's earned income		15 000
Deduct single person's allowance		2 605
Wife's taxable pay		12 395
Deduct tax payable at 25%		3 098
Wife's net pay (£15 000 − £3 098)		11 902
Comparison of tax liabilities:		£
Net income − with no election		34 235
Net income − with election (£23 597 + £11 902)		35 499
Savings − with election		1 264

Independent taxation of wife's income − 1988/89 Budget

From April 1990, husbands and wives will be independently taxed. Wives will have complete privacy and independence in their tax affairs and tax penalties on marriage will end.

Under the new system, all taxpayers, male or female, married or single, will be entitled to the same personal allowance, which will be available against income of all kinds, whether from earnings or savings.

In addition, there will be a married man's allowance, equal to the difference under the old system between the married man's allowance and the single allowance. This will go to the husband in the first instance, but he will be able to transfer the unused portion of it to his wife.

Husband and wife will be taxed independently on any capital gains they may have, with an annual exemption each, instead of one between them, as now. Transfers of capital between husband and wife will continue to be entirely free of tax.

Two further penalties on marriage will be abolished under the new system:
1   For new mortgages, after 1 August 1988, the £30 000 limit on mortgage interest relief will be related to the house or flat concerned, irrespective of the number of borrowers. An unmarried couple will no longer be able to get twice as much relief as a married couple;

2   From from April 1989, unmarried couples with children will be entitled to only one additional personal allowance, so that they no longer get more tax relief than a married couple.

An important aspect of the independent taxation of wife's income is the privacy of wife's investment income. It seems that even if the wife has no job, she could use her allowances against income from her savings, taking money out of the building society (where tax is deducted and is not recoverable) and putting it in National Savings where no tax is payable. Even if she has no capital but her husband has, he could transfer investments to her to use up her allowance against the dividend or interest. If he is a high rate taxpayer he may transfer enough assets to her so that her basic rate tax band is also available on what was his investment income.

Other changes 1988/89 Budget

1   *Convenant*
A covenant used to be a tax effective way of giving one's children (who are over 18 years of age or married) and grandchildren money, provided the deed of covenant lasted more than six years. The adult could deduct the basic rate of tax from the gift but the child or the grandchild could claim the tax back to the limit of the personal allowance.

Example
A father gave his son (over 18) through a legal deed of covenant, £1000 p.a. for 10 years, in 1987.

Gift	1000
less tax at basic rate (1987/88)	270
Son gets from father	730
Son reclaims tax	270
Son gets the full gift given by father	1000

Note: (a) Irrespective of the donor's marginal rate of tax, the donor could only deduct tax at basic rate
  (b) Donor could not benefit from the donation.

On all new covenants (with the exception of those for charities) made on or after 15 March 1988, tax relief has been abolished. For all new covenants, those receiving the payments will not be liable to tax on them and those making the payment will get no tax relief on them. The largest single group of people affected by this change will be parents of students, and there may be a parallel reduction in the scale of parental contribution to the maintenance grant for the children's education expenses.

2   *Business taxation*
The small companies' rate of corporation tax is cut to 25% (standard rate is 35%), in line with the basic rate of income tax.

3 *Business Expansion Scheme*
The amount of finance a BES company can raise in any 12 month period is now limited to £500 000, except where the finance is raised for ship chartering or for the provision of private rented housing, where the limit is £5 million.

4 *Personal Equity Plan*
The annual investment limit has been raised from £2400 (£4800 for married couples to £3000 (£6000 for married couples). The amount which can be invested in unit and investment trusts has been raised from £420 to £540 (£45 a month) or, if greater 25% of the total investment.

5 *Home improvement loans*
Tax relief on all new house improvement loans is abolished.

6 *Company cars*
The tax charge has been doubled.

7 *Subscription to charities*
Tax relief for payroll giving to charities was doubled: from £120 to £240 a year.

8 *Capital duty*
Whenever a new company was formed or an existing company sold new shares to the public, it had to pay a capital duty of 1%. This duty is abolished, because it discriminated against equity capital as compared with debt finance and bank borrowing.

9 *Unit trust investment*
The duty payable on all property put into a unit trust is abolished.

10 *Investment in woodlands*
The use of forestry as a tax shelter is abolished by taking out commercial woodlands out of the income tax system entirely, but parallel increase in planting grants is made available.

11 *Trusts*
The additional rate applying to income of discretionary and accumulation trusts is reduced to 10% for 1988/89. The overall rate, basic plus additional, is therefore 35%.

12 *Life Assurance Premium Relief*
LAPR on policies taken out on or before 13 March 1984 is reduced to 12.5% for premiums paid on or after 6 April 1989.

13 *PAYE calculations*
The new tax rates and allowances will be effective on the first pay day after 14 June 1988.

14 *Penalty for non-disclosure*
From 1988/89 tax year, measures are proposed including a more realistic penalty for failure to notify liability to tax, which will assist the Inland Revenue in obtaining the information it needs so that the tax liabilities of individuals and businesses can be properly settled. Some measures take effect immediately and others will not be implemented until 1992 at the earliest.

Capital Gains Tax (CGT)

Any surplus arising from the disposal of securities, land and other assets, after exemptions and reliefs, is either assessed to income tax (i.e. when the surplus is derived from a business dealing) or chargeable to CGT. Capital gains chargeable to CGT are taxed at 30% but the first £6600 (for 1987/88; for 1988/89, see below) of the gain (taking husband and wife together) is exempt. Gains up to £6600 can therefore be realised tax free. The exemptions cannot, however, be carried forward and some planning may be necessary to obtain the maximum benefit.

Many capital gains are created or swollen by inflation. Thus the surplus may not create gains in real terms up to the full amount. For gains made on disposals before April 1982, there was no relief for the inflationary element in them. But gains made on or after 6 April 1982, may be reduced by an 'indexation allowance'. The calculation and application of the indexation allowance was substantially amended for disposal made after 5 April 1985. The factor used to compute the indexation allowance is according to the following formula:

$$\frac{RD - RI}{RI}$$

Where RD = the Retail Price Index (RPI) for the month of disposal
RI = the RPI for March 1982 or the RPI for the month in which the expenditure was incurred, whichever is later.

The factor is rounded to the nearest third decimal place. If RD is less than or equal to RI then there will be no indexation allowance.

Significant changes were made in 1985 to the rules regarding the indexation allowance. It is no longer necessary to own an asset for one year before it qualifies for the allowance and the allowance can now create or increase the CGT loss.

Example 1: Indexation Allowance computation
X bought shares costing £8000 on 12 August 1985. He sold them on 4 October 1987 for £22000, and realised a gain of £14000. Suppose the relevant RPI figures were as follows:

August 1985 (RI)	= 376
December 1987 (RD)	= 404

The *Indexation Allowance* = $\frac{404 - 376}{376}$ = 0.074

	£
Purchase cost of shares	= 8 000
Indexation factor (£8000 × 0.074)	= 592

The chargeable gain for 1987–88:

Share disposal receipt	= 22 000
less cost	= 8 000
	14 000
less indexation allowance	= 592
Chargeable gain for 1987/88	= 13 408

Example 2: Calculation of CGT payable (1987/88)

If the aggregate net gains made in the assessment year of 1987/88, are less than £6600, no tax is payable. Any excess of the net gains over £6600 will attract a flat rate CGT of 30%.

	£
Chargeable gains (gross) (see example 1)	13 408
less allowance losses	4 000
Net gains	9 408
less basic exemption	6 600
Tax chargeable on	2 808
Tax payable at 30%	842

Example 3: Adjustment of capital losses against gains (1987/88)

Capital losses are calculated in a manner similar to capital gains, but the indexation allowance is *added* to the aggregate losses to determine the allowable losses. Allowable losses during the year of assessment are offset against chargeable gains for that year, and if the chargeable gains are insufficient to absorb all allowable losses, the surplus losses are carried forward to future years.
Suppose:

	£
Unabsorbed losses in 1986/87, carried over to 1987/88	10 000
Allowable losses during 1986/88	4 000
Chargeable gains during 1986/88	17 600

	£
Chargeable gains	17 600
less allowable losses (1987/88)	4 000
	13 600
less losses b/f (part) from 1986/87	7 000
	6 600
less basic exemption	6 600
CGT chargeable	Nil
Unabsorbed losses c/f to 1988/89 (£10 000 − £7000)	£3 000

Strategy regarding CGT liability (1987/88)

Although minimisation of CGT should not be allowed to override other aspects in portfolio strategy, the following should be borne in mind.

1 If net gains, after indexation allowance, are in excess of £6600, it may be worth realising losses to offset against excess gains.

2 If the chargeable gains are less than the basic exemption limit of £6600, it may be worth realising further gains to take full advantage of the basic exemption allowance.

Note: unlike allowable capital losses, chargeable capital gains cannot be carried forward.

3 If the net gains for the tax year do not exceed £6600 it may be beneficial to delay making disposals that realise a loss until after 5 April as there is no advantage in *reducing* gains which are already exempt from tax.

4 CGT is payable on 1 December in the next tax year. By delaying a disposal until after the end of the tax year (5 April) one can delay payment of the tax on the disposal by a full year.

5 Following changes in 1985, it is again possible to 'bed and breakfast' a shareholding in a Stock Exchange account in order to realise a gain or loss whilst retaining the investment. However, stamp duty is payable on such transactions (see Chapter 6).

Capital gains which do not attract CGT

1 Selling a chattel for less than £3000. Chattels with a predictable life of less than 50 years are exempt from CGT.

2 Sale proceeds of the principal private residence. If more than one house is owned as a residence, one house which is to qualify for the CGT exemption should be elected. The election must be made within two years of acquiring the second house. It is possible to vary the election subsequently, in which case different houses may qualify for the exemption for different periods.

3 Friendly society bonds.

4 Personal Equity Plans (within statutory limits).

5 Life assurance policies.

6 Business Expansion Scheme investments (on fixed disposal only).

7 National Savings investments.

8 Gild-edged and other fixed interest securities.

9 The donor of chargeable assets (e.g. to children) as gifts may defer the CGT liability on the gift if the donor and donee jointly elect that the chargeable gain be deducted from the base cost of the asset to the donee. The donor will then have no CGT liability on the gift. (The deferred charge, however, may be triggered if the donee goes abroad and, if not paid, the charge could revert to the donor.)

10 A tax loss on an asset which has become worthless or of very little value, even though the asset has not been sold, and this can reduce CGT on other chargeable gains. It is not worth making the claim until the claimant is in a position to use the loss because the claim has the effect of stopping further indexation allowance accruing.

11 If a person disposes of a business asset and reinvests the proceeds in another business asset within the preceeding 12 months or the following three years, he/she may be entitled to defer the gain on the fixed asset until disposal of the second asset – this is known as roll-over relief.

Changes in CGT introduced by the 1988/89 Budget

For disposals on or after 6 April 1988:

1   Base date for tax brought forward from 1965 to 1982, so that only gains or losses accrued since 31 March 1982 will be brought into account:

2   Gains will be chargeable to CGT, not at 30%, but:

(a) for individuals at the rates that would apply if they were treated as the top slice of income,

(b) for trustees of accumulation and discretionary settlements – at a rate equivalent to the basic *plus* additional rate (see below),

(c) for other trustees and for personal representatives – at a rate equivalent to the basic rate of income tax;

3   For 1988/89 the annual exemption limit is reduced from £6600 to £5000 for individuals and from £3300 to £2500 in settlements;

4   Retirement relief is extended for disposal taking place on or after 6 April 1988 for individuals when aged 60 or above or who retire earlier on the grounds of ill-health. In addition to the existing exemption of gains up to £125 000, relief is to be extended to 50% of gains between £125 000 and £500 000.

Changes in investment strategy caused by CGT changes

Until 15 March 1988 (Budget tax) taking profit in the form of gains had two advantages to the higher rate taxpayer: the CGT rate was lower at 30% and the amount chargeable was reduced by indexation and various exemptions. It was therefore almost axiomatic that a higher rate taxpayer, where possible, would prefer to take capital gains rather than receive income. Since 6 April 1988 the picture has changed dramatically, with both income and gains being taxed at the individual's marginal rate of 25% or 40%, and the focus has shifted to differences in the amount subject to tax, the timing of the tax charge, and (in the case of investment in companies) the combined tax burden of the company and the shareholder.

For the basic rate taxpayer, there was for a number of years no difference in the rate of tax, although for the past two years the rate on gains has been

3% higher than the basic rate of income tax. Thanks to the 1988/89 Budget, the basic rate taxpayer will experience a cut in CGT to 25%.

For some investors, such as retired persons, regular income is preferred to gain, and non-tax factors, such as ease of access, costs of transactions, risk of market fluctuations all tend to favour the receipt of income. Investors whose holdings go back to March 1982 will benefit from the change in the base date from 6 April 1965 to 31 March 1982, because any gains accruing between 1965 and 1982 become tax free; gains prior to 1965 were of course tax free. Some taxpayers, with adequate income, may prefer occasional 'lumps' of gain to regular income, because they could then realise gains in years when losses or other factors have reduced the marginal rate to 25%, or when the £5000 exemption could be used to eliminate a capital gains charge altogether.

Despite the fact that there is now no difference in the rates of CGT and Income Tax, certain features of CGT still make gains more attractive than income. Even the reduced annual exemption band of £5000, is worth £2000 of tax to the 40% taxpayer, and £1250 to the basic rate taxpayer. From April 1990 husband and wife will *each* have an annual exemption band, and that makes even more attractive a personal investment policy aimed at capital growth sufficient to use these tax free bands.

The change of the base date means that only real, not inflationary gains in excess of the annual exemption limit will now be taxed. By contrast, income receipts are taxable in full, sheltered to some extent by the indexed increases in personal allowances.

It would be incorrect to assume, however, that gains would in all circumstances be preferable to income. For some taxpayers, the existence of income tax reliefs may affect the desirability of taking income or realising gains. If income from other sources fluctuates sharply, receipts taxable as income may enable relief to be obtained from income losses or investment in BES shares, or even make it possible to utilise personal allowances. The imputation system allows the payment of ACT by a company (which partly reduces the company's tax liability for the year) to be passed as tax credit to the shareholder who receives a dividend. The tax credit covers a shareholder's income tax liability at basic rate. The workings of the imputation system mean that many more taxpayers may now prefer dividends to capital growth; particularly where shareholders already make full use of their capital gains exemption and are concerned for the future prosperity of the company as the overall tax cost, under the computation system, to shareholders and company, is generally lower.

Certain other exemptions or relief affect to a major extent the gains chargeable to tax. For example, gilts, qualifying corporate bonds and, subject to certain conditions, BES shares are exempt from tax on capital gains.

Inheritance Tax (IHT)

IHT was introduced from March 1986 as a successor to the Capital Transfer Tax, which, in turn, replaced the extended Estate Duty in 1974. Basically, IHT is charged on assets passing on one's death and gifts made within seven years prior to one's death. Lifetime gifts (excepts gifts to certain trusts and transfers involving companies) are generally exempt, except that if the donor dies *within* seven years of making the gift then IHT becomes charge-able on the gift. However, 'tapering relief' (see below) scales down the potential liability to IHT after three years have passed since the making of the gift.

Certain rules apply to 'gifts with reservation', i.e. where the donor retains possession of some benefit from the asset. For example, if the donor gives his/her house to his/her children but continues to live in it this may be a gift with reservation. Broadly such gifts remain part of the donor's estate and are ineffective for IHT purposes. It must be remembered that the law relating to IHT which preserves much of the legislation and practice relating to estate duty and capital transfer tax is complex and the investor who seeks advice on the subject which departs from the straightforward, should seek expert advice.

Gifts which do not attract IHT

1   Although a husband and wife are treated separately for IHT purposes, transfers between them are exempt provided the spouse receiving the transfer is domiciled in the UK.
2   Gifts not exceeding £250 in total in the tax year to any one person.
3   Gifts within the annual exemption of £3000. Unused exemption may be carried forward for one year only, and used only after the current year's exemption has been used up.
4   Gifts in consideration of marriage of up to £5000 to a son or daughter, £2500 to a grand child and £1000 in other cases. Whilst there have been major relaxations to the regime, providing new and better tax planning opportunities, there has been no significant reduction in the severity of the rates which apply at death. Therefore, the importance of estate planning has been increased, rather than reduced, by the IHT changes.

Inheritance Tax Rates (1987/88)

Band ('000)	IHT Rate (%)	Tax payable (£)	Cumulative tax (£)
0–90	0	0	0
90–140	30	15 000	15 000
140–220	40	32 000	47 000
220–330	50	55 000	102 000
330 +	60	—	—

Tapering relief

Years between gift and death	Percentage of full charge
3–4	80
4–5	60
5–6	40
6–7	20

Minimisation of IHT liability

In addition to those gifts which do not attract IHT, the following measures will help minimise IHT liability.

1   Making gifts to trusts. Trusts have an important part to play in IHT planning – for example, if the donor does not wish to give absolute interest to the beneficiaries at this stage, or if the donor is not yet able to determine in what proportion they should benefit. Different types of trusts may be used for different purposes, and thereby substantial savings made.

2   Where exemption from IHT is contingent upon the survival of the donor, the gift is called a Potentially Exempt Transfer (PET). Making PETs reduces IHT liability considerably, especially as after three years the liability is reduced by tapering relief.

3   It is possible to take out a special life assurance policy with reducing cover after three years to reflect the decrease in the potential IHT liability due to tapering relief.

4   Avoiding of making gifts with reservations, which are ineffective for IHT purposes.

5   Making gifts of appreciating rather than depreciating assets.

6   Making adequate provision for retirement through a company pension scheme or a retirement security scheme. The financial security thus achieved may give increased scope for lifetime giving.

7   A husband and wife are treated as separate persons for IHT purposes, therefore if the will is drafted in such a way as to pass the wealth direct to the next generation from *both* spouses rather than just from the surviving spouse, it will lead to considerable savings.

8   Certain business and agricultural properties, by making the best use of property reliefs, can be reduced by 50% or 30% in arriving at their value for IHT purposes.

IHT changes in the 1988/89 Budget

The two major changes are:

1   The raising of the threshold from £90 000 to £110 000, and

2   The establishing of a flat rate tax at 40% for transfers on or after 15 March 1988 which replaces the previous rates of 30%, 40%, 50% and 60%. For the wealthiest, the top marginal rate has therefore been cut by 20%,

and for those with modest estates of up to £220 000, the marginal rate has increased to or has remained unchanged at, 40%. The increase in the level of the threshold and the marginal rate make it more important than ever to ensure that the exemption bands are used to the full, and arrangements already made to utilise the exempt band will need to be reviewed to be kept up to date.

It is common for a husband and wife to provide in their wills that the entire estate of the first to die should pass to the surviving spouse. However, the effect of such an arrangement is to increase the eventual IHT charge on the total property owned by the couple, because only one exempt band is used on the second death. If the assets are sufficient, £44 000 of tax can be saved by leaving property, up to the value of exempt band of £110 000, to someone other than the spouse (e.g. children or grandchildren).

The effect of IHT changes on the use of trusts

1 *Accumulation, maintenance and possession trusts*
Since 1986, gifts into accumulation and maintenance trusts have been potentially exempt transfers (PETs), and since 1987, gifts into possession trusts have been exempt. Therefore, provided the donor survives for the required seven years, the changes in the rates and exempt band are unlikely to reduce interest in trusts for tax planning purposes.

2 *Discretionary trusts*
Gifts into these trusts remain chargeable as lifetime transfers, at half the rate applicable on death. Therefore *now* the maximum rate payable on transfers of unlimited amounts in discretionary trusts, is 20%, rather than 30%. If the assets qualify for business property relief, the effective rate is reduced to 10%.

A gift into a discretionary trust up to the exempt band incurs no tax now, and will, after seven years, drop out of the account, so that the nil rate band will be available for use again. Therefore, in circumstances where outright gifts are not appropriate these trusts for children and grandchildren can be used to multiply, over a period of years, the benefit of exempt band. This allows flexibility to the trustees in deciding how to use funds for the beneficiaries. Furthermore, where there is no tax charge on the payments into the trust, payments out to the beneficiaries within the first 10 years of the life of the trust are similarly not subject to tax.

The changes in CGT may now make it advantageous for some assets to be held from the outset in discretionary trust. Suppose, the settlor's exempt amount will be fully utilised, this gives an additional exempt amount of £2500 (half the amount of the individual capital gains allowance for 1988/89) and also enables any gains to be taxed on the trust at 35%, rather than on the individual at, possibly, 40%. Gains on assets held in life interest trusts will be taxed at 25%.

Deeds of covenant

New covenants to individuals will no longer achieve any tax saving for income tax purposes, however there is one situation for IHT where they may continue to be of use, viz. where an elderly person already makes full use of the annual exemption and in addition makes regular gifts out of income. The claim to IHT exemption for these gifts, provided the elderly person does not die within seven years of the latest of the series of gifts, may be simplified if they are made under a deed of covenant.

Portfolio planning and construction

By identifying the needs and requirements of investors (see above), an investor profile can be drawn up, and from that profile a 'tailor-made' investment folio can be constructed for each investor.

Several broad portfolio outlines are given below for various *groups* of taxpayer. The outlines can be adjusted to suit the requirements of the *individual* investor in each group.

Note: most sources of investment can alter their terms overnight and what was 'suitable' today may become 'unsuitable' tomorrow. Keep this general warning in mind as you study the portfolio outlines given below. Also note that an investment which gives capital growth also gives an element of hedge against inflation.

Non-taxpayer group

General profile: relatively low income, limited resources for investments, limited existing investments, mortgage payments, dependents.

General needs: good income, ready access to capital, safety of capital and income, some capital growth, short- and medium-term time horizons, life insurance cover of the breadwinner.

Portfolio outline

Investments	Income	Liquidity	Safety of capital	Safety of income	Capital growth	Remarks
NSB Investment Account	high	not instant	yes	yes	no	interest is paid gross
Banks:						
Current account	no	instant	yes	no income	no	
High interest deposit	high	instant and notice	yes	yes	no	ACT deductions – cannot be reclaimed

Investments	Income	Liquidity	Safety of capital	Safety of income	Capital growth	Remarks
Building society: Ordinary shares	good	instant	yes	yes	no	ACT deductions – cannot be reclaimed
Term shares	high	yes with notice	yes	yes	if income reinvested	withdrawal notice required; interest paid gross
National Savings Income Bonds	high	yes	yes	yes	no	monthly income; interest paid gross
National Savings Deposit Bonds	no	no	yes	yes	yes	interest added to capital
High coupon medium term gilts from National Savings Stock Register	high	yes	yes	yes	yes	interest paid gross
Index-linked gilts	no	yes	yes	yes	yes	provided interest rate does not rise
Income-orientated unit trusts-giving monthly income	good	yes	fair	fair	possible	tax deduction can be reclaimed
Life insurance, regular premium	no	no	yes	no income	yes	all proceeds tax-free

The liquidity element in all portfolios is extremely important. Its size, i.e. its proportion to the investment capital, will depend upon the size of such capital and individual's circumstances; if it is small then most of it will need to be absorbed in the liquidity cushion.

Basic-rate taxpayer group

General profile: average income, average resources for investment, some existing investments, some knowledge of investment market, cautious attitude to risk, regular job, pension rights, dependents, mortgage payments. *General needs:* liquidity, income and capital growth, safety of income and capital, medium- and long term horizons, insurance cover.

Portfolio outline

Investments	Immediate access to capital	Safety	Income growth	Capital growth	Risk element	Remarks
Bank investments	yes	yes	some	no	yes if interest rate rises	High interest and current accounts

Investments	Immediate access to capital	Safety	Income growth	Capital growth	Risk element	Remarks
High interest building society deposits	with notice	yes	some risk element	yes if income if not spent	yes if interest rate rises	
NSCs	no	yes	no	yes	yes if interest rate rises	
Medium-term gilts with highest net interest and redemption yields	no	yes	yes	yes	yes if interest rate rises	Excellent if interest rate expected to fall
Bank and building societic variable rate with highest net yields	no	yes	yes	some	no	suitable when interest rates expected to rise
Index-linked gilts, NSCs	no	yes	no	yes	no	especially if inflation expected to rise
Direct/indirect investment in equities, BES	no	some	some	yes	yes	as above, and when economic outlook is bright
Single premium Insurance Bonds	no	yes	no	yes	no	to benefit from CGT basic tax free limit. 5 % withdrawals
PEP and Friendly Society investments	no	yes	no	yes	no	highly tax efficient
Personal Pension Plans	no	yes	no	yes	no	highly tax efficient
Capital shares of split level investment trusts	no	yes	no	yes	no	mainly for capital growth
House purchase	no	yes	no	yes	no	mortgage interest relief

Investors with sufficient funds may pursue an active investment policy, i.e. frequent switching between markets – keeping a watch on dealing costs and growth orientated unit trusts.

Higher – rate taxpayer group

General profile: high income, sufficient investment capital, investment portfolio exists, knowledgeable of investment products, willing to take risk, agreeable to an active investment policy, own house, some dependents, good job, pension rights.

Portfolio outline

Investments	Liquidity	Capital growth	Safety	Income Tax Saving	Inflation hedge	CGT benefits	Strategy
Bank and Building Society accounts and deposits	yes	no	yes	no	no	no	choose instant access and highest net IT interest rates
NSCs and index-linked NSCs	no	yes	yes	yes	some/yes	yes	maximum entitlement; very tax effective.
Friendly Society savings	no	yes	yes	yes	some	yes	maximum entitlement; very tax effective
National Savings Yearly Plan	no	yes	yes	yes	some	yes	maximum entitlement; very tax effective
PEP	no	yes	yes	yes	possible	yes	maximum entitlement; very tax effective
Low coupon gilts	no	yes	yes	yes	possible	yes	highest net of tax plus CGT yield capital gain
Index-linked gilts	no	yes	yes	yes	yes	yes	most of the return is tax-free
Direct/indirect investment in equity with low dividend yield	no	yes	some risk	yes	possible	no	high capital, not income, growth
Capital share of split level ITs	no	yes	yes	yes	some	no	high capital, not income, growth
Single premium insurance bonds	no	yes	yes	yes	some	no	cheap switching, 5% of initial investment withdrawable tax-free p.a. tax free rolled up value
Personal Pension Plan	no	yes	some risk	yes	possible	yes	most tax effective long-term security
BES	no	yes	some risk	yes	possible	yes	risky – but highly tax efficient
Traded options, warrants	no	possible	some risk	no	possible	no	risky but highly tax efficient
Premium Bonds	no	no	yes	yes	no	yes	prizes tax free

General needs: maximum capital growth, minimum income tax liability, medium- and longer-term horizons, income and liquidity less important.

Note: IHT benefits of investments are very difficult to define with certainty. Therefore, although IHT benefits can always be a feature and consideration, yet the needs of the investors and their immediate dependents should always have priority.

This group of investor requires investments which are highly tax efficient in producing maximum capital growth in preference to income growth in order to avoid as much as possible of the income tax liability at higher rates. Minimisation of CGT is important also. These investors may also expect an active investment policy.

Retired persons group

General profile: cautious and generally averse to risk-taking, pension recipient, adequate savings for investment, limited dependents, own house outright, some investments, all levels of taxpayer.

General needs: safety of capital, easy access to funds, regular income for life, Tax free gifts to grandchildren, tax free transfers between spouses, medium- and long-term horizons.

Portfolio outline

Investment	Liquidity	Safety	Regular income	Tax savings	Remarks
NSB investment account and bank and building society deposits	yes	yes	yes	possible	liquidity and tax savings if non-taxpayer
National Savings Income Bond	yes	yes	yes	possible	liquidity and tax savings if non-taxpayer
Annuities	no	yes	yes	possible	Income for life, capital part tax-free; not suitable until over 70
Special term life assurance	no	yes	no	yes	tapering relief reduces IHT liability
Gifts: to spouses, lifetime gifts, charities, wedding gifts grandchildren	no	yes	no	some	to reduce IHT liability for donor and donee and keep wealth within the family or help charities.

Much will depend upon the amount of investment capital, state of health, amount of pensions and tax position.

Trusts

General profile: constrained in investment policy by the terms of trust deed, but most modern trusts have wide powers of investment and, if necessary, take advantage of TIA provisions; meet the income payments laid down in the deed; pay income tax at 45% on income not distributed and CGT at 30% beyond the the £3300 tax-free limit (1987/88).

General needs: highest tax-free income and capital gains commensurate with duties as trustees and the terms of the trust.

Portfolio outline: while the previous portfolio outlines are relevant as general guidelines, with trusts it must be borne in mind that trustees act in a fiduciary capacity and should act responsibly bearing in mind the interests of all the beneficiaries and generally should adopt the policy of a prudent business person. Therefore a portfolio outline for the trusts as a group, on the lines of previous portfolio outlines, will not only be too simplified but will also be misleading.

Charities

General profile: expected to serve some cause beneficial to the community; long life; exempt from the UK income tax and CGT; bound by terms of trust deed but can take advantage of ITA, most charities have wide investment powers.

General needs: highest growth and redemption yields; make payments which can be both capital and income.

Portfolio outline: as with trusts, it would be misleading to give one, even general, portfolio outline.

Non-residents group

General needs: may or may not return to UK; may or may not have financial commitments and dependents in the UK; income may be earned overseas and in the UK.

General needs: income growth; protection against inflation; capital growth; easy access to income; a measure of liquidity.

Portfolio outline: the investment needs of the non-resident group, if the UK is to be the investment base, are very much in line with the outlines for the different rates of taxpayer as far as balance is concerned with added emphasis on utilising to the full the tax advantages that are available. Investments which are free of UK taxes would be appropriate.

Interest on certain securities, such as the following, issued by the Treasury, is exempt from tax if the beneficial owner is not ordinarily resident in the UK. The exemption does not apply if the securities are held for the two purposes of a trade or business carried on in the UK. Examples of tax-free securities: 2% Treasury 1992; $6\frac{3}{4}\%$

Treasury 1995–98; 9% Conversion 2000; 11% Exchequer 1990; $13\frac{3}{4}$% Treasury 1993; $15\frac{1}{2}$% Treasury 1998.

If return to the UK as residents at some future date is likely, then capital orientated investments (e.g. unit and investment trust investments) are essential.

Portfolio management and review

Having successfully taken the aeroplane to a high altitude, the pilot does not switch off the engine! Likewise, having constructed a highly effective investment portfolio, there is an on-going need to monitor, review and manage the portfolio contents and performance, so that the high performance of the portfolio continues. While in some instances the active policy may well be 'steady-as-she-goes', in other circumstances a directional change, in composition, diversification and risk element, may be essential. For example, if interest rates are expected to rise, fixed-interest investments should be sold and proceeds transferred to variable and high-yielding investments. Obviously if the circumstances of the investor radically change, e.g. change in tax position, retirement, redundancy, disabling accident, the portfolio will need to be overhauled and restructured.

Interested and reasonably knowledgeable investors can structure, monitor and even manage their own investment portfolios by regularly studying investment publications like *Planned Savings, Money Which, Money Management, Investor's Chronicle* and by following the Stock Exchange securities price movements in *The Financial Times*, and by ignoring share tipsters and other unsolicited investment invitations. It is essential to continue measuring portfolio performance by its overall rate of return based on its average value over a period of time, and by comparing this level of performance with other possible 'mixes' of investments.

If technical complexities arise, then it is best to seek advice from professional advisers, e.g. banks, accountants, stock brokers, insurance brokers, solicitors – all of whom are required under the Financial Services Act to act in the best interests of their investor customers (see Chapter 10). In portfolio management it is a good policy to take the gain, cut the losses as soon as possible by selling and switching and to take only the affordable risk.

Portfolio diversification

A 'portfolio' is the total holding of investment securities by an individual or an institution. It may include fixed interest securities, preference shares, ordinary shares, indirect investments in domestic securities and direct and indirect investments in the securities of overseas enterprises. 'Diversification' of a portfolio implies the proportions to which funds are invested in the securities of various companies, sectors (e.g. engineering, electrical, banks, building) and investments in different overseas countries, so that if one company or sector or overseas market faces problems that depress the value of its securities, the investor is protected by not 'putting all-eggs-in-one-basket', i.e. by holdings in *other* companies, sectors and overseas markets.

The diversification of portfolios reduces investment risks, because it is not possible to predict with certainty how well any one particular investment will perform in the future. The fundamental basis of portfolio theory is that any asset is less risky held with others in a portfolio than when held by itself: this is due to the mutually neutralising effects of 'swings and roundabouts'. However, it is true to say that diversification is a cautious and somewhat passive approach and therefore cannot always maximise returns.

Investments in overseas enterprises (see Chapter 5) may be undertaken to obtain higher returns (through higher dividends or interests) and to benefit from the relative political and economic security and strength elsewhere. Most professional investors believe that for large portfolios 20 to 30 well chosen and well diversified securities will provide adequate diversification advantage. Too much diversification can be as ineffective as too little diversification. Smaller investors can obtain portfolio diversification via investments in unit and investment trusts which have in-built diversification in their investments. Diversification is as important for the small investors as for the larger investors.

Importance of 'timing'

Buying and selling of securities at the *right* time distinguishes a good portfolio management from an average one. To achieve the precision in timing requires an alert and vigilant check on market movements and expectations. For instance, some investment managers unloaded (sold) most of the equity element in portfolios under their care before Black Monday, 19 October 1987, while others did not forsee the stock market crash approaching. As a general rule of timing in buying and selling shares; it is often beneficial to sell when the market has been rising for some time, and to buy when the market has been falling for some period of time. It is only by chance (or insider knowledge) that one can buy a share at rock bottom price or sell it at its highest peak price.

Investors are often tempted to buy new shares (in anticipation of capital gains) but are put off selling the old ones (in the hope of higher prices later). Dealing at best prices is not easily achieved, however, the 'contrary thinking' formula suggests that if the market is highly optimistic on the first day of a new account period, it is better to wait till early buyers are out of the way, and more realistic prices emerge. A lethargic start to a new account period may be a good time to buy, especially if there is no good reason for the inactivity of the buyers. The last couple of days of a buoyant period may be a good time for buying; the short-term bulls may be selling to close accounts. The last two days of a dull account may be appropriate for selling, the short-term bears may be buying to close the accounts.

On the other nand, the classical examples of bad timing would involve *purchases* of long-dated gilt or other long-dated fixed-interest securities just before a *big rise* in interest rates, and *sales* of such securities just before a *big fall* in interest rates! Bad timing results from failure to read and interpret market signals correctly.

Timing in '*switching*' is equally significant. 'Switching' implies changing from one form of investment to another, or from one foreign currency to another according to the requirements of the time.

There are several kinds of switching.

1 Policy switching

If a basic rate taxpayer inherits a very large sum that takes his tax status into the higher tax band, then it is essential that the policy switching transfers his funds into such equities and gilts that would keep his tax status at the most efficient level. Thus policy switching implies changes of one form of investment for another according to an investment policy. Sometimes, it may be necessary to purchase short-dated marketable stock, even though the investment objective is the highest net redemption yield, because the interest rates are expected to rise steeply. At an appropriate later date, short-dated stock's proceeds can be invested in long-dated gilts yielding highest redemption yield.

2 Anomaly switching

If the yields on two similar stocks (with same coupon and date), get out of line, an anomaly switching may be required. This may happen when the Bank of England is unable to sell in full a new issue of government stock. It will offer the unsold portion later on at a lower price, i.e. at a higher yield. A similar anomaly may arise when the dividend yield on ordinary shares, because of their company's excellent performance, becomes higher than the stationary yield on the convertible stock to which such shares are linked, i.e. a discount arises on the convertibles. In such cases anomaly switching would benefit the invester by switching from low yielding to high yielding security. However, the anomaly must be sizeable to make switching worthwhile for the private investor. Institutional investors, with large investment, find switching quite beneficial even when the anomaly itself is quite small.

4 Switching discounts

Most unit trust groups provide a discount on switching *between their own funds* which helps to reduce the cost of changing investment direction. Selling a unit and buying another can be extremely expensive, especially if the investor has to pay the full initial charge (of usually around 6%) each time. However, there are wide discrepancies between the switching discounts on offer from the various unit trust groups (see Chapter 5).

Selected questions

Portfolio planning is an extremely important part of the CIB examinations and is crucial to investment decision making generally. The following questions have been selected from the many portfolio planning questions to show some of the variety in such questions. Try to answer them in point form before consulting the brief answers provided below.

Q1 A UK resident asks you to advise him whether it is appropriate for him to invest the sum of £10 000, which he has just inherited, in UK ordinary shares. He is aged 48, with a grown-up family and has a secure managerial position within a large company. What further information would you require before being able to confirm that UK ordinary shares would be a suitable choice, and what factors should he take into account in the selection of particular holdings?

Q2 There have been several articles in the press about the effect of the capital gains tax provisions in the Finance Act 1985. It has been suggested that the small investor aiming for growth need no longer be concerned with this tax.

    (a) (i) Outline the changes in capital gains tax resulting from the Finance Act 1985.

    (ii) Give examples to illustrate the effect of these changes in relation to a holding of quoted shares.

    (iii) Discuss the effect of this tax on the small investor aiming for capital growth.

    (b) In view of the changes to the capital gains tax in the Finance Act 1985, is it more beneficial to an individual UK investor to purchase gilt-edged securities direct or through the medium of a unit trust?

Q3 It is sometimes said that a successful investment policy is as much dependent on efficient tax planning as it is on the nature of the individual investments. Discuss this statement and give examples in the following circumstances:

    (a) if income is the primary objective;

    (b) if capital growth is the sole objective;

    (c) if a 'middle of the road' approach is required.

Q4   One of your customers, a young man of 24, has received £50 000 as compensation for an industrial injury. He is still working, but is concerned that a future deterioration in his physical condition might affect his earnings adversely. He is quite unaccustomed to dealing with amounts of this size and asks for your advice about investment. Outline the reply you would give him.

Q5   Your customer, Mr Universal, has recently sold half of his UK equities for £21 000 at a reasonable profit. He informs you that he has carried out the sales on the advice of his stockbrokers and he now intends to re-invest overseas. He says that he has a feeling that this is the right thing to do but, being cautious, he has come to you for advice.

(a) Outline the advantages and disadvantages of investing overseas.

(b) What type of investment would you recommend?

(c) Which countries would you choose to invest in? Give your reasons.

Q6   (a) What are the criteria that company securities must meet to qualify as Wider-range investments under the provisions of the Trustee Investment Act, 1961?

(b) What are your arguments for and against the continuation of the Trustee Investment Act, 1961?

(c) What points would you consider in forming and implementing an investment plan for a new company pension fund which has a starting capital of £5 million and is expected to receive in the future an estimated £1 million per year in contributions from the company and its employees? The trust deed contains the widest investments powers. Give reasons for your answer.

Brief answers

A1   *Given*: UK resident; investment capital £10 000 (inherited); age 48; grown up family; has a secure managerial position with a large company; desires to invest in UK ordinary shares.

Further information required: current income from all sources; financial commitments; attitude to risk/reward equation; existing investments; retirement age; pension amount receivable; current liquidity cushion; house ownership; liability to income tax rate, CGT and inheritance tax; likelihood of large financial expenditure soon.

Assessment: time horizon – 15 years; some risk acceptable; capital growth preferred; safety of capital; owns the house; has cash in bank and building society deposit; has reasonable insurance cover; sizeable pension payment in due course; higher rate taxpayer; no inheritance tax to pay.

Advice (on the basis of above assessment): investment in the UK ordinary shares suitable: £5000 in a BES investment trust; *if* the holding period of five years, and the risk of investing in smaller companies are acceptable, £5000 in a capital-growth orientated fund in the UK. *Alterative choice*: go for direct investments of £10 000 in around 12 leading quoted, including USM, companies, *provided* he has basic knowledge of methods of share buying, dealing costs and monitoring of the growth of shares bought. Companies chosen should be market-leaders and should have sector diversification. He should be able to understand financial press, reports, company accounts and communications, and be able and willing to sell and buy at the right time.

A2 (a) (i) The changes in CGT resulting from the Finance Act 1985:

- Indexation applies from the date of acquisition (or March 1982, if later). The 12 month 'waiting period' is abolished.
- Indexation will be available for losses and may turn a gain into an allowable loss.
- Where it is more favourable for the taxpayer, for assets acquired before April 1982, indexation will be calculated on the market value of the asset as at 31 March 1982 rather than on the original cost.
- The CGT will remain at 30% with index-linked basic exemption limits.
- On retirement at 60 (or earlier–ill health–retirement) the full £10 000 relief of a business or a part of it is available, the tapered relief (60–65) is now abolished.

  (ii)

- A CGT taxpayer bought shares for £1000 in 1975, sold them for £10 000 shortly after 5 April 1985 (market value as at 31 March 1982: £8000). Under the old rules, indexation allowance of 14% could only be applied to purchase price of £1000, i.e. £140. Under the new rules, indexation applied to value at 31 March 1982, i.e. 14% of £8000: £1120. Ignoring the annual exemption under the earlier method: capital gain could be £10 000 − (£1000 + 140) = £8860; CGT at 30%: £2658. Under new rules: capital gain = £10 000 − (£1000 + £1120) = £7880. CGT at 30%: £2364.
- An investor bought shares for £8000 on 1 April 1982, sold them on 9 April 1985 for £8300. The profit of £300 eliminated by capital loss of £1120 (£8000 at 14%), leaving a surplus of £820 (£1120 − £300) to offset against other gains.

  (iii) Display knowledge required for (i) and (ii) above.

- Look for investments aiming at capital growth for small investor in a way which also avoids CGT liability.

  (b)

- Knowledge of market conditions.
- Individual taxpayer's tax situation.
- A gain on sale of unit trust could be taxable, but gain *within* the trust is exempt from CGT.
- Gilt-edged securities purchased directly are now exempt of CGT, but the management abilities of the unit trust manager who gets his timing right and will be dealing in much larger sums could be a deciding factor in direct or indirect purchase of gilts.

Income Tax: are all tax allowances being utilised, e.g. for pensions, mortgages, friendly societies, insurance policies utilising the withdrawal facilities of insurance bonds?

CGT: are the annual personal allowance and index-linking being utilised?

IHT: how to overcome the probability of a large slice of the capital going to the Revenue? Are IHT allowances and thresholds being utilised? Are insurance type bonds to take capital out of one's estate for IHT purposes and also preserving the flexibility of annual tax-free withdrawals being utilised? The investor must be ready to unravel the whole arrangement if other overriding needs arise. Investment is not an exact science.

A3 (a) (i) *Basic rate or less than basic rate taxpayers*
- High yielding gilts
- Debenture and unsecured loan stock.
- Building societies, National Savings Bank investment account, income bonds, higher interest bank account, money funds.
- Guaranteed income bonds. Annuities (for elderly).

(ii) *Higher rate taxpayers*
- 5% withdrawal facility with single premium investment bonds.
- Using CGT 'manufactured' allowance on capital appreciation on equities.

(b) National Savings Bank ordinary account, (£70 of interest taxfree). Low coupon gilts. Single premium investment bonds. Friendly society bonds. Growth orientated equities, unit trusts, investment trusts. Business Expansion Scheme. Personal Equity Plan. Personal Pension Plan.

(c) A suitably diversified mix of (a) and (b) dependent on tax situation.

A4 *Identified needs of the customer:*
- Reduction in earnings on a long term basis.
- Adequate liquidity.
- Indirect investment, since he is unaccustomed to dealing with large amounts of money.
- Security of capital against loss, including inflationary.
- Growth orientated portfolio – until he is working which is easily switchable into income growth orientated if he suddenly requires income.
- Need for continuing advice.

Portfolio construction (assuming he is a basic rate taxpayer)

(a) Liquidity reserve (at least £20 to 25%), kept in:
- National Savings Bank investment account,
- Building society ordinary shares and short-notice accounts,
- High interest bank account.

(b) *Capital growth element of the portfolio* (75 to 80%):
- National Savings Certificates,
- National Savings Yearly Plan,
- Guaranteed growth bonds,
- Low-coupon long-dated gilts,
- Personal Pension Plan,
- Index-linked National Savings Certificate,

- National Savings Deposit Bonds,
- Growth oriented unit trusts.

A5 (a) *Advantages*

- Wider spread – UK market is small in world terms.
- Spread into investments not available in UK (e.g. private health insurance, electricity).
- Can provide currency hedge.
- Stronger economies than UK (e.g. Germany, Japan) can be tapped.
- By using appropriate timing, different market conditions around the world can be exploited.

Disadvantages

- Greater political risks (e.g. exchange controls, nationalisation).
- Currency exchange rate fluctuations.
- Higher handling costs.
- Difficulties in obtaining information about overseas company affairs.
    - (b) (i) Indirect investment: unit trusts and investment trusts (with overseas orientation)
        - (ii) Direct investment: UK quoted companies, including those with substantial overseas interests.
    - (c) Japan: size and strength of economy.

Germany: size and strength of economy

USA: size and strength of economy (even though currently suffering from domestic and international deficits).

Canada: expanding economy – growth potential high.

Australia: expanding economy – growth potential high.

Hongkong: more volatile market – high risk/reward ratio.

Singapore: more volatile market – high risk/reward ratio

South Africa: large natural resources (gold) – but politically risky.

A6 (a) *The criteria*

- (i) They must be securities of a fully listed company.
- (ii) Any shares must be fully paid except for new issues to be paid within nine months.
- (iii) The company must have a paid-up share capital of at least £1 million.
- (iv) The company must have paid a dividend on all classes of share capital in each of the five years preceeding the investment.
- (v) Company must be incorporated, securities registered and issued in UK.
- (vi) Not narrower-range securities.
- (vii) Principal and interest payable in sterling.
- (viii) Advice must be taken. Division carried out.
- (b) Arguments against continuation:
    - (i) The complexity of its terms and the difficulties of book-keeping.
    - (ii) The distortions in the size of narrower-range and wider-range funds caused by differing rates of growth and the effect of inflation.

    (iii) As a result of inflation a paid-up share capital of at least £1 million for wider-range securities is too small.

    (iv) Inability to invest in freehold of leasehold land or building.

    (v) Trustees not allowed to invest in insurance based products.

    (vi) Problems of investing in wider-range securities which are partly paid.

    (vii) Difficulty of interpreting what is expert advice.

    (viii) Dividend qualification unrealistic.

    (xi) No overseas companies allowed.

Arguments for:

    (i) Achieves fixed interest/equities balance.

    (ii) Encourages diversification.

    (iii) Requirement for advice protects beneficiaries, aids selection of sound investments.

    (iv) Wider-range investments should be in large, sound companies.

    (v) Avoids risks of direct overseas investments.

    (vi) It places restrictions on investment in an increasingly complex world of investment where risks are greater.

    (c) *Points in forming investment plan*

- Perusal of actuaries report.
- Pensioners' needs – when and the amount?
- Need for growth, bearing in mind index linking commitment.
- Who is to manage investments and at what cost?
- Is fund approved by the Inland Revenue and therefore tax free?
- Review of investments – how frequently?
- Spread of investments – fixed interest, equities, property, overseas.

Points in implementing plan

- Proportion of investments in each type of security, e.g. 20% in gilts, 10% in property, 70% in equities (30% overseas).
- Overall gross yield obtainable from each type.
- Timing of purchases.
- The amount of liquidity bearing in mind the ongoing requirement to meet payments to pensioners (this may be small at outset as it is a new fund) and the inflow of funds from contributors.
- The ongoing need to be aware of market conditions in the UK and overseas.

Specially selected question

Your customer, Mr Dogood, a widower aged 53 years with no children, informs you that he has decided to go to Africa for the next twelve years to help a well known charitable organisation. He has retired early from the company where he has been employed for 20 years. He will receive a deferred pension at the age of 65 and this pension together with his state pension, he feels, will enable him to live comfortably in due course. Meanwhile his house is up for sale and he will receive £100 000 for it after clearance of the mortgage and payment of all costs. He will need spending income of £7000 a year for the next 12 years. He will receive no payment from the charitable body for his work.

He requires your advice. He wishes to keep the real value of his capital as intact as possible, in order to purchase a house in which to live in retirement when he returns to the UK at the end of 12 years. However, he recognises that it may not be possible for him to purchase a house of the same standard as the one he is selling.

Required:
(a) How should his funds be managed to achieve his aims and what investment policy should be followed? Give reasons for the course of action you propose and point out the advantages and the risks involved.

(b) Prepare a portfolio showing types of investment and how his required level of spending income can be achieved.

Model answer

In view of Mr Dogood's absence for 12 years overseas professional management of his capital is advisable, and his professional advisers should have discretion to act in Mr D's best interest in his absence.

His adviser should suggest to him, with regard to his *tax situation*, that he should establish himself as a resident abroad for UK tax purposes, as soon as possible. He will then be subject to UK income tax on the proportion of his UK income relative to his world income and will also be free of capital gains tax on any investment charges in the UK.

In order to protect the value of Mr D's portfolio against inflation, which to some degree is inevitable, his adviser will ensure that some part of his portfolio is equity based.

The *advantages* that will accrue to Mr D from the above action will include: tax benefits, professional management of his funds in his absence and diversity of investment to minimise risk.

The *risks* that Mr D has to bear include: uncertainty of his portfolio performance measured against inflation and other economic conditions, e.g. a sudden stock market crash, an unforseen need for capital (e.g. due to ill health) at the wrong time in the investment cycle, fiscal and other changes affecting possible investments abroad.

Portfolio construction
In constructing the portfolio, Mr D's personal preferences about investment, his attitude to risk, state of his health should be ascertained from questioning him, it will then be possible to determine an appropriate investment approach. Bearing in mind the amount involved, it might be preferable to

pursue a conservative, though active, investment policy from the UK and avoiding investments in tax havens.

Mr D's investment folio may be as follows:

Approximate investments		*Gross income*
£50 000 (to include liquid reserves)	In five dated gilts-edged stocks with facilities to 'swear off' UK tax at say a return of 9.5% (maturity close to his date of return).	£ = 4750
£25 000	In 10 to 12 blue chip equities at a return of 4.5% (amounts could be varied).	= 1125
£25 000	In five unit trusts with some overseas interest and with some income paid and some growth orientated with an overall return of say 6.5% (amounts could be varied)	= 1625
	Total gross income	= 7500
	less Liability for UK tax based on world income return, say	= 500
	Yearly spending income for Mr D	= 7000

Updating

The financial press and publications, such as *Money Mail, Investors Chronicle* and Whillans' *Tax Tables* for the current year are essential reading to update your knowledge. A helpful *Tax Savings Guide*, is published by *Which* magazine annually. From time to time, 'Signpost' articles in *Banking World* provide extremely useful information. The most important sources of updated knowledge are the bi-annual CIB *Examiners' Reports*.

9 Practice of investment: (III) Sources of investment information

Syllabus coverage

Investment advice and professional management
services provided by the banks and other financial institutions
Stock market indices and statistical services:
SEDOL
FT-30 Index
FT/SE 100 Index
FT-Actuaries Indices
Extel
Investment fees and expenses

Introduction

The quality of investment information, its easy availability and the understanding of details of such information by active private investors, or by their investment advisers, is crucial in keeping the portfolio performance at a high level. The main sources of reliable investment information are the stockmarket indices, the financial pages of leading newspapers and magazines and specialised companies which provide fact sheets, digests and cuttings of news with comments of the listed and unlisted companies in the UK and overseas.

The average private citizens with investment capital seek two types of investment advice: occasional guidance, which can be obtained usually free of charge from the branches of high street banks, stockbrokers, merchant banks; and a comprehensive investment management of their portfolios. These comprehensive investment management 'packages' are not free, in fact they can be costly. Besides, the investment capital which may be accepted for such packages is rather large, say, in excess of £50 000, but the service in return will be highly 'personalised'. The clearing banks, merchant-banks, stockbrokers, also building societies provide comprehensive management services for their customers.

Some of the smaller investment management companies, authorised by law to do investment business, often offer the so-called 'active' management service at competitive fees. Such active management is typified by frequent 'switching' of investments. The customers feel satisfied that they are getting some service for their money. Yet it is not wholly certain that 'active' management always outperforms a more sedate, nonetheless, alert approach to investment management.

The fees and expenses of dealing in various kinds of investment are another important consideration in investment decisions, and a knowledge of this aspect of investment advice is expected from those who wish to become investment advisers.

Theoretical aspects

Investment advice and Professional Management Services

Since the Big Bang, it is possible for private investors to obtain comprehensive investment advice and management from 'under one roof'; for example, from stockbrokers, clearing bank groups, merchant banks. On the other hand, certain financial institutions provide specific, specialised investment services, for example, unit trusts and investment trusts. There are other financial institutions which are somewhere in the middle of these two sets of institutions, for example, building societies, insurance companies and some smaller authorised investment management companies. Broadly speaking, the professional providers of investment advice and management services to private investors may be divided into four categories: stockbroker firms, clearing banks, merchant banks and others.

1 Stockbroker firms

The services offered by various stockbrokers are not identical. Much depends on the investment objectives of clients, the size and nature of portfolio, the degree of discretion given by clients to their stockbrokers and whether the clients would prefer a cautious or active management policy to be pursued.

Typically, the stockbroker firms provide the following investment services to private clients:

(a) For occasional enquirers – appropriate advice and course of action in connection with matters such as takeover bid offers, rights issues offers, current security prices etc. Usually this service will be free of charge but an impression may be given that the broker is assisting a possible future client.

(b) For investors placing dealing instructions – brokers will carry out investors' instructions implicitly, without advice or comment. The investors will be charged the appropriate dealing costs (see below).

(c) For clients who want safe custody of their securities – brokers act as nominee companies or depositories and may deal with the paperwork involved.

(d) For absolute beginners – brokers give advice, guidance and recommendations in portfolio constructions which would aim to achieve investors' investment requirements.

(e) For clients who already possess investments – brokers provide assessment and appraisal of the existing portfolio, and if required and needed, advice on reconstruction of portfolio by the redeployment of capital.

(f) For small investors with capital between say £3000 and £25 000 – brokers first identify the income and/or capital needs of investors and then construct a portfolio of gilts and unit trusts. They may waive the fees for buying units from trust funds because the fund managers will pay brokers a commission of around 3%, but the client will pay dealings costs for gilt purchases. Brokers will usually send clients six-monthly valuations of their portfolios.

(g) For clients seeking discretionary management service – brokers would expect a portfolio size of £50 000 and over. Discretionary service is beneficial when timing is of the essence in switching of investments. On the other hand clients will need to watch out for simply 'churning', as distinct from logical switching. Churning implies frequent in and out transactions without investment justification but simply to earn more commission for the brokers. To avoid clients' suspicion of churning, brokers may charge fixed management fees which will include switching brokerage charges.

(h) For clients seeking methods, within the law, of tax avoidance – Brokers will need to know personal details of incomes and gains and financial assets before devising tax effective strategies. Clients cannot offset fixed management fees paid to brokers against taxable income or chargeable gains. However, brokers' commissions on individual deals are included in CGT calculations.

(i) For clients seeking portfolio valuation on a specific day (for probate or other purposes) – brokers provide this service quickly but charge fees for their work.

(j) For customers who want comprehensive personal financial planning – some broker firms provide such planning for capital in excess of £30 000. The service generally includes insurance, investment advice and management, income, pensions, property matters and tax planning. The portfolio in this connection may contain a mixture of around 15 securities. Brokers may charge a commission of around 2% on all changes in portfolio.

(k) For information-updating for clients – brokers send regular or occasional fact sheets and bulletins.

(l) For customers seeking regular valuations and reviews of their portfolios – usually portfolio sizes of around £20 000 will be required for such valuations and reviews, which will include recommendations for any changes considered to be appropriate.

With regard to brokers' professional investment services, two points should be noted.

(a) Brokers give 'no recourse' advice, i.e. they are not responsible to indemnify clients against subsequent financial loss arising from their advice given in good faith and, at all times, given in the best interest of their clients.

(b) If there is culpable negligence on the brokers' part, or if the brokers default, then aggrieved clients can appeal to the Council of Stock Exchange to be compensated from the Stock Exchange Compensation Fund.

2   Clearing banks' in-house investment services

The clearing banks have been involved in the provision of a fully-fledged investment advice management service through their specialist departments or divisions for many years. Prior to their preparations for the challenge of the Big Bang, they also operated in conjunction with stockbrokers on a shared commission basis. Increased competitiveness has brought the clearers more into the mainstream of investment advice and portfolio management business. To private investors the in-house clearing bank groups can provide the following professional investment services.

(a) A full discretionary management package for portfolio sizes in excess of £25 000. The package may include insurance, tax planning, pensions, wills, collection of dividends, making decisions on rights issues and takeover bids, and dealing with the paperwork. This service is particularly useful to busy people and to those who travel a lot and are away from the UK for long periods. Banks charge fees which compare favourably with the charges of unit trust fund managers.

(b) Banks have expertise in a wide range of investment and market sectors, including in overseas markets. Therefore portfolios constructed by the clearers can have the right balance and diversification to minimise risk and yet gain from the favourable opportunities at home and abroad.

(c) There are in-house unit trust funds of the clearers which are performing well, and can be very suitable for small investors.

(d) The clearers have financial muscle and this enables them to secure lower commission rates for their clients.

(e) By placing investment management work with the clearers, the investors enjoy the security of major financial institutions.

(f) Their branch network at home and correspondent relations overseas enables the clearers to monitor the world markets and use this knowledge for the benefit of their clients' investments.

A criticism is sometimes voiced against the clearers' investment portfolio management that the banks are not sufficiently active, expecially when equities are involved and, unlike the stockbrokers, they do not keep clients posted with fact sheets and bulletins, and also that banks simply divert a good proportion of their clients' money into their in-house unit trust funds.

It may be that banks seem inactive because they avoid churning. Since the banks are expected by law to act in their clients' interests to the best of their abilities, the diversion of funds into their in-house unit trusts funds may well be due to the better performance record of these funds.

3 Merchant banks' management and advisory services

Merchant banks accept larger size portfolios to manage, the minimum size tends to be £100 000. They insist on discretionary management, which is understandable because when managing portfolios of these sizes speed in switching is of the essence. Most of their investments are in equities. Their annual fees range from 0.5% to 1.25%, with reduced rates for the largest portfolios. Most of the merchant banks have in-house unit trust schemes. Most of their clients' investments are geared for growth.

There is a general belief that merchant banks produce better investment results for their clients, although facts do not bear this out, perhaps because they have been in the field of investment management for a long time and there has been a certain mystery about their activities. Generally speaking merchant banks are more interested in managing larger portfolios, such as those of pension funds.

4 Other sources of investment advice and management services

(a) *Institutions based in cities and towns* These are usually not large firms; in some cases they may be independent investment managers. They mainly provide highly personalised investment services, with continuity of management by a known and trusted person. They cater for virtually all the investors' financial requirements. They do not always have access to economic advisers and do not always offer the security of large and reputable financial organisations. Their charges vary.

(b) *Accountants, solicitors, insurance agents* The main field of activity of these people does not always directly relate to investment in all its complexities. Therefore they cannot always be expected to be fully aware of all the latest developments in the investment area and to be fully in touch with market trends and opinions.

Large accounting firms do however, provide all-embracing financial packages to wealthy clients. Even so they may refer their clients to brokers for advice on equity selection. They give personalised service on pensions, tax matters, executor services and life assurance. They can be expensive, charging an hourly rate of between £25 to £100, depending upon the location and reputation of the firm.

Stock market-indices and statistical services

Stock Exchange Daily Official List (SEDOL)

SEDOL is published by the Quotation Department of the SE in London for every working day. There are no regional SE official lists now, they have been amalgamated with London SEDOL.
SEDOL provides the following information.

1 All securities granted quotation on the SE appear in SEDOL, grouped together in various categories starting with the British Government stocks on the first page. The largest category includes Commercial and Industrial securities.
2 Against each quoted security is given its official quotation of the day. The bid-and-offer quotations are supplied by the market-makers and the spreads tend to be wider than those quoted to broker/dealers by market-makers. If a broker/dealer is unable to deal within the official quotations, he/she can insist on their alteration.
3 The following particulars for each security are given: when quoted xd; dividend payment date and rate; SEDOL Code number; Classification grouping number; name and description of the security; double-barrelled quotation at 2.15 pm; and the price at which business was done.
SEDOL does *not* include:
Yields, P/E ratios, dividend cover, highs and lows of listed securities for the year, issued share capital and information on company results. SEDOL is now available in microfiche as well.

The prices shown in SEDOL are for deals done in the Talisman system and appear in the Talisman computer. For the non-Talisman securities, mainly gilt-edged stocks, the prices come from the 'markings', i.e. when deals are done the names, types and prices of the securities are entered on slips, which are then put in boxes, and the prices collected from these boxes are published in SEDOL.

For the overseas registered securities, the buyers and sellers sign the transfer forms and their signatures have to be witnessed. The SEDOL and the Stock Exchange Official Year Book explain the transfer requirements for overseas registered stocks quoted on the London SE.

Usefulness of SEDOL

1 The prices shown in SEDOL have legal validity in the calculation of the CGT and Inheritance Tax liabilities.
2 It is a reliable guide for portfolio valuations and comparisons.

Complementary to SEDOL is the Stock Exchange Weekly Official Intelligence, which provides such investment information as is not included in SEDOL. For example, details of forthcoming company meetings, capitalisation and rights issues, new issues, takeover and merger developments and the short-dated bonds issued by the local authorities.

The Financial Times Ordinary 30 Share Index (30-Share Index)

The 30-Share Index is the single most widely quoted measure of the behaviour of the SE. It is called the 30-Share Index due to the number of shares which are its constituents. It is calculated on a 'real-time' hourly basis from the start of trading at 9 am.

A closing Index is produced soon after 5 pm on the basis of prices collected at the close down of the SEAQ system. The Index is reproduced on news agency tapes, radio and television and on the TOPIC information system. The Index produced at 5 pm appears each day on the front and back page of the FT, and on the SE page inside the paper. The closing Index is given more importance because it shows the 'high' and low points of its movements. It is the most widely quoted index for three reasons.

1 With only 30 constituents, their prices can be quickly collected, and since it is an unweighted Index, i.e. each constituent has the same weight, it is easily and quickly calculated without the need for elaborate computer programming.
2 Since it is based upon heavily traded market leaders' shares which are first to respond to any changes in stock market sentiment, it is a sensitive Index.
3 It goes back to 1935, and about a quarter of its constituents have remained in the 30 throughout its unbroken history, therefore its behaviour is clearly understood.

Of the original 30 shares, six were allocated to heavy industry, four to textiles, three to motors and aviation, three to electrical manufacture and radio, three to building materials, six to food, two to retail stores and three to miscellaneous industries. Once it becomes evident that some constituents have been taken over, they do not behave in the way typical of the market, or run into financial difficulties, they are taken out and replaced. There has been a steady shift of emphasis from heavy industry towards service industries. Oil, in the shape of BP, gained representation in 1977. In 1984, BT went into the Index, and so did, for the first time, a financial share, viz. Natwest Bank. Consequently, the word 'Industrial' was dropped from its title, and it was renamed FT Ordinary Share Index. The current 30 constituents are so chosen as to form a representative spread across British industry and commerce.

Technically, it is an 'unweighted' and 'geometric' Index. The mechanism of its construction is as follows. Each share counts equally, irrespective of the market capitalisation of each company. The Index is calculated by multiplying the 30 share prices (with each share divided by its value at the chosen base date) together and then taking the 30th root.

The advantage of using geometric method, in preference to the simpler arithmetic method, is that it makes it easier to make allowances for capital changes, and to replace constituents, without the need for rebasing. Secondly, the geometric construction damps down the impact of large rises and falls in individual constituents. For instance, if one constituent share doubled in price while another halved in price, both starting with 100, the geometric mean will remain 100 ($2/100 \times 2 \times 100 \times \frac{1}{2}$), whereas the arithmetic mean will be 125 ($200 + 50 \div 2$).

A drawback of using the geometric mean in constructing this Index is that it tends to bias the Index downwards over the longer term. This is partly a purely mathematical effect but, more importantly, it is due to the way that poorly performing constituents, like BL, tended to leave their negative drag impact behind them. When they are replaced, their successors enter at the same low levels, and this depressing effect is never fully offset by the high performances among the constituents. It is therefore suitable for long-term portfolio comparisons; unsuitable for short-term portfolio comparisons. Although every effort is made to keep the 30 constituents as representative of the UK industry and commerce as possible, they are not really sufficiently representative.

The FT-Actuaries Indices

The FT-Actuaries All-Share Index, along with some 40 component indices covering different sectors of the market, is published each day on the stock market report pages in *The Financial Times* (FT), and on Saturdays only an enlarged table is published in the FT giving the 'highs' and 'lows', not only for the current year but also for 'all-time', i.e. since 10 April 1962, when the FT-Actuaries series started. This Index is the professional investor's yardstick for measuring the level of the whole equity market because:

1 It accurately reflects the whole market, with over 720 (July 1987) constituents (initially 636) shares covering over 80% of the total market capitalisation;
2 It measures the market's behaviour over long periods;
3 It is a reliable yardstick against which to assess portfolio performance, because it behaves as an actual portfolio would behave; and
4 It helps investors to track the performance of particular sectors, and thereby to understand the structure of the whole market.

However, it moves sluggishly compared with the FT-30 Index, because it has a large number of inactive components which lag behind the market leaders. The Index began at 100 in 1962, but by 1987 it had reached 2000. The market capitalisation of each constituent is simply the number of shares in issue multiplied by the share prices, this gives the weighting to each constituent. Since this Index is constructed on a weighted arithmetical mean method, the values of all constituents are added and divided by the number of constituents to arrive at the market level for the day.

The FT collects the SE values prevailing at 5.0 pm, updates them with new earnings and dividend figures, and the arithmetical average is published at 6.0 pm. The design and management of the indices are the responsibility of Actuaries organisations. Constant monitoring keeps the Index consistent and useful, e.g. changes in capital of the constituent companies is reflected in their weightings, so that the Index is kept at the same level immediately before and immediately after each capital alteration, caused, for example, by rights issues and takeovers involving issue of new shares. In replacements, the new constituent company needs to be sufficiently large – market capitalisation of £60 million at present – and if possible the newcomer will be in the same classification sector. Changes in constituents are frequent, whether because of takeovers and mergers, or because of the need to maintain proper coverage of the market.

The Index is accepted by the stock market and the institutional research departments as the basis of analysis of companies. Each day investors can see the percentage movement of all the indices the previous day, and can compare with the values a year earlier. The Index provides information, such as the yield, P/E ratio and ex-dividend adjustments to date (i.e. fall in the share price by the amount of dividend, other things remaining the same) for each sector.

The indices include fixed interest, British Government securities, debenture and loan stock, preference shares. In addition, there are 18 indices of gross redemption or interest yields; these indices can be used to monitor the difference in yields between gilt-edged stocks and equities – the so-called yield gap.

A Table of Monthly Averages of Stock Indices is published in the first issue of FT after the last trading day in the month.

Financial Times – Stock Exchange 100 Index

In the early 1980s competition from the overseas markets was increasing, therefore it became imperative to obtain minute by minute information about the equity market. There were also pressing demands from the new Traded Options and Financial Futures markets. Until then there were only two indicators of equity performance: the FT-30, calculated hourly and FT All-Share, calculated daily. Thus to meet the growing demands, on 3 January 1984, the FT-SE 100 was established. This Index is now popularly called 'FOOTSIE'.

Footsie includes the 100 largest companies by market capitalisation: more than 100 could not provide quick information and less than 100 would not provide an accurate way of measuring the market. A base figure of 1000 was chosen to make the Index more tradeable on the futures or options markets as a high base contract figure usually produces whole number changes every day.

The constituents of Footsie are the top 100 UK registered companies, listed on the UK SE. These companies account for almost 70% of the total market value and include 74 industrials, 18 financials and the remaining 8 from oil, mining, investment trusts and overseas traded sectors. Some of the large market value companies are not its constituents because:

(a) they are resident overseas;
(b) they are subsidiaries of existing constituents;
(c) they do not intend to pay dividends; and
(d) they have large static shareholdings.

The replacement of constituent companies is kept to a minimum, but replacements do occur when a constituent has fallen below 110th in ranking and the replacement company, out of a reserve list of companies, has moved into the top 90, in market capitalisation. Acquisitions and mergers are the other main reasons for changes to the constituents.

The Footsie is a weighted arithmetic index, i.e. a change in price is weighted by the issued share capital of the company, so that a 5% movement in the 100th company has less 'weight' than a 5% movement in the largest company. The prices are taken from SEAQ and an Index is calculated by the SE computer each minute, of the day, from 9.01 am until approximately 5.30 pm each day.

The base value is recalculated whenever a constituent company issues more shares, thus only a price movement, and not an increase in the number of shares, has a direct effect on the index value.

Traded options on the Footsie are based on the same concept as those in individual securities. The main difference between the two is that index options are specially designed to enable investors to profit from price movements in the stock market generally, rather than in individual securities. Index options now account for about 10% of the daily contract volume of the traded options market. Like the FT All-Share Index, it is also useful for portfolio performance measurements.

The FT-Actuaries World Indices

These Indices are the latest addition to FT indices, and were launched in March 1987 to provide a new yardstick for investors around the world. The birth of these indices arose from the huge growth in the volume of cross-border equity investments in recent years as fund managers have sought to diversify their international portfolios. The main objective of these indices is to provide a set of measurements against which to judge the performance of these international fund managers.

They consist of individual indices for 23 different countries, a series of regional indices (e.g. Europe, North America, Pacific basin), and a World

Index. The indices are calculated in three separate currencies – the US dollar, sterling, and the local currency, and are based on the prices of some 2400 equity securities drawn from the 23 countries and represent 70% of the total market of the world's stock markets.

The indices are weighted arithmetic averages of the price relatives of the constituents as produced solely by transactions in the market place, adjusted for intervening capital changes.

The criteria for selecting the constituents for the indices are as follows:

1   Markets, companies and securities have only been included when direct holdings of shares by foreign nationals are allowed.

2   In each country, the aim has been to capture at least 70% of the total market value of all companies' shares listed on the domestic exchange.

3   The aim is to capture a fair proportion of the number of companies available, rather than just giant companies.

4   The number of companies from the US has been limited to 600, so as to keep the project manageable.

5   A number of smaller companies with a strong international following have been included, even so companies with a market capitalisation of less than $100 million at the end of 1985 have been excluded.

6   Only those companies and markets are included where the compilers are confident that a timely and reliable source of price movements is available.

Exchange Telegraph Company Statistical Services Ltd (EXTEL)

EXTEL specialises in the supply of financial and company information to the financial community and industry in the UK and overseas. The EXTEL cards and fact sheets are available for every company on the SE, many unquoted companies and companies in North America and Australia. These cards are handy substitutes for the information contained in the published accounts of the above mentioned companies, and provide details pertaining to profit and loss accounts; balance sheets; capital history; names of directors; net asset value; income priority percentages; and recent acquisitions, trading prospects, interim dividends and so on. A companion to EXTEL is the EXTEL Computing Ltd, which collects and disseminates international financial and business information. This information is useful in investment accounting, portfolio valuation, investment research, analysis and management.

Investment Fees and Expenses

These may broadly be called 'dealing costs', and can be divided into five sections: fees of broker/dealers and market makers; government taxes; contract levy; and unit trust fund managers' fees.

Broker/dealers' commission

Since the Big Bang, the rates of these commissions are not fixed by the Council of SE any more: the rates are now negotiable. In the Practical aspects (see below) the broadly typical broker/dealers' commission rates are listed. In justifying the payment of these commissions it needs to be said that broker/dealers in return do the work of negotiating the best price, dealing with the documentation, giving guidance and advice for first time buyers/sellers of securities, and carrying out clients' instructions.

Market-makers' turn

Investors indirectly pay the market-makers' turn on their purchases and sales of securities. The 'turn' is the difference between the bid and offer prices quoted by market-makers to broker/dealers, and it remunerates a market-maker for making a market in the securities concerned and to cover administration expenses. If the security prices quoted remained stable until the deal was completed, then the market-makers's turn would be both automatic and risk-free. However, market-makers' turn is not risk-free. They must buy and sell at the prices quoted whether or not they hold the security in question on their books. Suppose market-maker, A, quotes $125\frac{1}{2} - 129\frac{1}{2}$ of X PLC shares to a broker/dealer. The market-maker's turn is $4\frac{1}{2}$p per share. Suppose the broker/dealer buys 20 000 X PLC shares for a client at the beginning of Account. A on paper, should make a profit of £900. Suppose A has sold these shares without holding them, and the market in X shares is very active, and sellers of X shares are unwilling to sell at $125\frac{1}{2}$p per share. A will have to raise the offer price to obtain 20 000 X shares before the settlement day. If X shares have suddenly become very popular, A may have to raise the bid price to whatever level to attract sellers of X shares. Suppose A has to raise the bid price to 130p to buy 20 000 X shares, his/her reward on this deal will be a loss of £100! Changes in security prices may occur quite suddenly if large institutional buyers begin to buy or sell the securities.

Government taxes

VAT

It is payable at the standard rate (currently 15%) on broker/dealers' commission. It is collected by the broker/dealer on behalf of HM Customs and Excise authorities. On transactions where no commission is charged, no VAT is payable, e.g. purchases of unit trusts (but not sales) bear no commission charge, therefore have no VAT liability. Sales of units bear all those costs that share sold bargains bear.

Stamp Duty

This tax is also called 'Transfer Stamp', and is payable on all bought bargains, but not on sold bargains. The rate of stamp duty was reduced from 1% to 0.5% from 27 October 1986. There is a body of opinion which advocates complete abolition of stamp duty on the grounds that it makes UK dealing uncompetitive because no other country levies stamp duty.

Contract Levy

This levy is collected by broker/dealers on both bought and sold bargains on behalf of the SE. Its proceeds go towards financing the expenses of the Panel for Takeovers and Mergers and the Securities and Investment Board. It is charged at 80p for all equity bargains of £1000 and over and at 50p for bargains in gilts of £1000 and over.

Unit Trust fund managers' charges

If the units in a fund are sold through a broker/dealer, the transactions will be treated as share dealing transactions, but unlike bargains in shares, unit purchasers pay no commission and VAT. If they are purchased from a fund manager, then most fund managers make an initial fee of around 5% which is included in the offer price of the units. They have a bid-offer spread of about 6.5%. There is an annual management fee of around $\frac{3}{4}$% which is deducted from the income. These fees cover administration, portfolio management, registrar's, auditor's and trustee's fees. The bid price takes account of selling expenses of the underlying investments.

Practical aspects

The Rates of Commission charged by broker/dealers are negotiable, therefore there would be some marginal disparities, especially in London, compared with the rates given below:

(a) *Gilts, Debentures and Loan Stocks:*
    Consideration

up to £2500	£20
£2500–£5000	0.8%
on the next £10000	0.25%
on the next £485 000	0.125%
above £500 000 by negotiation	

(b) *Ordinary and Preference Shares UK:*
     Consideration

up to – £1212	£20
£1212–£7000	1.65%
on the next £93 000	05%
above £100 000 by negotiation	

overseas:
Consideration?

up to £1515	£25
£1515–£7000	1.65%
on the next 93 000	0.5%
above £100 000 by negotiation	

(c) *London Traded Options*
     £1.30 per option contract
     (0.75 per *plus* FTSE option contract)
     plus
     Option Money:

Up to £800	£20
£800–£5000	2.5%
on the next £5000	1.5%
on the excess	1.0%

Sources of information

Private individuals *need* sources of information to assist them through the maze of personal finance, investments and for investor protection. The sources of information given below are intended to meet that need.

Names of sources

	Telephone numbers (at the time of printing)
Advertising Standards Authority queries about adverts.	01-580 5555
Age Concern – *Your Taxes and Savings in Retirement* publication and advice:	
England	01-640 5431
Scotland	031-225 5000
Wales	0222-371 5666
N. Ireland	0232-245 729
Association of British Insurers (ABI)	01-248 4477
Association of Futures Brokers and Dealers (AFBD)	01-488 0898

Telephone numbers
(at the time of printing)

Association of Investment Trusts – useful info. material	01-588 5347
Bank of England – Information Division	01-601 4444
Banking Information Service – general information	01-626 8486
Banking Ombudsman – specific complaints	01-583 1395
Blay's Guides – mortgage rates, conditions	0753-880 482
British Insurance Brokers Association (BIBA)	01-248 4477
British Property Timeshare Association – helpful advice to would-be purchasers	01-437 9992
Building Society Association	01-437 0655
Building Society Commission – supervisory body	01-437 9992
Building Society Ombudsman – specific complaints	01-931 0044
BS Choice – investment rates, building societies	04493-287
BS Ratecall – investment rates, building societies	0898-700258
Chartered Institute of Bankers – quotation papers and examiners reports	01-623 3531
Citizens Advice Bureaux – national HQ	01-833 2181
Department of Health and Social Security (freefore)	0800-666 555
Department of Trade and Industry	01-215 7877
EXTEL – latest share prices	0898-500191/199
FT London Report and Latest Share Index- latest shareprices	01-246 8026
FT: *Self-Employed Pension Handbook* – useful publication	01-248 8000
FT StatsPack – performance of unitised funds	01-248 8000
Finance Houses Association	01-491 2783
Financial Intermediaries, Managers and Brokers Regulatory Organization (FIMBRA)	01-929 2711
High – interest bank accounts – top rates	01-588 1717
Inland Revenue – central office	01-438 6622
'Inland Revenue Ombudsman' – specific complaints	01-212 7676
Insurance Brokers Registration Council (IBRC)	01-588 4387
Insurance Ombudsman – specific complaints	01-242 8613
International Gold Corporation – *Krugerand Directory*	01-930 5171

	Telephone numbers (at the time of printing)
Investment Management Regulatory Organization (IMRO)	01-256 7261
Investors Chronicle, weekly financial magazine – useful information	01-405 6969
Investors' Gold Index – Commodity futures traded in London, New York, Chicago	01-828 5699
Legal and General Retirement Counselling	01-681 5177
Life Assurance and Unit Trust Regulatory Organization (LAUTRO)	01-379 0444
Life Insurance Association (LIA)	09278-5333
Lloyds of London – insurance information and coverage	01-623 7100
London International Financial Futures Exchange (LIFFE)	01-623 0444
London Stock Exchange	01-588 2355
Money Management Council	01-405 1985
Money Management Magazine – Bible for professional investors	01-405 6969
Mortgage Brain – mortgage rates, conditions	01-689 4686
Murray Noble's Open Market Annuity 'Hotline' – best rates for annuities	01-242 2343
National Association of Pension Funds	01-681 2017
National Association of Securities Dealers and Investment Managers (NASDIM)	01-283 4818
National Girobank HQ	051-928 8181
National Premium Bond and Stock Office	0253-72 1212
National Savings – information on *all* National Savings investments	01-605 9461
National Savings Bank – investment and ordinary accounts	041-649 4555
National Savings Certificate and SAYE office	0385-64 900
National Savings Stock Register	0253-69733
Occupational Pensions Advisory Service	01-405 6922
Office of Fair Trading	01-242 2858
Opal Statistics – performance of unitised funds	01-256-8011
Peat Marwick Mitchell + Co – useful investment publications etc	01-236 8000
Policy Network – buying/selling life policies	01-929 2971
Planned Savings – an essential publication for private investors	01-837 1212
Policyholders' Protection Board – specific complaints	01-248 4477

Telephone numbers
(at the time of printing)

Quotel Insurance Service – rates offered by
leading insurance companies 0276-62155
Registrar of Joint Stock Companies for
England and Wales 0222-388 588
Royal Mint – British gold coins 0443-222 111
Securities Investment Board (SIB) 01-283 2474
Solicitors Complaints Bureaux – specific
complaints 01-588 2355
Takeover Panel 01-628 2318
The Securities Association (TSA) 01-256 9000
Unit Trust Association 01-638 3071
Which? – articles on savings, investments,
money matters 0992-57773

Selected questions

The following questions, or parts of questions, have been asked in the CIB
Investment question papers in the past. You should be able to answer them
briefly from the knowledge achieved from the contents of the text in this
chapter. If you get stuck check the brief answers given below.

Q1 Investors are often unaware of the fees and expenses which will be
incurred in acquiring, maintaining and disposing of an investment, nor do
they always understand what services they should be getting in return for
these outlays. Identify the fees and expenses relating to the following types
of investment, and explain how these costs are justified.

(a) ordinary shares in a quoted UK company;
(b) a quoted British Government stock;
(c) an authorised unit trust;
(d) a single premium bond.

Q2 What arguments would you put forward in order to persuade your
customer, Mr Knowall, to let the bank manage his capital?

Q3 (a) Describe the main features of *The Financial Times* Actuaries Share
Indices.

(b) The extract overleaf from *The Financial Times* of 15 February 1986
shows some of the figures contained in subsections of the Equity Groups
of the FT Actuaries Share Indices. Taking into consideration the trends
since the date of this extract, and with the aim of achieving capital growth,
in which order of preference would you purchase ordinary shares in the
three subsections. Give reasons for your proposals.

	Index No	Gross Div. Yield % (ACT at 30%)	Est. P/E ratio (net)	High and Lows Index 1985/86		Since compilation	
				High	Low	High	Low
CAPITAL GOODS (214)*							
Electricals (13)	1742.13	4.36	15.51	1762.42 (12.2.86)	1289.36 (10.7.85)	1909.93 (3.6.83)	84.71 (25.6.62)
CONSUMER GROUP (183)							
Food Retailing (14)	1778.93	2.61	20.16	1852.45 (29.11.85)	1400.36 (1.3.85)	1852.45 (29.11.85)	54.25 (11.12.74)
FINANCIAL GROUP (119)							
Banks (7)	542.87	5.77	8.31	554.06 (25.11.85)	420.58 (15.4.85)	554.06 (25.22.85)	62.44 (12.12.74)
ALL SHARES INDEX (739)	719.01	4.14	—	719.01 (14.2.86)	581.88 (3.1.85)	719.01 (14.2.86)	61.92 (13.12.74)

* The figures in parantheses show the number of stocks per section.

Q4 An investor has in his portfolio several holdings of ordinary shares in leading UK quoted companies.

(a) What information can he obtain about these shares:

(i) from The Stock Exchange Daily Offical List;

(ii) from the two-page FT Share Information Service normally printed at the back of *The Financial Times*?

(b) What further information about these companies may he expect to find in *The Financial Times* from time to time?

Brief answers

A1 (a) *Fees and expenses relating to UK Ordinary shares:*

Negotiated broker's commission (minimum £20), VAT on commission, 0.5% stamp duty, contract levy of 80p for transactions of £1000 and over, and market-maker's turn.

Justification for these expenses:

Broker's commission – for negotiating the best price, dealing with documentation and giving advice. Market-maker's turn – for making a market in the shares, taking risk, administration expenses. VAT and stamp duty – are government taxes. The Contract Levy – to finance the Panel for Take-overs and Mergers and The Securities Investment Board.

(b) *Costs relating to a quoted British Government Stock*

These are similar to those relating to UK ordinary shares, *except* that stamp duty is not payable. Broker's commission rates though negotiated, are lower (minimum £20), market-maker's turn-narrower. Purchases from National Savings Stock Register involve even lower commission charges.

Justification

Lower charges because gilts are more marketable and traded on a cash basis.

(c) *Costs relating to investment in an authorized unit trust*

An initial fee of around 5% included in the offer price of units; a proportion may be passed on to agents. An annual management fee of around $\frac{3}{4}\%$ which is deducted from income.

Justification

To cover administration, portfolio management expenses, registrar's, auditor's and trustees' fees. The bid price covers selling expenses of the underlying investments, and some profit made by managers from dealing in units.

(d) *Costs relating to investing in a single premium bond*

Initial fee of around 5%, included in the premium. An annual fee of $\frac{3}{4}\%$, deducted form the value of the fund. The dealing costs of the underlying investments are reflected in the value of the units.

Justification
Fees cover limited insurance benefit, portfolio management, administration costs and an agent's commission.

A2 (a) A detailed series of indices showing earnings and yield averages, covering a wide range of equity groups, sub-sections and fixed interest securities, produced and published by the *The Financial Times* in co-operation with the Institution of Actuaries and the Faculty of Actuaries. Indices are base-weighted and so measure the change in value of hypo-thetical portfolio of shares, where the holdings are in proportion to the market capitalisation of the companies. The most widely used is the All-Share Index covering over 720 shares. A better indicator of longer-term trends in share prices than the FT Industrial Ordinary Index.

(b) The All-Share Index reached a peak on 16 July 1987, and since then has fallen back drastically after the stock market crash in October 1987.
Three Sub-sections' performance seen from the extract
Banks have been the strongest performers, followed by food retailing, with electricals having fallen slightly. Generally, gross yields had risen a little although banks were normally lower.

A3 He needs somebody more knowledgeable than himself to:
• make decisions on rights, takeover bids etc.;
• collect dividends and deal with paperwork;
• provide tax efficient service;
• use expertise in a wide range of investment areas and market sectors;
• secure lower commission rates through financial muscle;
• take opportunities on placings on favourable terms;
• provide the security of a major financial organisation;
• quote performance records if possible;
• limit risk by diversification;
• gain benefit from access to economic advisers; and
• utilise expertise in overseas markets.
Show him that it is your banking group which would do all the above services to his benefit.

A4 (a) (i) The Stock Exchange Daily Official List (SEDOL) can provide the following information:
• name and denomination of shares;
• whether they are Talisman or non-Talisman shares;
• the last bargain done on his shares;
• dividend rates and when they will be paid;
• whether the shares are ex-div or cum-div, the date when they went ex-div (if applicable);
• whether and when shares have gone ex-rights; and
• official quotation for main market shares at the close of business.
(ii) Shares denominations and names.
• shares classifications – industrial, commercial, financial.
• shares' high and low prices for the year.

- shares that have gone ex-dividend or ex-rights.
- share price changes from previous day's closing prices.
- shares' net dividends, dividend covers, gross dividend yields, P/E ratios, dividend payment dates.
  - (b) (i) details of interim and financial results with comments;
    - (ii) news of rights issues, scrip issues, takeovers, contracts, board changes and other developments affecting the company;
    - (iii) statistical information, such as the lists of active stocks, new highs and lows, major price changes, the Saturday list of dealings from the previous Thursday's SEDOL, and option business.

Specially selected question

Describe the main features of *The Financial Times* Industrial Ordinary Share Index, *The Financial Times* – Actuaries Indices, and *The Financial Times* – Stock Exchange 100 Index. How may these indices be of use to the investor?

Model answer

Financial Times Industrial Ordinary Share Index.
This Index goes back to 1 July 1935, when 30 leading shares were made its constituents, with a base number of 100. The allocation of the original 30 was into heavy industry, textiles, motor and aviation, electrical manufacture and radio, building materials, food, retail stores and a few others. Such constituents as became unrepresentative of the market were replaced by other more heavily traded 'blue chips'. However, there has been a steady shift of emphasis from heavy industry towards service industries. Oil became a constituent in 1977, and in 1984, the newly privatised BT entered the constituents. At the same time, the financial sector, in the form of National Westminster Bank share, was represented in the 30, for the first time. Hence the word 'Industrial' was dropped from its title, and it was renamed 'FT Ordinary Share Index', or simply FT-30. The constituent 30 ordinary shares are chosen to represent the spread across British industry and commerce. It is calculated on an hourly basis from the start of the London Stock Exchange (SE) business each working day at 9 am, on an hourly basis. The last index is constructed at 5 pm at the close down of the SE SEAQ system. This last Index is published each day on the front and back pages of *The Financial Times* (FT), and on the SE page on the inside of the paper. The hourly Index is reproduced on news agency tapes, radio, television and the SE TOPIC information system.

The FT-30 Index is the one single most widely quoted measure of the behaviour of the SE, for three reasons: it is easily and quickly calculated and does not require elaborate computer programming; it is sensitive to changes in the market mood; and its unbroken history goes back to 1935, therefore it is well understood.

Technically, it is an 'unweighted' and 'geometric' Index. Each share counts equally, irrespective of the market capitalisation of the company. And it is calculated by multiplying the 30 share prices together and taking the 30th root. The advantage of the geometric method is that it makes allowances for capital changes and for the replacement of constituents, without the need for rebasing. Furthermore, the geometric construction damps down the impact of large rises and falls in the prices of individual constituents. And herein lies the drawback of this Index: the more diverse the behaviour of the constituent share prices, the more likely it is that it will understate the market movements. It is compiled from a handful of shares, therefore it is not sufficiently representative. For example, a takeover bid of a constituent company gives an inadequate reflection of price changes in the market. Investors therefore may find it suitable for long-term portfolio comparisons, but unsuitable for short-term portfolio measurement.

The Financial Times – Actuaries Indices

The FT - Actuaries All-Share Index, along with some 40 component indices covering different sectors of the market, is published daily, in *The Financial Times*. The Index is calculated on the basis of weighted arithmetical mean. The weighting of each constituent company, of which there are over 720, is determined by its market capitalisation, i.e. the number of shares in issue multiplied by the share price. Changes in constituents are frequent in order to maintain proper coverage of the market. The base date of the Index is 10 April 1962, with a base number of 100. The Index is subdivided into sectors, giving an accurate guide to long-term market and sector movements and comparison. There are indices covering gilts, fixed interest loan stocks and preference shares. It shows average yields, price earnings, P/E ratios and earnings yields. However, this Index moves sluggishly compared with the FT-30 Index, because it has a large number of inactive components which lag behind the market leaders.

The index is the professional investor's yardstick for measuring the level of the whole equity market because it accurately reflects the whole market, measures the behaviour of the market over long periods, provides a yardstick against which to assess portfolio performance, and it helps to track the performance of particular sectors. The Index is accepted by the stock market and the institutional research departments as the basis of analysis of companies.

Financial Times – Stock Exchange 100 Index

This Index is now popularly called 'FOOTSIE'. It was introduced on 3 January 1984. It is a weighted arithmatic index of the 100 largest UK companies quoted on the SE, accounting for nearly 70% of the market capitalisation, and includes 74 industrials, 18 financials and the rest from oil, mining, investment trusts and overseas traded sectors. Some of the large

value companies are not included if they are non-UK resident companies
or are subsidiaries of existing constituents, or do not intend to pay dividend.
Replacements are kept to a minimum. The prices are taken, minute by
minute, from 9.01 am to 5.30 pm from SEAQ and the Index is calculated
by the SE computer. A major reason for its introduction was to provide a
base for contracts on the Traded Option and the Financial Futures markets.
Index options now account for about 10% of the daily contract volume of
the traded options market Traded options on the Footsie are based on the
same concept as those in the individual securities. The main difference
between the two being that the index options are specially designed to
enable investors to profit from price movements in the stock market
generally, rather than in individual securities. An investor may be right
about movements in the market as a whole, but wrong about the individual
shares in which he may invest. Like the FT All-Share Index, it is also useful
for portfolio performance measurements.

Updating

In addition to studying the sources of information described in this chapter,
your best source for updating information is by regularly reading the financial pages of leading daily newspapers, but chiefly *The Financial Times*.
Make a point to hear 'Money Matters' and 'Money Box' on BBC Radio 4,
and watch 'The Money Programme' on BBC2 and 'The Business
Programme' on Channel 4. Most college libraries subscribe to the press
cuttings service provided by McCarthy Information Services on news and
comments on listed companies in the leading newspapers and magazines.
They probably also subscribe to the *Stock Exchange Fact Book*, published
quarterly, which deals with securities in general. Find time to consult these
publications for updating. You must of course study carefully 'Signpost'
articles on Investment and related topics in *Banking World*.

10 Protection and rights of investors

Syllabus coverage

Financial Services Act 1986:
  SIB and SROs,
  Self regulation
  Disclosure of interests by directors
  Duties and rights of auditors
Banking Act 1987
Building Societies Act 1986
City Code on Takeovers and Mergers
Rights of shareholders:
  Company meetings and resolutions
  Voting rights
Protection for investors buying insurance and unit and investment trusts products

Introduction

In common law, with regard to sale of goods, there is a legal maxim, *caveat emptor* ('let the buyer beware'). This principle means that, when making a purchase, the buyer must use his own eyes to discover defects in goods if such exist and if he buys them without proper examination he has only himself to blame *unless* there has been misrepresentation on the part of the seller.

The implication of *caveat emptor* for investors is that they should not part with their money until they have fully considered not only the potential profits but also the potential risks of the investments offered to them. There are plenty of genuine investments and investment schemes, run by people who know that both the public interest and that of their own industry are best served by honest and competitive service. Genuine investment can be both profitable and interesting. However there are con-men, albeit in a tiny minority, in the wide range of direct and indirect investments available, and getting caught by a member of that tiny minority can be a devastating experience for the investor. Therefore, a little self-help goes a long way in helping both the regulators and the honest practitioners to keep the sharks at bay.

If there has been misrepresentation of facts by the seller of investment products in order to defraud the unwary investor, there exist institutional, associational and legal safeguards to examine complaints, to compensate the victims and to punish the guilty. There are ombudsmen for certain groups of investment institutions and if the aggrieved investors do not get satisfaction from a particular institution (for example, a bank or an insurance company) they can put their complaint to the appropriate ombudsman in an endeavour to obtain satisfaction.

The rules for investor protection are: first use self-help, but if the investment involves complexities seek professional advice, if the professional advice is negligent and if the investment product purchased has been misrepresented by the vendor then seek institutional and/or legal advice and redress.

Theoretical aspects

1 The Financial Services Act 1986

The Financial Services Act 1986 brings up-to-date and extends the coverage of regulation of investment business. It is the most comprehensive overhaul of investor protection legislation for 30 years. It defines investments and investment business, makes it an offence to carry on an authorisable investment business without the appropriate authorisation. It also makes changes to the law on collective investments, listing of securities, offers of unlisted securities, and insider dealing. It provides for a compensation scheme for investors with valid claims. The Act establishes a framework for investor protection, which includes wide-ranging statutory powers and new criminal offences. The provisions of the Act came into effect in phases, and the Act is now operational.

2 The Banking Act 1987

The 1984 Johnson Matthey Bankers (JMB) crisis, which put at risk their depositors' funds, pointed to the weaknesses of the 1979 Banking Act's supervision regulations. These weaknesses were principally the case with which JMB could lend the equivalent of their entire capital to a single, doubtful borrower, the failure of JMB auditors to spot the trouble and the slowness with which the Bank of England, the overseer under the Act of the management of UK banks, responded to JMB's imprudence. To lay the basis for a new and more effective supervisory regime for the UK banking system, the 1987 Banking Act was brought into existence. The provisions of the 1987 Act, including an extended deposit protection scheme, became effective in October 1987, replacing those of the 1979 Banking Act.

3 Building Societies Act 1986

This Act makes it possible for building societies to become banks and to undertake investment business which previously was outside the scope of their activities. Therefore, societies that opt to become banks will come under the jurisdiction of the Banking Act 1987, and for undertaking author- isable investment business under the requirements of the Financial Services Act 1986. The liquidity requirements of the societies are closely controlled, under the Act, by the Building Societies Commission which is a government body. The Act also requires all societies to participate in an Investor Protection Scheme which provides specific ceilings for investor protection.

4 The City Code on Takeovers and Mergers

The privatisation process during the past few years has once again brought the small shareholders, to some extent, on the stage of share ownership and control of commercial companies. However, the institutional investors are still the elite among the shareholders. Their decisions are crucial in the take- over and merger bids of private sector companies. This institutional eliticism undermines a fundamental principle of the Stock Exchange, viz., all inves- tors are equal. The City Code on Takeovers and Mergers was introduced by the Stock Exchange as a set of self-regulating rules, to prevent differ- ential offers being made to different classes of shareholders. Under the Code, a Takeover Panel is appointed to see, in conjunction with the statu- tory Monopolies and Mergers Commission, that the rules are observed in the takeover and merger bids. The Code aims to prevent institutions gaining control of the undervalued companies cheaply and freely on the Stock Exchange, and stripping the assets of the taken over companies to enrich themselves, while, at the same time, the smaller and weaker shareholders, employees and creditors, received a less than fair treatment. A weakness of the Code is that it does not carry the force of law, but the Panel can publicly reprimand and even refer the matter to the Department of Trade and Industry under the 1986 Financial Services Act.

5 Surveillance under Stock Exchange Rules

The Stock Exchange has no direct statutory authority over anybody and no legal powers other than those which members and companies freely contract to give it. The members agree to abide by its Rules as a condition of Membership, and companies do so by applying for, and willingly accepting the responsibilities of, a Listing. Within the limits of these voluntary agree- ments, the Stock Exchange has surveillance rules on the buying and selling of authorised securities by its members to protect the interests of investors. For instance, if you buy or sell securities on the Stock Exchange the Stock Exchange Rules regard you as the owner of the securities purchased or the net sale proceeds of securities sold from the moment those securities are dealt in on the Exchange, because the same day your broker will send you a Contract Note, setting out all the details of the transaction. It does not matter that there is a delay before you receive the share certificate or the net payment for securities sold. The Stock Exchange has a fund which may compensate you for fraud or failure by Stock Exchange members.

6 Rights of shareholders

Ordinary shareholders have a residual position, right at the end of the queue, when it comes to participating in the assets and profits of their company. To restore the balance to some extent, ordinary shareholders have a number of legal rights, not available to other classes of investors. These rights flow from the company law, the Stock Exchange Listing requirements and from the provisions of the City Code on Takeovers and Mergers. They have the legal right to receive their company's annual reports and accounts and a voice in the company's management. They have the right to attend general meetings of the company and there to discuss and vote on any matter on the agenda. They appoint and remove the directors to and from their company's policy and its day-to-day running. They appoint (or re-appoint) the auditors of the company and authorise directors to declare a dividend for the ordinary shareholders. Extraordinary general meetings can be convened by the ordinary shareholders to deal with special business. They are entitled to appoint a proxy (see below) to attend meetings, to request a poll (see below) and to vote on a poll. They have the first right to subscribe to any new share capital or convertible loan stock in proportion to their existing holdings, and, in the case of public limited companies, freely to transfer their shares.

Practical application

The Financial Services Act 1986

The Department of Trade and Industry (DTI) asked Professor L. C. B. Gower to carry out an exhaustive review of investor protection, which was largely provided by the terms of the Prevention of Fraud (Investment) Act 1958. In his final report Gower proposed that a new Act to replace the 1958 Act be passed. A White Paper, 'Financial Services in the United Kingdom: A new framework for investor protection', based largely on the Gower Report, was published in January 1985. The Financial Services Act 1986 implements the 1985 White Paper. The Act's provision came into effect in phases. It became fully operational in the summer of 1988.

The Government's objectives for the new system, as set out in the White Paper, are:

(a) The financial services industry of the UK should be able to provide services to industry and commerce, private investors and Government in the *most efficient* and economic way.

(b) The industry *must be competitive* both domestically and internationally. Regulations should stimulate competition and encourage innovation; it must be responsive to international developments and not a cover for protectionism.

(c) The system of regulation *must inspire confidence* in issuers and investors by ensuring that the financial services sector is, and is seen to be, a 'clean' place to do business.

(d) The regulatory framework must be clear enough to guide but not to cramp structural and other changes in the industry. It *must have the resiliance* not to be overcome by events.

Provisions of the Act

I The Act empowers the Secretary of State for Trade and Industry to authorise and regulate the carrying on of investment business. The Secretary of State has transferred the majority of his powers to a Designated Agency, viz. the Securities Investment Board (SIB).

II SIB is not a government department, it is a private limited company. It will nevertheless have substantial regulatory powers under the Act.

The executive chairman and members of SIB are appointed jointly by the Secretary of State for Trade and Industry and the Governor of the Bank of England. Its members are practitioners from a wide variety of investment activities and independent 'lay' members representing both the users of financial services and the public at large. The Act has armed SIB with a formidable armoury of regulatory sanctions ranging from reprimands, private and public, through crucial actions to obtain restitution of investor funds, where appropriate, up to suspension and – the ultimate sanction – withdrawal of authorisation from an investment business. Despite the formidable, legally backed regulatory powers, SIB is to be financed entirely by the financial markets themselves, with no contributions from the public purse.

The *responsibilities of SIB* may be summarised as follows:

1 To authorise the carrying on of investment business – it will determine whether firms are 'fit and proper' to carry on investment business, either by granting direct authorisation or recognising Self-Regulatory Organisations (SROs – see below) and professional bodies, membership of which will confer authorisation. Except for a few strictly limited exempt categories, it is a criminal offence to carry on investment business without authorisation. The penalty for doing so can include up to two years imprisonment,

and any contracts made in the course of unauthorised business will be invalid.

2 To effect a consistent level of both investor protection and overall efficiency in the financial markets – all investment carries some degree of risk, whether relating to business or general economic conditions. SIB will not take the risk out of risk capital. Its regulatory powers come into effect where the conduct of an authorised investment business appears to have been in contravention of the legal rules, or cast doubts whether it is indeed 'fit and proper', i.e. meets the standards of honesty, competence and solvency. SIB is also responsible to ensure that the system is flexible enough to be able to react to changes and developments in the various markets in order to maintain those standards.

3 To put into practice the principles of investor protection as laid down in the detailed rulebook, constructed by SIB and backed by the powers of the Act – SIB has the right to take an investment business to court to obtain restitution for clients where appropriate and, within limits, to carry out criminal prosecutions under the Act. The rulebook has a dual purpose: to outlaw malpractice and to require proper financial and management discipline within companies, because although deliberate fraud has been the cause of trouble in some cases, the lack of proper financial controls has often led to the collapse of the investment companies and investors losing their money.

4 SIB will keep a register, open to public inspection, of all authorised persons.

5 To recognise Self-Regulating Organisations (SROs) and other regulatory bodies – a recognised SRO is a practitioner-based body set up to provide proper regulations (to achieve investor protection standards laid down by SIB) of the investment companies under its jurisdiction. Each SRO has to demonstrate to SIB that its rules are equivalent to those of SIB and that it is able to ensure compliance with those rules by the member companies.

At present there are *five SROs* which, in broad terms, are likely to cover the following investment areas:

(a) *Association of Futures Brokers and Dealers (AFBD)*. AFBD's member firms will carry on business in connection with dealings and arranging and advising on deals in futures, options and contracts for differences, and managing portfolios of these types of investments.

(b) *Financial Intermediaries, Managers and Brokers Regulatory Association (FIMBRA)*. FIMBRA's member firms will, for the most part, have as their main activity advising on and arranging deals in life assurance and units in authorised unit trusts and similar collective investment schemes and/or providing investment advisory and management services to retail customers, and also advising on and arranging deals in securities, including Government and other public securities.

(c) *Investment Management Regulatory Organisations (IMRO)*. IMRO members will be engaged in investment management, management and operation of collective investment schemes, acting as trustee of regulated collective investment schemes, e.g. unit trusts, in-house pension fund management and acting as pension fund trustee, investment advice to institutional or other corporate customers, and advising on and arranging deals in investments.

(d) *Life Assurance and Unit Trust Regulatory Organisation (LAUTRO)*. LAUTRO's member firms will, for the most part, be insurance companies and friendly societies engaged in retail marketing of life assurance products, and operators of regulated collective investment schemes engaged in retail marketing of units in such schemes.

(e) *The Securities Association* (TSA – TSA is the result of the merger between the Stock Exchange and the International Securities Regulatory Organisation). TSA's member firms will carry on business in connection with such activities as dealing, and arranging deals, in shares, debentures, Government and other public securities, warrants, certificates representing securities, rights and interest in securities, and financial futures and options on securities and their derivatives and on foreign currency. They are also concerned with advising on deals in the above investments, with managing such investments or with arranging and advising on transactions in life assurance and collective investment schemes.

Recognised Professional Bodies (RPBs)

Professional bodies which could apply to be recognised by SIB include Law Societies and Institutes of Chartered Accountants. If they do not have 'recognition' then those of their members whose activities will be covered by the Act will have to join an appropriate SRO or seek authorisation from SIB directly. Thus SROs and PRBs would make up the self-regulatory part of the new system. SIB itself is not a self-regulatory body.

Recognised Investment Exchanges (RIEs)

It is possible for investment exchanges to obtain recognition from SIB which will exempt them (but not their members) from needing authorisation as investment businesses. For an investment exchange to become RIE it must satisfy SIB that it meets certain basic requirements, including adequate financial resources, proper conduct of business rules, a reasonably liquid and proper market in its products, procedures for recording transactions, effective monitoring and enforcement rules and proper arrangements for the clearing and performance of contracts.

Designated Investment Exchanges (DIEs)

SIB will draw up a list of overseas exchanges which have operating procedures broadly equivalent to those of RIEs, and give them the status of DIEs. Although 'designation' will not carry any guarantee to potential UK Investors, it will at least let them know that DIE meets certain basic criteria.

Ombudsman procedure

SIB can expect to receive a wide variety of complaints ranging from specific allegations of misconduct against firms to general complaints. SIB is required to have effective arrangements for the investigation of complaints against any 'authorised' person. SIB would prefer, however, for the benefit of investors, to see arrangements in place whereby such disputes can be resolved outside the court, for instance, through an Ombudsman procedure which would be able to result in an award binding on an investment business if the investor wished to accept it. An Ombudsman is an independently appointed official, empowered to investigate individual complaints of bureaucratic and institutional injustice.

AFBD have decided to deal with complaints through a Business Conduct Committee, chaired by a judge, and an internal Arbitration Committee. LAUTRO have made arrangements with the Insurance Ombudsman Bureau (IOB) to investigate complaints against LAUTRO life office members who are IOB members, and against policies issued by friendly societies. The IOB has also been asked to investigate complaints against unit trust managers. However, LAUTRO is responsible only for the marketing of unit trusts; IMRO is responsible for the investment management. IMRO has devised a Referee Scheme for conciliation and arbitration in respect of complaints against its members, which would also apply to unit trust managers in respect of their investment management function. It is possible, however, that the unit trust managers will join either the LAUTRO's extended IOB Scheme or the IMRO's Referee Scheme, so that a single standard may be applied to the business of unit trusts. TSA will establish a Complaints Bureau and a Conciliation Service, the operation of which will be subject to the supervision of an independent Lay Observer. An Arbitration Scheme will also be offered. TSA requires its members to see that complaints by customers are properly treated and to keep detailed records which can be inspected by TSA. The complaint against FIMBRA members will be initially investigated by an in-house Complaints Officer. Beyond that matters will go to the Formal Complaints Committee, chaired by a Lay Independent member of the Council of FIMBRA, for the appropriate disciplinary action.

Exemption from requirement to be authorised

There are certain restricted classes of person who are exempt from the requirement to be authorised. These include public bodies which perform investment business in the course of other duties (e.g. Department of National Savings); the Society of Lloyd's of London and its underwriting agents as far as investment business undertaken in connection with their insurance business is concerned (Lloyd's of London are regulated by the Lloyd's Act 1982); appointed representatives (e.g. 'tied agents') for whom an authorised business takes responsibility; wholesale money market institutions which are included on a list maintained by the Bank of England (see below); and the Bank of England.

The Act does not deal with the specific controls applying to banking (covered by the Banking Act 1987, and regulated by the Bank of England – see below) and building societies (regulated via the Building Societies Act 1986 – see below).

III The Act defines 'investments' and 'investment-businesses' and enables the Secretary of State to amend the definitions so that the definitions can be kept up-to-date when new forms of investment are developed.

1   *The main types of investments covered by the Act* are:

(a) Stocks and shares in UK or foreign companies.

(b) Debentures including debenture stock, loan stocks, bonds and certificates of deposit.

(c) Government and other public securities including gilt-edged stock, local authority bonds and bonds issued by foreign governments and international organisations.

(d) Warrants entitling the holder to subscribe for shares and bonds.

(e) Depository receipts for shares, bonds or warrants.

(f) Units in collective investment schemes including units in unit trust schemes and shares in an open-ended investment company.

(g) Options on currency, gold or silver and on any other investment.

(h) Futures contracts for commodities and other property.

(i) Contracts for differences whose value is linked to the value of any kind of property or to an index (e.g. a stock market index).

(j) Insurance policies which are investments – such as endowment and unit-linked policies – but not pure term insurance or policies which simply protect against risk, e.g. most permanent health and credit protection policies and general insurance such as fire and theft.

2   *Investment businesses*

A 'person' (i.e. any body or company with legal personality) will be carrying on investment business if, as a business, he/she:

(a) Buys and sells investments;

(b) Arranges for others to buy and sell investments;

(c) Manages investments belonging to others;

(d) Advises others on their investments; or

(e) Operates a collective investment scheme.

Exceptions

(a) A person who buys and sells investment for his/her own account *unless* he/she does so to make a market in them.

(b) Transactions within a group or a joint commercial enterprise.

(c) Trustees and personal representatives who manage or advise on investments *unless* they hold themselves out as providing professional investment services.

(d) A person who gives investment advice purely as a consequence of advice on non-investment matters – e.g. a tax consultant advising a client to sell shares for tax reasons.

(e) Advice included in a *bona fide* newspaper (but not a tipsheet).

(f) The administration of employee share schemes and the operation of 'share shops' set up to help employees to exchange shares in the company or group which employs them.

(g) Anything done to buy or sell more than 75% of the shares in a private company where both the vendor and the purchaser satisfy conditions.

(h) An overseas person without a permanent place of business in the UK entering into investment transactions in the UK only with or through authorised or exempt persons, or if the only activities he/she carries on in the UK result either: (i) from an unsolicited approach made by a person in the UK on the overseas business; or (ii) from an approach made by the overseas person in the UK which did not contravene the provisions of the Act relating to 'cold-calling' or 'advertising' (see below).

(iii) wholesale money market activities of those institutions which are admitted to a list maintained by the Bank of England and only those transactions which are above a specified monetary limit. The limit is £100 000 for debentures, loan stocks etc; and an underlying contract value of £500 000 for currency options, futures etc. Transactions below this limit are, however, permitted with established wholesale customers.

IV *Compensation of investors.* A Compensation of Unpaid Investors Scheme is set out which is, under the Act, subject to future consultation with those SROs who will be required to join it. It proposes that investment businesses contribute to the cost of compensation on the basis of equal proportions of gross revenue of each firm, up to a limit in any one year (the limit proposed being £100 million from all contributors *as a group* in any one year). Members of one SRO may be required to contribute up to the maximum in respect of claims against one of their fellows, and members of other SROs only, thereafter. The indications are that compensation under the scheme would be limited to private investors who lose money through an investment business's fraud, negligence or failure to comply with the rules. The maximum compensation, it is hoped, will be in the region of £30 000 to £50 000 in individual cases.

Where a participant firm has become insolvent and an investor satisfies the Compensation of Investors Schemes Manager that the firm is unable to satisfy his claim, the Scheme Manager shall pay to the investor out of the Compensation Fund the amount of the unsatisfied claim subject to the following limitations:

1   100% of valid claims of losses up to £30 000
2   90% of losses on a further £20 000 to an effective limit of £48 000.
3   The maximum amount paid out in claims cannot exceed a ceiling of £100 million in any one year.

Claims from the Scheme will only be met when no further redress can be secured from the defaulting firm, in other words, when the firm is bankrupt or otherwise unable to meet its obligations. Professional investors are not eligible and investors who have opted out of the protection of their client money will not be eligible to claim for loss of such money. An investor's claim for compensation shall be rejected if submitted more than six months after the investor became aware of the insolvency of the firm, unless the Scheme Manager considers that it ought in the circumstances to be allowed. The scheme came into operation on 27th August 1988 and it is not retroactive.

V *Auditors*. Provision is made to facilitate communication between the auditors of an authorised person and that person's supervisors. The SIB can require a directly authorised business to appoint an auditor (if it is not already required to do so by other statutes such as the Companies Act); accounts or other information reported by an auditor may be required to be submitted for a second examination by another qualified person; and no duty to which an auditor may be subject is to be regarded as being contravened if he/she reports to the supervisor of an authorised business in good faith any matter which is relevant to that supervisor's function. The circumstances in which such reports should be made are expected to be laid down in professional guidance but, in the event that some auditors are not subject to satisfactory guidance, the Secretary of State will have power to specify the circumstances in regulations.

VI *Insider dealing*. In broad terms it means dealing in securities of a company by persons 'connected' with that company whilst in possession of unpublished price-sensitive information. Connected persons do not only include directors and senior officials but also auditors, solicitors, merchant bankers and other professional persons acting on the company's behalf. The Act empowers the Secretary of State to appoint inspectors to investigate possible insider dealing. The inspector will be able to question connected people on oath and require papers and documents to be produced. The Act also extends this offence of inside dealing by Crown servants and to other public servants.

The Rules of SIB applying to investment business in the UK

SIB has produced a large volume of the rulebook covering a very wide area in terms of the scope both of the firms to whom it may apply, from 'entry' requirements of 'fit and proper' firms to compensation for the customer of any investment business which may still fall into insolvency.

The various rules and regulations have the force of law. They set limits to the freedom of the SROs to draft their own rules. They have to be applicable, potentially, to any kind of investment business. Breach of SIB's and SRO's rules may not only lead to disciplinary sanctions up to and including the withdrawal of authorisation of the firm but will also enable a person who suffers loss as a result to sue the firm in question. The courts may grant injunction and an order recovering profits made by the firm and restoring losses incurred by the investor. SIB itself may take up such cases on behalf of investors where it feels such action to be appropriate. It is because of these legal consequences that the Act provides for an approach to regulation based on *Rules* rather than codes on the Highway Code model.

The following is a brief account of SIB rules relating mainly to investors' protection

1   *Authorisation* This Act says that authorisation has to be obtained entity by entity, not on a group basis. Most of the rules apply only to firms regulated by SIB itself, not by SROs, RPBs, etc. Some rules, however, apply to firms authorised by other bodies (see below).

2   *Conduct of investment business*

(a) The rules apply to investment business done by authorised firms from the UK with persons overseas but do not apply to investment business done overseas with persons overseas. The rules apply to investment business done by overseas-based authorised firms in the UK from overseas.

(b) Certain kinds of business may be carried on without authorisation by 'appointed representatives', but the principal is responsible to the same extent as if he/she has expressly authorised it for anything said or done or committed by the representative. A firm to whom the rules apply and who has appointed representatives must therefore read the rules as applying to them as they would to him/her.

(c) The rules relate to authorised and recognised collective investment schemes (e.g. unit trusts) as they do to any other investment.

(d) The conduct of business rules apply to insurance companies and friendly societies only in respect of 'marketing' policies and the management and marketing of pension funds, but the financial rules do not apply because other regulatory systems exist to cover the remaining areas.

(e) Certain investment businesses are exempt from authorisation therefore firms carrying on such businesses are not subject to the rules: wholesale money market activities can be carried on by those firms that have been approved by the Bank of England.

(f) The rules will apply to those 'in-house' pension fund managers who under the Act require authorisation, but many of the conduct of business rules (e.g. financial resources rules and the Compensation Scheme) will be irrelevant to them by the nature of their activities.

(g) Adherence to the Take-Over Code (see below) is not explicitly required by the rules, since that would be unwarranted subdelegation to the Take-Over Board. But failure to adhere to the Code would call into question a firm's status as a 'fit and proper' investment business.

3 Investor protection

Investors are a heterogeneous group – large or small, rich or poor, expert or lay – and not all investors need equal degrees of protection. Therefore rules differentiate between a number of categories of investor, customer and investment and are supplied in some respects differentially.

4 Categories of investor

The categories of investor distinguished by the rules are:

(a) 'Professional investor': in effect an investor whose own business is the investment business to which the relevant rules apply, e.g. 'in-house' pension fund managers. It would be inappropriate to treat such an individual in relation to investment business done by him/her with his/her competitors or counterparts in the way in which an investor with no expertise needs protection.

(b) 'Business investor': an investor, normally a corporate entity, whose business although not 'investment business' involves various investment activities. For example, a chocolate manufacturer whose business involves buying and selling commodities such as cocoa and sugar and who therefore uses the cocoa, sugar and currency futures markets. Such an investor does not need the same protection in transactions relating to commodity or currency futures as an ordinary member of the public. Local authorities are also included in this category.

(c) 'Experienced investor': an investor competent to make up his/her own mind, who understands the risks involved in investments and markets and does not rely on the advice or judgement of the investment business he deals with or through, in making his/her decision. The rules permit authorised firms which have reasonable grounds for believing that an investor has this sort of experience and ability, to deal with him/her on a purely commercial basis.

(d) An 'execution-only' customer: such a customer is one who either carries on the same business as the firm with whom he/she is dealing (e.g. dealer to dealer) or a person who knows precisely the transaction he/she wishes to do and wishes it to be executed with no more ado. In such cases the obligation of the firm is limited to carrying out the execution requested.

(e) An 'occasional customer': one who seeks advice and assistance on one occasion with no expectation of creating a longer term business relationship, for example, the recipient of an inheritance who wishes to sell the investments and to reinvest them. In such cases firms need not do more to formalise the relationship than summarise in a letter their advice, terms of dealing and the customer's instructions to them, for the customer to confirm and give the go-ahead.

4 Categories of investment

(a) There are risks inherent in investment: a speculative overseas mining stock is different from gilt-edged stock, for instance. There are risks involved in gearing, in buying futures contract and of illiquidity, that is, of difficulty in reversing a contract. Therefore it is necessary to vary the protections imposed according to the risk and complexity of the investment product or transaction an investor is to acquire or enter into.

(b) Where investments are traded on or under the rules of a well-regulated exchange there is usually provision both to inform investors (and keep them informed) about the investments and their issuers and to maintain liquidity. These and certain other non-exchange traded instruments like US government bonds are categorised as 'marketable investments'. Other investments not traded on recognised or designated exchanges are categorised as 'not readily realisable'. Risk warnings must be given to would-be buyers of such investments.

(c) There is a category of 'marginal transactions', that is those involving gearing in the futures and options market where customers can be called for margin and rapidly incur large, possibly unbearable obligations. These transactions must also be preceded by risk warnings and governed by rules for the protection of the customer's funds and positions. Inexperienced investors may not be sold off-exchange futures etc. (because off-exchange marginal transactions pose greater risks of fair pricing, liquidity and protection of investors funds) except where their liability is limited in advance to a fixed sum.

5 *A firm's relationships with its customers*

(a) It should know its customers' relevant personal and financial circumstances. Armed with such knowledge, it should recommend investments which are suitable for each client, and make each client aware of the extent of risk exposure.

(b) When recommending life assurance policies or units in a collective investment scheme an independent intermediary (or a company representative) must recommend only a product which is at least as good as any other product available on the market (or as good as any other product available from his/her company or group). Firms effecting transactions with or for ordinary customers must take all reasonable steps to do so on the best terms available.

(c) The relationship between an ordinary investor and the firm must be governed by a 'full customer agreement' which sets out all the salient features of the relationship, including the services the firm is to perform, the basis for payment, arrangements for the custody of customer's assets and the periodic information to be provided to the investor. There is no requirement, however, for such agreements to be renewed from time to time.

6 *Disclosure*

Disclosure must play a key role in any regulatory system. It is a discipline on a firm and equips the investor to make considered judgements. It thus provides both high standards and competition. The disclosure requirements in the rules cover such key matters as recommendation of an associate, fees and surrender values, material interests of a firm or its associates, status (independent or company representative), and details of transactions effected and portfolios held, on contract notes and in periodic statements.

Advertisements must also contain certain items of information and not be obscure and misleading. Full particulars of life assurance policies and collective investment schemes must be provided to would-be buyers and in certain circumstances, a right is given to a buyer to cancel his/her purchase. Together these requirements in the rules will make available to investors, in a systematic manner, a very substantial amount of information.

7 *Restriction of business*

(a) If firms are permitted to advise on and sell life assurance policies and units in collective investment schemes otherwise than *either* on a fully independent basis *or* as the representatives of a company or group, the investors will be confused as to the nature of the service available to them and accordingly likely to make decisions based on erroneous assumptions. Banks and building societies must make a decision whether they want to act as independent advisers, helping clients to find the best products on the market for their needs or they can sell their own products – be it unit trusts, personal pensions, unit-linked life policies etc. This policy is called '*polarisation*'.

(b) The rules restrict the investments which may be sold 'off-the-page', i.e. to an investor made aware of the investment opportunity solely by way of newspaper advertisement or mail-shot leaflet, who may enter into an investment agreement merely by returning to the selling firm a tear-off slip or other application form together with initial payment, or credit card number or direct debit authority. In such circumstances the investor, in effect, self-selects the investment and the firm selling it will have had no reference to the rules on knowing its customer, best advice, suitable invest-ment etc. The only products which may be sold in this way are life policies, units in an authorised or recognised collective investment schemes and PEP schemes which meet certain criteria, and then only if specified material particulars and clauses are incorporated in the advertisement and the appli-cation form. Sales of securities for which a prospectus meeting the relevant requirements is available, are not affected by these rules.

8 *Unsolicited calls*

(a) The rules permit investment agreements entered into as a result of unsolicited calls principally to the sale of life assurance or units in regulated collective investment schemes or personal pensions: this puts unit trust sales on the same footing as unit-linked life policies.

(b) Investors have the right to cancellation of investment contracts to purchase life policies or unit trusts or personal pension schemes resulting from unsolicited cold calls, other than calls provided for in a customer agreement or where the investor is capable of protecting his own interests.

9 *Clients' money*

Uncommitted clients' money will be fully segregated from the investment business itself and given trust status so that, if the firm goes into liquidation, the money will clearly not belong to the firm's creditors. Clients' money balances will have to be regulated regularly.

10 *Compensation of investors* (see above).

11 *Investigation of complaints* (see above).

A summary of the investor protection provisions under the Act and SIB rules drafted under the Act

1   If an investment firm operates without 'authorisation' and without being 'exempted', it is committing a criminal offence. Authorised firms must continue to abide by the appropriate rules, and the relevant SRO, or SIB, has the power to arrange 'spot checks' of financial and other records and to impose disciplinary measures where appropriate.

2   Only 'fit and proper' firms can carry out investment business, and the task of being fit and proper includes consideration of adequacy of financial resources and the previous record of the firm and its officers.

3   A firm must have proper regard for a client's best interests in any advice given, to do its best to ensure that it is aware of that client's circumstnces and must subordinate its own interests to that of the client whether dealing as a principal or agent.

4   Firms are required to set out the basis of their relationship with their clients in customer agreement letters setting out the functions or services they are to provide, their responsibilities and charges or other basis for remuneration.

5   Firms must adhere to a proper complaints procedure, fully investigating and dealing with client complaints and keeping records of the complaints and produce them for a subsequent inquiry by the SRO if required. Unsatisfied clients must have access to an Ombudsman (or similar) system before resorting to the Courts.

6   Ordinary investors are entitled to the full protection of the rules. However, the 'professional', 'business' and 'experienced investors' do not need the same degree of protection.

7   With the exception of life assurance and unit trust sales, any transaction arising from unsolicited visits and telephone calls will be unenforceable by the investment firm. The customer has a 14-day 'cooling off period' during which to reconsider the transaction. In any case, unsolicited visits and telephone calls to sell investments are for the most part, banned.

8   A much wider disclosure of information relevant to life assurance must be given by the investment firms, enabling the customer to know surrender values, commission levels and the status of persons selling assurance (whether such persons are company representatives, tied to one range of products, or fully independent intermediaries acting as agents of the customer: polarisation of status).

9   Investment advertisements, including general mailshots, must give clear

warnings about matters such as the volatility or the marketability of the product advertised. Investment advertisements must be placed or approved by authorised firms.

10 All published recommendations must be fully researched and be capable of substantiation to ensure that although proper care has been taken in meeting the recommendations they are not a guarantee that the recommended product will rise in value or even maintain its value.

11 Investment firms must make proper arrangements for the segregation of clients' money.

12 There must be compensation arrangements in place in all sectors of the investment industry to protect clients' funds (up to defined limits) in the event of the collapse of the investment firms.

Banking Act 1987

To lay the basis for a more effective supervisory regime for the UK banking system, this Act was brought into existence. Its provisions, which became effective in October 1987, replaced those of the 1979 Banking Act.

One of the central aims of the Act is to establish the Bank of England as the legal supervisory authority and strengthen its statutory powers to prevent financial institutions taking in deposits illegally and thereby to protect the depositors. The following is a summary of the main provisions of the 1987 Banking Act.

1   The Bank of England (Bank) is empowered to investigate illegal deposit taking, and on its application to the Courts, the Courts are empowered to order the early repayment of deposits accepted illegally.

2   The two-tier system of 'recognised' banks and 'licensed-deposit takers' created under the 1979 Act is replaced by a unified system with a single category of 'authorised' institution.

3   All authorised institutions will have to meet the same statutory prudential requirements. In summary, these are that an institution's directors, controllers and managers are 'fit and proper' persons to hold their positions; that the business is effectively directed by at least two individuals; that, in the case of UK incorporated institutions, it has as many non-executive directors as are considered appropriate by the Bank, having regard to its circumstances; that the business is conducted prudently – which covers, *inter alia*, adequate capital, liquidity, provisions for bad and doubtful debts, accounting and other records, and internal controls; that the business is carried on with integrity and the professional skills appropriate to the nature and scale of its activities; and that, when authorisation is granted, the institution has net assets of not less than £1 million.

4   A UK-incorporated authorised institution is permitted to use a banking name provided it has at least £5 million of paid-up share capital and/or

undistributable reserves. Institutions authorised under the 1979 Banking Act may resurrect any banking name which they then had to drop, irrespective of whether they have £5 million of share capital and reserves. The Bank is empowered to object to the name or proposed name of an applicant, or authorised institution where it considers the name misleading or otherwise undesirable.

5   All institutions are required to notify the Bank of changes of their directors, controllers and managers. In addition, any person who becomes a 'significant' shareholder in a UK-incorporated authorised institution is required to notify the Bank; in brief, a 'significant shareholder' is defined as a person entitled to exercise, or control the exercise of, between 5% and 15% of an institution's voting power (or that of its holding company).

6   A person proposing to become a shareholder-controller of the UK-incorporated institution is obliged to give *advance* notice to the Bank. Similar requirements apply to existing shareholder-controllers who propose to take their shareholding over 50% or over 75%. The Bank is empowered to intervene in the merger or acquisition of a bank on prudential grounds. Failure to give the prior notice or proceeding when the Bank has objected are criminal offences, which could lead to prosecution. In addition, the Bank is able to take steps against those who proceed in spite of its objection, for example by freezing voting rights, and on application by the Bank the Courts are empowered to order the sale of shares concerned. The Bank can also object to an existing shareholder-controller which it considers does not satisfy (or no longer satisfies) the 'fit and proper' requirements.

7   The Treasury is empowered to direct the Bank to give a notice of objection to an overseas person proposing to become a shareholder-controller of a UK-incorporated authorised institution where, if the acquisition were to proceed, it could serve a notice of disqualification or restriction on the institution under the Financial Services Act 1986. This will effectively enable the Treasury to block an acquisition on the grounds that the proposed shareholder-controller is from a country which does not offer reciprocal access to UK entities in the field of banking, insurance or investment business.

8   Authorised institutions whose principal place of business is in the UK are obliged to report to the Bank exposures of over 10% of capital and to give *prior notice* of proposed transactions exposing them to the risk of losing over 25% of capital.

9   A Board of Banking Supervisors consisting of Bank officials and outside experts has been established to advise the Bank on supervision matters. The Board, which will report separately to the Treasury, is to make the Bank more accountable for the way it carries out its supervisory responsibilities.

10 It is a criminal offence for any person knowingly or recklessly to provide information for supervisory purposes which is false or misleading in a material particular. The Bank's powers to require information and documents for the purposes of supervision are extended to cover, *inter alia*, holding companies, subsidiaries, sister subsidiaries, director, controllers,

significant shareholders and managers of authorised institutions. Information received by the Bank can be disclosed to other regulatory bodies and government departments (but not to the Inland Revenue).

11 For each authorised institution an independent firm of accountants will make available to the Bank three separate annual reports: on its internal control system; on its accounting and other records; and on its prudential statistical returns.

12 UK-incorporated authorised institutions are required to notify the Bank of changes in their auditors. An auditor is required to give notice to the Bank if he resigns, does not seek reappointment, or decides to qualify his opinion on an institution's accounts. Auditors (and reporting accountants) are released from constraints on their disclosing to the Bank information about an authorised institution obtained in the course of their audit (or examination), provided the disclosure is made in good faith and the information is relevant to Bank's supervision of the institution concerned.

13 The Deposit Protection Scheme is extended to cover all authorised institutions, including overseas banks. In addition, the cover is increased to 75% of the first £20 000 (previously £10 000) of sterling deposits made with an institution's UK offices.

14 Overseas banks proposing to establish representative offices in the UK have to give *prior* notification to the Bank. The Bank can object to the name of the institution if it appears misleading and to require the provision of information and documents. In addition, the Treasury has reserve powers to impose an authorisation and regulatory regime on representative offices.

15 Any institution aggrieved by a decision of the Bank may appeal to a tribunal, which will determine whether the decision was lawful or not. Individuals may appeal in their own right against a finding by the Bank that they are not 'fit and proper' to hold their position with an applicant or authorised institution.

Thus the 1987 Banking Act provides a much more elaborate supervision system backed by stronger statutory powers. It is hoped that the enforcement of prudent practices would foster greater confidence in financial institutions which operate in the UK – and that would enhance the reputation of London as a financial centre.

Building Societies Act 1986

This Act came into effect on 1 January 1987. It provides a further spur to competition between banks and building societies. It has also opened up the possibility that some building societies may opt to become banks, in which case they will come under the supervisory regime of the Bank of England under the 1987 Banking Act. The Financial Services Act 1986 (FSA) will also create a number of challenges for building societies. The prime objective of FSA is to regulate any person who conducts investment business. As many building societies and their subsidiaries may carry out ancillary services of an investment nature for their customers they too fall under the FSA jurisdiction.

The main investment activities of the societies which will come under the requirements of FSA include:

1 Arranging for the provision of, and advising on, life insurance, including endowment policies linked to mortgages.
2 Establishing and managing of unit trusts.
3 Providing of personal pensions.
4 Establishing and managing of personal equity plans.
5 Arranging for the provision of services in connection with stocks and shares.

It will be a criminal offence to engage in investment activities of this nature without authorisation. Societies can obtain authorisation from either SIB or from one or more of the SROs, depending upon the breadth and mix of investment business activities undertaken.

Whether or not a society requires authorisation depends on its activities and the manner in which they are undertaken. Each society therefore will need to:

1 Determine whether any of its current or proposed activities constitute investment business; if not, it does not require authorisation.
2 Decide its policy on whether it will be an introducer or a representative; introducers (who restrict their investment service to introducing customers to authorised independent intermediaries on a commission basis), and representatives (who represent a single authorised life office or unit trust operator for a fee), do not require authorisation.
3 Choose to become independent investment intermediary or manager, then it will need authorisation from appropriate SRO(s) or SIB.

Investor protection in building societies

Prudential requirements

1 The law and regulations under which societies currently operate require that at least 90% of their total commercial assets (i.e. total assets less liquid and fixed assets) be in the form of loans for house purchase to individuals which are secured by first mortgage. Societies may not lend more than 100% of the valuation of the property. Residential property has generally risen in value. Consequently, losses as a result of bad debts are minimal, at the end of 1985 provisions for mortgage losses accounted for only 0.012% of mortgage assets of about £97 000 million.
2 The size of the societies' liquid funds and the manner in which these funds can be invested are closely controlled by regulations made by the

Building Societies Commission (set up under the Building Societies Act 1986), the government body responsible for the prudential supervision of societies. Broadly speaking, societies can invest their liquid funds only in authorised banks and government and government-guaranteed securities. A proportion of liquid funds must be in short term securities and in practice most investments are held on a fairly short term basis.

3 Societies are required, for the prudent operation of their business, to maintain adequate reserves and comprehensive accounting records and internal control systems.

Monitoring of building society activities

The Building Societies Commission monitors very closely the activities of building societies. Societies are required to complete detailed monthly, quarterly and annual returns on their activities to identify any potential difficulties at an early stage.

The statutory investor protection scheme

The Building Societies Act 1986, provides a new legislative framework for building societies and includes provision for a statutory *Investor Protection Scheme*. This replaces the voluntary scheme set up by the Building Societies Association in April 1982 and covers all 'authorised' building societies: 123 societies, out of a total of 131, at the time of writing. The statutory scheme is along similar lines to that which exists for the banks, with two important differences:

1 Unlike the banks' scheme, the building society Investor Protection Scheme does not have a permanent fund of money. The reason given for this by the Treasury is that 'experience suggests that calls on the scheme are likely to be much less frequent than those on behalf of depositors with small licensed deposit takers under the Banking Act Scheme.'

2 The level of protection is 90% of amounts up to £20 000. Hence an individual investor would be guaranteed a maximum of 90% of £20 000 regardless of how many accounts are held in the society. (Depositors of larger amounts than £20 000 can of course split their funds between two or more societies, but then they will lose out on the increasingly popular high interest accounts with a £20 000 minimum.)

When the investor/depositor protection provisions under the Banking Act 1987 and the Building Societies Act 1986 are compared, building societies appear to provide greater protection: for example, the maximum fund which could be raised under the Banking Act would not be nearly sufficient to repay the depositors of any one of the big four clearing banks, in the unlikely event of a bank losing all its funds.

City Code on Takeovers and Mergers

Takeovers (a contested bid for the share of a target company) and mergers (mutually agreed union between companies, usually of equal size and in the same industry) are not undesirable as such. It may well be that larger size will bring economies of scale, better management, better usuage of resources, rational horizontal and vertical restructuring, and a healthier industry by the cutting out of the 'dead wood'. However, takeovers can also be by predators, whose main motive is a quick gain by buying out an independent company, stripping its assets – possibly selling the site to property developers – at large profit, but with no regard for the welfare of shareholders, employees and creditors of the target company.

Takeovers of business companies can enrich the bidder and may be unfair to the smaller and weaker shareholders, employees and creditors of the target company. The City has been aware of this and has been trying to lay down a voluntary set of rules in order that justice might be served. The first informal City guidelines on the conduct of takeovers were published in 1959. They were not very successful, therefore in 1968 the *City Code on Takeovers and Mergers* was published. It has since been revised, and the current edition was published in 1985. In an attempt to ensure that the Code rules are adhered to a Takeover Panel has been appointed. The Panel operates under the watchful eye of the Bank of England.

The code represents the collective opinion of those professionally involved in the field of takeovers on a range of business standards. It is not concerned with the financial and commercial advantages or disadvantages of a takeover, which are matters for the company and its shareholders, or with the wider questions of monopoly formation and restraint of competition, which are the responsibility of the government, advised by the Monopolies and Mergers Commission.

The Code does not have the force of law, but those who wish to avail themselves of the facilities of the securities market in the UK must conduct themselves in takeovers according to the Code, otherwise they cannot expect to enjoy those facilities.

The provisions of the Code fall into two categories: (a) *General Principles* of conduct to be observed in takeover transactions and (b) a series of *Rules of Procedure*. The responsibilities under the Code apply most decidely to those who are actively engaged in all aspects of the securities markets, but they also apply to directors of target companies, to those who seek to gain control of a target company and to all professional advisers of the companies involved.

General principles

The following principles and the spirit of the Code will apply in areas or circumstances not explicitly covered by any Rule.

1   All classes of shareholders in the offeree company must be treated equally and fairly.

2   Interests of shareholders must be paramount, and directors and controlling shareholders must subordinate their own interests to the interests of *all* shareholders.

3   All relevant information and sufficient time must be given to shareholders to enable them to make a properly informed final decision.

4   All those concerned in a takeover transaction must ensure that the creation of false market in the securities of both the offeree and the offeror companies is prevented and shareholders are not misled by any false statements.

5   All takeover documents or announcements must be lodged with the Panel at the same time they are made.

6   All documents addressed to shareholders, especially profit forecasts, must be proposed with the same standard of care as is required under the 1985 Companies Act for the preparation of a prospectus.

The Code specifically forbids directors from buying the shares of a company because they know that a bid is in the offing. Insider dealing is a criminal offence under the 1980 Companies Act and under the Financial Services Act 1986. The directors, or their advisers or close relatives, of the offeree company must not make a deal with the substantial shareholders of the offeree company at above the bid price to ensure that the bid goes through. All shareholders must be treated equally and offered the same bid price. The directors in an offeree company must not resist a takeover bid simply because that if the bid is successful they may lose their jobs. The full reasons for their resistance must be conveyed to all shareholders in a properly constituted general meeting, and the shareholders must approve the decision to block the bid for good, or temporarily in order that the bidder may raise the bid price or that a second interested company may put in a higher counterbid. On the other hand, the directors must not do anything without shareholders' approval which could effectively frustrate a bona fide offer and the shareholders of the offeree company being denied the opportunity to decide on its merits.

Rules of procedure

1   As soon as the offeror company makes its intention known to the board of directors of the offeree company the directors must make an announcement of the offer to the shareholders. The board must be satisfied that the offeror can implement the offer in full.

2   The board of the offeree company must seek competent independent legal and financial advice on the offer, and the substance of such advice must be conveyed to the offeree company shareholders.

3   If a person (or persons acting 'in concert', i.e. together) acquires 30% of the shares conferring voting rights, by whatever means and over whatever period, that person must make an offer for the rest of the shares in cash or have a cash alternative.

4   If the offeree company has more than one class of equity shares, the offeror must make the offer to all classes of shareholders (including non-voting, 'A' ordinary shareholders) on comparable terms.

5   If the offeror has purchased shares in the offeree company during 12 months prior to making the offer, then the offer price must not be less than the highest price the offeror paid for acquiring the shares of the offeree company during the previous 12 months. This is to prevent a predator buying a company on the cheap, especially where there is a wide spread of share ownership.

6   An offer must be open for at least 21 days for the shareholders of the offeree company to accept the offer. The offer will become unconditional if and when a minimum level of shareholders (90%) have accepted the offer (see below). After the offer becomes unconditional, it should remain open for acceptance for another 14 days.

7   When an offer is announced all conditions to which it may be subject must be unambiguously made known. All conditions must be fulfilled or the offer must lapse within 21 days or the date on which the offer becomes unconditional, whichever is later.

8   Where an offer comes within the statutory provisions for possible reference to the Monopolies and Mergers Commission, it must lapse when it is referred to the Monopolies and Mergers Commission.

9   Once an offer is announced, the share transactions in all the companies involved must be reported by all parties to the Panel, the Stock Exchange and the Press. The Panel's executive staff are available throughout a takeover to advise whether the rules are being observed.

Amendment of Companies Act provisions on takeovers by the Financial Services Act 1986

The FSA amends sections 428–430 of the Companies Act 1985 which deal with the compulsory acquisition of shares following the takeover bid (Section 172 and Schedule 12). The present rules:

1   Enable an offeror company which has secured acceptances from the holders of at least 90% of the target company's shares (excluding shares held by it and its subsidiaries) to buy out the remaining shareholders (compulsory acquisition); and

2   Enable the minority to require the offeror company to buy them out (reverse acquisition) once it holds 90% of the shares *including* those held by it and its subsidiary.

In both cases, there is provision for appeal to the Courts. The main changes are:

1   The provisions in the FSA Schedule improve the position of dissentients (the minority), notably by tightening up the definition of the 90% threshold triggering the offeror's right to buy them out so as to exclude shares held by associates generally and not simply, as previously stated, those held by the subsidiaries of person making the offer.

2   The timetable governing the compulsory acquisition process is altered so that the dissentients are informed of their rights earlier and are permitted to exercise those rights without an inordinate delay.

3   Dissentients who want to take an arguable case to Court are protected against orders for costs.

The powers of the Panel

Although neither the Code nor the Panel have the force of law, yet in the case of quoted companies, they can exercise the following real powers:

1   A company, before quotation on the Stock Exchange is granted, is required to enter into a 'listing agreement' with the Stock Exchange which binds the company to certain rules and procedures, including the City Code. If a listed company breaks the rules and procedures it is deprived of the facilities of the Stock Exchange.

2   The Panel membership covers a wide range of services in the City, and a flagrant flouting of the City Code can lead the defaulting company into trouble from all sides.

3   The Panel can issue a public reprimand to transgressing companies, often in professional journals, which can be really harmful to the companies.

4   The Panel can refer matters to the appropriate SRO or SIB and even to the DTI, for examination under the Financial Services Act, and for appropriate punishment to the wrongdoer.

Appeals can be made by companies to the Panel's Appeals Committee to review the decisions of its executives.

Shareholders of the target company

They should examine themselves, or with the help of their financial advisers, the merits and demerits of accepting each offer. Broadly speaking, they should hold back their decision until the last day before giving their accept-ance to the offer; this will enable them to take advantage of any higher offer from the bidder or a superior bid from some other bidder. They should make certain that the securities offered in exchange for their shares meet their specific investment objectives. Accepting securities in exchange does not constitute a disposal for capital gains tax purposes, but accepting cash wholly or partly does. The dissentients should accept the offer, no matter how strongly opposed to it they may be, once it becomes unconditional.

Rights of shareholders

Under English law a company, upon registration, becomes a 'legal person' in its own right, able to sue and be sued in its own name. Its personality is separate from the shareholders who own it and the shareholder-directors who manage it. Therefore shareholders have rights against the company and its directors. However, the shareholders (ordinary shareholders – the equity holders) have a residual position when it comes to participating in the profits and assets of the company. To restore the balance somewhat shareholders have a number of legal rights, not given to other classes of investor, which flow from (a) company law (in particular, Companies Act 1948, 1967 and 1985), (b) the Stock Exchange Listing Requirements for companies and (c) the provisions of the Takeover Code.

Each shareholder of a company has the following legal rights:

1   To receive the annual reports and accounts 21 days before each Annual General Meeting (AGM). They contain, at the very least, a profit and loss account, a balance sheet, notes to the accounts, the auditors' report and directors' report. Their contents are governed by the 1967 Companies Act, and the Act emphasises 'disclosure'. Therefore in addition to profits, companies are required to declare such matters as turnover, exports, wages, the salary of the highest paid director, and the directors' interests in the company.
2   The right to receive due notification of general meetings, to attend such meetings and there to discuss and vote on any matter. All members may attend but only those with voting rights can vote on resolutions. The resolutions of the general meetings are binding on all members of the company.

General meetings are of three types.

(a) *Statutory meeting*: it must be held between one and three months after the issue of the trading certificate by the Registrar, to discuss exclusively the contents of the first statutory report, i.e. the means or otherwise of the first public issue of the company's shares.

(b) *Annual General Meeting*: the AM of a new company must be held within 18 months of its incorporation. Thereafter it must be held in every calendar year, and not more than 15 months after the last AGM. A 21-day notice in writing must be given to shareholders prior to AGM. The agenda is restricted to receive, discuss and, if approved, adopt directors' report and accounts; to declare dividends rate (the shareholder can reduce this rate but cannot increase it); to elect directors; to fix remuneration of auditors and any other competent business (e.g. removal of a director).

(c) *Extraordinary General Meeting*: all meetings, other than the statutory and AGMs, are referred to as extraordinary general meetings. A 14-day notice (21-day notice where a special resolution (see below) is to be discussed) must be given by the directors to the shareholders. Shareholders representing 1/10th of voting rights can, if allowed in the company's article of association (the internal rules of a company), requisition an extraordinary general meeting.

3 To appoint a proxy to attend meetings, to request a poll and to vote on a poll. Every shareholder who is entitled to attend and vote at a meeting has a statutory right to appoint a proxy to attend and vote on the shareholder's behalf. The articles usually require proxies (a written authorisation by the shareholder to another person also known as 'proxy' – to attend and vote on shareholder's behalf) to be deposited at the company's office in advance of the meeting. Proxy forms are sent along with notice of meetings. Having appointed a proxy, a member can still attend and vote, and the member's vote must be accepted by the company instead of the proxy's if the proxy has not already voted. A proxy has merely a negative obligation, i.e. not to vote against the instruction of the principal, if proxy votes at all. A proxy will become a binding contract if it is remunerated, i.e. where the proxy is a member's professional advisor.

Normally voting is by a show of hands: one-man-one-vote, regardless of the number of shares held. However, a 'poll' can be demanded either by five or more members, or by members representing 1/10th of the voting capital; then a member's votes will depend on the number of voting shares held: one-share-one-vote. Voting rights are specified in a company article. The minimum amount of support required to demand a poll protects the minority from provisions in the articles if they are designed to make it difficult to obtain a poll.

4 To share in the profits of the company either in the form of dividends or by an increase in the reserves. No company may pay dividends except out of its accumulated realised profits less its accumulated realised losses. Therefore, dividends paid to ordinary shareholders will vary with the *net* amount of accumulated realised profit, i.e. on the prosperity of the company. Even so ordinary shareholders, unlike preference shareholders, do not have an automatic right to receive dividends. A dividend is not a debt of the company *until* it is declared. In a solvent and prospering company, dividends once declared must be paid to shareholders as a matter of right. On the other hand shareholders may consider it more prudent to retain profits in the company and increase reserves. In that case, shareholders can *reduce* a dividend proposed by the directors; they cannot increase it for that would create serious liquidity problems for the company.

5 They have the right to subscribe for any new share capital or convertible loan stock. Company law stipulates that a company, wishing to raise new share capital, may not allot equity shares unless it has made an offer to the existing equity holders to subscribe on the same or more favourable terms

for such shares in proportion to their existing holdings. Shareholders must be notified in writing and the offer must be open for at least 21 days. No allotment of new shares may be made until either 21 days have expired or every offer to existing shareholders has been accepted or refused. If this stipulation is contravened then every officer of the company who knew of the contravention is liable to compensate any shareholders entitled to receive the offer for damages suffered or expenses incurred due to the contravention.

Convertible loan stocks besides being fixed interest securities carry important rights enabling the holders to convert stocks into a given number of ordinary shares on or before certain stipulated dates. These stocks, the law states, must be offered first to existing ordinary shareholders on a 'rights' basis since these stocks are, from the outset, potential ordinary shares. If this stipulation is contravened then all the officers of the company who knew of the contravention will be liable to the same penalties as under rights issue of shares.

6 To transfer their shares (in public limited companies) freely. The mere fact that one owns shares in a public company – a separate legal entity – does not give one the automatic right to take part in the management of the company. Therefore it matters little to the company whether X owns its shares or Y, so long as no person holds so many of its shares as to give rise to speculation of a takeover bid. Consequently, shareholders are free to transfer/sell their shares to whomsoever and whenever they choose. The Stock Exchange insists on free transferability. In the case of a private limited company shares however there will probably be a restriction on this right, that will be stated in its articles of association.

7 To elect and remove the directors of their company. The shareholders own the company, therefore can appoint or remove its directors. The usual method of appointment is by 'ordinary resolution' in a general meeting.

Before a meeting can validly proceed to do business there must be a *quorum*, i.e. the minimum number of suitably qualified persons who must be present. The articles provide the quorum for general meetings.

Any members may move a *resolution* for discussion. There are three types of resolution: Ordinary, Special and Extraordinary.

(a) *Ordinary resolution*: Whenever the law or the company's articles do not require a special or extraordinary resolution, an ordinary resolution will be used. The period of notice for moving an ordinary resolution depends on the type of meeting in which it is to be moved: 21 days for an AGM and generally 14 days for an extraordinary general meeting. A simple majority of members present in person or by proxy entitled to vote and voting, will pass the ordinary resolution.

(b) *Special resolution*: Normally a 21-day notice is required, and no amendments to the resolution can be accepted at the meeting. Special resolutions are required for a number of important company decisions, such as to allow the memorandum or the articles of association, to reduce capital, to change the name of the company. It requires a three quarter majority of members present in person or by proxy and entitled to vote and voting to pass a special resolution.

(c) *Extraordinary resolution*: Except for a 14-day notice period, an extraordinary resolution is similar to a special resolution. It is required for several other important decisions by the company, e.g. to wind up the company, to sanction variation of class rights.

The persons proposing to remove a director must give the company 28 days notice (special notice). The company will communicate the motion to the director concerned and to the members, giving at least 21-day's notice. The director may make written representations to the company which must be sent to members with the notice of meeting. At the meeting the passing of an ordinary resolution will remove the director.

Surveillance under Stock Exchange Rules

The first Stock Exchange (SE) Rules were accepted in 1812, and these form the basis of the present (October 1986) Rules. These Rules have been expanded to take account of the 1986 Financial Services Act's detailed requirements with regard to the keeping of records of transactions, disclosure, interest of the member firm and its remuneration and periodic statements of each managed portfolio. The rules are necessary because titles to stocks and shares are as important as real estate. Therefore the price and time at which securities are traded are essential matters of record (and recorded in Contract Notes) not only for the buyer and seller of securities but also for any potential subsequent inquiry as to whether the deal struck was a fair one or was arrived at as a result of breach of SE rules, such as trading through inside knowledge not available to the ordinary investor or member of public.

On receipt of the Contract Note (CN), the client should study its contents carefully to ensure that his/her instructions have been carried out by the stockbroking firm member of the SE. Once the client accepts the CN, it becomes binding on the member firm. Therefore, *SE rules or the 'Contract Note Contents'* specify precisely as to the details of information to be stated on a CN. A CN, according to the SE Rules, must contain the following:

1 The name and address of the member firm (member) and stating that it is a member of the SE: this implies that the transaction is subject to SE rules.
2 The name and address of client and his/her account number (if any).
3 The date and time of transaction, and whether it has been struck by the member with a third party or for its own account.

4   Whether the member has effected the transaction through the agency of a connected company.

5   Whether the member is receiving a second commission in respect of the transaction.

6   The full title of the security which is the subject of the transaction.

7   The nature of the transaction (bought or sold), its unit price, the total consideration (numbers dealt × unit price) and its other conditions.

8   In the case of a fixed income stock, the number of days for which income has accrued and the resulting amount of gross interest that is added to the consideration (or deducted from it, in the case of ex-dividend transactions).

9   If the transaction involves the conversion of one currency into another then the rate of exchange obtained for conversion, should be given.

10 The amount of commission or fees charged, and any taxes, duties etc.

11 If the commission is shared with a third independent party, then the identity of the third party and the percentage or amount shared with it should be stated.

12 With the purchase of units of a collective investment scheme, the percentage of the initial charge included in the price of units should be stated.

13 The settlement due date (no dates given where the transaction is for cash).

14 The CN must state that the transaction is subject to the SE rules.

15 If the security involved is not on the SE Daily Official List, a statement: 'This security is not officially listed on the SE', should be made.

16 For securities admitted to the Third Market the Statement: 'Effected in accordance with the rules and regulations governing the Third Market. This investment may carry a high degree of risk', must be made.

17 With the exception of CNs issued for transactions with considerations of £5000 or less, or expressing the nominal value in a currency other than sterling or involving insurance or property bond, an offshore or overseas fund or units in a unit trust, every CN shall include a 'PTM Levy' (Contract Levy).

18 Where a member has been approved by the Inland Revenue as a PEP manager, the following provisions regarding periodic statements in relation to managed portfolios shall apply:

(a) If the cash subscriptions of the PEP investor are invested according to the instruction of the investor solely in the units of a specific scheme, a statement at least every six months shall be sent to the investor giving the information as prescribed in the Rule on CNs.

(b) If the cash subscriptions are invested at the discretion of the member as PEP manager, solely in listed or USM securities and in the units of an authorised UT scheme, a statement at least every three months shall be sent to the investor as per the requirements of Rule 325(1).

(c) If the cash subscriptions of the PEP investors are to be invested in a PEP scheme other than in (a) and (b) above, a CN shall be issued to the investor in accordance with Rule on CNs immediately.

One danger seen in the new dual capacity membership system of the SE is that, because there is no longer a strictly independent intermediary, i.e. the jobber, brokers can in theory sell to each other at prices which might bear little relation to the market, thereby making profit for themselves. Furthermore, if the market maker has taken on a bad stock and made a loss on it, one of his dealers could attempt to unload it on an unsuspecting investor. Such practices are strictly prohibited by the SE rules on conduct of business which maintains a close watch on share dealing by member firms. The main *Dealing Rules* in this connection are as follows.

1 No member shall promote a false market, i.e. a market in which the collaboration of buyers and sellers contrive a price of share which is not justified by the assets, earnings or prospects.

2 A member shall not advise a client to use the services of another investment business which is connected with the member firm unless the client has been informed of the connection, nor shall the member advise a client to purchase or retain units in a collective investment scheme managed by the member firm or a connected company unless the client has been made aware of this at the time advice is given. No member shall deal as principal with a client unless given his written agreement.

3 A member shall before effecting a transaction disclose to the client the rate or amount of commission or any other payable charges.

4 A member shall maintain written rules governing dealings by partners and employees for their own accounts which shall be available for inspection by the Council of SE at all times. Personal dealings which would involve the person in conflicts of interest with any customer of the member firm or a conflict with his duty to any customer, are forbidden. This would mean that a stockbroking member firm's employees could not buy the firm's own issue if the firm was under a duty to avoid a fall in the price in the after market. The member firm will be required to take all reasonable steps to ensure that its employees obey the rule.

5 A member shall deal in equities for the best advantage of its clients, i.e. the price obtained by the client is as good as or better than the best price displayed on the SEAQ.

6 A market maker member shall report the following to SE in respect of every transaction, other than options and futures, affected by it: name of member firm, date and time of transaction, the security, the transaction price (excluding commission etc), number of shares, whether the transaction is a purchase or a sale. The reporting to SE deadlines for transactions effected by a market maker member are: effected between 9 am and 5 pm, within five minutes of effecting; effected after 5 pm should be reported

between 7.30 and 9 am the following day. Failure to report shall lead to a fine in accordance with a scale laid down by the Council of SE from time to time.

7   A member shall not deal on behalf of a client in London Traded Options without a signed letter of authority from the client after the client has been given a plethora of risk warnings of entering into any options or futures transactions.

With regard to *custody of investments*, members should keep separate accounts for themselves and for their clients because members cannot use clients' shares as collateral for the member firm's or its partners' or directors' investments. Periodic (at least twice yearly) written confirmation must be given to clients that the securities are in safe custody. At least once a year the member should deliver a statement of the securities held in safe custody on behalf of their clients.

If any member firm is discovered transgressing the stringent SE rules in any way, that member will be censured, suspended and even expelled by the Council of SE according to the seriousness of the offence. The SE insists that members submit monthly statements as well as quarterly balance sheets to the SE Council, so that, *inter alia*, the solvency margins (excess of assets over liabilities) can be watched on a regular basis. However, if a member firm defaults on its obligations, it receives a 'hammering', i.e. its membership lapses.

When the conventions of honesty, strict rules and periodic financial surveillance all fail to avert a member firm defaulting, then the ultimate investor protection comes from the *Stock Exchange Compensation Fund*. The Fund, which was set up in 1950, is administered by the Council of SE as an essential form of investor protection for those who transact their business through its member firms. The Fund does not protect against losses resulting from the rise or fall in the market value of investments. The Council of SE makes grants from the Fund to the clients of member firms of the SE who fail financially, up to a maximum of £250 000 per claimant of the defaulting firm. That limit is increased to £500 000 where losses over and above £250 000 are attributable to the misappropriation of securities registered, or cash deposited, in the name of a nominee company, i.e. a company which is owned by the member firm. In addition, where a claim arises as a result of losses incurred by lenders of securities to a failed SE moneybroker, there is no limit to the amount of the claim.

Losses arising from the transaction of SE business will normally be evidenced by a Contract Note issued by a member firm with the statement that the business has been done 'subject to the Rules and Regulations of the Stock Exchange'. If a claimant is not satisfied with the decision of the Council, he/she has a right of appeal to an Appeals Committee on which lay members of the Council form a majority.

There are three main resources of the Fund: the assets held by the

Council and earmarked for the Fund in the SE's balance sheet (about £5 million) plus other liquid assets and reserves of the Council; by means of a levy on member firms for general services (up to £5 million, in any one year); and, from the extensive insurance cover (between £5 million and £20 million), in case claims exceed given levels in any one year.

To meet the investor protection requirements under the Financial Services Act 1986 (FSA) and the anticipated changes after the 'Big Bang' in October 1986 – such as the integration of member firms with new owners and the entry of overseas securities houses to SE membership – the various agencies of the SE involved in prudential control were brought together in 1984 to form the *Surveillance Division* (SD). The SD, with enhanced surveillance capability, is responsible for identifying possible abuses or breaches of SE rules. The expanded inspectorate teams have direct access through desk top terminal to both Talisman's checking and matched bargain reports and SEAQ's price quotation information and trade reporting. These, along with other sources, provide a continuous picture of market trading. The SD's increased capacity, together with the new surveillance systems developed for the screen-based markets, the SE believes, will continue to ensure full and detailed monitoring of prices and dealings.

The staff of the Panel on Takeovers and Mergers work closely with the SD to investigate dealings in advance of publication of bid proposals, with the objective to establish whether there has been any breach of the rules governing secrecy and insider dealing, i.e. the abuse of privileged information.

The insider dealing investigation has become a better known aspect of the SD's work. The increased power given to DTI inspectors by the FSA mean even closer co-operation with the DTI and with its inspectors.

Protection for investors buying

Insurance investment products

The Policyholder protection Act 1975, ensures that in the event of an insurance company failure, its policyholders receives at least 90% of the 'reasonable' value of their policies. The Policyholders' Protection Board, which administers the 1975 Act, can impose a levy on insurance companies of not more than 1% of their net premium income, and also on the insurance brokers and agents up to a proportion of their commission earnings from the failed insurance company.

Investors can buy insurance investment products from press advertisements, insurance salesmen, insurance brokers or on recommendation of investment advisers. The following Regulations protect the interests of investors in insurance products.

The DTI is empowered under the Insurance Companies Act 1974, to regulate the content of insurance companies advertisements, so that no misleading and false statements are made. This Act also requires that any person selling a policy must reveal his connection with the insurance company concerned.

The Insurance Brokers (Registration) Act 1977, requires all those calling themselves insurance brokers to be registered with the Insurance Brokers Registration Council, which lays down the code of professional conduct for its members. Investment advisers who recommend insurance products act as 'accountable intermediaries' under the Policyholders Protection Act 1975.

Authorised unit trusts products

There are three 'watch dogs' who protect investors in unit trusts products.

1   A unit trust is a 'trust' in the legal sense: investments in a unit trust are held in trust by an independent and respectable trustee, like a major bank or a large insurance company. There is a trust deed which lays down how the money may be invested, how the price of units is to be calculated, how the income is to be distributed and how much the managers can be paid. The trustees ensure that the managers do not make extravagant or misleading claims regarding the performance of the fund by vetting all advertisements of the unit trust group.
2   The DTI plays a part in protecting investors in unit trusts by vetting each unit trust before 'authorising' its managers to sell units to the public. It approves the trust deed and the choice of trustee and the suitability of directors of the unit trust.
3   The Unit Trust Association (UTA) is the trade association of the unit trust industry, and the unit trust groups which are its members are required to comply with the UTA's code of conduct. The members of the UTA manage almost 90% of the money invested in unit trusts.

Investment trusts

Investment trusts are public limited companies, quoted on the Stock Exchange, therefore investors are protected by the stipulations of the Companies Act, and the listing requirements of the Stock Exchange. The Association of Investment Trust Companies is the trade association of investment trust companies, and members have to meet certain standards of entry; one of which is that a member investment trust must hold at least 60% of its assets in stocks and shares quoted on the Stock Exchange. This protects their shareholders by limiting the extent of high risk investment investment trusts could hold. Also they must not have more than 15% of their assets in one company.

Selected questions

It is not always easy to identify the chapter which is relevant to a specific question; this is especially so with this chapter. Investor protection is bound to become a big issue due to new legislation. It may be necessary to amend the questions asked in the past to bring them under the provisions of new enactments, and even to construct new questions. Study the following questions carefully and jot down the relevant points which form the scope of each question before looking at the brief answer below.

Q1 You are an ordinary shareholder in a company which is the subject of a take-over bid. What factors would you take into account in deciding what action to take?

Q2 Summarise briefly the provisions of the Companies Acts in relation to

(a) the rights of an offering company;

(b) the requirements for the passing of a resolution at an Extraordinary General Meeting;

(c) the disclosure of ownership.

Q3 (a) What are the normal rights of ordinary shareholders in a public company?

(b) What business is usually dealt with at the Annual General Meeting of a public company?

(c) Describe briefly the system of voting by proxy at public company meetings.

Q4 (a) Summarise the circumstances in which the shares of non accepting shareholders in an offer may be acquired under section 428 of the Companies Act 1985.

(b) After an offer has been made, in which circumstances is a minority shareholder in the offeree company entitled to require the offeror company to buy his/her shares?

Q5 Describe the provisions for the unpaid investor/depositor under the:

(a) Financial Services Act 1985;

(b) Building Societies Act 1986;

(c) Banking Act 1987.

Brief answers

A1 (a) Terms of the bid: cash, shares or other securities

- With cash offer: CGT problem, but attractive in a falling market.
- With securities other than ordinary shares: do they fit with investor's objectives?; are they listed?

(b) Value of the bid: is it more than the value of original shares? Is a higher bid likely?

(c) Prospects of offered shares as compared to original shares.

(d) Consideration of formal offer document: to compare the records and prospects of both companies; to examine the reason for the bid (integration, management quality); whether the board recommends acceptance; how many shares are already committed; whether the takeover panel rules are complied with; whether any cash offer is underwritten.

(e) Market reaction and public comment: if market price is above the value of bid then bid may be increased or a counterbid made; reference to Monopolies Commission may block the bid; professional advice should be sought and press comment studied for guidance.

(f) In case the offer becomes unconditional, choice will lie between accepting the offer or selling holdings in the market for a price that will be a few pence below the bid price; becoming a dissentient will serve no useful purpose.

A2   (a) If the offering company has secured acceptances from the holders of at least 90% of the offeree company's shares (excluding shares held by it or its subsidiaries) it has the right to buy out the remaining dissenting shareholders on the same terms as offered to those accepted by the assenting majority.

(b) A 14-day notice to all those entitled to attend the general meeting
- Resolution must be set out in full in the notice.
- Meeting must be quorate.
- 75% of those able to vote and voting for the resolution.

(c) A person acquiring a company's voting capital in excess of 5% of that issued, must notify the company of this fact within five days of acquiring.
- Certain exemptions for corporate bodies acting as trustees and for authorised unit trusts.

A3   (a)
- To receive the annual reports and accounts.
- To receive notification of general meetings, to attend, to discuss and vote (if eligible).
- To appoint a proxy to attend meetings.
- To receive declared dividends.
- To subscribe to any new share capital or convertible loan stock.
- To transfer shares freely.
- To elect and remove directors.

(b) Consideration of:
- Reports and accounts.
- Declaration of a final dividend.
- Election of directors.
- Appointment and remuneration of auditors.

(c) A properly appointed proxy may vote:
- On a show of hands if allowed by articles (unusual);
- On a poll.

A proxy may speak:
- At a meeting only if articles allow;
- To demand a poll.

A4 (a)

- If the offeror has required less than 10% of the shares of the offeree company, it must receive acceptances in respect of 90% of the outstanding shares (if it has acquired 9% before the bid it must acquire 90% of the remaining 91%) within four months of the announcement of the bid, to buy out the remaining shares, and giving them a two-month notice after the end of the four month period.
- If it has acquired, prior to the announcement of the bid, 10% or more of the shares of the target company, it must acquire, in addition, at least 75% of the remaining shares within four months of making the bid, to be able to buy out the remaining shares after the due notice.
- The offeror must offer the same terms to *all* shareholders.

(b)

- The dissenting minority has the right to change its mind and accept the offer when it becomes clear that the offer has become unconditional, i.e. when the offeror, in addition to shares already acquired, has acquired 75% or 90% (as appropriate) of the remaining shares. The bidder must give notice of this to the dissenting minority, whereupon the dissenting minority can, within three months, require the bidder to buy its shares at the same terms accepted by the majority.

A5 (a) Compensation of Unpaid Investors' Scheme: Investment business to contribute to the cost of compensation on the basis of equal proportions of gross revenue of each firm, up to a limit in any one year of £100 million from all contributors *as a group*. Members of one SRO will be required to contribute up to the maximum in respect of claims against one of their fellows, and members of other SROs only thereafter.

(b) Building Society Investor Protection Scheme: The level of protection is 90% of amounts up to £20 000. An individual investor is guaranteed a maximum of 90% of £20 000 regardless of how many accounts are held in a building society. In the case of joint accounts, each individual is guaranteed a maximum of 90% of £20 000.

(c) Banking Deposit Protection Scheme: All 'authorised' institutions, including overseas banks, are required to participate in the scheme. The level of protection is 75% of the first £20 000 of sterling deposits made with an authorised institution's UK offices.

Specially selected question

Takeover bids are an almost daily feature in the activities of the Stock Exchange in London. Spectacular battles, involving vast sums of money, often result.

Required:

(a) What measures are available for the protection of the UK Investor who has shares in a company involved in a take-over bid? What penalties can be imposed on companies involved in take-over situations?

(b) Outline the main items which should be contained in the offer document on companies involved in takeover situations?

Model answer

(a) Take-over activity is regulated by a code of practice, 'the City Code' administered by the Panel on Takeovers and Mergers. It began life as a working party in the 1960s and its members include all bodies concerned with investment and finance. It has gone through several revisions, the last revision took place in 1985. It is a voluntary body, and therefore does not have the force of law, although some consider it should have statutory powers.

Its main principles are mainly concerned with the provision of information to shareholders and responsibilities of the directors of both the bidding and target companies. They require that:

(i) All shareholders of the same class should be treated equally.

(ii) Directors of offering company should act in the best interests of its shareholders and obtain independent professional advice.

(iii) Shareholders of both companies must be given fullest information to enable them to evaluate the bid properly.

(iv) Creation of false markets in shares should be avoided.

The Panel comes down heavily on transgressors. It can:

- Privately admonish those concerned.
- Reprimand the offenders publicly.
- Refer offenders to their own professional body, e.g. the Stock Exchange can be asked to suspend quotations and refuse listings for proposed new securities to be issued.
- Refer matters to the DTI for examination under the Financial Services Act 1986, and for appropriate punishment to the transgressor.

Bids may be referred to the Monopolies and Mergers Commission on grounds that: it is detrimental to competition by merging two units in one industry; it is lacking in industrial logic by attempting to link up disparate businesses; it would create a monopoly or near monopoly; or for some other reason it would not be in the public interest.

(b) Offer documents will set out the terms and conditions of the offer. Terms take various forms such as; cash bid, share offer, mixture of shares and cash, choice of shares or cash, exchange of an equity for a convertible or other fixed interest stock, mixtures of shares and loan stock or other fixed interest security, three way mixture of shares, fixed interest stock and cash.

There may be conditions such as the offer being subject to a minimum acceptance level (usually within 51 to 90%), the offer not being referred to

Monopolies Commission, any necessary increase in capital being approved by shareholders of bidding company and the Stock Exchange granting listing for the new security.

Offer document will also contain information about both companies shareholders' anticipated benefits, effects on directors, management and employees, financial effects, tax implications and the time limit to accept the offer. If the directors of the target company agree to the offer, the offer document should state whether terms have been approved by the company's merchant bankers or other advisers. There will be detailed information on such matters as the companies concerned, including recent dealings, directors, shareholders, underwriting terms.

Updating

The 'Big Bang' and the Financial Services Act 1986 have opened the door to aggressive competition between investment institutions. Therefore investor protection has become even more important. The quality newspapers, the radio and the television are aware of this and any transgressions of the law or professional practice are fully reported and discussed. These should provide you with the best source of the on-going updating of this topic. Look out for *Signpost* articles in this area in *Banking World*.

Index